Freud Along the Ganges

Books by Salman Akhtar

Psychiatry and Psychoanalysis

Broken Structures (1992)
Quest for Answers (1995)
Inner Torment (1999)
Immigration and Identity (1999)
New Clinical Realms (2003)
The Alphabet of Psychoanalysis (in press)

Popular/Non-Fiction

Objects of Our Desire (2005)

Urdu Poetry

Ku-ba-ku (1976)
Doosra Ghar (1986)
Nadi Ke Pas (2004)

English Poetry

The Hidden Knot *(1985)*
Conditions (1993)
Turned to Light (1998)

Edited

New Psychiatric Syndromes (1983)
The Trauma of Transgression (1991)
Beyond the Symbiotic Orbit (1991)
When the Body Speaks (1992)
Mahler and Kohut (1994)
The Birth of Hatred (1995)
The Internal Mother (1995)
Intimacy and Infidelity (1996)
The Seasons of Life (1997)
The Seed of Madness (1997)
The Colors of Childhood (1998)
Brothers and Sisters (1999)
Thicker than Blood (2000)
Does God Help? (2001)
Three Faces of Mourning (2001)
Real and Imaginary Fathers (2004)
Mental Zoo (2005)
Cultural Zoo (2005)
The Language of Emotions (2005)
Freud Along the Ganges (2005)
Severe Personality Disorders (in press)
The Crescent and the Couch (in press)
Interpersonal Boundaries (in press)
Space and Intuition (in press)

Freud Along the Ganges

Psychoanalytic Reflections on the People and Culture of India

Edited by

Salman Akhtar, M.D.

OTHER

OTHER PRESS
New York

"Rabindranath Tagore and Freudian Thought," by Santanu Biswas © Institute of Psychoanalysis, London, UK.

"The Cloistered Passion of Radha and Krishna," by Sudhir Kakar and John M. Ross reproduced by permission of Oxford University Press, India, New Delhi.

Every effort has been made to trace or contact all copyright holders. The publisher will be glad to make good in future editions any omissions brought to our attention.

Copyright © 2005 Salman Akhtar

Production Editor: Mira S. Park

This book was set in 11 pt. Goudy by Alpha Graphics of Pittsfield, New Hampshire.

ISBN-13: 978-1-59051-090-2

10 9 8 7 6 5 4 3 2

Library of Congress Cataloging-in-Publication Data

Akhtar, Salman.
    Freud along the Ganges : psychoanalytic reflections on the people and culture of India / edited by Salman Akhtar.
        p. cm.
    Includes bibliographical references and index.
        ISBN 1-59051-090-9 (pbk. : alk. paper) 1. Psychoanalysis and culture–India.
    2. Ethnopsychology–India. I. Akhtar, Salman, 1946 July 31-
    BF175.4.C84F74 2005
    150.19'5'0954–dc22

                                                                    2005000265

To

my first mentor in psychiatry

PROFESSOR NARENDRA NATH WIG

with affection and gratitude

"One of the thorns in the flesh of Europeans who write or have written histories of Indian philosophy is that all philosophy is seen as contemporary by Indians. That is to say, they are interested in problems themselves, not in the mere biographical fact or historical, chronological fact. That So-and-So was What's-His-Name's master, that he came before, that he wrote under the influence—all those things are nothing to them. They care about the riddle of the universe."

—Jorge Luis Borges, 1967

Contents

Acknowledgments

I wish to thank the distinguished colleagues whose contributions appear in this volume. I am also thankful to Michael Vergare, M.D., who, as the chairman of the Department of Psychiatry and Human Behavior at Thomas Jefferson Medical College, gave unwavering support to my work. A number of psychoanalytic colleagues, especially Drs. Ira Brenner, Saida Koita, and Vamik Volkan, gave me useful advice during the preparation of this book. Many others, including Drs. Subhash Bhatia, Shiv Kumar Hatti, Naresh Julka, Rajnish Mago, Shantanu Maitra, Harish Malhotra, Ashwin Patkar, Tarnjit Saini, and J. Anderson Thomson, as well as Bharat Luthra, Nawab Warsi, Manail Ahmad, Shivani Nath, and Shankar Vedantam, helped in subtle and explicit ways. I also received helpful input from my uncle and aunt, Abu and Hamida Salim, who are distinguished academics in their own right, on certain aspects of this book. Anju Bhargava made some very important points for me to consider and greatly enriched the book. My secretary, Melissa Nevin, offered me devoted and skillful assistance.

"Going-on-being" (to use a phrase of Donald Winnicott) pleasantly, despite my occasionally infantile demands, she made my work easier. To all these individuals, I offer my sincere thanks.

Above all, though, is my gratitude to India, my motherland. The milk of its generosity flows as the blood of industry in my veins. For all my effort in preparing this book on India, there are no more apt words than those of Kahlil Gibran: "Work is love made visible."

Contributors

Salman Akhtar, M.D. Professor of Psychiatry, Jefferson Medical College; Training and Supervising Analyst, Psychoanalytic Center of Philadelphia, Philadelphia, Pennsylvania.

Santanu Biswas, Ph.D. Professor of English Literature, Jadhavpur University, Calcutta, West Bengal, India.

Komal Choksi, M.A., M.Phil. Doctoral student at the Clinical Psychology Sub-Program of the Graduate Center of the City University of New York, New York, New York.

Prakash N. Desai, M.D. Professor of Psychiatry, University of Illinois at Chicago; Co-Chief of Staff, Jesse Brown Medical Center, Chicago, Illinois.

Jaswant Guzder, M.D. Associate Professor of Psychiatry, Faculty of Medicine, McGill University, Montreal; Faculty Member, Canadian Psychoanalytic Institute, Montreal, Canada.

Sudhir Kakar, Ph.D. Training and Supervising Analyst, Indian Psychoanalytic Society, Goa, India.

Meenakshi Krishna, M.A. Freelance business consultant, London, England.

Hyman L. Muslin, M.D. Professor of Psychiatry, University of Illinois at Chicago, Chicago, Illinois (deceased).

Prajna Paramita Prasher, Ph.D. Faculty Member, Department of Film Studies, Chatham College, Pittsburgh, Pennsylvania.

Dwarakanath G. Rao, M.D. Adjunct Clinical Assistant Professor of Psychiatry, University of Michigan Medical School; Training and Supervising Analyst, Michigan Psychoanalytic Institute, Ann Arbor, Michigan.

Satish Reddy, M.D. Assistant Professor of Clinical Psychiatry and Medicine, Faculty Member, Columbia University Center for Psychoanalytic Training and Research, New York, New York.

Alan Roland, Ph.D. Training Analyst and Faculty Member, National Psychological Association of Psychoanalysis, New York, New York.

John Munder Ross, Ph.D. Training and Supervising Analyst, Columbia University Center for Psychoanalytic Training and Research, New York, New York.

Jeffrey B. Rubin, Ph.D. Private practice of psychoanalysis and psychotherapy, New York, New York.

Bhaskar Sripada, M.D. Clinical Associate Professor of Psychiatry, University of Illinois at Chicago; Faculty Member, Institute of Psychoanalysis, Chicago, Illinois.

Pratyusha Tummala-Narra, Ph.D. Teaching Associate, Department of Psychiatry, Cambridge Hospital/Harvard Medical School; Assistant Professor of Clinical Psychiatry, Georgetown University School of Medicine, Washington, DC.

Madhusudana Rao Vallabhaneni, M.D., FRCPC Lecturer in Psychiatry, Faculty of Medicine, University of Toronto; Faculty Member, Toronto Institute of Psychoanalysis, Toronto, Canada.

Preface

India has forever fascinated Western observers and yet its essence has always eluded them. Shades of gray have never appeared in their portrait of India. The country has either evoked a shudder at its poverty and overpopulation or elicited rosy idealization of its monuments and ancient civilization. The former stance, emanating from pitiful scorn, is evident in the biased coverage of India in the Western news media. Stories of malnourished children, bride burning, train accidents, caste tensions, people marrying animals in esoteric rural customs, and all varieties of superstitious surrender of logic abound in their presentation of India. The latter tendency, namely that of idealization, offers an equally unrealistic picture. India is seen as a land of omnipresent divinity, serene rivers, placid people, awe-inspiring palaces, and temples for spiritual rejuvenation. Regardless of whether the Western view is disdainful and devaluing or charmed and idealizing, the portrayal of India ends up being a caricature.

The fact is that India is the largest secular democracy of the world. It is a nation with a nuclear capability, booming economy, and a burgeoning middle class that is educated, electronically up to date, and robust in ambition. Its cities are teeming with energy and its citizens are proud of their country. Its rural areas, where a majority of the country's population lives, are coming out of their backward status. Primitive farming equipment is being increasingly replaced by modern machines for land cultivation. The literacy rate is rising throughout the country and so is the average life expectancy, which has gone from 38.7 years in 1950 to 62.9 years in 1998, the last year for which such data are available. To be sure, social and economic problems continue to exist. Some, such as overpopulation, are old. Others, such as the rise of Hindu fundamentalism, are new. And yet, the secular and democratic spirit of the nation shines through. Voter participation in regional and national elections is high, and the public debates over political and economic matters are informed and passionate.

India also has philosophical and aesthetic traditions that are truly majestic in their scope and depth. These range from the Vedanta's unifying existentialism to Ghalib's playful symbolism, from Bhagavad Gita's enlightened pragmatism to Gandhi's unflinching pacifism, from Khajuraho's informed hedonism to Kathakali's narrative corporealism, from Buddha's contemplative realism to Tagore's spiritual lyricism, from Nanak's divine eclecticism to Nehru's sophisticated secularism, and from Kabir's poetic mysticism to Rushdie's sardonic surrealism. That the fruits of such rich intellectual trends have not been brought to bear upon the psychoanalytic thinking of the West seems unfortunate.

It is also puzzling since psychoanalysis had an early (circa 1920) and promising start in India. Girindrasheckhar Bose (1885–1953), a Calcutta-based physician who later obtained a doctorate in clinical psychology, was the "father of Indian psychoanalysis." Deeply interested in the causes of mental suffering, Bose read the little that was then available of Freud in English. More to his credit, he evolved a depth psychology of his own that was experience-near, culture-specific, and often at variance from that of Freud's. Later, the two entered into a correspondence with each other. For nearly two decades (1920–1937), they discussed theoretical notions but also evolved a personal, though ambivalent, relationship. Bose was idealizing of Freud but also an independent thinker. Freud was delighted by finding someone with common interest so far away from his native Vienna but seemed unable to allow Bose a true collegial autonomy.

After an early blossoming, psychoanalysis in India underwent intellectual and professional stagnation. The racist overtones of the British analysts in pre-independence India, the economic crisis of the postwar era, and the religious orientation of India's masses all caused the mental health profession to renounce psychoanalysis and lean toward a medical orientation. That fact that psychopharmacology challenged the Indian belief systems less than psychoanalysis also facilitated this occurrence. Factors of poverty (which causes a shift of mental energy to concerns of daily living), an intact family (which diminishes loneliness), and the pervasive influence of religion (which gives meaning to otherwise unexplained life issues and offers a particular sort of soothing stoicism) all contributed to marginalizing psychoanalysis in the Indian setting. The subsequent decades witnessed an unfortunate lack of cross-fertilization of ideas between psychoanalysis and Indian thought. This seems to be the case despite the unmistakable echoes of Hindu mysticism in some of Freud's concepts.

Take the example of the death instinct concept in Freud's theorizing. Based on observations of children turning passive traumatic experiences into play, certain analysands returning over and over again to painful past experiences, the behavior of those who must go through similar calamities repeatedly, and the frightening nightmares of war veterans, Freud suggested that there might be a "demonic force" at work in them. This force seemed to work in opposition to the pleasure principle. It is as though these individuals never comprehend the futility of their repetitions. Freud argued that this force was aligned with a fundamental attribute of the mind that involved a search for reduction of all excitation to quiescence. This "Nirvana principle" was aimed at returning the living organism to its previous, inorganic state. He concluded that "the aim of all life is death," and thus gave voice to his celebrated concept of the death instinct.

Freud acknowledged borrowing the expression "Nirvana principle" from Barbara Low, a Sanskrit expert. The notion of the death instinct thus, from the beginning, had an Eastern touch. Gustav Fechner, the renowned physiologist whose "constancy principle" had led Freud to the Nirvana principle in the first place, was himself involved in Buddhism. And the French novelist Romain Rolland, from whom Freud obtained the related concept of "oceanic feeling," was an avid reader and biographer of the nineteenth-century Bengali mystics Sri Ramakrishna

(1836–1886) and Swami Vivekenanda (1863–1902). It thus seems that the Indian mystical tradition was a background conceptual source for Freud's death instinct. This may have been part of why the concept appeared alien to Western minds.

Freud's 1913 discourse on the essential kinship between humans and animals is also congenial to Hinduism while being far from the Judeo-Christian and Islamic tenets. With minor exceptions, the Hindu perspective on animals is a much gentler and understanding one. The idea of animal mentation is not frowned upon, eating meat is discouraged, and language is rich with animal metaphors. Keeping Freud's important observation that the Western civilization causes a vertical split between the child and his animal surround allows one to think of the fluid shifts in mental representations of the two that are possible at the base of the human psyche. Thus introjective-projective use of animal imagery, far from being primitive and pathological, might be truer to the essence of humanity. Adopting such a viewpoint could minimize the puzzled amusement or mocking horror of the West at the human–animal conflation in Hindu mythology and religious icons.

Other areas of overlap between psychoanalysis and Indian thought exist as well. Wilfred Bion's recommendation that an analyst meet his patient "without memory or desire" has striking similarities with J. Krishnamurthi's detached perceptual realism, for instance. Another example is the overlap between the regard British independent analysts, especially Nina Coltart, have toward lying fallow and the positive emptiness of the mind and the *Vipaasna* meditation of the Vedantic and Buddhist traditions. (Fascinating to note here is that Bion was born in India and Coltart turned to Buddhism toward the later part of her life.)

Still other areas open for further investigation are the ways in which the Hindu concepts of *punarjanam* (reincarnation), *karma* (action with its undeniable antecedents and inevitable consequences), and *vidhi* (destiny) overlap with the psychoanalytic notions of deposited self representations, internalization of parental ego strengths and weaknesses, transgenerational transmission of trauma, "fate neurosis," and repetition compulsion. While it is tempting to focus upon the different worldviews from which these concepts arise, their courageous juxtaposition might be more heuristically rewarding in the long run. The recent contributions of Indian psychoanalysts, Western psychoanalysts interested in India, and the psychoanalysts of the Indian diaspora support this point.

However, cross-currents between psychoanalysis and Indian thought can also become turbulent. This risk is heightened if one transports personality development models from the West in an unaltered form to India and ends up pathologizing the Other. The graphic psychosexual vocabulary typical of the early psychoanalytic theory can also offend. Psychoanalytic works written in this manner can injure Indian cultural pride and lead to hermeneutic conundrums of considerable magnitude. To avoid this, one needs not only scholarly rigor but also a genuine respect for intracultural viewpoints and interdisciplinary input. A greater reliance on contemporary psychoanalytic formulations (which view human bonds as the core psychic agenda and bodily imagery as the means to realize desired relational configurations) might also benefit. The capacity for conceptual surprise and willingness to learn from the Other must also be in place. However, concerns for political correctness should not be allowed to blind the penetrating gaze of curiosity or silence the skeptical voice of speculation.

With such caveats in place and with affectionate enthusiasm for both India and psychoanalysis, I offer *Freud Along the Ganges* to the reader. It is my loving tribute to India and an expression of the profound attachment I have to my motherland. Its central idea is to bring the rich cultural traditions of India to enter into a dialectical exchange with the multilayered conceptualizations of psychoanalysis. The encounter I have arranged is aimed at enriching both these idioms, and its message is directed toward both the Indian and psychoanalytic communities. Contributions from both Indian and Western authors of repute contained here help us delve into the microcosm of Indian family life, the mysteries of homosexuality and androgyny, the mythopoeisis surrounding the Indian lore of the Ganges River, the meditative practices of Vedanta and Buddhism, the mixture of different eras and various religious heritages in the fabric of contemporary Indian culture, the music of female subjectivity in the Indian diaspora, and the maudlin extravaganza of Bollywood. This vivid collage of ideas demonstrates that Indian thought and psychoanalysis can indeed enrich each other, and that such enhancement might extend from knowledge to affect and from contemplation to praxis.

PROLOGUE

Psychoanalysis in India

Salman Akhtar and Pratyusha Tummala-Narra

The field of repression in normal life is very much wider than is usually believed. Our ideas of morality, crime, punishment, chastity, social duty etc. all owe their motive powers to this source.

Girindrashekhar Bose (1921, p. 151)

Few practitioners in Western psychoanalytic circles are familiar with the interesting saga of the development of psychoanalysis in India. Indeed, many colleagues would be surprised to learn that psychoanalysis began in India very early (circa 1920) in the course of its history and that this happened almost independently of Freud's direct involvement. Such a dramatic advent, however, did not lead to sustained growth and popular acceptance. Indeed, a prolonged period of a marginalized, even moribund, existence followed, though the situation has recently begun showing signs of reversal. There is renewed enthusiasm for the discipline in India, and the participation of Indian psychoanalysts in the meetings of the International Psychoanalytic Association is on the rise.

These ups and downs in the history of Indian psychoanalysis are the topic of this chapter. We provide a brief survey of the nodal points in this narrative and their sociocultural background. We introduce the dramatis personae, highlight the theoretical contributions, and bring the reader up to date with some comments on the current psychoanalytic interest in India and the people of the Indian diaspora.

GIRINDRASHEKHAR BOSE

Psychoanalysis in India began with the work of Girindrashekhar Bose, a psychiatrist who received his medical degree from Calcutta Medical College in 1910, and his master's degree in experimental psychology from the University of Calcutta in 1917. In 1921 he received the first doctor of science degree in psychology awarded in India, for his thesis entitled "The Concept of Repression." Bose's keen interest in psychiatry was preceded by his interest in hypnotism and magic. He was born in 1887, the youngest of nine children of the *Diwan* (estate manager) of a *Maharaja* in Bihar. His family moved to Calcutta after his father's retirement, where he received his schooling. He married at age 17, which was not unusual for his era, and had two daughters (Sinha 1966). Bose's family life was highly influenced by Hindu philosophy and Indian cultural traditions, including a belief in the supernatural (Kakar 1995, P. Mehta 1997).

By 1914 Bose developed his psychoanalytic ideas almost independently of Freud. Although he had heard of Freud's discoveries soon after he began his psychiatric practice, he had access only to newspaper and lay magazine articles in Western psychoanalysis, as English translations of Freud's works were not available (Sinha 1966). His technique included suggestion, recall of memories, and encouraging associations.

In 1921 Bose published a book entitled *Concept of Repression*. It is a highly interesting treasure trove of ideas. Its main thesis revolves around what Bose called the theory of opposite wishes. According to this theory, no wish exists without a counterpart in the psyche. A wish to hate is always accompanied by a wish to be hated, a wish to love by a wish to be loved, an exhibitionistic wish by a voyeuristic one, and so on. Individually, all wishes are pleasurable. Unpleasure arises only in conflict with its opposite. The mind resolves such conflict by vacillation between the two wishes, by compromise formation, or, most often, by fulfilling one of the wishes. The repressed wish, however, continues to exert its effect. It is at this point that Bose makes a suggestion that moves his otherwise one-person model to a sophisticated two-person psychology. He declares that the repressed wish

> finds satisfaction by the mechanism of identity. It is obvious that the manifest wish and its opposite latent one can not both have satisfaction at one and the same time. The latent wish, which in its manifest form, would exactly correspond to the situation of the object, finds satisfaction by the subject identifying himself with the object. Unless this identification takes place, the object's not apprehended by the psyche of the subject and remains a non-entity as far as the subject is concerned. This identity is the bond of relation between the object and the subject and on it depends the true appreciation of the nature of the object. [Bose 1921, pp. 122–123]

This remarkable passage contains the seeds of ideas regarding projective identification and intersubjectivity long before these concepts were explicitly developed in the West. Given the fact that in any interaction each partner has a subjectivity and is treating the other as an object, Bose's statement that "the aim of all reactions is to bring about a state of identity between the subject and the object" (p. 126) seems to be the unknown precursor of the relational and intersubjective emphasis in North American psychoanalysis.

Bose also gave a unique and original twist to the concept of castration anxiety. He proposed that the castration threat appears convincingly frightening to the oedipal boy not only because of its talion aspect or its narcissistic dimension but also because the wish to be a female already exists in the boy's unconscious. The push factor of castration gets combined with a pull factor of a deep, early maternal identification from which the boy had only reluctantly emerged and that continued to exert its pressure from within. Once again, the sophistication of Bose's thought is striking. Not only did it anticipate the notion of primary femininity proposed some fifty years later by Stoller (1976), it also allowed for a layered model of gender multiplicity that is a far cry from Freud's (1905, 1925) phallocentric monism.

While these two ideas, namely the theory of the opposite wish and the boy's preoedipal wish to be female, constitute the central contributions of Bose's book, it contains valuable insights regarding many other topics of psychoanalytic interest. These range from poetry to martyrdom, from travel to jurisprudence, and from religion to the significance of smell in emotional life. Examples include the following. "Death is painful to the ordinary man but even this is sought by a patriot or a martyr who is not necessarily pathological" (p. 54). "The beneficial aspect of exercise is always explained on physiological grounds and the psychological factor is usually lost sight of" (p. 100). "It has been common knowledge that smell has a specially close relationship with feeling and memory. A whiff of perfume would often rouse up long-forgotten memories, cheerful or depressing as the case may be" (p. 163). In a world replete with suicide bombers, fitness fanatics, and vast cosmetic and vestmental paraphernalia to evoke "retro" effects, Bose's observations sound entirely fitting indeed.

Bose also makes useful comments on treatment technique. Note the following: "It is always desirable that analysis be conducted in such a way as to avoid all excessive reactions" (p. 111). A similar attention to tact is evident in Bose's comment that during the activation of intense negative transference, "the patient needs most careful handling and it is best to avoid all further analysis so long as this phase lasts" (p. 111); clearly by "analysis" Bose means "interpretation," since he is not recommending interruption of the treatment. If true, this oscillating stance between "handling" and "analysis" is very much in accord with what, many decades later, Balint (1968) would describe as optimal technique in his book *The Basic Fault* and what Killingmo (1989) would refer to as desirable adjustments in the analyst's interventional attitude with fluctuations in the analysand's level of mental functioning.

Bose's book also comments on dreams, making an astute link between the nightly dreams and real-life writing of a play:

> A dramatist, in creating his characters, has to conjure up the cravings of each and thus he gives expression to such wishes. The hero is not the only character through whom repressed desires find vent. Every character in a good drama represents some phase or the other of the author's repressed or latent cravings. So also in dreams. [p. 156]

While expressing a viewpoint that, for the Western world, will be voiced much later by Fairbairn (1952), Bose's perspective on dreams and creativity is hardly in discord with that of Freud. This brings us, full circle, back to the letters the two exchanged with each other.

THE BOSE–FREUD CORRESPONDENCE

Bose began a correspondence with Freud in 1921 and their exchange of letters lasted until 1937. It involved numerous discussions concerning the organizational and theoretical aspects of psychoanalysis (Akhtar 2001, Ramana 1964). Bose expressed his admiration for Freud's discoveries in his initial letter, stating, "Along with my friends and relations I have been a warm admirer of your theories and science" (quoted in Ramana 1964, p. 117). He sent a copy of his book with his initial letter to Freud. Freud responded to Bose in May 1921:

> I acknowledge the receipt of your book on "The Concept of Repression" and am glad to testify [as to] the correctness of its principal views and the good sense appearing in it. My surprise was great that Psycho-analysis should have met with so much interest and recognition in your far country. [Quoted in Ramana 1964, p. 117]

Over the next seventeen years, the tone of the correspondence between the two men was polite, with an occasional but clear disagreement around theoretical matters, especially Bose's theory of opposite wishes and his conception of the castration threat. Freud's response to Bose's ideas was mixed, in that while he commended Bose for his insights, he was not convinced of their validity. Along with a letter dated January 31, 1929, Bose sent Freud a series of his papers on various topics, and requested that Freud draw his attention to his paper entitled "The Genesis and Adjustment of the Oedipus Wish." Freud conveyed his thoughts about Bose's ideas in the following statement in a letter dated March 9, 1929: "Your theory of the opposite wish appears to me to stress rather a formal element than a dynamic factor. I still think you underrate the efficiency of the castration fear" (Ramana 1964, p. 125). Bose responded by stating, "I do not deny the importance of the castration threat in European cases; my argument is that the threat owes its efficiency to its connection with the wish to be a female. . . . The desire to be a female is more easily unearthed in Indian male patients than in European ones" (pp. 125–126). Bose further described the relevance of his theory of opposite wishes in explaining various psychic phenomena (i.e., sadism and masochism, exhibitionism and voyeurism).

Freud's feelings toward Bose's ideas are captured well in his letter dated May 12, 1929: "I wonder what the relation of the opposite wish to the phenomena of ambivalence may be" (p. 127). While he seemed to be intrigued by Bose's efforts, he was clearly unprepared to address the cultural specifics of Bose's ideas. In a letter addressed to Bose on December 13, 1931, Freud wrote, in response to receiving an ivory statuette of *Vishnu* (the Preserver of the Universe) for his seventy-fifth birthday from Bose, "As long as I can enjoy life it will recall to my mind the progress of psychoanalysis and the proud conquests[1] it has made in foreign countries" (p. 128). It appears from Freud's comments that he, in some ways similar to some of his European contemporaries, was more interested in a theoretical conquest than in Indian mental life as elaborated by Bose and his colleagues.

Interestingly, Bose, while highly influenced by Freud's theories, had actually created an Indian psychoanalysis with separate, distinct theoretical notions. He was committed to the integration of traditional Indian philosophy with the Western notion of unconscious processes. Bose's letters reflect both a curiosity about Freud and a cautious interpretation of Freud's response to him. In a letter dated January 26, 1922, Bose wrote,

A friend of mine Mr. J, Sen—a celebrated Indian artist and an ardent admirer of yours—has drawn from imagination a pencil sketch which he thinks you ought to look like. I am sending you the original keeping a copy for myself which I would like to compare with your photo when it arrives. Needless to say he has not the slightest information about your features. [Quoted in Ramana 1964, p. 118]

On March 1, 1922, Freud replied, "The imaginative portrait you sent me is very nice indeed, far too nice for the subject. You will soon have occasion to confront it with the photo and see that the artist did not take into account certain racial characters" (pp. 119–121).

Freud and Bose never met, although each extended invitations to the other to visit him in his native country.[2] Bose's daughter and son-

---

1. Freud's use of the word *conquests* is telling. Not only does it express his ever-present longing for a "conquistador" (Gay 1988), it also reveals an unfortunate tendency of psychoanalysis to colonize other idioms of thought rather than enter into a mutually enhancing, dialectical relationship with them. Applied psychoanalysis especially needs rectification in this regard.

2. Freud did meet another, world-renowned Indian luminary, namely the Nobel

in-law, however, did meet Freud briefly during their visit to Vienna. Bose, in a letter dated October 4, 1932, wrote, "My daughter had been hearing about you ever since she was a little child and she has written to me a glowing account of her impressions about yourself. I only wish I had the opportunity of conveying my thanks to you personally." Freud responded in letter dated November 8, 1932:

> I could not read your kind letter without feelings of embarrassment. In fact, I do not deserve the gratitude of your children owing to the fact that I and my daughter were full in work, my wife and her sister not speaking your language and difficulties in our household making it hard for us to invite them for meals. [Quoted in Ramana 1964, pp. 128–129]

How much of this difficulty in inviting Bose's daughter for a meal emanated from Freud's real problems and how much from inner ambivalence is hard to say. One does wonder about the latter, though, given Freud's mixed reaction to Indians in general and to Bose's theoretical independence from him in particular.

Despite their polite, and sometimes warm, correspondence, several realities in the lives of these two men contributed to their disconnection. It is not that they did not have important similarities. Both enjoyed a privileged economic background. And both worked under the yoke of ethnic oppression (i.e., Viennese anti-Semitism in the case of Freud and British colonization in the case of Bose). Yet their sociopolitical worlds stood in sharp contrast from one another, with Freud identified with European intellectual traditions and Bose with the Indian cultural ethos. Bose's theoretical ideas were tied to Hindu philosophy, whereas Freud's theories sharply questioned religious authority. Moreover, Bose was interested in the cultural specificity of the psychoanalytic idea, while Freud was devoted to formulating a universal theory

---

Prize–winning poet Rabindranath Tagore. Biswas (2003) has recently provided an account of this encounter (included here as Chapter 3). Freud's reaction was one of strong ambivalence. On the one hand, he said that Tagore "is a wonderful sight, he really looks like we imagined the Lord God looks" (quoted in Goldman 1985, p. 293). On the other hand, in a prejudicial remark, he wrote to Ferenczi a few days later that "my quota of Indians has now been filled for quite a long time" (quoted in Falzeder and Brabant 2000, p. 290).

of the mind. It is not surprising that these differences led to the two men forming a deeply ambivalent relationship.

THE PSYCHOANALYTIC HISTORY IN INDIA

The Origins of Indian Psychoanalysis in Calcutta

Bose founded the Indian Psychoanalytic Society in 1922 and, with the assistance of Ernest Jones, established its affiliation with the International Psychoanalytic Association in the same year. While Bose began conducting informal analyses with members of his Calcutta-based group right away, formal analytic training through the Indian Psychoanalytic Institute did not begin until 1930 (Akhtar 2001, Sinha 1966). The Indian Psychoanalytic Society consisted of fifteen original members, nine of whom were academicians in psychology or philosophy and five of whom served in the medical corps of the Indian Army (Kakar 1995).

The objectives of the Indian Psychoanalytic Society, as outlined by its original members, included the "cultivation and furtherance of the science of psychoanalysis" (Ramana 1964, p. 114) through scientific discussion, creating facilities for work, providing lectures, and translating psychoanalytic works into English. The members of the society were actively involved through the 1940s in meeting these objectives. Two major developments in psychoanalytic practice and discourse were the establishment of Lumbini Park Mental Hospital in 1940, the first inpatient psychotherapy facility in India, and the publication of *Samiksa* (Sanskrit for "analysis") in 1947, the society's official journal in English (Ramana 1964, Sinha 1966). Bose further established psychoanalytic teaching in the undergraduate and postgraduate psychology courses at the University of Calcutta, where he served as the chairman of the Department of Psychology from 1929 to 1949. Postgraduate students and medical students also undertook psychoanalytically informed training at Lumbini Park (Sinha 1966).

Early Indian Psychoanalysts

Several Indian psychiatrists, such as Tarun Sinha and C. V. Ramana, were trained by Bose and H. P. Maity, and became actively involved in the practice of and training in psychoanalysis. Sinha, Ramana, Mitra, and Desai, in particular, were involved in the publication of *Samiksa*, the structuring of psychoanalytic training, and the running of the Lumbini Park clinic. Following Bose's death in June 1953, S. C. Mitra and Tarun Sinha served successively in the role of president of the Indian Psychoanalytic Society. The society created a school, called *Bodhayana*, in 1949 for children with emotional disturbances. In 1959 Sinha initiated the publication of *Chitta*, a Bengali-language magazine aimed at educating the lay public in psychology and psychoanalysis (Sinha 1966).

The extent to which such initiatives influenced the lay public is unclear, but there is no question that these analysts' efforts created a lively intellectual space for psychoanalytic inquiry in Calcutta. The discourse of Indian psychoanalysts between 1920 and 1950 indicates their concern with the Indian culture, including the adaptive and defensive uses of Hindu mythology in their patients' mental lives, the study of Indian sculptural motifs such as the *lingam* as representing phallic aspects of the oedipal situation, and studies of the Hindu family (Kakar 1994). The writings of Bose and his contemporaries, while certainly influenced by Freud, were unique in that they considered the psychological lives of Indians from the standpoint of appreciation of Indian culture and traditions. In effect, Indians were subjects of inquiry and not exoticized or pathologized objects of examination. The struggle to pursue this form of inquiry into the Indian psyche has continued in contemporary psychoanalysis in India and in Western countries.

The Colonial Context

British colonialism significantly influenced the development of psychoanalysis in India, not to mention the profound impact it had on the Indian psyche at large. Two of the original members of the Indian Psychoanalytic Society, Owen Berkeley-Hill and Claude Dangar Daly, were British army officers. Tragically, both men used psychoanalysis as a vehicle of cultural prejudice and oppression in their studies of the Hindu personality (Hartnack 1987). They displayed an astonishing lack of curiosity in the experiential individuality of their Indian subjects and in the positive aspects of Indian culture. Their work, largely propelled by their wish to maintain the colonizer's superior position, contributed to what P. Mehta (1997) has defined as a "split-self representation" within the Indian psyche; this consists of the "intrusive dominating foreign British self and the native, submissive, inferior Indian self" (p. 457). Both Berkeley-Hill and Daly published articles in *Samiksa* and the *International Journal of Psycho-Analysis* portraying Indians as inferior and infantile. They even spoke of a need for the British to take the role of enlightened parents for the Indian people. Berkeley-Hill (1921) wrote a paper entitled "The Anal-Erotic Factor in the Religion, Philosophy, and Character of the Hindus," in which he used Jones's (1918) work on anal eroticism as a springboard for describing the modal Hindu character as given to greed and hoarding besides being "insanely short tempered and vindictive" (p. 336). He stated:

No one can deny that as a general rule the Hindus exhibit a disastrous propensity to quarrel, especially in the family circle, and to this trait is added, what is still worse, vindictiveness. Reference has already been made to the miserliness, meanness and pettiness of the Hindus, and as these traits are so well known there is no call to notice them further. . . . The tendency to dictate and to tyrannise is such a notorious trait of all Oriental character that it is not surprising to find it a prominent feature of Hindu character. [p. 336]

Daly, who did not work with a single Indian patient, stated, "In the Hindu, we have a psychology that differs considerably from the European, its equivalent with us being found in pathological cases" (1930, p. 210). In an applied psychoanalytic paper entitled "The Psychology of Revolutionary Tendencies" (1930), he expressed his opinion about the Indian freedom fighters such as Gandhi and Ghosh. He portrayed them as displaying childlike reactions to their overwhelming and pathological love of India, which he said symbolized the oedipal mother. Daly added:

When we realize the nature of the Hindu's unconscious tendencies, we must see how easy it is for the young Hindu to form revolutionary groups . . . . They have engraved on their ego an ideal of the mother whose incestual love is denied them, and insatiable unconscious hate of any power that comes between them and their primitive desires. [p. 209]

Having thus "established" Hindu infantilism as the basis of the Indian freedom movement, Daly found it logical to recommend that the British act as parents for them. He even felt that psychoanalysis could help the British adopt and maintain this role:

It is only by a deep study of the psychology and needs of the Indian people, and the application of the knowledge obtained by psychological research, that the British government can hope to continue to rule them to their best advantage in the present, and perhaps guide them to final liberation from their psychological fixations in the future. [p. 197]

What is striking in all this is the utter unawareness of distortions arising from a racist countertransference, confusion of group with individual psychology, and the disregard of actual sociopolitical variables in an oppressed people's rebellion. In all fairness, however, it should be acknowledged that in 1930, when Daly's paper was written, psychoanalysis was too intoxicated by the discovery of the unconscious, and omissions of the sort mentioned above were hardly rare. Yet the prejudicial attitude is difficult to overlook. As a result of it, such writings come across as having more to do with British imperialism and its racist propaganda than with genuine psychoanalytic study. They also reflected the author's defensively contemptuous reaction to the Indian independence movement, which threatened their identities and existence within India.

Despite such prejudices, the British analysts served as links between the Bengali intellectuals of Calcutta and the International Psychoanalytic Association based in London and Vienna. Berkeley-Hill, in particular, was involved in the training of second-generation Indian psychoanalysts, and became the president of the Indian Psychoanalytic Association (1927–1938). And yet, the details of Berkeley-Hill and Daly's relationship with the Indian psychoanalysts remains a bit unclear, which is not surprising given the precarious nature of any open discussion or opposition expressed against analysts' ideas. They represented the ruling class, after all. Their writings on Indians were likely not discussed at any significant length in the meetings of the Indian Psychoanalytic Society. Hartnack (1987) points out that Bose, in an obituary of Berkeley-Hill, wrote that he would be missed by the "mental sufferers" of India, but he did not mention himself or any other sane Indian in this context.[3]

---

3. Bose's irony closely resembles Freud's remark regarding the Gestapo. Upon being asked to declare in writing that he was not inconvenienced by the Gestapo in any way, Freud is known to have written that the Gestapo has been good to him, wryly adding that he "can most highly recommend the Gestapo to everyone" (Gay 1988, p. 628).

THE CONTEMPORARY SCENE

Postindependence Psychoanalysis

The gradual decline of psychoanalysis in India, after its independence from the British in 1947, was at least in part related to the extensive poverty, resulting from prolonged colonial rule, the country's partition, and war. Sinha (1966), in his account of the development of psychoanalysis in Calcutta, stated that the major problems in the spread of psychoanalytic ideas were encountered immediately after World War II, in part due to restrictions on food supply and physical mobility. In describing the situation in Bengal, he stated, "Thousands died and many fell victim to mental disorders. There were no arrangements to house them or to treat them with care or medicines" (p. 436). Commenting upon India's partition, he wrote that "refugees started swarming in and around Calcutta and many of them became mentally sick. There was an acute economic crisis in the Society" (p. 437). With the increasing need to attend to these external realities, the physical and emotional resources involved in the practice and teaching of psychoanalysis became even more limited than before.

By the mid-1950s, psychoanalysis, as developed by Bose and the pioneering first and second generations of Indian psychoanalysts, had entirely lost its foothold in academic psychiatry. More unfortunately, there was a demise of originality in psychoanalytic thought specific to Indian mental life. Kakar (1994) noted that the number of Indian analysts (thirty) in 1994 remained more or less unchanged in the previous fifty years.

Several contemporary analysts of Indian and non-Indian descent have speculated on the decline of interest and/or rejection of psychoanalysis in postindependence India (Akhtar 2001, Kakar 1995, P. Mehta 1997, Roland 1988, Sinha 1966). One reason for the ambivalence entailed the anticolonial feelings of the early twentieth century Indian intellectuals, who wished to maintain their distinctly Indian identity. Many of them emphasized spirituality and metaphysics, affirming the Indian identity and even implying superiority over Western materialism (Kakar 1994). The writings of European analysts on the Indian psyche, which lacked a genuine appreciation of Indian culture, further fueled the rejection of psychoanalytic ideas. Indeed, there is little disagreement on the pervasiveness of colonial and anticolonial intentions in the discourse on Western and Indian psychology (Kakar 1994, P. Mehta 1997). One recent example is Kurtz's (1992) book on the impact of multiple mothering on character formation in India. According to him, a modal Indian child develops easy attachments to other female figures in his environment because the mother–child physical closeness in India is not accompanied by a deep emotional bond between them. Kurtz does not recognize that lack of bonding with the mother does not lead to a movement toward healthy socialization with others. It breaks the heart of the self and results in narcissistic withdrawal, if not schizoid regression. The assertions Kurtz makes appear racist and incredible. He states, "During the period of physical contact, there is not the same sort of attention or mirroring as would be expected in the West to accompany intense physical contact or breast feeding" (p. 100); "healthy, empathic mirroring seems to be entirely absent here" (p. 252). Such assertions appear

> contrary to (a) common sense, (b) the instinctive behavior of higher mammalian mothers, (c) Carstairs's observations of numerous Hindu mother–infants dyads, (d) my own informal, though numerous, observations in this regard, (e) Kakar's and Roland's analytic reconstructions, (f) the Hindu myths of profound mother–child love, (g) idiomatic expressions in many Indian languages (e.g., *Aankh ka taara* in Hindi, suggesting that a baby is literally the gleam in the mother's eye), and (h) the portrayal of mother–infant dyads in countless Indian paintings from antiquity to the present. The striking picture presented by Kurtz, of a "disjunction between physical ministration and emotional attention in Hindu mothering" (p. 51), comes from descriptions by Western anthropologists who have largely witnessed poverty-ridden households. And are the distracting pressures of poverty to be equated with lack of love? [Akhtar 1997a, p. 1017]

It is this sort of attitude that alienated (and, continues to alienate) Indian thinkers and academics from psychoanalysis. Yet another reason for the rejection of psychoanalysis in India had to do with the divergent attitudes toward religion inherent in the Indian and the Freudian psychoanalytic contexts. Western psychoanalysts interpreted religious experience in terms of psychopathology, compensations, and compromise formations (Freud 1927, 1930). Such antireligious sentiment stood in sharp contrast to the pervasiveness of religious or spiritual practice among Indian analyst and analysands alike. In fact, as Roland (1988) pointed out, many leading contemporary Indian psychiatrists who most vehemently reject psychoanalysis are involved in Indian spiritual practices.

The West–East psychoanalytic discord also arose from the powerful individual and collective orientations of the two societies, respectively. In the West, autonomy and separateness are upheld as ideals to strive for, while in the East, premium is placed upon attachment and interdependence. In the West, the matter of sociological theoretical concern is "optimal distance" (Akhtar 1992a, Escoll 1992, Mahler et al. 1975) and in the East, it is "optimal closeness" (Edward et al. 1981). As a result, the Indian ideal of interdependence on one's family, especially the mother, gets devalued in classical psychoanalytic models. Freud is known to have said in exasperation to an Indian patient, "Oh, you Indians with your eternal mother complex!" (as quoted in Kakar 1994).[4] The individual versus collective frameworks have technical implications as well. Western patients, regardless of the intensity of their transferences, almost always "remember" that their analyst is not actually a relative of theirs. Indian patients, in contrast, frequently relate to the analyst as an extended family member or guru who is not only personally involved in the treatment process but is also integral to their actual lives outside the treatment setting (Kakar 1995).

Together these three factors (revolt against colonialism, pervasive involvement of religion in life, and an overall collective bent of psychological experience) led to a gradual decline of psychoanalysis in India. The early tension between psychiatry and psychoanalysis, initiated by Bose himself, became further entrenched with the rise of biological psychiatry throughout the nation, especially because it was less challenging to the Indian cultural beliefs. And yet, small pockets of psychoanalytic interest survived here and there. Actually there is some evidence of a renewed interest in discipline across the nation.

---

4. One wonders how Freud would respond given an opportunity to reflect upon the contradiction between his exasperation over Indians' love of their mothers and his own lifelong devotion to his mother, often at the cost of excluding his wife and children during his visits to her (Gay 1988).

Regional Differences in Practice of Psychoanalysis in India

Indians are markedly heterogeneous with respect to geography, race, language, religions, and customs. G. Mehta (1997) has aptly called India a "land of fabulous contrast," where every river, lake, and mountain is the repository of divine mythologies of the Hindus, Muslims, Christians, Buddhists, Sikhs, Jains, Parsis, and Jews alike. It is a common experience for many Indians who visit a different region of India to feel like foreigners, due to differences in language, food, and customs. The contradictions of India are numerous, and the ability to live with them is encompassed in one's identity as an Indian. It is not surprising, then, that the practice of psychoanalysis by analysts also has distinct forms in different parts of India.

This began with the migration of several Bengali analysts from Calcutta. Two of the leading psychoanalysts of the Indian Psychoanalytic Society, Desai and Ramana, moved to Bombay and the United States, respectively, between 1934 and 1955. The institute in Calcutta continued to struggle under the heroic leadership of Hironmoy Ghoshal, who recently passed away, and D. N. Nandi. There are younger individuals like Jhuma Basak and Varsha Bhansali who, along with others, continue to strive for the preservation of psychoanalysis in Calcutta. *Samiksa* is still in publication, and the Calcutta analysts are making valiant efforts to learn and grow by participating in International Psychoanalytic Congresses.

A second analytic training institute was established in 1945 in Bombay (now Mumbai), with the leadership of the Italian analyst Emilio Servidio. Bombay also became the home of the Psychoanalytic Therapy and Research Center, and the Indian Council on Mental Health, a psychoanalytically oriented school and college counseling center. While the Calcutta (now Kolkata) analysts identified themselves as classical Freudians, the dominant orientation of the Bombay group is one of object relations, specifically the work of Melanie Klein and Wilfred Bion. This group is represented by Aiveen Bharucha, Manek Bharucha, Sarosh Forbes, and Shailesh Kapadia.[5] It has held a few collaborative meetings

---

5. For a complete listing of qualified psychoanalysts in various parts of India, see *Membership Handbook and Roster of the International Psychoanalytic Association* (2003, p. 603).

with their Israeli and Australian colleagues. Some of its members (e.g., Kapadia 1998) have published papers of clinical interest employing notions from ancient Hindu mythology.

The few psychoanalysts that are in New Delhi are a mixed group. Mallika Akbar and Madhu Sarin are clinically devoted, while others, for instance Ashok Nagpal and Ashis Nandy, are mostly academically and sociologically inclined. Sudhir Kakar, the most widely published and internationally known psychoanalyst of India, has moved from New Delhi to Goa. He is largely Eriksonian in orientation, with a strong influence from social sciences. His oeuvre is simply too vast even to list here. Suffice to say that he has published extensively and meaningfully on personality development, sexuality, youth, love relations, Hindu–Muslim conflict, and mysticism within the Indian context (Kakar 1990a,b, 1991a,b, 1993, 1996). After Freud, Kakar is the only analyst throughout the world to receive the highly coveted Goethe Prize; this was bestowed upon him by German Federal President Roman Herzog on March 22, 1998, in the Goethe town of Weimar, Germany.

In Ahmedabad, B. K. Ramanujam, drawing from Freudian theory, has made significant contributions in psychoanalytic work with children and families at the Bhikubhai Manekbhai Institute of Mental Health. It is worth noting that the B. M. Institute provides low-cost psychoanalytically oriented treatment to patients, which has been made possible through the funding of the eminent Sarabhai family (Akhtar 2001, Roland 1988). Two practicing analysts in Ahmedabad, namely M. M. Trivedi and Smita Gouthi, are members of the International Psychoanalytic Association.

Kakar (1995) attributes the strong influence of Klein and Bion's ideas on the work of the Bombay analysts to the high degree of westernization in Bombay. He also suggests that classical models of psychoanalysis tend to be either rejected in their entirety or accepted without critical examination and utility within the Indian context, reflective of the aftermath of colonization. The universalistic bias of many Indian analysts, according to Kakar, is related to patients' reluctance or refusal to seek help through analysis. Kakar's work is likely to parallel the smaller group of analysts and psychoanalytically oriented psychiatrists and psychologists who constitute a middle ground between the classical analysts and the biologically oriented psychiatrists in India. These individuals, primarily trained in Western countries, are well versed in contemporary psychoanalytic theory, make efforts to understand the Indian psyche in its own right, and modify modes of psychoanalytic therapy to help Indian patients. Consequently, they are defining new professional identities as Indian analysts (Roland 1988).

Moving Beyond the Colonial and Anticolonial Discourse

Psychoanalysis in India continues to be in a formative state. There are several areas of inquiry, specific to the Indian context, that need further psychoanalytic investigation, including the impact of linguistic and religious differences on the shaping of the psyche. There has been a lack of attention directed to issues specific to women, and the role of poverty and other sociopolitical conditions in one's mental life. Furthermore, colonial terminology continues to prevail in the psychoanalytic writings on Indians, by both Indian and non-Indian analysts.

These gaps in Indian psychoanalysis may in part reflect a relative absence of the contributions of intersubjective perspectives, which emphasize the unique constitution of the analyst, patient, and their relationship (Mitchell 1988). In his classic early study on high-caste Hindus, Carstairs (1957), while acknowledging the potential impact of his Scottish background on his role as an interviewer/observer, does not truly elaborate the relevance of this issue in his findings. Similarly, most Indian analysts, in their written works, have not discussed the significance of countertransference in the analytic process. The further examination of the relational aspects of the analytic encounter would be particularly relevant in the Indian context, in light of the limited applicability of a homogenized Western psychoanalysis to the distinct aspects of Indian society.

THE DIASPORA ANALYSTS

Not only did psychiatry become increasingly phenomenological and psychopharmacological in India, Indian psychiatrists living abroad also followed the same path. Few Indian psychiatrists of the diaspora pursued psychoanalytic training. The reasons for this seem varied.

First, Indian physicians have generally come from joint families and, as children, have grown up with a large number of relatives. Such lack of aloneness in childhood, while having immensely salutary effect on personality formation, is not infrequently accompanied by lack of self-reflectiveness, a quality necessary for developing interest in psychoanalysis. Second, the minds of Indian physicians seem to have a split in the "hard" and "soft" aspects that deal respectively with scientific and spiritual and/or artistic matters. The latter aspects either are expressed in personal (and not professional) lives or emerge only during the later phases of life span in the form of meditation and religiosity. This split also precludes interest in psychoanalysis. Third, till recently the American psychoanalytic profession did not act in an encouraging fashion toward Indian psychiatrists and this also resulted in the latter's disinterest in the field. Fourth, the paucity of Indian role models within the psychoanalytic profession might also be a contributing factor here. Finally, the highly expensive requirement of personal analysis in the course of analytic training might also have played a discouraging role. [Akhtar 2002, pp. 1–2]

Fortunately, this trend of Indian psychiatrists avoiding psychoanalysis is reversing. Many are now deciding to obtain psychoanalytic training in the Western countries of their residence. They seem to be following in the footsteps of the few but outstanding Indians who emigrated to England during the 1940s and 1950s and became psychoanalysts. This group includes Masud Khan, Narain Jethmalani, Prakash Bhandari, and Harwant Singh Gill. Arriving in England in 1946, Khan trained in psychoanalysis and rapidly rose through the ranks and became a towering, if controversial, presence on the British psychoanalytic scene. Hobbled by emotional and physical ailments of his own, Khan nonetheless became the associate editor of the *International Journal of Psycho-Analysis* and, at least at the beginning of his career, was a highly sought-after analyst and supervisor. A gifted and prolific writer, Khan published numerous papers, which have been collected in four books (Khan 1974, 1980, 1983, 1988). His contributions, especially his paper on cumulative trauma (1963), his relationship with the great British psychoanalyst Donald Winnicott, and his tragic professional downfall have become a part of psychoanalytic legend (Cooper 1993, Limentani 1992, Sandler 2004). Khan's fame and notoriety aside, British analysis also saw Gill's (1982, 1987, 1988) papers dealing with clinical and developmental issues as well as the principled clinical and didactic contributions of Baljeet Mehra and Kamal Mehra.

Moving across the Atlantic, one encounters eleven practicing analysts of Indian origin in the United States and three in Canada. The former group consists of Salman Akhtar, R. Rao Gogineni, Rajiv Gulati, Shireen Kapodia, Saida Koita, Purnima Mehta, Monisha Nayar, Dwarkanath Rao, Satish Reddy, Bhaskar Sripada, and Dushyant Trivedi. The latter group consists of Jaswant Guzder, Madhusudana Rao Vallabhneni, and Dushyant Yajnik. While most of them have provided outreach services to the Indian community, taught in psychoanalytic institutes, and contributed to psychoanalytic literature, it is Akhtar who has been most prominent in this regard. Among his important contributions are his papers on optimal distance (1992a), pathological optimism and inordinate nostalgia (1996), immigration (1995b, 1999a), forgiveness (2002), and terrorism (1997b, 2003a). These papers, alongside his earlier contributions to the understanding of personality disorders as well as his other contributions, have been gathered in five books (Akhtar 1992b, 1995a, 1999a,b, 2003b).

Besides the United States, England, and Canada, there are three other countries with practicing psychoanalysts of Indian origin. These are France, Germany, and Australia, where Shama Hirdjee and Harbans Nagpal; Tapasi Gupta; Dev Aterya and Shahid Najeeb; respectively, practice.

CONCLUSION

We have offered this wide-ranging survey of the events and dramatis personae in the history of Indian psychoanalysis with three aims in mind. First, we wish to familiarize Western psychoanalysts with a lesser known facet of our field's evolution. Second, we want to remind Indian readers of the remarkably early advent of psychoanalysis in their nation; this is not to kindle maudlin nostalgia but to reopen the mental space that had existed earlier for new imagination and conceptual growth. Finally, our hope is that the crosscurrents between psychoanalysis and Indian thought that we have merely mentioned here might become foci of attention from others. We hope that this chapter will stir further psychoanalytic interest in themes that were dear to Bose (ambivalence, early identification with mother, the role of poetry in relieving mental anguish, man's desperate need for his fellow beings, and death's integral relationship with life) as well as themes that pertain to cross-cultural relativism of psychoanalysis. All this, we think, might lead to a greater cultural elasticicity in psychoanalytic theory and technique. In a world with rapidly intermingling demography and cultures, such broadening of psychoanalytic concepts would be indeed welcome.

REFERENCES

Akhtar, S. (1992a). Tethers, orbits, and invisible fences: clinical, developmental, sociocultural and technical aspects of optimal distance. In *When the Body Speaks: Psychological Meanings in Kinetic Clues*, ed. S. Kramer and S. Akhtar, pp. 21–57. Northvale, NJ: Jason Aronson.

——— (1992b). *Broken Structures: Severe Personality Disorders and Their Treatment*. Northvale, NJ: Jason Aronson.

——— (1995a). *Quest for Answers: A Primer for Understanding and Treating Severe Personality Disorders*. Northvale, NJ: Jason Aronson.

——— (1995b). A third individuation: immigration, identity, and the psychoanalytic process. *Journal of the American Psychoanalytic Association* 43:1051–1084.

——— (1996). Someday and if only fantasies: pathological optimism an inordinate nostalgia as related forms of idealization. *Journal of the American Psychoanalytic Association* 44:723–753.

——— (1997a). Review of "All the Mothers Are One: Hindu India and the Cultural Reshaping of Psychoanalysis." *Journal of the American Psychoanalytic Association* 45:1014–1019.

——— (1997b). The psychodynamic dimension of terrorism. *Psychiatric Annals* 29:350–355.

——— (1999a). *Immigration and Identity: Turmoil, Treatment, and Transformation*. Northvale, NJ: Jason Aronson.

——— (1999b). *Inner Torment: Living Between Conflict and Fragmentation*. Northvale, NJ: Jason Aronson.

——— (2001). Psychoanalysis and India. In *The Freud Encyclopedia: Theory, Therapy, and Culture*, ed. B. Erwin, pp. 275–276. New York: Routledge.

——— (2002). Psychoanalysis and psychiatrists of Indian origin. *The Forum: Newsletter of the Indo-American Psychiatric Association* 67:1–2.

——— (2003a). Dehumanization: origins, manifestations, and remedies. In *Violence or Dialogue?: Psychoanalytic Reflections on Terror and Terrorism*, ed. S. Varvin and V. D. Volkan, pp. 131–145. London: International Psychoanalytic Association.

———— (2003b). *New Clinical Realms: Pushing the Envelope of Theory and Technique.* Northvale, NJ: Jason Aronson.

Balint, M. (1968). *The Basic Fault.* London: Tavistock.

Berkeley-Hill, O. (1921). The anal-erotic factor in the religion, philosophy, and character of the Hindus. *International Journal of Psycho-Analysis* 2:306–338.

Biswas, S. (2003). Rabindranath Tagore and Freudian thought. *International Journal of Psycho-Analysis* 84:717–732.

Bose, G. (1921). *Concept of Repression.* Calcutta: Sri Gouranga Press.

Carstairs, G. M. (1957). *The Twice Born: A Study of a Community of High-Caste Hindus.* Bloomington, IN: Indiana University Press.

Cooper, J. (1993). *Speak of Me As I Am: The Life and Work of Masud Khan.* London: Karnac.

Daly, C. D. (1930). The psychology of revolutionary tendencies. *International Journal of Psycho-Analysis* 11:193–210.

Edward, I., Rushin, N., and Turrini, P. (1981). *Separation-Individuation Theory and Application.* New York: Gardener.

Escoll, P. J. (1992). Vicissitudes of optimal distance through the life cycle. In *When the Body Speaks: Psychological Meanings in Kinetic Clues,* ed. S. Kramer and S. Akhtar, pp. 59–87. Northvale, NJ: Jason Aronson.

Fairbairn, W. R. D. (1952). *An Object Relations Theory of Psychoanalysis.* New York: Basic Books.

Falzeder, E., and Brabant, E., eds. (2000). *The Correspondence of Sigmund Freud and Sandor Ferenczi: 1920–1933,* vol. 3. London: Belknap.

Freud, S. (1905). Three essays on the theory of sexuality. *Standard Edition* 7:135–172.

———— (1925). Some psychical consequences of the anatomical distinctions between sexes. *Standard Edition* 19:248–258.

———— (1927). The future of an illusion. *Standard Edition* 21:5–56.

———— (1930). Civilization and its discontents. *Standard Edition* 21:57–145.

Gay, P. (1988). *Freud: A Life for Our Time.* New York: Norton.

Gill, H. S. (1982). Life context of the dreamer and the setting of dreaming. *International Journal of Psycho-Analysis* 63:475–483.

———— (1987). Effects of oedipal triumph: collapse or death of rival parent. *International Journal of Psycho-Analysis* 68:251–263.

———— (1988). Working through resistances of intrapsychic, environmental origin. *International Journal of Psycho-Analysis* 69:535.

Goldman, S. (1985). Sigmund Freuds briefe an seine patientin Anna v. Vest. *Jahrhuch Der Psychoanalysis* 17:293–294.

Hartnack, C. (1987). British psychoanalysts in colonial India. In *Psychology in Twentieth-Century Thought and Society,* ed. M. G. Ash and W. R. Woodward, pp. 233–251. New York: Cambridge University Press.

Jones, E. (1918). Anal-erotic character traits. In *Papers on Psychoanalysis*. London: Balliere Tindall and Cox, 1948.

Kakar, S. (1990a). *The Inner World: A Psycho-Analytic Study of Child and Society in India*. London: Oxford University Press.

——— (1990b). *Intimate Relations: Exploring Indian Sexuality*. Chicago: University of Chicago Press.

——— (1991a). *Shamans, Mystics, and Doctors: A Psychological Inquiry into India and Its Healing Traditions*. Chicago: University of Chicago Press.

——— (1991b). *The Analyst and the Mystic: Psychoanalytic Reflections on Religion and Mysticism*. Chicago: University of Chicago Press.

——— (1993). *Identity and Adulthood*. London: Oxford University Press.

——— (1994). Encounters of the psychological kind: Freud, Jung, and India. In *Essays in Honor of George A. De Vos*, ed. L. B. Boyer, R. M. Boyer, and H. F. Stein, pp. 263–272. Hillsdale, NJ: Analytic Press.

——— (1995). India. In *Psychoanalysis International: A Guide to Psychoanalysis Throughout the World*, ed. P. Kutter, vol. 2, pp. 16–122. Stuttgart-Bad Cannstatt, Germany: Frommann-Holzboog.

——— (1996). *The Colors of Violence: Cultural Identities, Religion, and Conflict*. Chicago: University of Chicago Press.

Kapadia, S. (1998). On borderline phenomena. *International Journal of Psycho-Analysis* 79:513–528.

Khan, M. M. R. (1963). The concept of cumulative trauma. *Psychoanalytic Study of the Child* 18:286–306.

——— (1974). *The Privacy of the Self*. New York: International Universities Press.

——— (1980). *Alienation in Perversion*. New York: International Universities Press.

——— (1983). *Hidden Selves*. New York: International Universities Press.

——— (1988). *When Spring Comes*. London: Chatto and Windus.

Killingmo, B. (1989). Conflict and deficit: implications for technique. *International Journal of Psycho-Analysis* 70:65–79.

Kurtz, S. (1992). *All the Mothers Are One: Hindu India and the Cultural Reshaping of Psychoanalysis*. New York: Columbia University Press.

Limentani, A. (1992). Obituary: M. Masud R. Khan (1924–1989). *International Journal of Psycho-Analysts* 73:155–159.

Mahler, M. S., Pine, F., and Bergman, A. (1975). *The Psychological Birth of the Human Infant*. New York: Basic Books.

Mehta, G. (1997). *Snakes and Ladders: Glimpses of Modern India*. New York: Doubleday.

Mehta, P. (1997). The import and export of psychoanalysis: India. *Journal of the American Academy of Psychoanalysis* 25(3):455–471.

Membership Handbook and Roster. (2003). London: International Psychoanalytic Association.

Mitchell, S. (1988). *Relational Concepts in Psychoanalysis: An Integration.* Cambridge, MA: Harvard University Press.

Ramana, C. V. (1964). On the early history and development of psychoanalysis in India. *Journal of the American Psychoanalytic Association* 12:110–134.

Roland, A. (1988). *In Search of Self in India and Japan: Toward a Cross-Cultural Psychology.* Princeton, NJ: Princeton University Press.

Sandler, A. M. (2004). Institutional responses to boundary violations: the case of Masud Khan. *International Journal of Psycho-Analysis* 85:27–42.

Sinha, T. C. (1966). Development of psycho-analysis in India. *International Journal of Psycho-Analysis* 47:427–439.

Stoller, R. (1976). Primary femininity. *Journal of the American Psychoanalytic Association* 24(5, suppl):59–78.

MIND

2

The Development of Gandhi's Self

Prakash N. Desai and Hyman L. Muslin

> Not by the weak, not by the unearnest,
> Not by those who practice wrong disciplines
> Can the Self be realized. The Self reveals
> Himself as the Lord of Love to the one
> Who practices right disciplines.
>
> *Mundaka Upanishad (III.ii.4)*

Gandhi was born in 1869 in Porbandar, a town on the western peninsula of India. Over the centuries the peninsula had produced rugged men, adept at war and great seafarers. The family occupied a special position in the community since the father, Karamchand (Kaba) Gandhi, was a diwan or prime minister of a small princely state. His father held the same position before him. The family was of the caste of merchants and storekeepers called Modh Banias, a subcaste of the third of the four divisions of Hindus. Staunchly religious, they belonged to a sect known as the Vaishnava, devotees of Vishnu; in fact, alongside the Gandhi home was a Vaishnava temple dedicated to Lord Krishna.

The childhood and adolescence of Gandhi unfortunately did not provide him with the experiences necessary to develop a self of vigor. Throughout his childhood, Gandhi demonstrated through his behaviors that he experienced intense inferiority and diminutive assertiveness. Gandhi demonstrated early in life the deficits associated with diminutive self-experience of worth, which ordinarily becomes transduced into the actions of assertiveness. Early in life he manifested the long-held need for a leader, his ideals for himself being insufficiently formed and unable to provide him with a compass by which he could set his sights and strive for an identified goal.

In 1925, when Gandhi was 56 years old, he was persuaded by his associates to write his autobiography, a distinctly Western enterprise (Parekh 1989). He acceded to his followers' wishes and in doing so produced a document that is remarkably similar to the material of psychoanalysis in content and form. He revealed the significant interactions of his childhood with his parents in great detail, not omitting his expectations and disappointments.

Throughout the autobiography the material is presented in a form akin to free associational thinking, and thus it reveals unconscious connections ordinarily not revealed in conversation. As a result of Gandhi's capacity to disclose these materials of his background without restraint, and especially owing to his method of reporting, the psychohistorian's task in studying Gandhi not only is made easier but also ensures a high degree of validity of the material of Gandhi's development. In describing and collating the material of his childhood, we also utilize the discussions of the childhood Gandhi had with his secretary, Pyarelal, and with his nephew, Prabhudas Gandhi, in South Africa.

PUTLIBAI, MOTHER GANDHI, AND MOHAN

In Gandhi's view, his mother was the key to his equilibrium. When he left home for England to become a barrister, he had to have his mother's permission to go. He could not leave without her blessings, something not inconsistent with his culture. When he came to England, his separation feelings centered on her, although he also left behind his wife and child. His mother was easy to idealize, a woman who busied herself each day of her life for others. She was in charge of a large household. Often there was a small army of children, friends, and associates of her husband to feed, sufficient to keep her from any direct contact with any of her children including her youngest, Mohan. His care was assigned to his sister, Raliatbehn, four years his senior. From her description (P. Gandhi 1957, Pyarelal 1965), Gandhi was a hyperkinetic child, difficult to control perhaps, and clearly lacking the minute-to-minute internal monitoring and calming/soothing necessary to institute intra-psychic peace. There were many laps for Mohan to fill, many shoulders for him to lean on but clearly none sufficient to diminish the pervasive anxiety in his childhood.

Yes, Putlibai, the mother whom Gandhi described as filled with saintliness, was easy to idealize. She was, of course, deeply religious, which meant that her routines included daily prayers and daily visits to the temple. And then there were her fasts. At times she kept two or three consecutive fasts going as dictated by the vows she had taken. Gandhi recalled that during one period of religious observance, the four months of the rainy period when some Hindus impose fasting vows on themselves, his mother vowed not to have her single meal of the day without seeing the sun. In what seems from his description an anxious period for him he described the following scene:

> During another Chaturmas (the four-month rainy period) she vowed not to have food without seeing the sun. We children on those days would stand, staring at the sky, waiting to announce the appearance of the sun to our mother. Everyone knows that at the height of the rainy season the sun does not condescend to show his face. And I remember days when at the sudden appearance of the sun, we would rush and announce it to her. She would run out to see with her own eyes but by that time, the fugitive sun would be gone, thus depriving her of her food. "That does not matter," she would say cheerfully. "God did not want me to eat today." And then she would return to her round of duties. [M. Gandhi 1957, p. 5]

It seems clear that one of the origins of Gandhi's use of the fast lies in the remembrances of his mother's decisions to deprive herself in an act of strength to further her causes in the service of amalgamating with her God and doing it with cheer.

However, Putlibai was unable to meet the boy Mohan's needs. And it turned out that his older sister also could not perform these maternal functions. On one occasion during a festival in Porbandar before Gandhi was 3, he wandered away from his sister, and, after hours of her frantic search proved to no avail, strangers brought the youngster home. Mohan simply did what was apparently now commonplace for him: he wandered away from home. His father then hired a maid to guard him. She was Rambha, who became a devoted servant to him and the family. Although his mother had now become to him a figure whom he recognized as an extremely important person in his household, the 3-year-old Gandhi now experienced an entire body of experiences that reflected the deprivations of the ordinary teachings and ministrations of a mother: he was hyperkinetic; he was besieged by fear of thieves, ghosts, and serpents. Darkness had become a terror to him. He could not "sleep in the dark, as I would imagine ghosts coming from one direction, thieves from another and serpents from another. I could not sleep without a light in the room" (M. Gandhi 1957, p. 20). Rambha provided some of the missing guidance and calming that allowed Gandhi to internalize some measure of her devotion and soothing. For example, she gave him a device for calming himself sufficiently to ease the fear of ghosts and spirits. It was a mantra in which he would repeat the name of the god Rama. The recitation of the mantra ushers in the experience of the presence of God that allows the chanter to feel himself no longer lonely and empty but joined with what has been invoked.

Another manifestation of the deprivation in Gandhi's development was his pervasive fear of aggression, always associated with attacks of intense feelings of inferiority, and with it the massive fear of rebuff or implied rebuff. So Gandhi (1957) writes in his autobiography of his behavior in school:

> I used to be very shy and avoided all company. My books and my lessons were my sole companions. To be at school at the stroke of the hour and to run back home as soon as the school closed, that was my daily habit. I literally ran back, because I could not bear to talk to anybody. I was even afraid lest anyone should poke fun at me. [p. 6]

And further, "the daily lesson had to be done because I disliked being taken to task by my teacher as much as I disliked deceiving him." And again, "The least little blemish drew tears from my eyes" (p. 7). Pyarelal (1965) reported of his interviews with Gandhi family members that Mohan was known to be an inhibited youngster with his peers who stayed away from vigorous play. Prabhudas Gandhi (1968) told of Gandhi's fear of authority throughout his childhood. Gandhi himself said, "I was by nature blind to the faults of elders. . . . I had learned to carry out the orders of the elders, not to scan their actions" (M. Gandhi 1957, pp. 6–7).

The psychological markers that emerge in the accumulated data reveal Gandhi to have been an inhibited youngster filled with fears of bodily harm and fears of being shamed. There was no direct outlet for aggression in the usual forms characteristic of a boy in his culture since his aggression was tied up in conflict. The aggressive drive had become externalized—projected—onto the symbols of evil, which were then experienced as agents of destruction, the ghosts and spirits that Gandhi feared even into his second decade of life. And so the psychological markers of Gandhi's fears of aggression betoken a missing accent of support for his assertiveness in the formative years of his life. Gandhi's mother became aware at one point during his childhood that her son kept his hands "in his pockets" when his brother attacked him (P. Gandhi 1957). When she criticized him for his lack of aggressiveness, he criticized her for encouraging aggression. Her mirroring at that phase was much too late to alter Gandhi's lack of aggressive strivings, now well defended and massively inhibited. The fear of aggression took on added significance in Gandhi's later development, affecting, as it did, all phases of his leadership and his political and religious attitudes, such as his lifetime devotion to *ahimsa* (nonviolence).

KABA, FATHER GANDHI, THE MINISTER

A primary deficit in the support systems of a developing self—in Gandhi's case, a deficit in the mirroring of his assertiveness and vigor, one of the factors that led to his lifelong concerns over aggression—is often compensated for by an identification with an idealized parent from whom one can derive strength for an enfeebled self (Kohut 1971). Gandhi, already in early childhood, was a distressed person at many levels, phobic of the dark whence thieves and serpents would emerge, frightened and inhibited about his and others' aggression and in dire need of support to alleviate the painful weakness of his self. It was not to be, however, for Gandhi to derive the support of merger with a person whom he could idealize and then with whom he could identify.

Karamchand Gandhi was of moderate means but given to a leadership position, settling disputes (not only within the family but also those between princely states). He had a reputation for being incorruptible and intransigent. Mohan was the youngest of four children of Putlibai and Kaba Gandhi. Gandhi thought of his father as given to carnal pleasures "to be married for the fourth time (to Putlibai) when he was forty" (M. Gandhi 1957, pp. 3–4).

Kaba Gandhi chose to resign his diwanship rather than compromise his integrity when palace intrigue created such an imperative. In 1873, when Mohan was about 4, the father took on another assignment in Rajkot, a five-day journey by a bullock cart, and the family was not reunited until 1876. Thus, the father was physically absent during the crucial years when Gandhi was 4 to 7 years old. Gandhi was reported to be his father's favorite, and was admired by both his parents and was a concern to both. His father, however, could not offer himself as a target for idealization. Kaba Gandhi's duties did not allow him time for sufficient involvement with his youngest son, who, from his reported experiences, certainly was in intense need of a parent who might calm and soothe and reassure him that he was not alone. Gandhi remembered his father as "lover of his clan, truthful, brave, and generous, but short tempered" (M. Gandhi 1957, p. 3). Gandhi did identify with his father in several respects, and thus developed an exacting, if not rigid, conscience. In his maturity he certainly identified with his father's mission as a public servant and leader of men. However, the core experience of self-regard, the experience that allows the self to experience a sense of certitude and rectitude, was diminished for many years in Gandhi's development until he was able to accrete to himself the experience of firmness necessary for leadership from a succession of teachers whom he petitioned for their wisdom and strength.

Apart from his inhibitions, phobias, and vulnerability to rebuffs, all denoting manifestations of his enfeebled self, Gandhi's lack of vigor and certitude persisted throughout his early years in the form of self-doubting and self-demeaning. Gandhi (1957) related of his intellectual qualities that "[My] intellect must have been sluggish and my memory raw" (p. 5), when describing his childhood and achievements of childhood. He also said of his talents and abilities in these years:

> I had not any high regard for my ability. I used to be astonished whenever I won prizes and scholarships. But I very jealously guarded my character. The least little blemish drew tears from my eyes. When I merited or seemed to the teacher to merit a rebuke it was unbearable for me. I

remember once having received corporal punishment. I did not so much need the punishment as the fact that it was considered my dessert. I wept piteously. [p. 15]

In relation to physical activity and the ability to exhibit aggression expected of youngsters, Gandhi was always inhibited, whether it was to avoid playing with his chums or in organized school athletics. Gandhi would stand apart and say, "Carry on, but I cannot join you" (M. Gandhi 1957, p. 29). His response to physical attack was unusual: when boys engaged him in a physical confrontation he would not hit back. Of physical exercise, Gandhi wrote: "Dorabji Edulyi 'Gimi' was the headmaster then. He was popular among the boys as he was a disciplinarian, a man of method and a good teacher. He had made gymnastics and cricket compulsory for boys of the upper standards. I disliked both. I never took part in any exercise, cricket or football, before they were made compulsory" (M. Gandhi 1957, p. 15).

A well-known anecdote about Gandhi and his father adds an understanding of Gandhi's interactions and his difficulty in identifying with his father. At 15 he stole "a bit of gold" out of his brother's armlet to clear a debt. He could not bear the waves of remorse he incurred from his deviant behavior—already a sign of a strong conscience. He resolved to clear up his crime by confessing to his father, not directly but through a written statement. In Gandhi's words can be found his fears:

I did not dare to speak. I was trembling as I handed the confession to my father and asked his forgiveness. I wrote it on a slip of paper and handed it to him myself. In this note not only did I confess my guilt but I asked adequate punishment for it and closed with a request to him not to punish himself for my offense. He read it through and pearl-drops trickled down his cheeks, wetting the paper. For a moment he closed his eyes in thought and then tore up the note. . . . This sort of sublime forgiveness was not natural to my father. I had thought that he would be angry, say hard things and strike his forehead. [M. Gandhi 1957, pp. 27–28]

This remembrance reveals Gandhi to be understandably frightened of his father, who was a tempestuous man given to explosions. Young Mohan had witnessed eruptions before and therefore feared the consequences of these tirades. Perhaps Mohan's fears of the ghosts and thieves in the dark had roots in the episodes of his father's outbursts, his fears thus representing a displacement phenomenon from the inner pictures of his father onto spirits who would attack him at night. Apart from this conjecture is the data of Gandhi's methods of adjusting to this volcanic figure, methods he was to use throughout his life in dealing with judges and administrative officials of the British Empire. He confessed to his father that he was in the wrong and asked "adequate punishment" for the crime. Thus Gandhi learned early in life a tactic for disarming and defusing the aggressor by confessing the crime and insisting on "adequate punishment." The quality and quantity of hostility in the aggressor is neutralized when the one to be punished demands the fullest measure of punishment, that is, when the wrongdoer immediately becomes penitent and thereby evokes forgiveness.

Another incident in Gandhi's involvement with his father, well known to students of Gandhi, occurred at the time of his father's death. Gandhi, then 15, had been married for two years at that time. During these two years his father had become desperately ill from the accident that occurred at the time of Mohan's wedding. He required nursing care from all members of his family including Mohan, who gave himself totally to the care of his venerated father. On the last night of his father's life, Gandhi, relieved of his nursing duties by his uncle, went to the room he occupied with his wife, Kasturba. During sexual intercourse or shortly thereafter, they were interrupted by a servant who knocked at the door and announced that Kaba Gandhi was in extremis. He had died as soon as Gandhi left, in the arms not of his son, who wanted his final blessing, but of his brother, Gandhi's uncle.

Gandhi and students of Gandhi have always highlighted this episode as a manifestation of the taint on Gandhi's sexual nature that this single episode of "wrongdoing" left on his vulnerable self. Yet another consideration should be pointed out: the circumstances of Kaba Gandhi's death, which did not offer Gandhi the important blessings to which he was entitled, left Gandhi even more needy than he had been for the teachings and other strengths of a leader. In the Hindu rites of passage all that a father possesses he passes on to the son through the final embrace, a final infusion of strength (Kaushitaki Upanishad 1.5.17). In his autobiography, Gandhi (1957) begins the chapter following the one describing the death of his father and the anguish it evoked with a complaint that "I failed to get from my teachers what they could have given me without any effort on their parts" (p. 31). The major teacher he is referring to—from the view presented here—is his father. This chapter in his autobiography contains other references to what he did not derive from those around him in the way of religious and other teachings: "I was not fortunate to have more good books of the kind read during that period" (p. 33). Speaking of the Bhagavad Gita and a well-known scholar whose interpretations of the Hindu devotional work he studied in his later years, he said in this chapter, "I wished I had heard it in my childhood from such a devotee" (p. 33). This chapter, coming directly after the one describing his father's death, also contains a thinly veiled complaint about another relative to whom he had turned with questions on the theory of creation, in which he had become interested after reading a book of the Laws of Manu, a Hindu lawgiver. This cousin, like his father, also turned him away without adequate regard for his needs for direction: "When you grow up," so said his cousin to him, "you will be able to solve these doubts yourself" (p. 34).

Characteristically, Gandhi turned against himself because of his sexual activity while his father, unbeknownst to him, was dying; he denigrated his impulses by calling them an act that reflects only blinding passion. "It is a blot I have never been able to efface or forget, and I have always thought that, although my devotion to my parents knew no bounds and I would have given up anything for it, yet it was weighed and found unpardonably wanting because my mind was at the same moment in the grip of lust" (p. 31).

Here we see Gandhi explicitly articulate what many children conclude when they find their parent unloving: the defect must be within me, not within my parent.

Young Gandhi began seeking out replacement figures to give him the self structure he was missing, especially the guidelines and the affirmation that would enable him to experience more firmness and more worth for his self. And so in childhood he related to his boyhood friend in the manner of a student to the master—seeking direction and strength with which he could identify. This search for strength and standards would become a constant feature of his persona until well into his middle life. Sheik Mehtab, who was his childhood chum, became the first in a long line of leaders with whom Gandhi attempted to bond in a quest for direction. Unfortunately, his quest for direction was in conflict with another lifelong dynamic: his resistance to the direction-giver.

Perhaps as an adaptation to a milieu that offered inconsistent often contradictory ideals, prejudice against Untouchables for example, alongside a posture of piety and compassion, a paradox that left him in a state of uncertainty, he developed a keen ability to perceive and focus on contradictions. From a schoolmaster who told him to copy from a classmate the correct spelling of the word *kettle* during a high school examination to the mother who admonished him to fight back, situations were always arising in which he perceived a fundamental contradiction from his caregivers and proceeded to shame those—as his mother—who seemed to endorse a contradictory position. In these youthful events and in Gandhi's perception of them, we see in nascent form the Gandhi who would defiantly set himself against adversity as if to compensate for his sense of fragility. Testing himself, he repeatedly attempted to master his surroundings; these tactics—by setting him against authorities—became a feature of his self, a special form that his inhibited aggression took. The cure for his anxieties consisted in pitting himself against the source of anxiety and attempting to master his fears.

Gandhi's proclivity to attribute to his mentors supernatural powers and wisdom and to become the perpetual student of these masters and their knowledge was always, however, limited by his inability to plunge totally into these involvements, the syndrome in psychoanalysis called the defense transference. This syndrome refers to the displacement of characteristics from significant persons in one's past to latter-day figures, who are then resisted (defended against) because of disappointment with the original significant persons. Thus, the current relationship is always limited or incomplete. This pattern of never fully accepting knowledge from his teachers or even from his religious books was to coexist throughout his life along with his strivings to merge with each new leader he met or body of knowledge with which he became acquainted. Characteristic of Gandhi is that, although he never completely abandoned himself to the teachings of his mentors, he always imbibed something from them. Easily disappointed at the lack of perfection in his mentors, he never, however, gave up the search. He was committed to self-transformation.

GANDHI AND HIS BODYGUARD

The first surrogate for father Kaba and mother Putlibai, Sheik Mehtab, was a kind of bodyguard to Gandhi, because of Gandhi's fears of harassment from his schoolmates. Gandhi (1957) very much admired his young leader's courage: "My friend knew all these weaknesses of mine. He would tell me that he could hold in his hand live serpents, could defy thieves and did not believe in ghosts. And all this was, of course, the result of eating meat" (p. 21). Owing to the influence of the Jain religion, which emphasized nonviolence (*ahimsa*) and therefore barred killing and eating meat, and to similar strands in Hinduism, the Vaishnavas of Gujarat, Gandhi's family regarded meat eating as an absolute taboo. But Gandhi followed his idealized young Sheik Mehtab secretly into the practice of meat eating, a major instance of rebellion against the tenets of the Vaishnava sect. Gandhi's need to identify with his leader was so intense that he committed what would be to his family a cardinal sin. The secret meat eating went on for a year, always with trepidation and at times nightmares. Gandhi (1957) reported, "A horrible nightmare haunted me. Every time I dropped off to sleep it would seem as though a live goat were bleating inside me and I would jump up full of remorse" (p. 22). Here we have the earliest equation of inner strength or weakness, later to become another lifelong conviction of self-experience formulated by Gandhi as a consequence of diet. He concluded that it was meat eating that gave power to conquer and resist, something that he along with other Hindus lacked and the Muslims and the Christians were well supplied with. And hence, the Hindu servitude. Gandhi went through life making many dietary experiments trying to achieve strength and coherence from these supplies. He became an adept regulator of all manner of inputs and careful monitor of outputs, including food, speech, actions, sexual activity, and excretory functions. These assumptions and experiences describe the difficulty Gandhi experienced in what McKim Marriott (1990) has conceptualized as the transactions of "mixing" and marking.

Sheik Mehtab had other ambitions for his protégé: smoking and visiting prostitutes were also on this agenda. Neither of these activities was ultimately compelling to Gandhi, and both were failed actions that Gandhi never continued.

THE YOUNG GANDHI AND HIS BRIDE

When Gandhi and Kasturba were married, each at about 13 years of age, to him it was as if he were going to a party with drumbeating, processions, good clothes to wear, and a strange girl with whom he could play. Another room of Kaba Gandhi's household was now to be shared by these two shy children, who were coached before the event of marriage in the behaviors of the sexual act. Further, the cultural strictures against contact between a young married couple made it impossible for Gandhi ever to meet and have a conversation with his young wife in a public setting. All their activities, social, intellectual, and sexual, were carried out at night in their shared room in Kaba Gandhi's house. Yet another restriction against their contact was that they were not allowed to stay together for any lengthy period of time—again a common social practice in a marriage between two very young people. Kasturba actually spent almost half her time at her father's dwelling in these initial years. During the first five years of their marriage, she and Mohan lived together for an aggregate of only three years.

In Gandhi's (1957) autobiography, the middle-aged Indian leader of 56 years of age, a devotee of celibacy since he was 37, looked back on his childhood marriage and disparaged his behavior: "I was devoted to the passions that flesh is heir to. I had yet to learn that all happiness and pleasure should be sacrificed in devoted service to my parents" (p. 10). He equated his sensual appetite for his wife with becoming stricken with disease and premature death. Looking back on his early years with his wife, he insisted that his lust for her was responsible for her illiteracy. He wrote, "I am sure that, had my love for her been absolutely untainted with lust, she would be a learned lady today; for I would have conquered her dislike for studies; I know that nothing is impossible for pure love" (p. 13).

And, of course, there is the incident most tragic to Gandhi—his father's dying associated with the sexual behaviors in which he and Kasturba were engaged: "And yet as though by way of punishment for my desire for pleasure, an incident happened which has ever since rankled in my mind . . . and fills me with shame" (p. 12).

Although many of his remembrances of the early days of his marriage are filled with self-vituperation, Gandhi does allude tentatively and briefly to his fondness for the girl he lived with: "I must say I was passionately fond of her. Even at school I used to think of her and the thought of nightfall and our subsequent meeting was ever haunting me. Separation was unbearable. I used to keep her awake till late in the night with idle talk" (p. 13). However, as soon as this remembrance is ended, his next association reveals again the emergence of the negative value that he, at 56, placed on sexuality. He said: "If with this devouring passion there had not been in me a burning attachment to duty, I should have fallen prey to disease and premature death" (p. 13).

Unfortunately, the marriage in its early phase could not deliver to Gandhi the full measure of self supplies of which he was in need. Once again, as with all his attachments, came restraints.

When Kaba Gandhi died, 15-year-old Gandhi was enrolled as a student in high school with his older brother. He continued with his studies until age 18, when he and the family had a decision to make about his future. By then he had a child, even though he and Kasturba continued in their prescribed roles as solely nocturnal friends and lovers. The decision as to the future of Mohan was made by a family advisor, a brahmin friend of Kaba Gandhi, Mavji Dave, who advised Mohan to journey to London and become a barrister. Within the confines of his culture, and specifically his caste, Gandhi had to obtain the permission of his mother and the Sheth, the head man of the Modh Bania caste. His elder brother, who would finance his trip to London and his subsistence in London, agreed to the decision to journey to London. His mother, in her anxiety over his living in a foreign place, turned to Jain monks and other relatives to give her direction. Gandhi agreed to take a vow against imbibing liquor, eating meats, and making intimate contact with women, and by this gesture enabled his mother to give her consent to the project. Gandhi, however, was not given permission by the head man of the caste, and so he became an outcast from his caste.

In 1887, shortly before his trip to London, Gandhi traveled away from his home, alone, for the first time in his life. In describing his preparatory visits to relatives and others, as he attempted to obtain financial support for his London education, Gandhi commented, "I have already said that I was a coward. But at the moment my cowardice vanished before the desire to go to England, which completely possessed me" (p. 37). Gandhi (1957) wrote, "The high school had a send-off in my honour. It was an uncommon thing for a young man of Rajkot to go to England. I had written out a few words of thanks. But I could scarcely stammer them out. I remember how my head reeled and how my whole frame shook as I stood up to read them" (p. 39). The reaction of fear and trembling in the face of a challenge to exhibit himself was an earlier response to his life circumstances.

These descriptions, which represent Gandhi's introspective observations of his inner mental life, tell us of the shakiness of his self and tell us at the same moment of his courage to continue in the face of the anxiety he was experiencing. This was no small feat for a young man whose development was lacking in a vitally important regard: the mirroring of his assertiveness, which was insufficient to help him become a robust engager in life. When Gandhi describes his agitated mother, Putlibai, who was one of his major purveyors of whatever worth and vigor he possessed, it becomes clear that, with her fears of the world outside of their home, she could only infect him with the virus of fear of the world and further that his own resources would never be sufficiently strong for him to master the malevolent land of wicked women, wine, and meat eaters.

From then on, that is, the London years, Gandhi was determined to fight his feelings of inferiority and fragility. His body and soul both became the targets of his intense experimentation. Gandhi took literally Hindu assumptions of the transformations that occur in the body and mind with every input and output of food, of words, and of actions. Gandhi knew well that only intense heat separates base metal from gold. Gandhi was to develop an elaborate code of diet, not just avoidance of meat eating, but notions common to both folk and classical Hindu medicine about a variety of properties associated with food that enhance cohesiveness or lead to too much excitation or dullness. As we observed earlier, Gandhi became an adept regulator of all inputs and a careful monitor of all outputs. But all of this was aimed at transforming his body from fragility to resilience. With equal devotion and fastidiousness he approached the problem of spiritual purification. These developments were yet to come.

And so the first phase of Gandhi's development came to an end. He was sent out to the world of foreigners and by these directives was implicitly instructed to master his world—but with what self equipment? He was a product of his milieu, from which he had failed to incorporate into his own self the ingredients necessary for adaptation, even survival, in the Western world. No one or no institution had been available to fill up the self lacunae of weakness and inferiority. No wonder he was to spend so much of his life seeking out figures to emulate, mentors to guide him, to be "marked" by their wisdom and power, encouragers to invest in him as he tried to transform and perfect his self.

GANDHI IN LONDON

And so Gandhi, seeking models of strength, seeking encouragement for his assertiveness, entered the Western world.

The transition to life in London was an understandable hardship for the young man who was without adequate command of the English language or knowledge of English manners and dress. It was made somewhat easier by a new guide in London, Dr. P. J. Mehta, who advised him on many matters, including living arrangements, dress, and attitude. The London years of Gandhi—perhaps in part reflecting the appetite for support that was evoked by the separation from Mother India and from Mother Putlibai—were especially eventful as he began his lifelong involvement with the principles and the works of Hinduism as well as with many other forms of different philosophies and thoughts. It was also in London that Gandhi, with trepidation, began to display more assertiveness in academic studies, in public service, and in social intercourse. As Gandhi described his London years in his autobiography, the unremitting search for direction in each of the many activities that he initiated was striking. Another facet of his London years is revealed in these strivings to join with the culture to which he was exposed in adopting the dress, the manner of speech, and even the dancing and music of the turn-of-the-century London culture.

Gandhi came to London as a foreigner, inappropriately dressed and ill equipped in manner and speech. But, more important he came with a self filled with fears for his future, indeed fears for his life. An intrapsychic state of disarray fueled his by-now pervasive quest for direction and calming to give him a measure of intrapsychic peace. Here is Gandhi (1957) on arrival in London, already filled with the shame at being the only person in white flannels (i.e., inappropriate for the autumn season): "The shame of being the only person in white clothes was already too much for me" (p. 43). In his introduction to his new mentor,

Dr. Mehta, a meeting arranged by Mavji Dave, he revealed "Indian manners" by picking up the latter's top hat and disturbing the fur of the hat. This breach of etiquette elicited an angry warning from the urbane mentor: "Do not touch other people's things" and "Do not ask questions as we usually do in India on first acquaintance; do not talk loudly; never address people as 'sir'" (p. 44). Describing his initial disarray on landing in London, he attempted to evoke his mother's loving presence to soothe himself but it was not successful:

> I was very uneasy in the rooms. I would continually think of my home and country. My mother's love always haunted me. At night the tears would stream down my cheeks and home memories of all sorts made sleep out of the question. It was impossible to share my misery with anyone. And even if I could have done so, where was the use? I knew of nothing that would soothe me. Everything was strange—the people, their ways, and even their dwellings. There was the additional inconvenience of the vegetarian vow. Even the dishes that I could eat were tasteless and insipid. England I could not bear but to return to India was not to be thought of. [pp. 44–45]

Gandhi's complaint—remarkable for him—that the vow he had made to his mother was an inconvenience masked the psychological conflict caused by his need to continue to uphold the pledge not to eat meat and the burden of his having to carry his mother and his culture on his back. One of his new friends in London railed at him for sticking to a promise made to an "illiterate mother" who knew little of the conditions in London. His friend read to him from Bentham's *Theory of Utility* to influence his thinking. His landlady became uneasy at his refusal to eat her food. But, even as he was "at his wit's end" (p. 46), he remained adamant against adopting the eating habits of the Londoners and continued to remain bonded to his mother. He could not mix with British ways, which entailed taking in products that alter his body constitution. Such steadfastness was for him an assurance of his strength in facing the odds.

Gandhi now began to search in earnest for a vegetarian restaurant, when, as if he had received a visit from his mother, he found the now-famous vegetarian restaurant on Farrington Street. "The sight of it filled me," he said in his remembrances, "with the same joy that a child feels on getting a thing after its own heart" (p. 48). Through the vow of vegetarianism he rekindled his bond with his mother in absentia as he later did with the use of fasts. A new world of contacts with the vegetarians of London now opened up for Gandhi, especially in the persons of figures who were highly idealizable targets for him, to pattern himself on, and from whom to derive self support. Two English physicians, Drs. Allinson and Oldfield, befriended him and encouraged him to assert himself at the meetings of the Vegetarian Society, which he joined and which—with Oldfield's backing—soon elected him to its executive committee. In fact, his newly heightened assertiveness now fueled his literary strivings and he published ten articles in local vegetarian journals. His newly enhanced capacity for assertiveness likewise was revealed in his founding his own vegetarian club with the famous English translator of the Bhagavad Gita, Sir Edwin Arnold, as vice president, Dr. Oldfield as president, and Gandhi as secretary (M. Gandhi 1957). He continued, however, to suffer from experience of inaptitude even as he expanded his activities with increasing vigor. He said of a meeting in which he was to speak, "I had not the courage to speak, and I decided to set down my thoughts in writing. I did not find myself equal to reading it and the president had it read by someone else" (p. 60).

It was, however, during his London years that Gandhi was first able to experience himself as a competent student and to complete a major course of study without tutoring. Indeed, he even went beyond the required studies and read Roman law in Latin, an unnecessary and arduous task that he embraced in the spirit of pitting himself against adversity. Only a short time had passed since he had viewed himself as an inept student in Samaldas College in India, the college he entered and left shortly after high school. Gandhi had difficulty throughout his student years with all manner of schoolwork, including multiplication tables, geometry, and Sanskrit. Reading, apart from its role in his studies, had not been a routine activity for him; in London he read widely, including for the first time the daily newspaper, and began his initial study of the Gita.

Toward the end of his second year in England, Gandhi began his acquaintance with religions, yet another institution and/or mentors with which he could identify. Characteristically, his interest grew out of his meeting people involved in a special activity with which he could become involved, in this case theosophy. At this time Gandhi began studying the Gita, the Hindu holy book that had become a pan-Indian text of Hindu devotional practice. From these new friends he was introduced to Sir Edwin Arnold's *The Song Celestial*, an English translation of the Bhagavad Gita. He also became acquainted through the same friends with other English notables in religious circles, such as Madame Blavatsky and Annie Besant, both important theosophists.

His readings in comparative religions included the New and Old Testaments, and Gandhi found yet another guide, Jesus. He found that the Sermon on the Mount went "straight to my heart" (p. 68). The sections on nonviolence were especially to his liking as they echoed convictions familiar to him from the Hindu and Jain notions of *Ahimsa*. Seeking pathways for guidance dominated these experiments with religious truth for Gandhi in London in 1890.

Another institution to which Gandhi was drawn in London was that of the English gentleman. "I undertook," he said in his autobiography, "the all too impossible task of becoming an English gentleman" (p. 50). So he bought new suits at a local store and even a chimney-pot hat. Not content with these purchases, he "wasted" ten pounds on an evening suit made in Bond Street, a remarkable extravagance for a young man from a small town in India. In his rush to become a London gentleman, Gandhi did not stop at acquiring new clothes; his hair became an object of care to him for the first time. There were, however, other details that go toward the making of an English gentleman. After all, Gandhi was unacquainted with the music and dancing of the West, nor was he knowledgeable in other languages of the West, especially French. He started taking dancing lessons to remedy one of the missing skills. He found to his dismay, though, that he had no sense of rhythm. Since he could not move in time with the piano, dancing skills could not progress. Instead, he bought a violin, but this was also not productive. One last skill he vainly attempted to develop was elocution. At that juncture he stopped his rush toward becoming an English gentleman and gave up the violin, dropped his dancing lessons, and became a more serious student of the law.

Finally, at the end of his three-year stay in London, Gandhi had gone a long way in beginning his development in several spheres especially in the realm of becoming more assertive. However, it was to be his plight throughout his life to have to endure painful waves of inadequacy. As he said, "The shyness I retained throughout my stay in England. Even when I paid a social call the presence of half a dozen or more people would strike me dumb" (p. 60). As if to accent the self deficit he retained even at the end of this highly successful period of his life, Gandhi recounted the painful story of his farewell dinner in London for all his vegetarian friends:

> When my turn for speaking came, I stood up to make a speech. I had with great care thought out one which would consist of a very few sentences. But I could not proceed beyond the first sentence. I had read of Addison that he began his maiden speech in the House of Commons repeating "I conceive" three times, and when he could proceed no further, a wag stood up and said, "The gentleman conceived thrice but brought forth nothing." I had thought of making a humourous talk taking this anecdote as the text. I therefore began with it and stuck there. My memory entirely failed me and in attempting a humourous speech I made myself ridiculous. "I thank you gentlemen for having kindly responded to my invitation," I said abruptly and sat down. [p. 61]

This section has set about to highlight the psychological markers in Gandhi's background that pervaded his self throughout his early life and therefore became a vital part of the forces that were instrumental in the later political and spiritual life he came to lead and the decisions he took that became part of the history of South Africa and India. Of the markers that were illuminated were those that described the narcissistic deficits he experienced emanating from the unique deprivation in his background. These psychological markers, the deprivation experiences that led to fixations within a self, were a result of the deficiencies in caregiving that his psychological surround engendered. He experienced enfeeblement and inferiority in his self as well as lack of direction and certitude. The fixation process results in a self so affected by deprivation that it urges the reenactment of the archaic needs or conflicts until a resolution is afforded by a particular environment of gratification, or this unconscious process is neutralized through the subject achieving insight, or the reenactment continues without abatement throughout a person's lifetime. In Gandhi's need system the repetition compulsion of the archaic strivings resulted in his attempts to accrete to his self the longed for supplies of worth that when psychologically ingested would become experienced as self-worth. Similarly he became repetitiously caught up in a person or institution, a movement, a religion, from whom or from which he could gain the missing strength and direction for his flagging self. These patterns, those repetition-compulsions to alleviate his narcissistic deficiency, became a pervasive part of his self to ease his intrapsychic pressure lasting up to his middle years. For Gandhi, these archaic strivings were never able to be fully realized. Gandhi's uneasiness about unfolding himself to anyone precluded a complete exposure of himself and his dependency, and therefore he resisted a complete bond with any sources of worth or strength. And yet, he was open enough to take in something from what was offered and begin to accrete for himself self structure. Thus, Gandhi entered and left his involvements with people or institutions without the infusions necessary to achieve complete intrapsychic peace. This psychological restraint against the total internalization of the psychological supplies he needed is the so-called defense transference as previously described, the defense he instituted against becoming dependent on human or other objects onto whom he unconciously transferred the powers and male violence associated with his childhood caregivers. So Gandhi went through a great deal of his life with his needs initiating courses of actions designed to alleviate his intrapsychic distress in tandem, however, with these restraints unfortunately acting as a screen to protect him from exposure to "too much" dependence. In these early experiences are to be found the roots of his later embrace and articulation of the concepts and values of nonattachment (*Anasakti*) and nonpossession (*Aparigraha*).

RETURNING HOME

When Gandhi returned to India, his newly found cohesion was turned into chaos. His revered mother had died before he returned home. Thus, once again in his young life, Mohan had been deprived of an infusion of sustenance from a dying parent. His grief was intense, but he did not decompensate. Immediately after his return, Mohan attempted to establish himself as a barrister in Bombay. He failed in his debut in the small claims court; overly anxious, he was unable to conduct his assigned hearing. Two years later, following his failure and his persisting inability to obtain cases, he joined his brother in Rajkot, where he essentially worked as a law clerk until his departure, which his brother arranged, to work in South Africa. His self once more in a state of apparent vulnerability, Gandhi attempted to merge with yet another target of idealization.

That ideal was the poet and merchant Raychandbhai, a Jain and the son-in-law of Dr. Mehta's elder brother. The connection between the loss of Gandhi's mother and Raychandbhai's place in his life at this time is revealed in the title of the chapter in his autobiography in which we learn about the death of his mother: "Raychandbhai." During the two years of Gandhi's' stay in India, Raychandbhai functioned as an ideal of knowledge and spirituality for him. Gandhi (1957) acknowledged his influence: "Three moderns have left a deep impress on my life, and captivated me: Raychandbhai by his living contact, Tolstoy by his book *The Kingdom of God Is Within You*; and Ruskin by his *Unto This Last*" (p. 90). Raychandbhai was a highly successful jewel merchant, but he viewed his business life as peripheral to his spiritual life. According to Gandhi, he not only possessed a profound intellect but was also the embodiment of a great religious leader. By his example and his teachings, he encouraged Gandhi to adopt the Jain system of thought, which centered on the doctrines of *ahimsa* and self-negation. For two years as disciple of Raychandbhai, Mohan "scrutinized his life minutely at close quarters" (Pyarelal 1965, p. 274). In the end, however, he rejected Raychandbhai as his guru: "And yet in spite of this high regard for him, I could not enthrone him in my heart as my Guru. The throne has remained vacant and my search still continues" (M. Gandhi 1957, p. 89). Speaking of the tradition of Guru, Gandhi said, "I believe in the Hindu theory of Guru and his importance in self-realization. An imperfect teacher may be tolerable in mundane matters, but not in spiritual matters, only a perfect *gnani* (a knowing one, a seer) deserves to be enthroned as a Guru" (p. 89). In conversations with Pyarelal, Gandhi commented that his disappointment with Raychandbhai stemmed from the fact that Raychandbhai mixed business with religion, disregarded ordinary rules of health, and believed in the observance of orthodox caste rules. Gandhi regarded these lapses, neglect of ordinary rules of health and diet, as the cause of Raychandbhai's early death. Once again Gandhi experienced contradictions; once again he experienced a disillusioning lack of perfection in a leader and had to reject Raychandbhai as his guru. In his relationship with Raychandbhai, Gandhi could not restrain himself from arguing, from questioning, from criticizing; in short, he could not enter into a guru–pupil relationship, a relationship without challenge from pupil to guru.

When Gandhi arrived in South Africa, he was filled with relief at having escaped circumstances that had been demeaning to him both professionally and socially. His legal activities had proven disappointing, and his social life had not been uplifting in any respect. In sum, his environment—particularly at the time of his mother's death—had not provided him with the support and guidance he had previously received in London. Furthermore, his interaction with Raychandbhai had resulted in an unsatisfying stalemate; he would continue to receive religious direction from Raychandbhai for some time, but, as he said, the throne reserved for his guru—an idealized parent—was destined to remain empty. In point of fact, the short stay in India appears to have reactivated Gandhi's earlier self-distress.

SOUTH AFRICA

Gandhi's entry into the culture of South Africa was dramatic. Almost as soon as he landed, he was embroiled in disputes with a hostile environment. The young Mohan had now become Mohandas, a respected adult. But, when he was traveling as a first-class passenger to Pretoria to assume his duties as a barrister, he was suddenly ordered out of his first-class accommodations by an indignant railroad official who had suddenly discovered this person of color occupying the suite of a white man. When the young barrister refused to leave, he was forcibly taken out of the seat by a guard. Later, on that same journey to Pretoria, Gandhi was beaten on a coach because he was again not in a proper place for a "coolie"—the designation given to Indians living in South Africa. Thus was Gandhi initiated into a major social problem of the Indians in South Africa. Confronted with a group of people viewed as inferior by their "rulers" and who were subjected to oppression by these rulers, Gandhi's identification with them shortly became his trigger to action. As he said:

> I began to think of my duty. Should I fight for my rights or go back to India or should I go on to Pretoria without minding the insults and return to India after finishing the case. It would be cowardice to run back to India without fulfilling my obligation. The hardship to which I was subjected was superficial—only a symptom of the deep disease of colour

prejudice. I should try if possible, to root out the disease and suffer hardship in the process. [p. 112]

It is this very sentiment that led to Gandhi's work on behalf of the "colored people" in South Africa. More importantly, it served as a seed for his universally recognized role in helping India obtain independence from its British rulers in 1947. Our not addressing these later aspects of Gandhi's life does not minimize their significance. Actually, the opposite is the case. We end our essay at this juncture in Gandhi's life because the rest, true to the saying, is history indeed!

REFERENCES

Gandhi, M. (1957). *An Autobiography: The Story of My Experiments with Truth.* Boston: Beacon.

Gandhi, P. (1957). *My Childhood with Gandhi.* Ahmedabad: Navajivan.

Kaushitaki Upanishad I.5.17(1962). In *The Upanishads* (Part II), trans. F. M. Müller. Whitefish, MT: Kessinger, 1984.

Kohut, H. (1971). *Analysis of the Self.* New York: International Universities Press.

Marriott, McK. (1990). Constructing an Indian ethnosociology. In *India Through Hindu Categories*, ed. M. Marriott, pp. 20–46. New Delhi: Sage.

Parekh, B. (1989). *Colonialism, Tradition and Reform.* London: Sage.

Pyarelal (1965). *Mahatma Gandhi, The Early Phase.* Ahmedabad: Navajivan.

3

Rabindranath Tagore and Freudian Thought

Santanu Biswas

> Expression flows from the plenitude of experience, and, in turn, kindles
> experience in kindred souls. Then the expression acquires the status of
> a symbol, and serves as a perennial source of meaning. To the symbol,
> belongs the meaning. The substance is beyond expression.
>
> *K. Seshadri (1983)*

The most significant psychoanalytically inspired assessments
of Rabindranath Tagore's works have come from Rangin Haldar
(1924, 1928, 1931), Sarasi Lal Sarkar (1927, 1928, 1937, 1941), Amal
Shankar Roy (1973), and Sitansu Ray (1979, 1996).[1] Although Roy
and Ray have cited a few arbitrarily chosen remarks by Tagore on

---

1. Halder's paper of 1924 may not have been published. It has been referred to
by Hartnack as follows: "Rangin Chandra Haldar . . . read a paper in Bengali on the
Oedipus Complex in Rabindranath Tagore's poetry" at the Indian Psychoanalytical
Society on November 1, 1924 (Hartnack 2001, p. 181). In January 1928, he presented
a paper in English at the Indian Science Congress based on the same research. This
paper may not have been published either, though an abstract of it may be found (Indian Science Congress Association 1928, p. 346). A third version was read by Freud
and subsequently published in the *International Journal of Psycho-Analysis* in 1931 (Bose
and Freud 1964, p. 13). Similarly, Sarkar's paper dated 1926 is an early version of his
research read at the Indian Science Congress (Indian Science Congress Association
1926, p. 356).

psychoanalysis in their respective works, it is fair to say that these scholars have not seriously attempted to unravel any part of Tagore's own notion of Freudian thought. Ratul Bandyopadhyay's book on Tagore (1994), on the other hand, which contains excerpts from several letters and articles by Tagore and others on psychoanalysis in one of its chapters, accounts for only one relatively less important strand of a larger story. In this chapter, which is archival rather than analytical in nature, I shall seek to narrate that untold story as closely and clearly as possible.

It is probable that Tagore had come to know of Freudian psychoanalysis as early as 1915. One of the comments Tagore made during his long meeting with Kalidas Nag in March that year, even without the mention of Freud, or of such terms as *psychoanalysis* or the *unconscious*, seems to suggest that he was describing a finding associated with the name of Freud. One is not sure of the source of Tagore's knowledge of psychoanalysis, if any, at this stage, so the only noteworthy point in the text under consideration seems to be the indication of the time around which Tagore had made this new discovery. According to Nag (1986), in reply to his question on the novel *Chaturanga* [*Four parts*] (1916), Tagore first "explained in detail the relationship between Sachis, Damini, and Sribilas [three of the important characters]" and then went on to say the following:

> To the authors of yesteryears life meant desire and frustration, union and separation, birth and death, and certain other similarly imprecise events. Therefore, the play called life had to end either in a cherished and revered union, or with a scene devoted to death's vast graveyard. *Since a few days now*, our impression of our life has been changing—it seems we were so long loitering about the entrance—after a long time we seem to have discovered the way to the inner chambers *for the first time*. We are awake at the outer side of our consciousness—there we are consciously fighting battles, striking others and are being struck by others. But within these strikes and counter strikes, these ups and downs, something is being created in our ignorance of it. The arena for that gigantic game of creation is our submerged consciousness [*magnachaitanyalok*]. *It is a new world, as if gradually coming into existence before us.* [Nag 1986, pp. 183–184, my italics][2]

---

2. Unless otherwise indicated, translations of the texts cited in this chapter are mine.

Sigmund Freud (1856–1939) and Rabindranath Tagore (1861–1941), as contemporaries, had obviously heard of one another. Moreover, they had friends in common: Albert Einstein, Romain Rolland, Thomas Mann, and possibly others. But neither Tagore nor Freud appears to have felt the urge to correspond with or to meet the other, not even when Tagore was in Vienna in 1920, and not until Prasanta Chandra Mahalanobis and his wife Nirmal Kumari Mahalanobis, as Tagore's companions during his tour in Europe in 1926, took the initiative to facilitate a meeting of the two men.

It was on October 25, 1926, the day before an indisposed Tagore was to leave Vienna for Hungary, that he invited Freud to tea. Freud responded to Tagore's invitation and spent an afternoon in the poet's company at Hotel Imperial in Vienna where Tagore had put up with his group. At the time of the meeting, there were at least four other persons present in the same suite. They were Prasanta Chandra Mahalanobis, an avid reader of Freud's writings by his own admission and the one who took the only photograph of Tagore and Freud; Nirmal Kumari Mahalanobis, whose tour-account entitled *Kabir Sange Iyoropey* [*In Europe with the Poet*] (1969) is one of the important sources of information on the meeting; Anna Freud, who possessed sufficient participatory curiosity in her father's intellectual pursuits as to recognize the importance of the meeting; and Martha Freud, his wife, who did not follow English and hardly knew psychoanalysis. Since no one, Tagore and Freud included, had taken the initiative to record the text of their discourse, one is forced to depend on the reactions, primarily of Freud, in order to form an idea of the impressions they might have left on one another.

Freud's only reactions were quick, brief, and epistolary. In a letter written to Anna von Vest, dated November 14, 1926, Freud reported he was impressed by Tagore's appearance:

> Tagore invited us to pay him a visit on 25th October. We found him ailing and tired, but he is a wonderful sight, he really looks like we imagined the Lord God looks, but only about 10,000 years older than the way Michelangelo painted him in the Sistine. [Goldman 1985, p. 293]

In a separate letter to Sandor Ferenczi, dated December 13, 1926, Freud reported his meeting with Tagore, in terms of a less ambiguous final clause:

I have had so little occasion to write to you that I don't know what I have already and what I haven't yet told you. Eg., that on October 25 I called upon Tagore about his request; that last week, another Indian, Dos Gupta,[3] a philosopher from Calcutta, was with me—my quota of Indians has now been filled for quite a long time. [Falzeder and Brabant 2000, pp. 289–290]

Ernest Jones, commenting on the meeting in his biography of Freud, translated the last line of the excerpt as, "My need of Indians is for the present fully satisfied," and concluded that Tagore "did not seem to have made much of an impression on Freud" (1957, p. 128).

The following other factors appear to reinforce Jones's assessment of the meeting: that no one bothered to record the meeting, that Tagore never spoke about the meeting, that the *Neue Freie Presse* had described the meeting as "futile," that Tagore had not visited Vienna during his subsequent tour of Europe in 1930, that Freud had not contributed to *The Golden Book of Tagore* in spite of being asked to by its editor Ramananda Chatterjee, twice, and, that neither before nor since had Freud and Tagore corresponded with each other. Nevertheless, Jones's assessment might be incomplete from one point of view. Notably, Freud's remarks on Tagore are consistently laconic but never neutral. Besides, Freud's comment about Indians, made nearly two months after meeting Tagore, was largely a reaction to his latest meeting with Dos Gupta. Moreover, Tagore's persona had evoked the image of God in Freud's mind. In the final analysis, therefore, Freud's impression of Tagore may have been one of ambivalence rather than of indifference. As for Tagore, he appears never to have written anything on this meeting, not even when he found himself involved in a debate on psychoanalysis shortly after his return to India.

Most probably Tagore spoke on a "psychoanalytical" work for the first time in 1927, in reaction to a paper read by Sarasi Lal Sarkar at the Indian Science Congress in January 1926,[4] although he seems to

---

3. According to Sonu Shamdasani (1996, pp. xxi–xxii), this could refer to Surendranath Dasgupta, the famous Indian philosopher and author.

4. Dr. Sarasi Lal Sarkar was a founding member of the Indian Psychoanalytical Society in 1922 but became an associate member in 1934 for not undergoing a training analysis. His paper was published as Sarkar (1928).

have learned about the paper after Sarkar had spoken to him about it in the presence of Anil Kumar Bose some time later.

According to Sarkar, a peculiar fact about a large number of poems and other writings by Tagore is that a set of three images—concerning rhythm, song, and movement—occurred exactly in that order in an amazing frequency. For example, the following stanza cited and translated by Sarkar:

Break, break, oh break the prison house,
Strike at it hard yet harder,
How sweet the bird sings,
How abundantly pour forth the rays of the sun today.

Sarkar explained these lines thus:

In this [stanza] the words "Break, break, break" in the first line sound like the beat of a drum and convey the suggestion of a rhythm. The [line] "How sweet the bird sings" has the association of a song, while the pouring forth of the sun's rays suggests the idea of a movement. [1928, p. 241]

According to Sarkar, the origin of this structural peculiarity—peculiarity because the poet did not consciously intend it and yet it pervaded his works—must be looked for not in the "conscious plane" of the poet's mind but in a "more submerged plane" of it (p. 242). From this premise Sarkar went on to equate the "peculiarity" with the experience of the Indian mystics on the one hand and with dreams as Freud described them on the other, drawing upon the words of the mystics from the *Swetashvatara Upanishad* (pp. 257–260) and that of the Freudians from the works of Ernest Jones, William James, Charles Bandouin, Poul Bjirre, and translations of selections from Freud's works by M. D. Eder, for the purpose (pp. 251–257). Sarkar believed he had found the explanation for this strange sequence in Tagore's deep dependence, conscious as well as unconscious, on the formula of the Godhead as given in the Upanishads; namely, *Santam, Sivam, Adwaitam,* or the being who is Harmony, Beneficence, and without a second. Sarkar explained the connection between the ternary imagery and the attributes of the Vedantic Godhead, thus: "Rhythm is a very natural figure for representing the Principle of Harmony. The figure that all movements are proceeding towards the goal situated at the Infinity is a very natural way of representing the Eternal One without a second. . . . The principle of Bliss is a complex idea, "which Tagore represented in terms of the "light of music" or the "light of a song" (pp. 250–251).

Reacting to this paper in a letter to Kadambini Datta dated May 29, 1927, Tagore wrote:

> Sarasibabu's method of evaluating poems cannot lead us to lively poetry. If I judge a friend physiologically, I may grasp the principles of physiology but lose my friend. A poem is admired for the enjoyment it imparts; we derive enjoyment by savouring it and not by analyzing it. First rhythm, then songs, and finally movement, poetry has no meaning at this level. Poetry includes everything at once and is indivisible. Looking at a flowing river we cannot describe it in parts and say that the waves came first, then came the water, and finally the flow. It is all that at one and the same time. [1960, pp. 124–125][5]

For an account of Tagore's views on psychoanalysis proper, however, we have to depend on A. K. Bose's essay, in which the text of Tagore's long meeting with Sarkar and Bose himself over Sarkar's paper is reproduced at length.

In Bose's essay, Tagore is extremely critical of Freud and the Freudians. He began by saying:

> You have created great trouble for me by dragging me into the realm of Psycho-analysis [English in the original]; I am not able to understand any of it. That apart, why are you unable to use your own insight to see things? Why should you accept everything that Freud says? It cannot be denied that we have lost our ability to think independently. [A. K. Bose 1928, p. 341]

Tagore was also critical of the fundamental premise of psychoanalytical operations as he understood it, and asked at one point, "How can the world created by an individual in his own mind be understood by another individual having a different mind?" (p. 341). In another important remark he affirmed that his "main fight with the school of

---

5. Whether or not Sarkar's findings are valuable as literary criticism or valid as psychoanalytical observations, the man himself remained extremely passionate about this one idea over a period of fifteen years. This is evident from the different publications on the same theme in 1927, 1928, 1937, and 1941.

Freud" was on the question of the priority of the sex instinct: "I think sex instinct does not come at the beginning; self-assertion comes before it. The instinct of self-assertion is older than sex instinct, and the influence of the former inseparably pervades our life" (p. 341). Finally, Tagore questioned whether psychoanalysis was a science at all: "The main ingredient of psychoanalysis is dreams. Can this ingredient be measured in a definitive way as the ingredients of the other sciences can be?" (p. 342). Tagore may not have read Freud at this stage; all we know is that he had read the critical writings on Freudian thought published in what he described in this meeting itself as the Today and Tomorrow Series. Could this possibly be Tagore's first reaction to his recent meeting with Freud?

In July 1927, Tagore made two other significant remarks on psychoanalysis in "The Principle of Literature." He stated that, in spite of any practical utility or intellectual value that psychoanalysis might possess, it had "no part to play in literature," and that, even if its findings were true, its employment in art was inappropriate and therefore unacceptable (1927a, pp. 9, 11–12). These remarks were made by Tagore in the context of a different debate, however, one that concerned the effects of the use of realism—in the form of the representations of poverty presumably qua Marx and the representations of the body and of sex presumably qua Freud—in modern Bengali literature, especially those that were published in the literary journals *Kallol* [*The Roaring Wave*], *Kali Kalam* [*Pen and Ink*], *Pragati* [*Progress*], and the like.

Girindrasekhar Bose, president of the Indian Psychoanalytical Society, replied to many of Tagore's explicit and implicit allegations against psychoanalysis as reported by A. K. Bose, in a long letter published in the July–August 1928 issue of *Prabasi* [*The Sojourner*]. According to Bose, the reported conversation of Sarkar and Tagore had no relation at all to psychoanalysis because it contained no verifiable discourse on the unconscious:

> Psychoanalysis discusses only those matters that take place in the unconscious mind. . . . In terms of a special process, psychoanalysis ascertains the existence of all those things that happen . . . in the unconscious mind. Since there is no direct way of knowing what happens in the unconscious, the psychoanalyst determines it in terms of a thorough study of such matters as the thoughts that come to an individual's conscious mind, all

that he witnesses in his dreams, his behaviour with regards to everyday matters, his errors and slips, the irrational concepts nurtured by him, and all those emotions that arise in his mind against his own wish. . . . I have already said, no proof pertaining to the activities of the unconscious can be of the nature of direct evidence. No sooner a certain activity is perceived than it ceases to remain unrecognized, and hence falls outside the purview of psychoanalysis. It is not that direct evidence is the only form of evidence. In the courts of law, a convict may even be hanged on the strength of indirect evidence; moreover, there is a place for speculation in all the sciences. It is only when an indirect evidence has all those qualities for which a scientist or lawyer would have considered it to be as valuable as direct evidence in his field, that it is accepted by the psychoanalyst, otherwise not. . . . No one has the right to deny the claims of the psychoanalyst without having carried out a thorough discussion on the evidence on which these claims are based. The objections of Tagore to psychoanalysis as reported had been raised many years back in the West. Only those who have explored the unconscious, and no one else, can state as to what does or does not exist in it. . . . A scientist cannot reject a system of thought merely because it would hurt someone's self-respect or religious faith. A scientist cannot decide in advance as to what may or may not exist [in the unconscious]. One is obliged to accept what is revealed by the investigation. . . . The affairs of man are inspired by sexual instincts, the ego and so on. Man is often driven by his sexual instincts in the unconscious; therefore, it is impossible to state without having studied the unconscious first hand as to the ratio in which the instincts of self-assertion and sexuality had determined a particular act [of an individual]. In the essay referred to, both Tagore and Sarkar have spoken in oblivion of the distinction between the conscious and the unconscious; hence, their opinion on psychoanalysis is not acceptable. . . . The opinion of poets, philosophers and others is not always scientific in nature. The psychoanalyst never claims that only sex regulates man's life. Neither does the psychoanalyst claim that he alone has found the origin of all the mental faculties. A psychoanalyst only investigates the extent to which man is driven by his unrecognized mind. He has seen that a large part of the unconscious is occupied by sexual instincts. No psychoanalyst will ever accept the words of others without having conducted an investigation himself; therefore, it is unfair to call him a victim of slave mentality. [pp. 583–584]

Sarkar must have read Bose's letter. Whether because of that or not, in none of his subsequent publications on the same "peculiarity" (1937,

1941) did Sarkar explicitly mention Freud or psychoanalysis. One must mention, however, that Sarkar always retained the section on the latent and the manifest layers of dreams and of poetry from the previous versions of his paper where it had been avowedly derived from the writings of Freud. He even added a section on the ego and the superego, without the mention of Freud, in his publication of 1941 based on the same research.

Tagore, too, must have read Bose's reply to his objections to psychoanalysis—*Prabasi* being the journal it was published in—and, probably for that reason, when he once again remarked on the subject in the section entitled "Sahitya Bichar" ["The Evaluation of Literature"] in the book *Sahityer Pathey* [literally, *Along the Literary Path*] in October–November 1929 (1989, pp. 435–561), he temporarily refrained from voicing many of his earlier doubts. Instead, he only asked whether "the analytical technique was worthy of respect in the task of evaluating literature." Tagore's own reply to the question is based on the understanding that a literary work as a whole was greater than the sum of all its constituent parts, with the excess being a "mystery that underlies all creation." Tagore wrote: "In every creative work it is this that is unique, that which is diffused in the components but cannot be measured in terms of the components. . . . Therefore, literature ought to be viewed in its totality." The problem with psychoanalysis for Tagore was that "many people"—implying Sarkar in particular—with a fondness for "psychoanalytical jargon" displayed "the mentality to diminish the glory of the un-analyzable totality of creation" (1989, pp. 496–497).[6]

With reference to one of Tagore's comments on mysticism reported in A. K. Bose's article (1928), Sarkar sought Tagore's clarification in a letter to Amiya Chakravarty dated October 10, 1931. Tagore replied to this letter not directly addressed to him, in October itself; and the same was published in the December 1931 issue of *Bichitra* under the title "Psycho-Analysis." In this letter Tagore stated that he did not remember the reported remark on mysticism, but he resumed his denunciation of psychoanalysis in terms of the following critical comment on the discipline:

---

6. Tagore reiterated the same point in an allusion to psychoanalysis in one of the Hibbert Lectures, entitled "The Music Maker," delivered in Oxford in May 1930, and published later on as *The Religion of Man* (1931).

I have read your letter to Amiya. I do not want to enter into the realm of psychoanalysis without having the right to do so. This field of science is still in an embryonic stage, which is why it provides the best opportunity to say anything one wishes to. Such opportunity to term the bitterness of one's own mind a science and circulate it in the form of slander, is truly hard to come by. In this so-called division of science anyone can assume the role of a scientist, there is no need to go through any rigorous examination in order to be selected. Another road to insulting the individual has been opened in Bengal. Those who revel in slander will be delighted. [Tagore 1931b, p. 717]

Between 1927 and 1938, barring the remarks already mentioned, Tagore had very little to state on psychoanalysis. Only a few comments appeared in his essays on literature and art—such as in the article "Sahitya Dharma" ["The Religion of Literature"] published in Bichitra [The Various] (1927b)—which were written with the aim of combating contemporary literary realism not on ethical but on artistic grounds. Otherwise, a stray comment or two on psychoanalysis or on Girindrasekhar Bose were reported in Shanibarer Chithi [literally, Saturday's Letter], a literary journal edited by the conservative young poet Sajanikanta Das, who supported and instigated the conservative predisposition of Tagore for a long time. Apparently, Das was extremely critical of Marxian and Freudian thought for what he considered their bad effects on contemporary Bengali literature, and he often appealed to Tagore for words in support of his viewpoint. It would be wrong to assume from this, however, that Das was opposed to psychoanalysis per se. He was only but thoroughly opposed to much of what some of the poets of his time wrote. This explains why Das at once condemned psychoanalysis for vulgarizing modern Bengali literature, and thought that his own critique of modernity had been vindicated when Rangin Haldar (1928) the editor of Shanibarer Chithi at the time, explained why modern Bengali literature, especially in its vulgarity, was not psychoanalytical at all! The decade-long Tagore–Das dialogue on these issues that lingered on until Tagore's death, therefore, is far more problematic than it looks, especially when set against the hint of a favorable transformation in Das himself around 1940, as suggested both in his autobiography (1977) and in Jagadish Bhattacharya's Rabindranath O Sajanikanta (1973).

Tagore had started to read the works of Freud sometime around 1938 or 1939, doing so, most probably, in order to understand a subject that Amiya Chakravarty, whom Tagore loved and admired a great deal all his life, refused to ignore as a poet. Tagore and Chakravarty shared a very strong bond that was initiated around 1917, when Chakravarty was 16 and Tagore 56, and continued until the death of Tagore. Deeply disturbed by the suicide of his bright elder brother Arun, young Chakravarty had sought solace from Tagore, who had gone through a similar experience himself at the age of 23 when Kadambari Devi, his favorite sister-in-law, had committed suicide. Between 1921 and 1933, Tagore assigned important responsibilities to young Chakravarty at Visva Bharati, the newly founded university, made him his literary secretary, and they toured large parts of the world together. Tagore wrote at least five poems about the young man, and the two poets exchanged over 200 letters between them. The pain felt by both when Chakravarty left for Oxford to study for his Ph.D. in 1933 is a powerful indicator of the dynamics of the bonding in question.

During his stay in Oxford, Chakravarty started to write a new type of poetry under the strong influence of Stephen Spender and W. H. Auden who, as we know, had been influenced by Marx and Freud since the 1920s. Notably, Chakravarty had met both English poets more than once. As for Tagore, he could, albeit problematically, relate to modern European literature as a reader even in 1927. In his article "Sahitya Dharma," for instance, Tagore both condemned modern European literature for "outraging the modesty of the Muse" and for producing a "confused uproar," and condoned these flaws in view of the general respect for science in Europe and the horrid experiences of war to which the Europeans were subjected. It is perhaps noteworthy that he described the same elements in contemporary Bengali literature as "borrowed and artificial shamelessness" and "inexplicable/ irrational confusion" (1927b, pp. 174–175). By 1933, however, Tagore had estranged himself almost completely from postwar European literature, ostensibly owing to its obscurity. One of Chakravarty's major achievements is that, between 1933 and 1937, he painstakingly made copies of poems and other works available to Tagore from Oxford, familiarized him with the works of Havelock Ellis, Eliot, Joyce, Masefield, Yeats, Spender, Huxley, Auden, Cecil Day-Lewis, Louis MacNeice, and others, raised questions and evoked new ideas in Tagore through his letters, and thus helped Tagore to change his opinion on modern European literature. In 1938, soon after his return to India, Chakravarty published many of his Freudian and Marxian poems in *Khasda* [*Draft*].

It is obvious that Chakravarty took certain Freudian and Marxian principles seriously as a poet. More to the point is that, around this time and possibly for the first time, Tagore considered it necessary to read the primary texts by Freud, Jung, and Adler. Nanda Gopal Sengupta, who had joined Visva Bharati University as a professor and who also worked as editor of Tagore's works, both on Tagore's request, and who, moreover, had become private tutor in the Tagore household a little later, was able to observe Tagore from close quarters between 1937 and early 1939. In his book, Sengupta described Tagore's involvement with psychoanalysis as he saw it as follows:

> Towards the end of his life Tagore's interest was mainly centred on studying science. He also read a great deal on experimental psychology. I saw him reading and marking the works of Freud, Adler, and Jung! He was also keen to write something on psychoanalytical theory—which he could not manage to do in the end. He had entrusted Professor Benoy Gopal Ray of Visva Bharati University [later, after Sengupta had joined *Yugantar*] to write on the subject in a simple language, just as he had entrusted Rathindranath to write on life science. The excellent essay by Rathindranath has recently appeared in the form of a book. I published Benoy Ray's work serially in [the newspaper] *Yugantar* [*New Epoch*], perhaps it has not been published in book form. [1958, p. 44]

The withering away of Tagore's resistance to psychoanalysis and the process leading to his recognition of its worth is a complicated matter. It roughly started to take shape when Tagore was in Mongpu between September 12 and the second week of November 1939. One day Tagore picked up a poem by Chakravarty called "Chetan Shyakra" ["Consciousness, the Goldsmith"] that he had already read in the past. This time, Tagore not only liked the poem very much and wrote a long letter to the poet to let him know of his reaction, but he also felt compelled to begin to revise his opinion of Freudian thought. He elaborately explained in this letter to Chakravarty dated October 22, 1939, why repressed material from the author's unconscious could be used in literature if it served a special artistic purpose. Most probably, his reading of Freud had sensitized him to react in the way he did to this poem.[7] Here is an excerpt from Tagore's letter:

---

7. Notably, Tagore's letter to Chakravarty in question was written within a month of Freud's death on September 23, 1939.

This poem of yours is an excellent example of modern poetry. The kind of poetry that appears simple owing to the poet's whimsical relaxation is worthless stuff, but that which is truly simple is often the hardest to accomplish. In this poem of yours that impossible simplicity has appeared in the form of an effortless realization.

Since I am staying in the mountains, a simile pertaining to the mountains is crossing my mind. The tinge of blueness above the far-away mountain peaks reveals a bright white fountain making its journey towards the earth. It is clean, it is clear. Its scarf has been weaved by the subtle play of light and shadow. The music of the flowing water cannot be heard from afar but the unheard joy of its rushing forth reaches the mind. Here I find in the form of a symbol the far off, ancient mode of our own compositions. I have savoured its offerings for a long time, I have also offered some myself, do not ignore it. For, if the religion of poetry is to impart aesthetic enjoyment to the readers, then one must accept the validity of this form of aesthetic enjoyment too. But then, it must not end there. The same fountain descends upon the plain lands and becomes colourful after mixing with a bizarre catalogue of things. So many broken, distorted and detached things it picks up and carries along with it in the course of its flow; so many noises combine themselves with its murmur, with no regard for similarity of tone, perhaps even the washerman's donkey lets out a loud bray standing on its bank. . . . It incorporates everything while flowing on. Nothing resists it totally; triviality mocks it but does not oppose it. . . . In this muddy deluge, sprinkling muddy water towards the sky, let the verse of the new poets dance effortlessly like an unclothed child. Footnote: I would like to say something on the modern situation; if I get the time for it I will. [1974, pp. 364–366]

Albeit along an oblique path, Tagore had allowed his own poetry to be informed by psychoanalysis a month or so later. Toward the end of his stay at Mongpu, possibly in November 1939, Tagore, encouraged by Das, started to experiment with a kind of poetry that flowed from his mind more or less uninhibited by any restriction or effort. These poems usually consisted of short and absurd lines worked out backward from the rhyming words in terms of a meter. Initially Tagore ostensibly considered these a kind of madness and did not appear to take any of it seriously. In a similar vein, on November 21, 1939, Tagore drew a cartoon of a four-legged animal standing on two legs atop the head of an unconcerned bird, as a gift for Sajanikanta Das. He called it "*Sahitye Abachetan Chitter Srishti*" ["Creation of the Unconscious Mind in Literature"] and promised Das a satirical poem that would similarly bring out the absurdity of all such works. Das published the cartoon together with one of Tagore's "meaningless" verses in his journal in November 1939. By early 1940, however, Tagore regarded these very poems as extremely special in his lecture to the students at Visva Bharati (2000, pp. 474–475). No wonder, he had continued to compose them throughout the 1940s, and, instead of discarding them, published most of them in his last collection of poems, *Chhada* [*Verse*] (1941).

Whereas Das was ecstatic about the cartoon, Chakravarty was strongly displeased with both the pieces. He disagreed with Tagore on the manner in which the latter had criticized the misuse of psychoanalytical principles in literature and asked if he could dedicate his forthcoming collection of poems, containing pieces concerning the unconscious mind, to him:

> In *Shanibarer Chithi* you have laughed at the excessive excitement over the unconscious mind in your poem. How enjoyable the poem has been is difficult to say, but if someone claims citing it that you have meant to say that there was no place for this new type of poetry painted by the colours of the unconscious mind, I will never accept it. That is because you have liked many modern English poems in which aspects of the colourfully glowing submerged consciousness have partly made themselves manifest in unique forms. What appears asymmetrical to the superficial glance has, under the spell of a deep impulse, or, captured by the environ of a strange experience, led us to a deeper symmetry in your own collection [of short prose pieces] *Lipika* [*Sketches*] and in other works. In a number of your songs and paintings, the play of a consciousness beyond emancipation is evident, whose manners transcend the confines of rule-abiding art and thus produce a special flavour. Experiments with it have been going on in many forms but due to the lack of an inner symmetry, the results have often been laughable, which is what you have pointed at in this issue's sketch and verse. The outsiders are misunderstanding it. [Guha 1995, pp. 275–276]

This letter helped Tagore overcome his last hindrance of habit. On November 27, he replied:

> There is no reason to feel abashed about dedicating your new book of poems to me. Behind every creation there is the interplay of consciousness and the unconscious. While painting a picture I find the shape of a

line suddenly emerging from the depths of the un-thought—the thinking mind thereafter takes possession of it. I am trying to understand the mystery of the expression of poetry in the modern mind—if its appearance is not artificial then we will have to accept it—it would be a mistake to regard the hindrance of habit as insurmountable. [1974, p. 324]

Most probably in late 1939 itself, Tagore had entrusted Ray, the young lecturer in philosophy at Visva Bharati, to write on psychoanalysis as mentioned by Sengupta. Tagore himself had even corrected Ray's manuscripts. But, above all, in 1940, Tagore wrote his most comprehensive final essay on modern Bengali poetry, entitled "Nabajuger Kabya" ["The Poetry of the New Age"]. In this essay, Tagore explained what he meant by "modern poetry" in detail, almost exclusively in terms of elaborate comments on what part psychoanalysis should and did play in it, and illustrated his observations with selections from the two collections by Chakravarty entitled *Khasda* and *Ekmutho* [*A Fistful*]. Tagore's final assessment of psychoanalysis must have evolved gradually in the course of late 1939 and early 1940, for we know that he had intended to write on psychoanalytical theory sometime in late 1939, had expressed his wish to write on the "modern situation" in October, had shown interest in "the mystery of the expression of poetry in the modern mind" in November, and, had completed "Nabajuger Kabya" in March–April of the following year. This also explains why Tagore never had the reason at any point thereafter to change his views on the matter. In "Nabajuger Kabya," he wrote:

I have heard that today's poetry is based on the theory of the unconscious. The games played by the unconscious mind are incoherent and disjointed. The part of the mind that makes our expressions meaningful is largely inactive there. Meaningfulness brings universal recognition, but where the ties of meaning have been snapped the mind of each individual travels along an eccentric path of his own, the road maps of which are likely to be confusing.

But since art is not science, its essence is earnestly unique. In order to derive enjoyment from it, one has to make the special effort to go to its premises. It does not subscribe to any general theory, as does science.

This specialness of the poet or the artist, which in English is termed uniqueness, is undoubtedly founded upon the unconscious mind. Founded upon, yes; but if everything is regarded as products of unconscious activities then we are left with nothing but dreams.

However, a dream is not an entirely fuzzy thing either. Dreams are like heads of scattered landmasses projecting upwards in a flooded field. One of the proofs that all those unexpected dream-scenes do haunt the mind in a special way is the nursery rhyme. Outliving much of the laboured literature, these have survived still. They are made up of fantastic dreams and yet they provide enjoyment—or else human babies would not have responded to them.

> The little boy went fishing along the bank of the river of cheese
> The frog took away his fishing rod, the kite snatched his fish.

It is not easy to construct a dream-image such as this. All the images in it are absurd, but images they truly are. Perhaps their striking brightness is owing to their very meaninglessness. The support of meaning is not required here. . . . A little boy is fishing in a river, and in this occupation he is unlawfully obstructed by two creatures—I can clearly see it, it is in terms of this that it imparts enjoyment.

The disjointed structure of unconscious thoughts may be employed in poetry if its employment is appropriate; if the process helps create a special picture, or imparts a special form of enjoyment. Such specialty in poetry cannot be overlooked.

Following the spread of Freudian psychology, the Western world seems to have discovered a mine [of knowledge]. Literature can no longer help being influenced by it. These unexpressed materials lying buried have been used for different kinds of expressions. It is not that unconscious imagination had no part to play in poetry written before, but that it played its part as if from the background. Now it has appeared manifestly on the stage. One must assume that such manifestation has a particular purpose, a particular contribution to make, otherwise one must regard it as a nuisance; I do not have the courage to level an allegation of that magnitude against the present age. [1974, Appendix, pp. 361–363]

"Contrary to the usual course of development," wrote Jawaharlal Nehru on Tagore in *The Discovery of India*, "as he grew older he became more radical in his outlook and views." Tagore's admiration for the Russian Revolution, his rejection of narrow nationalism, and his general concern for broader humanitarian issues are cited in support of the argument (1946, p. 340). Though not touched upon by Nehru, Freudian thought, too, is a case in point. Around the time "Nabajuger Kabya" was written, on March 27 and 28 to be precise, Tagore wrote at least two poems in which references to certain fundamental aspects of psychoanalysis seem to be patent. These are "Aspashta" ["Unclear"] and "Rater Gadi" [literally, "The Night Car"], both published in April–May 1940 in the collection entitled *Nabajatak* [*The New Born*]. It seems Tagore had already started to regard psychoanalysis as an activity that lent expression to and thus empowered the weak, mute, and crippled thoughts imprisoned in the unconscious. Here are a few lines from the poem "Aspashta" to give us an idea:

> The pains that sway within the blood
> Beyond clear awareness
> Bubbles they are in the flow of thought
> Lacking fixed identity.
> The morning light that fills the sky
> Will wipe this picture out,
> Its mockery will nullify
> The deception of being unconscious.
> Whatever survives within the net
> Of the conscious mind,
> In this vast denseness, Creation
> Will sign and certify.
> Yet some obsessions, some mistakes
> Of their waking author
> Will stain the fabric of his life
> Colouring line on line.
> In life therefore the night's bequest
> Enfolds the works of day
> And in the gaps of labouring thought
> Are scattered everywhere.
> What intelligence mocks as false
> That is the root of truth
> The sap it secretly impels
> Flows into flower and fruit.
> Beyond sense, the senseless
> Casts its coloured shade—
> Reality forges shackles,
> Illusion makes our toys.
> [1983, pp. 702–703]

In April–May, Tagore wrote the Preface to *Chokher Bali* [literally, *Eye Sore*] (1902) on the occasion of its publication as part of his complete works. Therein he described the technique he had adopted for the novel as "analytical," both in material and in method:

> The story constituting *Chokher Bali* has been made intense by the jolt it is given from within by a mother's jealousy. This jealousy allowed Mahendra's [the son's] vice to expose its tooth and claw in a way that a normal situation would not have allowed it to. As if the doors of the cages had been opened, and out came the ferocious events without any restraint. The method followed in literature of the new era is not one of providing a chronological description of events, but of revealing the innermost story to the reader with the help of analysis. This procedure made itself manifest in *Chokher Bali*. [1985, p. 193]

This is the first of Tagore's retrospective descriptions of some of his major earlier works as "analytical" or "psychoanalytical."

On November 13, Tagore wrote Poem 9 for the collection *Rogshajjaye* [*On the Sick-Bed*], in which he wished to see repressed material freed from the unconscious and thus rendered complete an d proper; and, significantly, the mystery of nature revealed to man in the process:

O ancient dark
Today in the gloom pervading my illness
I view in my mind
In the endless darkness of the first hour
You sit in creative meditation
How terribly alone,
Mute and blind.
I witnessed today in the eternal sky
The effort of laboured composition in a sick body.
The cripple cries from the depths of sleep:
The craving for self-expression flames secretly
From the molten iron womb, in tongues of fire
Your fingers, unconscious
Weave the illusion of an indistinct art;
From the primordial womb of the ocean
Huge masses of dreams
Deformed, incomplete
Rise suddenly in swelling motion.
They wait in the dark

To receive from time's right hand
A finished body.
Hateful ugliness will take harmonious form
In the new light of the sun.
The idol-maker shall chant the invocation
The Almighty's secret purpose shall gradually be revealed.
[1983, pp. 794–795]

In November–December, Tagore wrote the preface to *Nouka Dubi* [*The Wreck*] (1906), describing its technique of narration as "*manobikalanmulak,*" or "psychoanalytical," going by Tagore's own translation of the word (1936, p. 403; see also Devi 1943, p. 79). The prefaces to *Chokher Bali* and *Nouka Dubi* together reiterate Tagore's point regarding the prevalent demand on literary composition:

The demand of the times has changed. These days the curiosity about stories has become psychoanalytical [*manobikalanmulak*]. The weaving of incidents has become redundant. Therefore, in order to explore the mystery of the mind in an unusual state, a grave mistake was allowed to inflate the lives of the hero and the heroine—extremely cruel, and yet evoking our curiosity. The ultimate psychological question associated with it is, does the root of the faith of our women in the everlastingness of her relationship with her husband lie deep enough for her to disdainfully tear apart the net of her first love based on unconsciousness? But such questions do not have a universal answer. [1985, p. 347]

Notably, the fact that there was no one answer to the question did not deter Tagore from creating and exploring an instance in which the answer was a categorical yes.

On January 5, 1941, Tagore wrote the untitled introductory verse for the collection *Chhada*, an excerpt from which is as follows:

From the outside I view
A rule-enclosed meaning
What mystery lies within it
No one knows a thing.
What are these in fancy's flow
Sinking and rising
What they were they answered not

From whence they were arriving.
[1941 (1983), pp. 873–874]

Finally, on February 4, a few months before his death on August 7, 1941, Tagore wrote the following poem for the collection entitled *Aragya* [*Recovery*], which contains his final assessment of Freudian thought in the form of a tribute to its less valued offerings to literature:

The metrical web I have learnt to weave in speech
That web entraps
What had remained elusive,
Evading conscious awareness
Hidden in mind's depths.
I want to bind it with a name, but it refuses
The name's identity
If it has a value
That value is revealed through use
Day by day.
Though sudden recognition may beguile
Its wonder, it has no place
In human habitation: for a while it remains
Scattered on the shores of the mind
Nourished in secret, yet passing into the sand each day
At the insult of exposure.
Insignificant in the marketplace, this unwanted withered indigence
From time to time has offered the gift of the unfamous
To literature's great island of language
Like a lifeless coral.
[1941 (1983), p. 837]

Having arrived at the end of the survey, we must now address the most important question, namely, did Freud's works influence Tagore the author in any way? With regard to *Chaturanga*, or parts of it, until the source of Tagore's supposed knowledge of psychoanalysis evident in his discussion with Nag is known, nothing definitive can be said one way or the other. As for *Chokher Bali* and *Nouka Dubi*, in spite of Tagore's description of these novels as "analytical" and "psychoanalytical," respectively, Freudian thought could not have influenced their composition at all. There are two main reasons for this. First, in the several letters that Tagore wrote to different persons about these novels during or shortly after their composition, there is no mention of the term *manobikalanmulak*, nor any statement warranting that description.[8] Notably, Tagore had probably coined the term *manobikalan* in 1927, but certainly not before the mid-1920s.[9] And second, *Binodini* [*Name of the Heroine*], or ur-*Chokher Bali*, had been completed way back in 1899, the year Freud's first psychoanalytical work, *Die Traumdeutung* [*The Interpretation of Dreams*], which sold a meager 351 copies in the first six years, was published. Nonetheless, the use of the equivalent term for *psychoanalytical* in this case brings out the influence of Freud on the manner in which Tagore read some of his own evidently non-psychoanalytical literary works around this time. Moreover, the introductory verse to *Chhada* indicates that Tagore's sudden and excessive penchant for rhyme was partly due to his preoccupation with his own preconscious mind. In addition to that, Tagore did write in favor of releasing, empowering, or realizing certain types of repressed material in some of the poems written, in sickness or in health, in the final years of his life, including a glowing tribute to the unconscious mind in one of his very last poems. With regard to the contents of these poems in particular, especially against the corresponding backdrop of his revised opinion of psychoanalysis, it seems likely that Tagore was actively concerned with, if not inspired by, Freudian thought.

---

8. These letters, written to Pramatha Nath Sen and others, may be found in Prasanta Kumar Pal (1988, 1990), and in Prabhat Kumar Mukhopadhyay (1936).

9. From Haldar's article (1928) we know that the word *manobikalan* had become reasonably well known in Calcutta by 1928; also that the word *psychoanalysis* used to be translated most generally as *manobishleshan* until Girindrasekhar Bose, with the help of Jogesh Chandra Roy, translated the word as *Manobyakaran*. Later on, Bose changed it to *manosamikshan* (see also Biswas 1971). As for the time of the coinage, one may argue as follows: from his book *Bangla Shabdatattwa* [*Bengali Linguistics*] it appears that whenever Tagore had to use a foreign word, he preferred to coin a Bengali equivalent of it instead of using the word untranslated, or an unsuitable translation that was available (1936, 1974). Since Tagore appears to have used the word *psychoanalysis* (in English) in a Bengali discourse for the first time when he spoke to Sarkar in 1926, it seems likely that Tagore had started to look for a Bengali equivalent around that time, and found it sometime around 1928. But the more interesting fact is that he almost never used the word *manobikalan* right up to late 1931, preferring the word *psychoanalysis* itself in his Bengali discourses. However, from 1938, that is to say more than a decade after he had actually coined the term, Tagore started to use it with amazing frequency. This gives us the impression that Tagore's acceptance of this particular coinage of his was at once delayed and drastic, which is but a reflection of his changing notion of psychoanalysis itself.

By the end of August 1940, Tagore had completed one of his last short stories entitled "Laboretori" ["The Laboratory"], for the collection *Teen Sangi* [*The Three Companions*] (December 1940). The story is about the construction of a huge state-of-the-art laboratory, single-handedly, by a scientist and businessman named Nandakishore, and especially the manner in which his radically dutiful widow, Sohini, deals with the threats to the survival of this symbol of her late husband's ideals from fraudulent relatives, cunning people, and her beautiful and promiscuous daughter Nilima. But the immediate problem in the story concerns a brilliant young doctor of science named Rebati, who is chosen by Sohini to be the director of the laboratory, and who does not have the courage to resist being manipulated by his dangerously pragmatic boss, her seductive and self-seeking daughter, and his orthodox, superstitious, old paternal aunt, all at once. It is irreverently established in terms of the ending of the story that, of these three women, each of whom had radically different expectations of Rebati, it was his aunt he feared and who influenced his decisions the most. In the penultimate line of the story the readers are told that her shadow fell on the wall and the words "Rebi, come away" were heard. Rebati, responding like a timid schoolboy, at once follows his aunt out of Sohini's premises, presumably forever.

Some of the important threads of the story seem to have rich psychoanalytical implications or resonances. The story of Nilima, for instance, hinges on her suspension throughout the narrative in a state of ironic ignorance as to who her biological father was. Unlike in Sophocles, Nilima's oedipal situation is extended to the readers as well. The irony is diffused by Sohini, toward the very end, with the revelation that Nandakishore was not Nilima's biological father! The most important character from our point of view, however, is Professor Chowdhury, who is interested in several branches of science—such as chemistry, botany, engineering, physics, and mathematics—as well as in poetry and psychology. In course of his discussions with Sohini, one of the topics often taken up is Rebati's fear of his aunt and his fear of other women as a consequence. Chowdhury describes it as a matriarchy that exists not in society but in the "pulse of Indian men." He reiterates this concept several times in the story and consistently speaks of or alludes to Rebati as a grown-up infant. Chowdhury's concept of matriarchy with regard to Rebati in particular is strongly reminiscent of the mother complexes encountered in psychoanalysis, and, as such, Chowdhury begins to resemble the figure of an analyst. Extremely significant, too, is the form of Chowdhury's lengthy discussions with Sohini that make up more than half of this long short story. The two of them are, almost always, engaged in long one-on-one discussions somewhat akin to the discourse of the analysand and the analyst. Notably, Sohini, whose own character represents the partial sublimation of erotic and destructive impulses, regards these discussions as a unique space that enable her to express the truth about herself freely and fearlessly. For example, in reply to Chowdhury's remark: "Bravo! What courage you have to tell the truth," Sohini replies: "It is easy to speak the truth to someone who enables the truth to come out of you. You are so simple, so true." The same point is reiterated in the course of a subsequent session: "Look, Professor, you are that special friend of mine to whom I can speak without any hesitation about the wickedness that smears my character. When the mind gets a clear outlet to reveal the tarnished side of the character, it gives a sigh of relief." To this Chowdhury replies: "For those who can see the complete picture, there is no need to suppress the truth. Only half-truth is a shameful thing. It is in our nature to see things in their totality. We are scientists" (Tagore 1988, p. 771). Written four months after the completion of "Nabajuger Kabya" and three months before the composition of Poem 9 of *Rogshajjaye*, part of the form and almost every important constituent of the content of this story may have been influenced by the clinical discourses and the Oedipus complex described by Freud.

REFERENCES

Bandyopadhyay, R. (1994). *Bitarkita Rabindra Prasanga* [Controversial Tagore issues]. Calcutta: Best Books.

Bhattacharya, J. (1973). *Rabindranath O S ajanikanta* [Rabindranath and Sajanikanta]. Calcutta: Ranjan.

Biswas, B. (1971). *Rabindra S habdakosh* [Glossary of Tagore's words]. Calcutta: World Press.

Bose, A. K. (1928). Rabindranath o manobishleshan [Tagore and psychoanalysis]. *Prabasi* June–July, pp. 340–343.

Bose, G. S. (1928). Rabindranath o manobishleshan. *Prabasi* July–August, pp. 583–584.

Bose, G. S., and Freud, S. (1964). *The Beginnings of Psychoanalysis in India: Bose–Freud Correspondence.* Calcutta: Indian Psychoanalytical Society, 1999.

Das, S. K. (1977). *Atmasmriti* [Autobiography]. Calcutta: Subarnarekha.

Devi, M. (1943). *Mangpute Rabindranath* [Tagore at Mangpu]. Calcutta: Prima, 1998.

Falzeder, E., and Brabant, E., eds. (2000). *The Correspondence of Sigmund Freud and Sandor Ferenczi: 1920–1933,* vol. 3. Cambridge, London: Belknap.

Goldman, S. (1985). Sigmund Freuds briefe an seine patientin Anna v. Vest. *Jahrbuch derPsychoanal* 17:293–294.

Guha, N., ed. (1995). *Kabir Chithi Kabike: Rabindranath ke Amiya Chakravarty: 1916–1941* [The Poet's Letters to the Poet: From Amiya Chakravarty to Tagore: 1916–1941]. Calcutta: Papyrus.

Haldar, R. (1928). Art o manobikalan [Art and psychoanalysis]. *Shanibarer Chithi* May–June, pp. 719–724.

——— (1931). The working of an unconscious wish in the creation of poetry and drama. *International Journal of Psycho-Analysis* 12:188–205.

Hartnack, C. (2001). *Psychoanalysis in Colonial India.* New Delhi: Oxford University Press.

Indian Science Congress Association. (1925–1931). Abstract of papers presented at the congresses.

Jones, E. (1957). *The Life and Work of Sigmund Freud,* vol. 3. New York: Basic Books.

Mahalanobis, N. K. (1969). *Kabir Sange Iyoropey* [In Europe with the Poet]. Calcutta: Mitra O Ghosh.

Mukhopadhyay, P. K. (1936). *Rabindrajeebani* [The life of Tagore], vol. 2. Calcutta: Visva Bharati.

Nag, K. (1986). *Biswapathik Kalidas Nag* [World-Traveller Kalidas Nag]. Calcutta: Writers Workshop.

Nehru, J. (1946). *The Discovery of India.* New Delhi, Bombay: Jawaharlal Nehru Memorial Fund and Oxford University Press, 1982.

Pal, P. K. (1988). *Rabijeebani* [The Life of Tagore], vol. 4. Calcutta: Ananda.

——— (1990). *Rabijeebani* [The Life of Tagore], vol. 5. Calcutta: Ananda.

Ray, S. (1979). On artistic creativity: Tagore, Freud and neo-Freudians. *The Visva Bharati Quarterly* July, pp. 5–13.

——— (1996). Tagore, Freud and Jung on artistic creativity: a psycho-phenomenological study. *Analecta Husserliana* 48:329–341.

Roy, A. S. (1973). *Rabindra Manas: Manosamikshaner Drishtite* [Tagore's mindscape: From the Point of View of Psychoanalysis]. Calcutta: Calcutta Publishers.

Sarkar, S. (1927). Rabindra kavye parikalpanar ekti bisheswatta [A speciality in the planning of Tagore's poetry]. *Manasi o Marmabani* [literally, The Mind's Idol and the Heart's Message] November–December, pp. 403–410.

———— (1928). A peculiarity in the imagery in Dr. Rabindranath Tagore's poems. *Calcutta Review* August, 241–280.

———— (1937). Rabindra kavye tal gan gatir troyee parikalpana [The ternary planning of rhythm, music and movement in the poetry of Tagore]. *Bichitra* January–February, pp. 76–85.

———— (1941). *Rabindra Kavye Troyee Parikalpana* [The ternary planning in Tagore's poetry], Calcutta: Tapasi.

Sengupta, N. G. (1958). *KachherManush Rabindranath* [Tagore: The person close to me]. Calcutta: Orient.

Seshadri, K. (1983). *Heritage of Hinduism.* Madras: C. P. Ramaswami Aiyar Foundation.

Shamdasani, S., ed. (1996). *C. G. Jung: The Psychology of Kundalini Yoga.* Princeton, NJ: Princeton University Press.

Tagore, R. (1927a). The principle of literature. *The Visva Bharati Quarterly* July, pp. 5–13.

———— (1927b) Sahitya Dharma [The religion of literature]. *Bichitra* July–August, pp. 171–175.

———— (1931a). *The Religion of Man.* Calcutta: Visva Bharati 2000.

———— (1931b). Psycho-Analysis. *Bichitra* September–October, p. 717.

———— (1936). *Bangla Shabdatattwa* [Bengali Linguistics]. Calcutta: Visva Bharati, 1995.

———— (1960). *Chithipatra* [Letters], vol. 7. Calcutta: Visva Bharati.

———— (1974). *Chithipatra* [Letters], vol. 11. Calcutta: Visva Bharati.

———— (1983). *Poems: Rabindra-Rachanabali* [The Collected Works of Rabindranath Tagore], vol. 3. Calcutta: Paschim Banga Sarkar.

———— (1985). *Novels: Rabindra-Rachanabali*, vol. 7. Calcutta: Paschim Banga Sarkar.

———— (1988) *Short Stories: Rabindra-Rachanabali*, vol. 9. Calcutta: Paschim Banga Sarkar.

———— (1989). *Essays: Rabindra-Rachanabali*, vol. 10. Calcutta: Paschim Banga Sarkar.

———— (2000). *Introduction to the Texts: Rabindra-Rachanabali*, vol. 16. Calcutta: Paschim Banga Sarkar.

4

Multiple Mothering and the Familial Self

Alan Roland

> It has been said that the Hindu grows old, not when his hair turns grey, but when he loses his mother. Before going on a journey and on returning, most Hindus touch the feet of their mothers. This apotheosis of motherhood is not the cult of a physical fact, but the idealization of the sublime qualities of motherhood.
>
> *Lila Majumdar* (1953)

An Indian woman artist from a Christian community in Kerala voiced the following thought in a therapy session: "Americans seem to have to be one thing. I and my Indian friends are able to be many different kinds of persons in different situations. I feel very comfortable slipping back and forth from being a professor to being a painter to being a mother and wife. I can't understand these American women who are conflicted between having a career and a family. I don't have to be one set self or have a single identity. In fact I avoid like the plague having a set identity." Nandita Chaudhuri, a professor of psychology in the postgraduate program in child development at Lady Irwin College in New Delhi, expressed a similar thought in feeling very comfortable experiencing herself in different ways in various relationships. She, too, dislikes the feeling of having to have a consistent identity or sense of self (personal communication). Thus, a South and a North Indian woman, one Christian and the other Hindu, both have similar experiences of a self that is far more relational and contextual than is an American's.

I have formulated these women's experiences as an integral part of the familial we-self, a self that experiences itself as highly contextual to relationships and tasks, and can easily live with dissonances and contradictions (Roland 1988, 1996). Nandita Chaudhuri conceptualizes it as a fluctuating I-we self in different relationships (personal communication). In an Indian setting, the self always experiences itself as intimately connected to the other(s) in a we relationship, rather than the dualistic I and you relationship in Euro-Americans. On the other hand, Catherine Ewing, a psychoanalytic anthropologist at Duke University, has looked to French psychoanalysis and DeLeuze's postmodern theory of the decentered self to take into account these same phenomena in Pakistani women (Molino 2003a). She had found the theories of ego psychology, self psychology, and British object relations theorists to have too integrated a view of the self to be useful in formulating her observations of Pakistani women. Gananath Obeyesekere, another psychoanalytic anthropologist, has similarly eschewed using ego psychology, self psychology, and British object relations theory in his analysis of Sri Lankans as he sees their views of the ego and self as too tied in with Western individualism (Molino 2003b).

A theoretical issue immediately arises from this simple yet profound statement by my South Indian patient. It calls for a rethinking and revision of psychoanalytic theory. My own approach is to keep the categories of psychoanalytic theory, in this case, the self; but then to alter the content and structure of the self as well as its norms in relationship to the sociocultural context of the person. Ewing, on the other hand, is oriented toward a more universal theory, that of the decentered self, as one that stretches across cultures. The problem with this is that it doesn't allow for the comparative analysis necessary to distinguish, as in this case, Indians or Pakistanis from Euro-Americans. Her thinking is based on the assumption of psychological universalism, that the underlying psyche of everyone is similar across cultures, and that only behavior is affected by culture. This contrasts with my approach, which assumes that culture affects the deepest layers of the psyche.

OTHER DIMENSIONS OF THE FAMILIAL SELF

There are other major dimensions of the familial self that I have previously formulated (Roland 1988, 1996). One is we-self regard, which is central to Indian relationships. Maintaining and enhancing the esteem of each other is always more important than the truth of any given matter. Thus at conferences the speaker is rarely challenged. Idealizations or idealized selfobjects are more salient than in America, whether of persons living or deceased, or of the various gods and goddesses. Similarly, empathic attunement or mirroring selfobjects is more emphasized. However, what is mirrored differs, inasmuch as Indians are more attuned to complex familial relationships, and less so to individualized aspects of children, which in American society is greatly emphasized for the development of an individual identity. Moreover, empathy is much more attuned to conscious nonverbal communication than in the West.

Particularly important to we-self regard is the reputation of the family as a selfobject, where how one behaves in public is central to family esteem, and family reputation is central to one's own esteem. Similarly, in the pervasive hierarchical relationships, subordinates are culturally expected to be loyal, deferent, and obedient to superiors to enhance their esteem; reciprocally, superiors are to be respectful and nurturing of subordinates to maintain their esteem. If this reciprocity is not observed, there can be considerable anger. In American-style hierarchical relationships, Indians often experience wounded esteem when their superiors are directly critical or are not nurturing and responsible.

Another important dimension of the familial self is a dual-self structure. There is a social presentation of self to observe the social etiquette of hierarchical relationships and the expected *dharma* or moral precepts of these relationships. Then there is a highly private self where all kinds of thoughts, feelings, and fantasies are kept to oneself but only revealed in a highly contextual way in certain relationships (Nandita Chaudhuri, personal communication). As part of this private self, there is a strong wishing, wanting libidinal self always in some tension with proper etiquette in hierarchical relationships. Thus, Indian patients can keep secrets to a much greater extent than the typical Euro-American patient. An example is Shakuntala, who kept her two main inner struggles to herself for over a year and a half rather than to reveal them to her Indian therapist because she felt he would be judgmental or not understand (Roland 1988). Authenticity, a prime value of the North American self, is if anything negatively valued as it would interfere with proper behavior in the hierarchical relationships. On the other hand, where there is little assertive individualism in the American sense, a great deal of individuality resides in the private self. An Indian psychoanalyst, Madhu Sarin, and a psychologist and psychotherapist, Rashmi Jaipal, both of whom lived in New York City for some years, the former returning to practice in New Delhi, both ventured that they experience decidedly more individuality in Indian relationships than in Euro-American ones (personal communication).

A third dimension of the familial self is a highly contextualized conscience, where moral behavior or *dharma* is much more oriented toward the time, the place, the nature of the relationship, and the natures of the persons involved. To act the same way in all relationships is considered immoral. This, obviously, is consistent with the highly contextual experiencing of the self. In addition, there are strong superego imperatives never to express anger directly toward a superior. Thus, in therapy sessions Indian patients frequently and early on voice great anger and resentment toward those they feel have unfairly treated them. But it is extremely rare for even the slightest ambivalence to be expressed directly to the analyst. When it finally happens, which took a couple of years of three-times-a-week analysis in the case of one man, he came to the next session in an anxiety state. This had to be connected to the ambivalence expressed in the previous session. This enabled him to be somewhat more direct in his criticism a few sessions later. He again came into the next session in an anxiety state, which again had to be interpreted as being related to his criticism of me. After this cycle repeated itself a few times, a negative transference became established. Besides the superego imperative, patients are reluctant to voice anger directly to the therapist because of the fear of losing a nurturing relationship.

Then, there are different kinds of ego boundaries than in the typical Euro-American. Outer emotional boundaries are more permeable than in Americans, with less space around oneself, in semi-merger relationships. Euro-Americans, for instance, can often experience themselves as being swallowed up in an Indian setting. But for Indians this is balanced by strong inner boundaries of a private self, which is greatly respected. While there is less attention to developing a more individual identity to be asserted in social relationships, there is on the other hand an acceptance of all kinds of idiosyncratic tendencies in a child since it is recognized that a child comes to this life with all kinds of tendencies from past lives.

Still another dimension of the Indian familial self are multiple levels of communication. While there is a great deal of verbal communication, although sometimes ambiguous, there is also extensive, conscious nonverbal communication through gestures, behaviors, and moods. These different levels may or may not be consistent with each other. Some may be oriented toward observing the deference of a hierarchical relationship while other nonverbal communications convey how the person really feels or what they want. Indians are sensitive to all of these although sometimes being puzzled as to what the person really means.

A different kind of cognition is also present in the Indian self. First, there is the much greater emphasis on contextual thinking where even time has its auspicious and inauspicious moments and music is to be played only at certain times of the day or seasons (Ramanujan 1990). Also cited by Ramanujan is metonymic thinking where there is a monistic assumption of the reality of the universe in contrast to Western dualism. Thus, an idol of a goddess is not a symbolic representation of her as in the West but rather a partial manifestation. Then there is the Hindu penchant to live on different levels of reality cultivating ambiguity and dissonance (McLean 2000). Major scientists may be deeply involved in astrology or palmistry as ways of ascertaining one's destiny without experiencing any conflict whatsoever with their scientific endeavors.

DEVELOPMENTAL ISSUES

Important developmental issues have been raised by a psychoanalytic anthropologist, Stanley Kurtz, in a provocative book, *All the Mothers Are One: Hindu India and the Cultural Reshaping of Psychoanalysis* (1992). Kurtz calls for a rethinking of psychoanalysis to take into account that there is multiple mothering in an Indian family, in contrast to the usual Euro-American nuclear family upon which psychoanalytic observations and theory have developed. His book raises a number of questions.

How does the familial self develop within the Indian extended family? What are the effects of multiple mothering? What are the effects of social change in the urban educated middle and upper middle classes on the familial self and multiple mothering? What is the relationship of the spiritual self and spiritual quest to the familial self and multiple mothering? To what extent does psychoanalytic theory need amending to take into account the familial self, multiple mothering, and its development?

To address these questions, one becomes involved in what seems like a wrestling match between anthropology and psychoanalysis, between ethnographic fieldwork in rural areas and psychoanalytic reconstructions and infant observation in the cities. Then, there is a further critical issue in psychoanalysis, itself, in India as to what extent it remains unreflectedly grounded in Euro-American norms of development from whichever model, or to what extent it frames a significantly different normative developmental theory rooted in the Indian experience (Carstairs 1967, Kakar 1978, Roland 1988). Kurtz cites the ethnographic observations of four anthropologists (Minturn and Lambert 1964, Seymour 1975, and Trawick 1990) that while there is a great deal of physical gratification of the infant and very young child by the mother, there is not a strong emotional bond with the child: "healthy, empathic mirroring seems to be entirely absent here" (Kurtz 1992, p. 252). He further cites the psychoanalytic anthropologist Robert LeVine (1977), who summarizes a number of ethnographic observations in different Asian and African rural cultures, that while there is a great deal of early physical gratification there is little empathic or emotional engagement of the mother with the infant and toddler.

Kurtz infers from these observations that the mother by her relative noninvolvement actually pushes the child into the hands of the in-law women of the family, who take over a great deal of the child care. This then enables the male child (Kurtz restricts his theorizing to boys) to separate emotionally from the mother, to eventually renounce incestuous ties to her, and to develop an ego of the whole with the entire family. In the importance of the in-law women of the family, Kurtz sees all the mothers are one, that is, the in-law women are equal to the mother. The psychoanalytic view, on the other hand, emphasizes an early and continuing strong emotional tie to the mother, as well as ties to other women of the family.

Which view is more accurate? Is it a question of a different methodology where the ethnographic observations of Western anthropologists, in contrast to Indian and Western psychoanalysts, do not take into account the nonverbal, empathic emotional relatedness, so characteristic of Indian relationships and mothering? And is there a cultural/ psychological bias on the part of these Western anthropologists that views normality as only being grounded in the highly individualized Western empathic relatedness, which is so rooted in the culture of individualism? Or is it a question of observations in rural India versus those of the educated middle and upper middle classes in urban India? Infant observation, conducted by persons in psychoanalytic training in Mumbai and based on the practices of the British Psychoanalytic Association, do not confirm the ethnographic rural observations. Could it also be a question of rural poverty that colors the ethnographic observations, a possibility that Salman Akhtar (2000) raises in his review of Kurtz's work? It may be difficult to fully answer these questions until anthropologists work among the urban educated and psychoanalysts among the rural population. Then, there is the central question that Kurtz raises as to whether psychoanalytic developmental theory needs revision to take into account not only the familial self but also multiple mothering in the Indian extended family. However, developmental theory would have to be significantly broader in scope than the libidinal, psychosexual one that Kurtz overwhelmingly uses, expanding it to include object relations theory, self psychology, and ego psychology.

MULTIPLE MOTHERING

In urban educated Indians, it is not only the various in-law women who are involved in child care, but also the entire family—fathers and older siblings, female and male, servants, and neighbors, also including the women of the mother's extended family—is involved. Thus, there is a great deal of caring for children from everyone. While much of the anthropological literature emphasizes the mother-in-law–daughter-in-law conflicts, I have found from two women patients that they were extremely upset when their mothers-in-law were not sufficiently involved with them and their children. The Indian woman becomes a much more integral member of her in-laws' family than is usual in North America, and expects a great deal of intense emotional involvement even when it can be conflictual.

Sa'ida, for instance, whom I saw three times a week in psychoanalytic therapy for a month in 1980, was in considerable conflict with a truly difficult mother-in-law (Roland 1988). Unconscious reactions from past family relationships made handling her mother-in-law much more difficult. As these reactions came to light during the therapy, it helped her considerably. Eleven years later when I returned to Mumbai, I found her once again quite upset with her mother-in-law but for completely different reasons. For practical business reasons, Sa'ida, her husband, daughter, and son had to move out of her in-laws' flat to a new, luxury one. Sa'ida was terribly upset because her mother-in-law was not visiting them, sleeping over, or being involved with Sa'ida and her children. We strategized how to get her mother-in-law more involved, taking into account that the move seemed to evoke an earlier abandonment when her mother-in-law had lost her own mother at age four. What was striking, however, was Sa'ida's expectation of her mother-in-law's being deeply involved with her and her children, and feeling deeply hurt when she wasn't.

One must also differentiate the role of multiple mothering depending on the age of the child. For an infant, mothers report welcoming the child care provided by the mother-in-law and sisters-in-law and others, since the mother also has other tasks to perform in the family besides child care, such as cooking, serving, and cleaning. My own impression is that the mother herself has a familial we-self with others of the extended family, and expects the child to develop similar ties. There is a strong tie to the family qua family. Identifications with the mother and other women of the family in early childhood certainly further this process, what Kurtz calls an ego of the whole. In the urban educated, I do not see the mother pushing the child into the hands of the in-law women by her noninvolvement, but rather encouraging multiple ties with herself and still remaining central to the child.

With older children and adolescents, the urban educated mother wants a more central role in guiding and setting standards for her child, which may be in conflict with the hierarchy of the in-laws. Traditionally, the daughter-in-law usually has to give in to the standards of the mother-in-law. Now, however, much maneuvering may take place or sometimes open conflict. An example of this mother-in-law–daughter-in-law conflict and maneuvering came out in a discussion with graduate child development students at Lady Irwin College, who mainly come from urban educated professional (in contrast to business) circles. In one case, the mother-in-law wanted her son's flat furnished in a certain way that the daughter-in-law didn't like. The daughter-in-law agreed to everything but after some time cited that first one and then another of her mother-in-law's decisions simply didn't work. After a month or two, the flat became exactly as the daughter-in-law had wanted. The same could easily go for child rearing as the educated mother cites the authority of various child-rearing articles or books to her mother-in-law. The mother actually mediates her child's relationships with the other women of the family as well as with her husband, while still observing the deference of the hierarchical relationships. Complexity of relationships are intrinsic to Indian families, as well as subtlety of communication, which children naturally pick up. The mother can apparently be stricter with teaching her children the proper etiquette of hierarchical relationships than the in-law women of the family. Interestingly enough, one of the child development professors at Lady Irwin College was surprised about her experience in field work with college-educated South Indian women in matrilineal families; contrary to her expectations, these women were less able to cope with their own aunt's or mother's expectations than North Indian women with their mothers-in-law. The latter women felt inwardly freer to challenge the decisions of their mothers-in-law even if it had to be done circuitously.

Returning to the initial statements of contextualized selves, one can say that it is from the multiple emotional ties in an Indian extended family, whether living in a unitary or joint household, combined with very different expectations and etiquette in various hierarchical relationships, that the statements of a highly contextualized self make a great deal of sense.

PSYCHOANALYTIC THEORIZING

Kurtz conceptualized the development of the preoedipal child as separation-integration, *ek-hi*, in contrast to the separation-individuation of American ego psychology. What Kurtz means by this is that the infant and toddler are emotionally pushed away by the mother into the hands of the in-law women, so that the male child eventually develops an ego of the whole integrated with the family, and renounces incestuous ties to the mother. While Kurtz has made an important contribution to psychoanalytic theorizing by emphasizing the role of the in-law women of the family—and we can now add many others in the family and neighbors for urban Indian families—and the family unit as a whole, I would strongly question his notion of separation-integration. My own observations are that the mode of relating and development from early childhood in India is much more along the lines of a symbiotic dependency and interdependency with the mother and the other women of the family in early childhood. I have termed it *symbiotic reciprocity*, as dependency and obedience are exchanged for strong expectations of being taken care of, and actually enhance the esteem of the caregiver. A libidinal, wishing and wanting self is cultivated from early childhood, with strong restrictions oriented around observing the social etiquette of hierarchical relationships being inculcated from around age five through adolescence. This is implemented as much or more by the mother as by the in-law women and father, and can be quite strict. Inner separation of images of self and other also take place by the accord afforded to a child's developing private self, which is not to be intruded upon, and where a great deal of individuality resides.

SOCIAL CHANGE IN THE URBAN EDUCATED

Important changes are also taking place in the urban educated. In January 2003, the population of the urban educated middle and upper middle classes was put at approximately 250,000,000, with gradually increasing affluence (Ashis Nandy, personal communication). Many of the college-educated women work and have careers, not infrequently making as much as or more than their husbands. They are therefore less willing to put up with more traditional hierarchical relationships with both their in-laws and husbands. This has created more conflict, with increasing numbers of the urban educated seeking counseling or psychotherapy since around 1995, according to mental health workers in various Indian cities. Often, the families live in unitary households, and since the mother frequently works, and in-law or even own family child care is not always available, there is increasing dependence on *ayahs* (housekeepers). On the other hand, fathers are now more involved in child care than was traditionally the case. There is, in general, a more individualized approach to children than before without it gravitating into American-style individualism, taking more into account the child's wishes and inclinations. This plays out later in teenagers and young adults having a much greater say in their educational and occupational choices, as well as in marriages, than traditionally.

THE SPIRITUAL SELF AND FAMILIAL SELF

There is still another theoretical point concerning the relationship of the spiritual self and quest to Indian family relationships. Originally, Carstairs (1957) posited that merger with the spiritual is a reflection of the early mother–infant symbiotic relationship. This is in keeping with Freud's (1930) notion. Kakar (1978, 1991) has taken a similar tack, though in a much more sophisticated and complex way, citing Winnicott's (1965) work. Kurtz disagrees with both since he doesn't see an early mother–infant merger relationship in India. Instead, Kurtz theorizes that the ego of the whole, the child's identification with the entire family, is the basis for spiritual merger.

While the emotionality and idealizations of Indian family relationships play a major role in devotional spiritual practices, and the observance of *dharma* or moral precepts in family relationships enhances inner transformation, the paradox is that as people become more involved in spiritual realization, they become more individuated from the intense familial emotional tugs and pulls. Thus, the spiritual self not only is in continuity with the familial self but also is an important counterpoint. To posit merger with the spiritual self to be related either to an early mother–infant symbiosis or to a child's identification with the family developing an ego of the whole, is to miss the point and become seriously involved in reductionism.

REFERENCES

Akhtar, S. (2000). Book review of: *All the Mothers Are One: Hindu India and the Cultural Reshaping of Psychoanalysis* by Stanley Kurtz. *Journal of the American Psychoanalytic Association* 45:1014–1019.

Carstairs, G. M. (1957). *The Twice Born: A Study of a Community of High-Caste Hindus.* Bloomington: Indiana University Press.

Freud, S. (1930). Civilization and its discontents. *Standard Edition*. 21:57–145.

Kakar, S. (1978). *The Inner World: A Psychoanalytic Study of Childhood and Society in India*. Delhi: Oxford University Press.

——— (1991). *The Analyst and the Mystic*. Chicago: University of Chicago Press.

Kurtz, S. (1992). *All the Mothers Are One: Hindu India and the Cultural Reshaping of Psychoanalysis*. New York: Columbia University Press.

LeVine, R. A. (1977). Child rearing as cultural adaptation. In *Culture and Infancy: Variation in the Human Experience*, ed. P. H. Leiderman, S. R. Tulkin, and A. Rosenfeld, pp. 15–27. New York: Academic Press.

Majumdar, L. (1953). Position of women in modern India. In *Great Women of India*, ed. S. Madhavananda and R. C. Majumdar, pp. 112–127. Calcutta: Advaita Ashrama Publication Department.

McLean, A. (2000). The collision of world views: theory and implications for psychotherapy with Hindu Indians in America. PhD diss., Rutgers University.

Minturn, L., and Lambert, W. W. (1964). *Mothers of Six Cultures; Antecedents of Child Rearing*. New York: John Wiley.

Molino, A. (2003a). Interview with Catherine Ewing. In *Culture, Subjectivity, Psyche: Dialogues in Anthropology and Psychoanalysis*. Middletown, CT: Wesleyan University Press.

——— (2003b). Interview with Gananath Obeyesekere. In *Culture, Subjectivity, Psyche: Dialogues in Anthropology and Psychoanalysis*. Middletown, CT: Wesleyan University Press.

Ramanujan, A. K. (1990). Is there an Indian way of thinking? In *India Through Hindu Categories*, ed. M. Marriott, pp. 41–58. London: Sage.

Roland, A. (1988). *In Search of Self in India and Japan: Toward a Cross-Cultural Psychology*. Princeton: Princeton University Press.

——— (1996). *Cultural Pluralism and Psychoanalysis: The Asian and North American Experience*. New York: Routledge.

Seymour, S. (1975). Child rearing in India: a case study in change and modernization. In *Socialization and Communication in Primary Groups*, ed. T. R. Williams, pp. 1–58. The Hague: Mouton.

Trawick, M. (1990). *Notes on Love in a Tamil Family*. Berkeley: University of California Press.

Winnicott, D. W. (1965). *The Maturational Processes and the Facilitating Environment*. London: Hogarth.

5

Hindu–Muslim Relations in India: Past, Present, and Future

Salman Akhtar

> The Indian state will not identify itself with or be controlled by any particular religion. We hold that no one religion should be given preferential status, or unique distinction, that no one religion should be accorded special privileges in national life or international relations for that would be a violation of the basic principles of democracy and contrary to the best interests of religion and government.
>
> *Sarvapalli Radhakrishnan* (1967)

Hindus and Muslims have lived together in India for over 1,200 years. The saga of their coexistence, however, is far from smooth. It is characterized by the contradictory hues of strife and synchrony, hatred and harmony, and conflict and cooperation. While different eras might have witnessed one or the other extreme of such polarities, both ends of this emotional spectrum have usually been evident throughout the mutual history of these groups. Moreover, when it comes to the love–hate economy within their relationship, neither of these groups has acted entirely one way or the other. Neither can claim to be merely a victim and neither can be labeled simply a perpetrator. Both have loved each other and both have hated each other. In the end, their story is one of a close but ambivalent sibling bond.

As a result, which facet of their history gets highlighted, under what circumstances, by whom, for what purpose, and with what consequences, becomes an important point to consider. It is in this spirit that I offer the following exploration of the recent crisis in Hindu–Muslim relations in India. The threat posed by this crisis to India's secular, multicultural, and democratic fabric has drawn urgent attention from the worldwide community of social scientists (Gopal 1991, Hasan 1991, Jafferlot 1996, Kakar 1996, Ludden 1996, Manuel 1996, Mukherjee 1991, Rudolph and Rudolph 1993, van der Veer 1994, Varshney 2002). This chapter constitutes a modest attempt at integrating and extending their valuable contributions.

SOME CAVEATS

First, the subject lies beyond the clinical realm that is the area of my expertise as a psychoanalyst. Well versed in depth psychology of individuals, I find myself ill-equipped to explain matters involving large groups of people. Although my tenure on the Group for Advancement of Psychiatry's Committee on International Relations (1996–2001), my work in the area of immigration and cross-cultural psychotherapy (Akhtar 1995, 1999a,b, Akhtar and Choi 2004, Huang and Akhtar, 2005), my reading of the post-Freudian psychoanalytic literature on large-group psychology (especially Volkan 1988, 1997, 2004), my participation in the International Psychoanalytic Association's Working Group on Terror and Terrorism (2002–present), as well as my own work toward understanding terrorism (Akhtar 1997, 2003) have given me some insights in the realm of social turmoil, the field still remains somewhat unfamiliar to me.

Second, in addressing the specifics of the Hindu–Muslim conflict, one faces the risk of overlooking the fact that such conflicts and the prejudices that fuel them are universal. It is therefore important to remind oneself that the roots of ethnic, racial, and religious prejudice (at least in its ubiquitous, mild, and dormant forms) are to be found in the ordinary and inevitable experiences of human childhood: "stranger anxiety" of infancy, later disappointment with maternal care, anger at the father for being the "invader" of the mother's body, resentment of younger siblings as unwelcome intruders, repudiation of pregenital sexuality, and the need for an Other for the purposes of self identity consolidation (Akhtar 2003, Bird 1956, Parens 1999, Spitz 1965, Sterba 1947, Thomson et al. 1993). Together these factors give rise to a universal vulnerability to prejudice. However, more than such ordinary childhood frustrations is needed to turn this seed of prejudice into a cactus of actual hatred of others. Factors pertaining to the real world (e.g., economic hardship) and to group psychology (e.g., intensification of emotions and lowering of critical judgment, as noted by Freud in his 1921 paper) are required to transform this hatred into ethnic violence. All in all, while the factors giving color to a specific ethnic conflict might vary from situation to situation, the factors preparing a human being for possessing such potential are universal. Study of a particular situation, therefore, teaches us about both that situation and the human condition in general.

Third, any consideration of the topic of the Hindu–Muslim conflict warrants a serious reading of the history of these two groups in India, and this brings its own hurdles. The material is too voluminous to cover and emanates from too many vantage points. Dichotomies that pervade this literature exist along the religious–secular, Muslim–Hindu, left–right, intracultural–extracultural, and Indian–non-Indian schisms. Historical tracts written by liberal Hindus and Muslims accord well with each other, while those authored by conservative Hindus and Muslims differ sharply in their accounts. British, North American, and European scholars bring their own perspectives. Different historians offer varying interpretations of the same historical fact, and even the facts they report often do not coincide with each other. One views a Muslim emperor's effort to bring Islam and Hinduism together as heretic and the other views it as admirably secular. One emphasizes the early Muslim invaders' atrocities while the other highlights the later Muslims' contributions in the realm of architecture, music, and films. One says that Muslims caused the partition of India while the other reminds us that a large number of Muslims were strongly against it. One underscores the differences between the Hindu–Muslim communities while the other brings out their similarities and overlaps. And so on.

Fourth, writing on matters of interfaith strife stirs up anxiety and conflict. On the one hand, there is the risk of offending those Hindus and Muslims whose viewpoint is different from mine. On the other hand, it would be shameful to skirt honesty for the purpose of appeasing others. It is not easy to find a way out of this conundrum.

Fifth, in focusing upon the conflictual aspects of Hindu–Muslim relations, one runs the risk of overlooking that the majority of individuals from both these groups are friendly and affectionate toward each other. The current rift between the two communities is largely engineered by the Hindu nationalists of the right who receive ample justification from the outrageous political stands taken by the narrow-minded Muslim religious leaders[1] of the country.

Sixth, a certain amount of personal bias becomes impossible to avoid in this sort of undertaking. No matter how hard one tries for it not to be the case, the picture one paints ends up receiving color not only from one's professional discipline but also from the deepest core of one's personal identity. I am no exception in this regard. It is therefore best that I put my cards on the table and let the reader know that I am politically a democrat, religiously a nonpracticing individual, and professionally a psychoanalyst. I was born into a highly creative, politically active, nationalist Muslim family of North India and have deep and abiding love for my motherland.

Finally, reading chapters such as this is not done in a state of psychic equanimity and neutrality. Feeling validated or invalidated in his own ethnopolitical convictions and thus narcissistically exalted or injured, the reader is himself vulnerable to regressive simplification, emotionality, and partisanship. Therefore, both positive and negative verdicts on this chapter need to be taken with a grain of salt.

It is with these caveats in mind that my contribution should be approached. In it I present my understanding of the nature of the current increase in the Hindu–Muslim strife in India. I also outline some psychoanalytically informed social interventions to minimize this problem. However, I begin with my reading of the history of the Hindu–Muslim coexistence in India. A background of this sort should be helpful since

> present-day conflicts cannot be fully understood without first understanding how historical hurts and grievances survive from generation to generation as "chosen traumas." These psychological "genes" exist within many large groups and can be manipulated by leaders in subsequent generations to mobilize the group. [Volkan 2004, p. 51]

---

1. A recent example of such outlandishness is the *fatwa* issued by Mufti Abdul Quddus Rumi, a Muslim cleric in Agra, which excommunicated fifty-four Muslims and nullified their marriages because they declared that singing the nationalist song, "Vande Matram," was not un-Islamic (*India Abroad* 2004).

HISTORICAL BACKGROUND

Hindus had lived in India for many centuries before scattered settlements of Muslim traders began to appear along the Southern coastal areas of the country. This development, also evident in parts of Sindh and Gujarat, occurred around the early eighth century. Invaders representing various Middle Eastern regimes also appeared on the scene around this time. One of them, Mohmmad-bin-Qasim, an emissary of Hajjaj bin Yusuf, the Umayyad governor of Baghdad, went as far as to establish his control over Sindh and parts of Punjab by 713 A.D. However, his administration soon faltered and a sustained dynasty formation did not follow. Muslim life in India returned to its relatively quiet status.

As the years passed, a modicum of cultural exchange between Hindus and Muslims occurred. Musical instruments of the two began to acquire hybrid forms. Patterns of attire were subtly affected and the necessity to learn each other's language was felt. Even folklore began to be shared. The most striking cross-cultural accomplishment of this era is the translation of the great Indian collection of fables, the *Panchtantra*, into Arabic around 750 A.D. (Mani 1975). All in all, life seemed relatively peaceful.

This changed with the massive and invasive influx of Muslims into India, beginning around mid-eleventh century A.D. Indeed, their history from then onward reveals a complex and contradictory pattern of plunder and patronage, bloodshed and beautification, coercion and cooperation, and repression and reform. The Turkish, Afghan, and Mongol invaders of the northwestern provinces of India were indeed plunderers. They showed little respect for the culture of the local masses and had no hesitation about denuding respected Hindu palaces and sacred temples of their valuable objects. The pain caused by their desecration of Hindu icons and shrines continues to throb in the Indian psyche even though nearly a thousand years have since passed.

The most significant and permanent military movement of Muslims into North India occurred in the late twelfth century A.D. and was carried out by a Turkish dynasty that arose from the ruins of the Abbasid Caliphate. The road to their conquest, however, was prepared by Sultan Mahmud of Ghazna (Ghazni in today's Afghanistan), who conducted more than twenty raids into Northwest India between 1001 and 1027 A.D. and established a large but short-lived empire in Punjab.

Mahmud Ghaznavi (the name by which he was widely recognized) only gave the impression of wanting to conquer and rule. Actually, he was more interested in robbing the local treasuries and Hindu temples that stored gold and precious jewels for religious purposes. His goal was to use this wealth to finance his campaigns in Central Asia where he *did* want to build an empire. Little did he know that one of his raids (1026 A.D.), at the magnificent Hindu temple of *Somnath* in the Junagadh district of Gujarat, would be evoked as a "chosen trauma" (Volkan 1997) by the Hindu consciousness many centuries later.[2] At the risk of straying from the chronological progression of events, let me clarify the reasons behind Somnath temple's demolition becoming a persistent and ever-aching emblem of Muslim atrocities toward Hindus. First and foremost, the sheer grandeur of the shrine made its demolition hard to fathom and mourn. Second, its demolition was not a one-time occurrence; the temple was reconstructed again and again by Hindus, only to be destroyed each time by one or another Muslim invader or ruler (at least six such attacks occurred; those in 1026, 1297, 1394, 1413, 1459, and 1669 A.D., are well documented). As a result, the site became a chronic reminder of large-group humiliation for Hindus. Finally, the fact that the two Muslims considered most nefarious by Hindus (Mahmud Ghaznavi and Aurangzeb) were both responsible, at different times, for the temple's demolition, also fixated the trauma in an emotionally powerful way.

While this deep wound would reappear in a later part of our discourse, for the time being allow me to rejoin the advancing march of time after Mahmud Ghaznavi's invasions. As I do so, I note that the next wave of Muslims who arrived in India included other plunderers like Mohammed Ghauri as well as imperial expansionists of the Middle East with aims to establish their rule over parts of India. The latter group did not view themselves as the keepers of Turkish, Afghan, or Iranian outposts; they were truly Indian rulers. Qutub-uddin Aybak established the first Muslim headquarters in Delhi, the heart of India, in 1193 A.D. He and the subsequent Muslim rulers were well grounded in the local

---

2. The *Somnath* temple was finally rebuilt after India's independence from the British in 1947. The impetus for its reconstruction was provided by Sardar Patel, the first home minister of postcolonial India, during his visit to Junagadh in November 1947. The ruins of the old temple were pulled down in October 1950 and Rajendra Prasad, the first president of the Republic of India, performed the idol installation ceremony in May 1951 (Jafferlot 1996).

idiom, took pride in their new nation, and sought ways for its improvement. This trend continued and, with the passage of time, the Indian-born progeny of these Muslim rulers began to ascend to power. They built major highways (e.g., Sher Shah Suri constructed the road known as the Grand Trunk Road today), created *sarais* (roadside inns) for travelers, and even founded new cities (e.g., Ahmed Shah, Sikander Lodhi, Adil Shah, and Quli Qutub Shah founded Ahmedabad, Agra, Bijapur, and Hyderabad, respectively). They invested funds in building canals, stepwells, and underground water channels. They also constructed buildings of great splendor, many of which (e.g., Fatehpur Sikri, the Red Fort of Delhi, and the Taj Mahal) continue to be the source of national pride today. Muslim rulers also established *Karkhanas* (small-scale factories) in Khurja for pottery, Moradabad for brassware, Mirzapur for carpets, Firozabad for glassware, Farrukhabad for printing, Saharanpur and Nagina for woodcarving, Lucknow for *chikan* and *zardozi* (two types of embroidery) work, and Srinagar for papier-mâché.

To be sure, the ancestral religion of these rulers was Central Asian, but even that began to have pliability and admixture. A near-pagan taint had already seeped into Islam via the Sufi movements of Persia and Afghanistan, which utilized devotional singing, dancing, and trance-like states; their dialogue seemed to be with a God who was friendlier and more human than the strict and foreboding God of the Quran. This trend received further color from the pantheistic culture of India that placed idol worship as a stepping stone for spiritual self-realization and union with God.[3]

There were considerable differences in the way various Muslim regimes responded to this encounter between their ascetic monotheism

---

3. On the surface, the distinction between Islamic monotheism and Hindu polytheism is obvious. However, a closer look reveals that the matter is much more complex. While not declaring Mohammad or his son-in-law Ali to be gods, the reverence Muslims have toward them as well as many other subsequent seers and sages tends to distribute their worshiping attitude a bit more widely. Conversely, while having a vast array of deities, Hinduism ultimately proposes one supreme God. The related matter of idol worship is similarly complex. On the surface, Muslims do not worship idols and Hindus do. However, the Muslim turning toward Mecca during prayers, rituals Muslims perform during Hajj (pilgrimage to Mecca), and the Muslim regard for various *mazaars* (graves) and *dargahs* (shrines) in India look suspiciously like idol worship to me. Conversely, all thoughtful Hindus know that the idols they worship are merely iconic way stations to a supreme God that is boundless and beyond reification.

and the more relaxed and colorful spiritual life in the land they were governing. Some emperors like Ghyas-uddin Balban (1200–1287 A.D.) and Alamgir Aurangzeb (1618–1707 A.D.) recoiled, asserted their religious ancestry, suppressed local customs, levied extra taxes upon Hindus, demolished Hindu temples, and forced Hindus to convert to Islam. Others reacted with ambivalence. Ala-uddin Khalji (1255–1316 A.D.), for instance, plundered Hindu kingdoms in South India and yet married a Hindu princess and opened the gates to prominent Hindus and Jains to participate in his administration. Still others went much further in adapting to India. Firoz Shah Tuglaq, who reigned from 1351 to 1388 A.D., conducted discourses with Hindu saints, commissioned Persian translations of important Sanskrit texts, and erected a pillar to commemorate the life of the great Hindu King Ashoka (who reigned from 273–232 B.C.) at a prominent place in his palace. Without openly violating the *Shari'ah* (the Islamic law), Firoz Shah Tughlaq, and many Muslim emperors after him, made sure that the policy of the state was based increasingly on the opinion of their court advisors and not on religious considerations. They supplemented *Shari'ah* by framing *Zawabit* (their own state laws), which, in cases of conflict, overrode the universal Muslim law.

Jalaluddin Mohammad Akbar (1542–1605 A.D.) married a Hindu princess, Jodha Bai, and later their son, Jahangir, ascended to the throne of India. Akbar appointed three Hindus (Raja Mansingh, Raja Todar Mal, and Raja Birbal) to the nine-member advisory council (*nav-ratna*) to their court.[4] He incorporated Hindu etiquette in his personal behavior (e.g., he often wore a *tilak* [Hindu sacramental marking] on his forehead) and banned certain practices (e.g., marriage between cousins) associated with Islam. Akbar even sought to create a hybrid religion (*Din-e-Ilahi*), which had attributes of Islam and Hinduism. His grandson, Shah Jahan (the builder of the Taj Mahal), was deeply interested in the Hindu culture, and his great-grandson, Dara Shikoh (the elder brother of Aurangzeb, to wit), translated *Upanishads* into Persian. Dara Shikoh himself authored a book, *The Meeting of the Two Oceans of Sufism and Vedantism*, that elucidated the intellectual confluence of these traditions (Radhakrishnan 1975).

---

4. A fourth member, the great singer Tansen (1535–1592 A.D.), is reported to be a born Muslim by some and a Hindu convert to Islam by other historians. What remains certain is that he died a Muslim and is buried in Gwalior, Madhya Pradesh.

Despite such rapprochement, tensions frequently flared up between Hindus and Muslims. However, not all such friction was religion-based. Most of it resulted from territorial battles that cut across the lines of religious faith. For instance, the Mughal emperor Akbar's general was Raja Mansingh, a Hindu Rajput. Aurangzeb fought his three brothers (Dara Shikoh, Shujaa, and Murad) for the throne with the help of Hindu allies, and each of his brothers had Hindu allies themselves. Muslim rulers of Deccan and Gujarat had similar alliances, and when the Marathas fought the Mughals, Shivaji's campaign had many Muslim lieutenants. In sum, Hindus and Muslims stood with each other on the basis of their political alliances more often than they did on account of their religious faith. Sher Shah Suri's appointment of Hemu Bhargava as his chief of intelligence and Sultan Mohammad Adil's later appointment of him as his prime minister are striking examples of such strategic pluralism of the times.

The Muslim–Hindu blending of culture, however, went beyond the mixture of blood, politics, and religion. It also became evident in architecture, music, and language. Muslim kings frequently employed Hindu artisans and the resulting confluence of aesthetics gave a uniquely charming texture to their buildings. Mosques built by Muslim rulers in India, for instance, began to have four minarets, in contrast to their Middle Eastern counterparts, which had only one. The single-minaret mosques were efforts to replicate the *Ka'bba* (the "first mosque") in Mecca. The four-minaret mosques reproduced the Hindu motif of symmetry in design and architecture.

Music was another realm in which Muslim–Hindu cooperation led to impressively productive results. Indeed, Manuel (1996), who has written extensively on this topic, declares that music might be the only sphere in which the followers of these two religions have led a completely harmonious existence over the last one thousand years. The talent of Hindu musicians was regularly nourished by their regional Muslim rulers.[5] Some, among the latter, made innovative additions to

---

5. Aurangzeb was an exception in this regard, but he treated Muslim musicians with an equal degree of contempt. In realms other than music, too, his harshness was directed at both Hindus and Muslims. He saddled Hindus with all sorts of religious, social, and legal hardships and he instituted severe punishments for Muslims over their omission of five daily prayers and fasting during the month of Ramazan.

the Indian classical singing; the most outstanding example of this is Sultan Hussain Shariqi of Jaunpur who introduced *Khayal* (a particular genre of classical Indian singing) in Indian *gayiki* (singing), circa 1430 A.D. Amir Khusrau (1253–1325 A.D.) evolved the sitar by conflating the features of the South Indian *rudraveena* (a South Indian drone instrument) with various Persian and Afghani drone instruments, and Mian Sarang, an eminent musician in the dying Mughal court of Mohammad Shah Rangeelay, invented a remarkable string instrument that was named *sarangi* after him. Currently the preeminent exponents of *Dhurpad*, a deeply devotional Hindu raga, are Muslim singers, especially the Dagar brothers.

Muslim intermingling with the Hindu mainstream of North India also resulted in the birth a new language, Urdu (circa 1500 A.D.). Derived from lexical betrothal of Persian, Turkish, and Arabic nouns and adjectives to the verbs and adverbs of the local *Braj-bhasha* and *Awadhi* dialects, Urdu (itself a Turkish word meaning "military barracks") became the language of the commoners, while Persian was retained for judicial and administrative transactions of the court. This led the litterateurs to shun Urdu at first. Gradually, however, a distinguished cadre of Urdu writers and poets emerged that ranged from the pioneering Wali Gujarati through the great Mir Taqi Mir and playful Nazir Akbarabadi to the immortal Mirza Ghalib. Even Bahadur Shah Zafar (1775–1862 A.D.), the last Mughal king of India before the country came under British domination, wrote poetry in Urdu.

The language, with its lyrical cadence, became a deeply loved medium of expression for vast segments of North Indian population regardless of their religious affiliation. Many Hindus came to be recognized as great contributors to Urdu literature. This vast list extends from Har Gopal Tafta (a favorite disciple of Ghalib), Daya Shankar Nasim, and Ratan Nath Sarshar, through Munshi Premchand and Braj Narain Chakbast, to Anand Narain Mulla, Raghupati Sahai ("Firaq Gorakhpuri"), Krishna Chandra, Mahindra Nath, Tilok Chand Mehroom, Upendra Nath Ashk, Kanhayya Lal Kapur, and Jagan Nath Azad. The most authoritative source on Ghalib's work in contemporary India, Malik Ram, was a Hindu and so is the eminent Urdu scholar, Gopi Chand Narang, who currently heads the national Sahitya Academy. Besides directly contributing to it, Hindus also took a lead in publishing Urdu literature, a tradition that has ranged from Munshi Nawal Kishore, the original publisher of the great *Diwan-e-Ghalib*,[6] through *Biswin Sadi's*[7] pseudonymous "Khushtar Garaami," to Amar Nath Varma, the founder of the current Star Publications in New Delhi.

With British rule over India (1858–1947) came subtle divisions among Hindus and Muslims, largely at the behest of their colonizer's divide-and-rule policy. The most virulent aspect of this tactic was the establishment of separate, religion-based electorates for the two communities. However, as van der Veer (1994) reminds us,

> this is not to say that there was no division of Hindu and Muslim communities in the pre-colonial period. There was: the division was not a colonial invention. But to count these communities and to have leaders represent them was a colonial novelty, and it was fundamental to the emergence of religious nationalism. [pp. 19–20]

Nonetheless, Muslims continued to feel deep loyalty to India, and the early uprisings against the British rule had prominent Muslim participation. The legendary Tipu Sultan of Mysore,[8] Begum Hazrat Mahal of Oudh, and Nawab Ali Bahadur of Banda (who fought the British alongside Maharani Lakshmibai of Jhansi in the 1858 battle of Kalpi) readily come to mind in this connection, though an actual list of such freedom fighters is certainly much longer. Countless is the number of Muslim soldiers who fought shoulder to shoulder with their Hindu counterparts against the British on the battlefronts of Lucknow, Patna, and Meerut.

All in all, Hindus and Muslims led a peaceful coexistence during the nineteenth and early twentieth centuries. In the Gangetic plain

---

6. The collection of poems by the great Urdu poet Mirza Asad-ullah Khan Ghalib.

7. A popular Urdu magazine published in New Delhi.

8. The Indian liquor baron Vijay Mallya, a Hindu, recently bought the fabled sword of the Muslim king Tipu Sultan (1749–1799 A.D.) at a London auction for over $3 million. Calling the sword a unique piece of Indian history, Mallya said that he had bought it to restore the "rightful legacy" (quoted in *India Abroad*, April 16, 2004, p. A-18) to Karnataka, the South Indian state to which Tipu Sultan belonged. Mallya's grand gesture underscored the essentially secular and multicultural spirit of India.

state of United Provinces (later named Uttar Pradesh) especially, a hybrid culture of sublime elegance prevailed; the *Ganga-Jamani tehzib*[9] of Lucknow was the epitome of such confluence (Mohan 1997, Oldenburg 2001, Sharar 1920). Hindu nobility kept *taazias* (an Indianized replica of Prophet Mohammed's grandson Hussain's tomb) during *Moharram* (the month in the Islamic calendar in which Hussain was killed in a battle in Karbala, Iraq). Raja Tikait Rai and Raja Bilas Rai went as far as building their own *imambaras* (Shia religious shrines) in Lucknow to house *alams* (scepters) representing the 680 A.D. battle of Karbala. The Hindu Lambadi community in Andhra Pradesh had (in fact, continues to have to this day) their own genre of *Moharram* lamentation songs in Telegu. Much more curious was the emergence of the small Hussaini Brahamin sect in the rural Punjab (Sikand 2004). They practiced an intriguing blend of Muslim and Hindu traditions and based their name on the claim that their Hindu ancestors had traveled to Karbala and fought in the army of Hussain. They believed that the sacred Hindu text, *Bhagavad Gita*, had foretold the event of Hussain's death at Karbala. They also held Hussain's father, Ali, in great respect and referred to him as *Om Murti*.[10] While most extreme in their hybrid beliefs, Hussaini Brahmins were by no means the only Hindu community that straddled the frontier between Hinduism and Islam.

Muslims, on their part, took delight in participating in the *Diwali* and *Dusshera* festivals. They joyously played *Holi* (the Hindu festival of colors) all across North India. Wajid Ali Shah (1827–1887), the famous Nawab of Oudh, learned *Kathak* dance from Hindu teachers of Banaras. He sometimes dressed up as Krishna and at other times as a Gopi to celebrate the love of Krishna and Radha in his palace. Abdul Rahim Khankhanan (1556–1627) and Malik Mohammad Jaisi (circa 1500) wrote outstanding devotional poetry about this paradigmatic romantic couple of Hinduism. In Southern parts of the country, too, Muslims intermingled peacefully with Hindus and their regional culture

---

9. This phrase metaphorically means "hybrid culture," evoking the confluence of the two great rulers of India, namely Ganga and Jamuna.

10. A stylized way of addressing someone as a divine incarnation. These Hindus frequently had Dutt and Mohiyal as their last names. Their recent generations have by and large abandoned the mixed religious heritage of the group, finding it embarrassingly deviant.

was a shared one. Muslims of Andhra Pradesh, Tamil Nadu, Karnataka, and Kerala spoke Telegu, Tamil, Kannada, and Malyalam, respectively, and not Urdu. In Bengal, Islam especially assimilated many values and practices that were not in conformity with the precepts of the Quran.[11] All in all, throughout India, regional commonality determined linguistic, sartorial, and culinary preferences to a greater extent than did religion. Interethnic strife was infrequent.

Such placidity centerstage notwithstanding, trouble was brewing in the wings. This was constituted by the foundation of the Muslim League in 1906 and Rashtriya Sevak Sangh (RSS, in short, a paramilitary organization dedicated to turning India into an exclusively Hindu nation) in 1925. The Muslim League was pro-Muslim and anti-Hindu. The RSS was pro-Hindu and anti-Muslim. Both promulgated discrimination and prejudice. And, despite their narrow nationalisms (Muslim nationalism of the League and Hindu nationalism of the RSS), both were opposed to India's independence struggle with the British. Another similarity between them was their receiving inspiration from events outside India. The Muslim League gained strength from the *Khilafat* movement (the adversarial relationship between the Turkish Caliph and the British government of that time) and the RSS drew fervor from its ideological links with the European fascists; Veer Savarkar "wrote approvingly of the occupation of Sudetenland by Germany on the grounds that its inhabitants shared common blood and language with the Germans. In the late 1930s, both *Hindu Outlook* and *Maharatta* praised Franco, Mussolini, and Hitler" (Jafferlot 1996, p. 51). All in all, both the Muslim League and the RSS sowed the seeds of organized hatred between the outer fringes of the Hindu and Muslim communities. This was later exploited by the British.

Then came the freedom movement of the mid-twentieth century. Initially united with their Hindu brethren in opposing the British rule, Indian Muslims found themselves suddenly caught up in an immensely painful dilemma. Feeling unfairly treated in the distribution of political power, some Indian Muslims sought not only independence from

---

11. Such "Hinduization" of Islam in Bengal, especially the local Muslims' love of the Bengali language, would later play a role in the 1971 birth of Bangladesh as a separate nation.

the British but also secession from the country in order to form their own nation. The Muslim intelligentsia was divided, with prominent activists on both sides of the dreaded choice. Mohammad Ali Jinnah, who had been dubbed the "Ambassador of Hindu–Muslim Unity" in 1916 by Sarojini Naidu (*The Encyclopedia of Asian History and Asia Society* 1988) and who had harshly rejected the idea of Muslim secession from India proposed to him by immigrant Muslims in London a few years ago (Collins and Lapierre 1975), now became the chief spokesman of a virulent ethnic megalomania. Liaqat Ali and Sikander Mirza also took the side of carving out a separate nation for Muslims, arguing that Hindus and Muslims were fundamentally different[12] and that Muslims could not expect fair treatment in a post-British independent India. Maulana Abul Kalam Azad, Khan Abdul Ghaffar Khan ("Frontier Gandhi"), Rafi Ahmad Kidwai, the Ansari brothers, Hakim Ajmal Khan, Mohammad Yunus, and Ansar Harvani were among the outstanding nationalist Muslims fiercely opposed to the country's partition. The first group felt that they were Muslims first and Indians later. The second group felt the opposite. Muslim masses were torn.

The radical Muslims, hell-bent upon seeking a separate country, were unwittingly aided by the right-wing Hindu ideologues like Veer Savarkar and Madhav Sadashiv Golwalkar, who also subscribed to the idea that Hindus and Muslims of India were two entirely irreconcilable nations. They wanted the Muslims "traitors" to be kept away from grabbing power in a government that would be formed once the British left. Lord Mountbatten, the last Imperial Viceroy of British India, was also in a hurry to hand over an empire that had lost its raison d'être with the post–World War II economic crisis. He facilitated the tragic partition of India. The country's body and soul were mutilated in 1947 and what was India ended up becoming India and Pakistan in a dark moment of the subcontinent's history. "Never before in South Asian history did so few decide the fate of so many. And never before did so few

---

12. Fascinatingly, the claim that Hindus and Muslims of India are two irreconcilable nations is made by both the Hindu and Muslim extremists. The thinking of the Muslim League's Mohammad Ali Jinnah and Shiv Sena's Bala Saheb Thackeray seems to be in complete agreement on this matter.

ignore the wishes and sentiments of so many in the sub-continent" (Hasan 1991, p.108). Gandhi protested to no avail and wept.[13]

This macabre territorial surgery was accompanied by a major population exchange whereby a large number of Hindus from Punjab, Sindh, and Bengal moved into "India" and a multitude of Muslims migrated from United and Central Provinces (Uttar and Madhya Pradesh, respectively), Bihar, Bengal, and a few other areas to the newly formed Pakistan. Looting, chaos, and communal violence accompanied this exodus. The degree to which both Hindus and Muslims sank in this bloody orgy of dehumanization and sadism is beyond description. Trains would arrive from what is now Pakistan filled with corpses of Hindus killed by Muslims. Entire families of Hindus were frequently murdered by Muslims, who also tortured Hindu children and pregnant women. Not ones to be left behind, Hindus killed numerous Muslims, raped Muslim women escaping India, castrated Muslim men and threw bucketsful of circumcised penises in mosques to taunt the Muslim community. A diabolical nightmare of religious persecution was unleashed on both sides and humanity was degraded in the name of Allah and Ram. All in all, ten million Hindus and seven million Muslims moved across the newly created boundaries and nearly 300,000 individuals were killed in the process.

While the Muslims who moved to Pakistan were traumatized by the sudden dislocation, the suffering of Hindus who came to the vivisected India was greater. The former were pursuing a dream, the latter pushed into a nightmare. The former, even in the midst of suffering, were buoyed with nationalistic optimism while the latter had little reason for hope. Most among the former had opted to emigrate, while the majority among the latter were forced out of their ancestral lands. The trauma of exile was great in the latter and its mourning blocked by necessities of adapting to new circumstances.[14] It would take another

---

13. He was assassinated on January 30, 1948, less than 6 months after India's independence and partition. His murderer, Nathu Ram Godse, had strong ideological ties to the right-wing Hindu nationalist leader Veer Savarkar. The "crime" for which Gandhi allegedly "deserved" to be killed was his kindness and "indulgence" toward Muslims!

14. I have elsewhere elaborated on the differences between immigrants and exiles when it comes to the matters of nostalgia, future orientation, and overall social adjustment (Akhtar 1999b).

fifty years before the psychosocial working through of this massive trauma would resume. Until then, the pain would remain subject to trans-generational transmission. Let me not rush, though, and return to the immediate postindependence period.

After the partition, both sides sought to deal with the refugees who had freshly arrived in their respective countries. Independence from the British was a heady affair, and nation building was a priority. Gradually, the dust settled. India glowed with national pride and chose an insistently secular fabric for its constitution. Here credit is owed to the enlightened vision of those Hindus (including Jawahar Lal Nehru, Rajindra Prasad, Sarvapalli Radhakrishnan, and C. Rajgopalacharya) who opted for making the territorially amputated India a secular rather than a Hindu religious state. The basically liberal and forgiving majority among the Indian Hindus accepted this secular constitution and embraced with relative equanimity those Muslims who had chosen to stay in India.

This group of Muslims received treatment in the postpartition India that was roughly equal to that offered to the majority Hindus. India's secular constitution offered them safety and by in large protected their cultural and educational institutions. If there were poor, illiterate, and hungry among them, they differed little from the Hindus in the same boat. If there were occasional outbreaks of violence against them, these were regularly followed by communal contrition and reparative gestures. Outside of such situations, most Muslims muddled along in a fashion similar to their Hindu brethren and some truly prospered and acquired great fame and success. The contributions of these Muslims to the contemporary Indian culture over the last fifty years are indeed remarkable.

Let me name the most influential among these: presidents of India, Zakir Hussain, Fakhruddin Ali Ahmed, and A. P. J. Abul Kalam; parliamentarians like Maulana Abul Kalam Azad, Rafi Ahmad Kidwai, M. C. Chagla, Ansar Harvani, Humayun Kabir, and Najma Heptullah; jurists like Chief Justice Hidayatullah, who also served as the acting president of India for a brief period of time; diplomats like Abid Hussain, India's ambassador to the United States from 1990 to 1992; film actors like Yusuf Khan ("Dilip Kumar"[15]), Yaqub, Zakaria Khan ("Jayant"),

---

15. Muslims frequently adopted Hindu names while entering the film industry and Hindus often took on Muslim *nom de plumes* while contributing to Urdu literature. The complex societal factors underlying such choices certainly deserve further attention.

Rahman, Sheikh Mukhtar, Hamid Ali Khan ("Ajit"), Badruddin Ahmed ("Johnny Walker"), Mehmood, Firoze Khan, Abbas Khan ("Sanjay"), Amjad Khan, Naseeruddin Shah, Shahrukh Khan, Salman Khan, Aamir Khan, and Saif Ali Khan; film actresses like Naseem, Fatima Bai ("Nargis"), Begum Paara, Surraiya, Mumtaz Jahan ("Madhubala"), Mahjabeen Ara ("Meena Kumari"), Shakila, Waheeda Rehman, Saira Banu, Mumtaz, Zeenat Aman, and Shabana Azmi; movie directors like Mehboob Khan, M. Sadiq, Kamal Amrohi, Nasir Hussain, and Farhan Akhtar; Bollywood music makers like Mohmmed Rafi, Talat Mehmood, Naushad, Shamshad Begum, and A. R. Rahman; Urdu poets[16] and film lyricists like Sahir Ludhianvi, Shakeel Badayuni, Jan-Nisar Akhtar, Majaz, Ali Sardar Jafri, Makhdoom Mohiuddin, Kaifi Azmi, Majrooh Sultanpuri, Rahi Masoom Raza,[17] Shaharyar, Nida Fazli, and Javed Akhtar[18]; journalists like K. A. Abbas, Hamid Dalwai, and M. J. Akbar; physician educators like Mahdi Hasan; ornithologists like Salim Ali; sportsmen like Nisar Ahmad, Mushtaq Ali, Abbas Ali Beg; Mansoor Ali Khan ("Nawab of Pataudi"), and Azharuddin; artists like M. F. Hussain; theater personalities like Habib Tanvir, Shaukat Azmi, and Firoz Khan; fiction writers like Ismat Chughtai, Qurrat-ul-Ain Haider, Razia Sajjad Zaheer, and Wajida Tabassum; litterateurs like Sajjad Zaheer, Aal Ahmad Suroor, Ehtisham Hussain, Mohammad Hasan, Safia Akhtar, Baqar Mehdi, Zoe Ansari, and Shams-ur-Rehman Farooqui; academicians like Irfan Habib, Asghar Ali Engineer, Mushirul Hasan, and Zoya Hasan; art and antique collectors like Salaar Jung III of Hyderabad; exponents of vocal and instrumental classical music of India like Bade

---

16. The works of these poets and their predecessors directly pertaining to India's topography and culture has been collected in a four-volume set, *Hindustan Hamara* (Akhtar 1975). Besides such overt reference, Urdu poetry has drawn more subtle and profoundly significant themes from ancient Hindu thought. The impact of Advaitic Vedantism especially is evident in poems of Mirza Ghalib and the more recent poet Ali Sardar Jafri.

17. A Shia Muslim from Ghaziabad, Uttar Pradesh, Rahi Masoom Raza, wrote the screenplay and dialogues of the fifty-two-hour-long television series based on the great Hindu epic *Mahabharata*, shown to rapt audiences across India during the early 1990s.

18. The husband–wife duo of Javed Akhtar and Shabana Azmi defies categorization. They are film personalities, stage and television performers, political presences, and social activists of immense virtuosity and international stature.

Ghulam Ali Khan, Allaudin Khan (the teacher and former father-in-law of the world-renowned Ravi Shankar), Allah Rakkha, Bismillah Khan, Ali Akbar Khan, Begum Akhtar, the Dagar Brothers, Amjad Ali Khan and Zakir Hussain; and, finally, Muslims of the Indian diaspora, like the novelist Salman Rushdie, the artist Raza, the filmmaker Ismail Merchant, the academic Aqeel Bilgirami, the journalist Fareed Zakaria, and community organizers A. R. Nakadar and S. M. Abdullah.

The contributions of these individuals to Indian society can only be denied by the truly irrational. Yet a culturally subversive effort to do precisely this is evident in today's India. Before describing this sinister scenario, however, I would like to conclude my historical survey[19] and move on to an overall picture of the Hindu–Muslim tension in India and complex forces that fuel such prejudice from within both these communities.

MUSLIM CONTRIBUTIONS
TO THE HINDU–MUSLIM TENSION

The current rise of anti-Muslim prejudice in India might make it seem out of place to mention, but the fact is that Muslim community has also contributed to the difficulties it faces in India. The ways in which they have, wittingly or unwittingly, contributed to the Hindu–

---

19. While there might be inadvertent omissions in this account, given my modest knowledge of history, there are some matters that I have deliberately bypassed in the service of narrative economy. Prominent among these are the massacres by Nadir Shah, Ahmed Shah Abdali, and Taimur Lung (the infamous "Tamerlane" of the West); Muslim–Muslim battles over the Delhi throne; Faizi's and Firdausi's literary and historical works; the gardens made by Mughal emperors; the fine arts of calligraphy and miniature painting under the sponsorship of Muslim rulers; the north-south difference in Hindu–Muslim relations; the complex saga of Sikh–Muslim relations; the Muslim *Nawab*–Hindu moneylender tension created by the British strangulation of finances in Oudh; the impact of the *Khilafat* movement in Indian–Muslim politics; the role played by the Deoband *ullema* (Muslim scholars) and academics of Aligarh Muslim University in the social concerns of Indian Muslims; the patriotic and exhortative songs written by Muslim poets (e.g., Jan Nisar Akhtar's "*Awaaz do hum ek hain*") during the Indo-Chinese and Indo-Pakistani wars; the details of both the *Babri Masjid* destruction and Gujarat riot; and, finally, the literature (e.g., Tharoor 2001) that has evolved about various communal riots.

Muslim strife can be grouped under five categories: (1) some of their inherent characteristics, (2) their ongoing "love affair" with a nostalgically idealized past, (3) prejudicial attitudes held by some members of their community, (4) the absence of secular and progressive leadership in the Muslim community, and (5) certain constitutional exceptions and privileges enjoyed by them. Together, these five factors have a synergistic effect of alienating Hindus.

Inherent Characteristics

The religious faith of Indian Muslims originated in Saudi Arabia, a place that is outside India. Their chief holy cities include Mecca and Medina, Jerusalem, and Karbala and Najaf, which happen to be in Saudi Arabia, Israel, and Iraq, respectively. In offering *namaaz* (daily prayers), all Muslims of the world turn to face Mecca; Indian Muslims are no exceptions in this regard. Such commitments and practices have the potential of making them appear not fully Indian to Hindu eyes. There is little, however, that Indian Muslims can do about this except to point out that extraterritorial religious loyalties are not to be equated with extraterritorial political loyalties. They can also remind their critics in this regard that such extraterritorial religious loyalties are the credo of vast segments of the world's population, including the Hindus living outside India. However logical such a rejoinder might be, it might still fail to correct the emotionally charged perception of Muslims having foreign ties. The situation is not helped by the fact that Indian Muslims have retained names that have Persian, Turkish, and Arabic origins even though this is too not in any way different from the progeny of migrant groups in other parts of the world.

Pathological Nostalgia

More problematic is the Muslim attitude of covert self-aggrandizement. In a self-deceptive act of ethnic elitism, they establish a mental link between themselves and the grand Islamic empire that once spanned from South Eastern Europe and Africa through the Middle East to India. By fabricating a kinship with the Turkish sultans of centuries ago, an Indian Muslim can put a Band-Aid of illustrious ancestry over the wounds of his daily hardship. This defensive maneuver, however, creates a dreamy quality to existence and cleaves the imaginative potential from the sunlight of effort.

A more severe problem is that the average Muslim has not fully accepted the fact that his co-religionists are no longer the rulers of the land. A mentality of *pidram sultan bood* ("my father was a king") prevails at a preconscious level and creates abhorrence of actual praxis and toil. It is as if the individual is saying, "Look, we have already made the Taj Mahal so we do not need to study hard for college or medical school entrance examinations." Such exaggerated nostalgia perpetuates complacency and a cryptic air of unearned superiority.

Prejudicial Attitudes

A third aspect of Muslim psychosocial life hurtful to Hindus is that some Muslims, especially those whose relatives moved across the borders during the country's partition, continue to have emotional ties with Pakistan. Mostly dormant, this proclivity can become overt during an Indo-Pakistan cricket match or during a border skirmish between the two nations. Fortunately, with each passing day, partition is receding back in time and memory; the numbers of those with pro-Pakistan feelings seems to be diminishing in tandem. It must also be emphasized that such individuals did not and do not represent the sentiments of the majority among Indian Muslims.

A bigger problem is that many Muslims hold secret prejudices against Hindus. They regard Hindus as having plebian minds, low valor, and gaudy aesthetics (for the last mentioned point especially, see Kakar 1996, p. 182). They hold scornful attitudes about Hindu animistic mythology and reified gods. In this, they are empowered by their religion, which declares all idol worshipers as *Kuffar* (plural of *Kafir*, meaning "the blasphemer") and by the socially irresponsible rhetoric of their religious leaders.

Absence of Progressive and Secular Leadership

Indian Muslims also suffer from the fact that they have never had a progressive, liberal, and secular leadership. It is not that their community has not produced such individuals. It has. However, in a trend set with the Muslim League–Congress schism of the early twentieth century, most of the postindependence secular Muslims stayed within the folds of the Congress party. Some joined the Communist Party of India. In either case, secular Indian Muslims never developed an en bloc, separate political voice of their own. An unfortunate consequence of this was that religious Muslim leaders became the community's political spokesmen also. A recipe for social disaster was set. Bound to orthodox beliefs and literal interpretations of the Quranic law, the Muslim clerics took every opportunity to steer the Muslim masses toward thinking that their faith was continually endangered in India. Using the age-old device of encouraging a sense of victimhood, they strengthened their grips on Muslim masses and thus became a political lobby of considerable importance with the central government. This frequently resulted in administrative decisions being made that were not only deeply annoying to Hindus but, in the long run, harmful to Muslims as well.

Take the example of the October 15, 1988, banning of Salman Rushdie's (1988) controversial novel, *The Satanic Verses*, in India. The ban attacked the right to freedom of expression that lies at the foundation of a democratic society. It strengthened the hand of right-wing Muslims in India, for instance Imam Bukhari of Delhi, who had engineered anti-Rushdie riots in Bombay. And, it perpetuated the image of Muslims in the Hindu eyes as an overindulged minority. All in all, the decision to ban made by Rajiv Gandhi (the Congress Party's leader and the prime minister of India at the time) was a shameful capitulation to the Muslim religious leadership; it was a terrible decision that might have done more harm than good in the long run.

Constitutional Privileges

The Indian constitution allows Muslims to have a separate family law governing matters of marriage, divorce, and inheritance. The renowned *Shah Bano* case, involving a divorced Muslim woman who had sued her former husband in order to get alimony, had brought this dilemma out in the open. While the ever-just Supreme Court of the country ruled in her favor in 1985, the then prime minister, Rajiv Gandhi (representing the Congress Party) overruled the verdict, largely as an appeasement of the right-wing Muslim politicians and religious leaders. This was truly unfortunate, as an opportunity for initiating an important paradigm shift was lost. To perpetuate separate laws for Hindus and Muslims is to create an imbalance. And, for Muslims to enjoy and feel entitled to such privilege is shortsighted, to say the least. It certainly does not help their cause for social justice and equity.

All in all, the foreign religious loyalties of Muslims, their covert nostalgic attitude of superiority, their ethnic prejudices, the lack of secular leadership in their community, and their reveling in having separate constitutional privileges all tend to create serious difficulties in the Hindus forming harmonious relations with them. To complicate matters, the Hindus bring their own negative attitudes toward Muslims to the table.

HINDU CONTRIBUTIONS
TO THE HINDU–MUSLIM TENSION

In light of the historical and social accounts provided above, it is not surprising that Hindus experience a certain ambivalence toward their fellow Muslim citizens. The vicissitudes of this tenuously balanced love–hate economy are such that a tilt toward intensified hate is an ever-present possibility. A flare-up of unrest in the predominantly Muslim state of Kashmir, a border skirmish with Pakistan, an India–Pakistan cricket match, news regarding anti-Hindu activities in the neighboring nation of Bangladesh, an economic policy of the government that threatens the majority interests, and a civic dispute regarding arrangements about the way one community's religious festival affects the other's existence for a mere day or two are all potent triggers to tip the scales of the Hindu ambivalence toward heightened mistrust and dislike of Muslims.

Even in the absence of such intensified aggression, subterranean negative images of Muslims lurk in the minds of many Hindus. A population survey conducted by Varma and colleagues (1973) revealed that such anti-Muslim prejudice is more marked in lower middle class Hindus than in those who are truly poor. Adorno and Frenkel-Brunswick's (1950) early observation that socioeconomic marginality, not socioeconomic class, is a crucial factor in the origin of ethnic prejudice was thus supported by the Varma study. Another finding of this investigation was the close association of anti-Muslim sentiment with ethnocentrism, politico-economic conservatism, and antidemocratic attitudes. Those who were prejudiced believed that Muslims are given to "escapist activists like poetry, music, and dance" (Varma et al. 1973, p. 158) besides being clannish, smelly, unkempt, and dirty.

There also exists a myth that Muslims might one day outnumber Hindus since they are polygamous and produce many more children than Hindus. The reality is that according to the 1992 census of India, there were 2.5 million fewer females than males among the Indian Muslims. So where are the alleged four wives for each Muslim man going to come from? To wit, the incidence of polygamy was 15 percent among the tribals, 8 percent among Buddhists, 7 percent among Jains, 6 percent among Hindus, and 5 percent among Muslims; these findings have also been reported in a recent book by Jagruthi (2004). And in the same census figures the Muslim birth rate was only marginally higher (0.01 percent) than that of Hindus. Given these facts, how is it possible that they will outnumber Hindus? And yet, the myth persists.

Were it only for such malevolent notions, matters might not be so bad after all. However, the situation has become worse over the last two decades. India's proud metropolitan centers have lost their spirit of ethnic camaraderie. Violence threatens to erupt readily through a thin veneer of tolerance. "Narcissism of minor differences" (Freud 1918, p. 199) has become sadism of manufactured animosities. This unfortunate turn of events seems to have resulted from the confluence of the following five unconscious factors operating in certain sections of the Hindu majority.

Post-Muslim Domination Trauma

The history of Muslims in India is a complex and contradictory tapestry of larceny and largesse, blood and blossoms, and domination and devotion. They came from foreign lands, plundered, and established their empire that extended quite widely over the country's terrain. Although over the course of time they became increasingly assimilated into the Indian culture and enriched it by their profoundly significant contributions, the fact that a minority had been the ruler of a majority left its indelible mark on the latter's collective psyche. This wound continues to affect the national recall of this historical fact. In the words of Kakar (1996):

There are two overarching histories of Hindu–Muslim relations—with many local variations—which have been used by varying political interests and ideologies and have been jostling for position for many centuries. In times of heightened conflict between the two communities, the Hindu nationalist history that supports the version of conflict between the two assumes pre-eminence and organizes cultural memory in one particular direction. In times of relative peace, the focus shifts back to the history emphasizing commonalties and shared pieces of the past. [p. 24]

I, however, believe that the traffic between the predominant historical paradigm and ethnic conflict goes in both directions. Kakar suggests that in conflictual times people prefer a Hindu nationalist version and in peaceful times people prefer a secularist version of history. I agree with him but add that the opposite might also be true. In other words, when a Hindu nationalist version of history is preferred, then conflict between the two communities ensues, and when a secularist version is preferred, then peace between them results. Further complexity is added to the situation by the retrospective embellishment of Muslim atrocities by one group and of Muslim contributions by the other. Fact and fiction get mixed up, as they often do in the creation of history (Loewenberg 1995). The ground gets well prepared for a harvest of hatred and gleefully welcomes the poisonous seed of further divisiveness.

Postpartition Unresolved Mourning

The refugees from those areas of pre-1947 India that became Pakistan were not able to fully mourn their trauma. Regardless of whether their losses were of lives or property or only of psychosocial continuity, their pain was great and a deep mourning of it was not possible. Deprived of the "protective rites of farewell" (Grinberg and Grinberg 1989), physically overwhelmed, emotionally shattered, and lacking the possibility of "emotional refueling" (Mahler et al. 1975) from their lost motherland, they suppressed their anguish. The need to reestablish their lives in a new land also shifted the tension away from inner sadness. Surviving occupied them more than reminiscing.

However, their unresolved grief and its associated emotions of hurt, shame, rage, and sadness became susceptible to transgenerational transmission. A tear shed at the mention of an old neighborhood, a sigh heaved at the sight of a sewing machine the like of which was lost to looting during the riots, an absentminded caress of a scar, and an un-explained silence in response to a seemingly innocent question, all became encoded signals to carry this grief into the souls of the next generation. Also passed was the unspoken (and not entirely unreasonable) fear and dislike of Muslims. It took the second or third generation of these refugees to open up the wounds of partition for understanding and resolution. Movies and plays regarding partition of India and its bloody aftermath have only recently begun to be made. Otherwise silence had prevailed, and under the cloak of wordlessness, pain and hate were being passed on to the next generation.

Postcolonial Villain Hunger

A certain amount of ethnic xenophobia is perhaps ubiquitous. It results from the universal tendency to externalize aggression. This helps human beings demarcate their own group boundaries and protects them from feeling weak and helpless vis-à-vis life's hardships. Having someone to blame keeps sadness and mourning in abeyance. Anger makes one feel strong. Paranoia becomes a psychic vitamin for threatened identity and powerful anodyne against the pain that results from genuine self-reflection. This is the essential dynamics of what I call a "villain hunger." And this hunger gets readily activated when a large group's identity is threatened from external or internal sources. Most such threats are constituted by economic upheaval, but sometimes the sudden disappearance of a well-known enemy can also destabilize the group. The fall of the Soviet Union, for instance, created a vacuum in the American large group dynamics and, in part, led to their finding a new enemy in the form of Islamic fundamentalism (not that these Muslims did not invite such an occurrence).

Within the Indian context, independence from the British had a similar effect.[20] After nearly two decades of patriotic exaltation, the masses gradually realized that the mere departure of the British hardly

---

20. Pakistan, formed with the heady notion of Muslim fraternity, also began to develop a similar "villain hunger" once it no longer had Hindus to demonize. The most striking result of such need for enemies was the Punjabi–Bengali tension, which ultimately led to the formation of Bangladesh. The subsequent anti-Hindu activities in Bangladesh and the Shia–Sunni strife in Pakistan (not to mention the anti-Ahmadi violence) testify to the ever-unquenched nature of man's need for enemies.

made their problems vanish. *Swaraj* (self-governance) gave them pride but did not take away poverty, epidemics, overpopulation, regional conflicts, and so on. Needing someone to blame for their continuing hardships, people unconsciously sought a new villain and Muslims appeared "suitable reservoirs for externalization" (Volkan 1997). After all, they had ancestors who had come from foreign countries, caused bloodshed, and became rulers of the land (disregard that this was hundreds of years ago). The fact that their religion originated outside of India confirmed that they were basically "not Indians."

The rampant national hunger for an enemy was exploited by the right-wing Hindu leaders who publicly emphasized the negative aspects of Muslim history. The *Jana Sangh* stalwart Balraj Madhok, who had earlier (1970) proposed a program for the "Indianization" of Muslims, now declared that they "have no legal or moral claim or right on this country" (1983). His call, along with similar rhetoric from other right-wing Hindu leaders, turned Muslims into the hated Other. However, like events in the individual mind, matters of large-group psychology are also multidetermined (Waelder 1936). The departure of the British seems to be one among many factors leading to the intensified anti-Muslim sentiment in India over the last two or three decades. Another factor was an intramural economic threat.

Post–Mandal Commission Economic Threat

In August 1990 the government of India, led by the secular and socialist-leaning *Janata Dal* (a major political party in India), implemented the final report from an advisory commission that had earlier been set up to study ways to improve the economic lives of the country's lower socioeconomic class. This commission, led by Justice A. K. Mandal, recommended that 27 percent of all federal level jobs be reserved for the "backwards classes." Coupled with an already existing quota of 15 percent for the untouchables and 7 percent for the tribals, this meant that 49 percent[21] of government jobs were now out of the reach for the ma-

---

21. Such quotas were arrived at to reflect the proportion of these group's population in the country. The total of reserved jobs was restricted to 49 percent in accordance with a ceiling set by the Supreme Court to maintain the credibility of the equal-opportunity clause of the constitution.

jority of Hindus. This resulted in a jolt of economic threat to the Hindu middle and lower classes. In their vulnerability, the right-wing Hindu leaders found an opportunity to mine political capital. They began to exploit the group frustration and to stir up a sense of victimization in the group. They fueled its rage and offered Muslims as the scapegoats for its aggression. The BJP (Bhartiya Janata Party) leadership had clearly sensed an opportunity to snatch power from the secular forces at the national level.[22]

Post-migration Hypernationalism and Its Boomerang Effect upon India

The smoldering passions stirred up by the right-wing Hindus in India received further impetus from the immigrant Indians (commonly known as nonresident Indians, NRIs) in the United States. This group was largely composed of physicians, academics, and technocrats. Their encounter with the North American culture of consumerism, competitiveness, sexual freedom, broken families, and multiculturalism produced interesting results. On the one hand, these Indians rose rapidly in the ranks of economic hierarchy. Indeed, by the mid-1990s, immigrant Indians had become the most affluent ethnic group (including the white Anglo-Saxons) in the United States (Mead 2004). Armed with first-class educational credentials, unburdened with student loans that plagued their American counterparts, and given to disciplined hard work, these immigrant Indians acquired great material success; the self-mocking quip by an Indian colleague that "no Indian shall die without a Mercedes" paints a fitting, if facile, verbal portrait of this group. It also hints at the gnawing uncertainty about the inner self that propels the need to own palatial houses and status-brandishing cars. There was evidence of pain here.

---

22. Hitherto marginalized in national level politics the Hindu nationalist party BJP, which had a mere two seats in the 534-member national parliament in 1984, garnered eighty-six seats by 1989, 118 seats by 1991, and a whopping 328 seats by 1993. The BJP leadership "told India's electorate that if the countries of Western Europe and the United States can call themselves Christians, India should be free to call itself Hindu" (Rudolph and Rudolph 1993, p. 28). That this was against the country's constitution apparently did not matter!

The Hindu community among the Indian immigrants was especially shaken up by finding itself to be a small minority in a nation largely made up of Christians. Even Muslims, with their multiple nationalities (Indian, Pakistani, Bangladeshi, Iranian, Saudi Arabian, Iraqi, Palestinian, Syrian, Egyptian, and so on) seemed to outnumber them in the United States. Not used to being a minority or being a target of prejudicial attitudes, this community was quite traumatized. Judging from their reactions, the members of the NRI Hindu community seem to belong to three groups. The first group was constituted by those who were able to adjust to this "ethnic downgrading" with wry humor, pride in efficacy, and a bicultural transformation of identity. They did have occasional bouts of nostalgia, but these tended to diminish with the passage of time (Akhtar 1999a,b). Their turning to religion had a "soft" and private quality, and their inner definition of India remained pluralistic and secular. Their self-esteem was sustained by their professional and familial achievements as well as by the fact that they helped India by investing funds, pro bono teaching and consultancy, and the construction of schools and clinics, especially in rural areas in the country. In contrast, the second group was constituted by individuals who became overidentified with the West in a massive "counterphobic assimilation" (Teja and Akhtar 1981). They renounced all sense of belonging to the Indian community and its rich traditions.

The third group of NRI Hindus resorted to defensive hypernationalism and ethnic grandiloquence. This helped in easing the pain of temporal discontinuity and made it possible for them to withstand ethnic caricature by the American community. They valiantly attempted to rectify the frequently biased and negative portrayal of India in the North American press. Unfortunately, their hypernationalism also had some problematic aspects, including (1) the mistaken equation of Indian culture with Hinduism; (2) a conviction that mankind's wisdom sprang only from Hindu religious thought; (3) an insistence that while Hindu culture provided concepts and imaginative potential to both the West and Far East, nothing significant from those regions contributed to the Hindu culture; (4) an exaggerated and paranoid sense of cultural victimization by the West; and (5) a doomsday scenario suggesting that Christian evangelists proselytizing in India would gradually convert so many people to their faith that the demographic dominance of Hindus would be threatened. Not surprisingly, a close liaison developed between the North

American NRI's holding such sentiments and the VHP–BJP politburo in India.[23] This ethnocentric twinship benefited both parties. Celebrations of Indian heritage in American cities became increasingly the solipsistic serenade of Hinduism, with VHP and BJP leadership often appearing at them. In turn, the Hindu nationalist NRIs of the United States began funneling huge amounts of money to support the anti-secular agenda of these political parties in India.

RECENT FIASCOS

The five factors mentioned above (namely, the lasting impact of Muslim rule over India, the unresolved grief over partition, the villain hunger subsequent to the departure of the British, the impact of the Mandal Commission report, and the dark fraternity between the diaspora Indians' hypernationalism and the VHP–BJP political juggernaut back in India) combined, in various permutations and at different levels of abstraction and consciousness, to make Hindu masses immensely susceptible to manipulation by the right-wing leaders of their community. Muslim religious leaders' outrageous proclamations provided further fuel to this fire. Hindu nationalist parties benefited greatly from all this and rose to power, and ultimately formed the national government.

There now began a virulent drumbeat that sought to evoke religious fervor in the Hindu masses. Right-wing leaders of the *Sangh Parivar* (BJP, VHP, RSS, Bajrang Dal, etc.) evoked "chosen traumas" (Volkan 1997), that is, old injuries to the group's pride, and with their fiery rhetoric created a sense of "time collapse." As a result, centuries-old wounds acquired the emotional intensity of yesterday's laceration and the fundamentally kind, multivocal, and pluralistic Hindu religion was hijacked by these "destructive pied pipers" (Blum 1995, p. 18) of the right. In North India,

---

23. VHP–BJP stands for Vishwa Hindu Parishad–Bharatiya Janata Party; the former represents the cultural front and the latter the political operations of the right-wing Hindu nationalist sentiments in India. This hypernationalism of the diaspora Hindus has striking parallels with the Muslim immigrants of London coming up with the idea of Pakistan during the 1940s (Collins and Lapierre 1975) and the Sikh immigrant community of the United Kingdom and Canada aiding and abetting the *Khalistan* (a separate nation for the Indian Sikhs) movement of the 1980s.

at least, the vast and deeply evocative pantheon of Hinduism was reduced to a monolithic exaltation of one particular deity, namely Rama. This was done in order to stir up the emotional delirium needed to destroy a 1528 A.D. mosque (*Babri Masjid*) that was presumably built by a Muslim ruler, Mohiuddin Babar (reigned 1530–1540 and 1555–1556 A.D.), on the site of Rama's birthplace (*Ramjananbhoomi*).

The fever spread widely. In the United States, Hindu nationalist NRIs took out ads in ethnic newspapers of the Indian community soliciting money for the construction of *Ramjananbhoomi* and implicitly endorsing the destruction of *Babri Masjid*. The very people who felt so proud of India thus openly mocked the country's secular constitution. No one seemed to notice this contradiction. There was madness in the air.

Back in India, L. K. Advani, a prominent BJP leader, undertook a 10,000-kilometer *Rathyatra* (travel by chariot), which took him across many North Indian states to the site of this mosque in Uttar Pradesh.

> The Toyota van in which the BJP leader traveled was decorated to make it resemble the chariot of the legendary hero Arjuna, as shown in the immensely popular television serial of the *Mahabharata*. Advani's chariot aroused intense fervor among the Hindus. Crowds thronged the roads to catch a glimpse of the *rath*, showered flower petals on the cavalcade as it passed through their villages and towns, and the vehicle itself became a new object of worship as women offered ritual prayer with coconut, burning incense, and sandlewood paste at each of its stops. [Kakar 1996, p. 49]

All along the way, Advani called for the destruction of this Muslim place of worship[24] and "there were incidents of violence between Hindus and Muslims in the wake of the *rathyatra*" (Kakar 1996, p. 49). In a clever political ploy that added a dreamlike quality to all this, Advani chose *Somnath* as the starting point of his sojourn. The message was loud and clear. By destroying *Babri Masjid*, the Hindus would

---

24. Advani's *rathyatra* had an uncanny similarity with the Serbian leader Milosevic's tour of Yugoslavia to stir up Serbian nationalism. At each stop of his rambling sojourn, Milosevic reminded the Serbs of their defeat by the Ottoman Turks nearly 700 years ago. At each stop, the remains of the defeated Serbian King Lazar were buried and exhumed in order to inflame Serbian passions against the Bosnian and Kosovar Muslims, who were declared to be the descendants of Turks. A genocide of the latter group followed.

be avenging Mahmud Ghaznavi's 1020 A.D. attack on *Somnath* temple. That the two events would occur in different cultural contexts, under different political systems of government, for different purposes, and would be separated by nearly 1000 years, did not seem to matter. Such is the power of large-group regression (Freud 1921) and the activation of its unmourned traumas (Volkan 1997, 2004). Under the sway of emotions, people lost their critical abilities and submitted to their mesmerizing leader. Personal morality got sacrificed on the alter of resurgent large-group identity.

On December 6, 1992, the *Babri Masjid* was destroyed by a frenzied Hindu mob "with prominent members of BJP, VHP, Bajrang Dal, etc. aiding and abetting the destruction. No police/Center Forces were used by the State government to stop the destruction" (Prasad et al. 1993, p. 113). The entire nation watched this horrible event in utter disbelief on television. The Muslim citizens of India were humiliated to the bone. The liberal Hindus of the country felt remorseful and outraged at what the right-wing zealots had done. To the country's credit, and to the credit of the liberal Hindus, a nongovernmental citizens' tribunal headed by three Hindu judges, namely Justices O. Chinappa Reddy, D. A. Desai, and D. S. Tewatia, conducted a thorough investigation and, on the basis of a

> voluminous body of evidence, eye-witness accounts, and submissions, the honourable judges concluded: "There is a moral certainly that there was a well-laid conspiracy to demolish the Babri Masjid," and indicted the top leaders of the BJP, VHP, RSS, Bajrang Dal and Shiv Sena for hatching the conspiracy. They also held the Government of India "guilty of culpable negligence and a willful refusal to discharge its obligation as a Constitutional Government" and observed that its "inaction was deliberate and with full knowledge of the likely outcome." [Prasad et al. 1993, p. x]

Existing parallel to such shiningly secular jurisprudence was the persistent knife of anti-Muslim hatred, still bloodthirsty and in search of victims:

> In Bombay in early January, a month after the destruction of the Babri Masjid, the militantly Hindu, Muslim-hating Shiv Sena acted out the fiery images and language of its campaign videos by torching Muslim homes and shops. The Bombay elite's sense of being in charge and safe

in India's most cosmopolitan city was shattered when roving bands searched for Muslim names in elegant apartments along hitherto sacrosanct Marine Drive, Club Road, and Malabar Hill. [Rudolph and Rudolph 1993, p. 29]

Never having suffered such national-level humiliation, the Muslim community of India was stunned. Indian Muslims living abroad became queasy about visiting their own motherland and those who lived in India felt robbed of civic dignity. As time passed, three unfortunate reactions to this onslaught became crystallized in the Indian Muslim community: (1) many became fearful and silent; (2) others turned to regressive, pan-Islamic fanaticism, with individuals like Imam Bukhari of New Delhi's *Jama Masjid* counting himself among the "brothers" of Osama bin Ladin; and (3) a few Muslims resorted to destructive acts against Hindus and their properties, which, in turn, evoked greater violence toward the Muslim community.

In 2002 some members of this last-mentioned group set fire to a train passing by the town of Godhra in the state of Gujarat, and in the process killed about sixty Hindus, including women and children. This cruel and deplorable act was followed by the massacre of over 2,000 Muslims in Gujarat, especially in the city of Ahmedabad. Hindu mobs killed Muslims, raped their women, destroyed their property, and burned their shrines. They cut the water and electric supplies to Muslim areas, creating pogroms of terror and despair. They even leveled the grave of the great (and arguably the first) Urdu poet, Wali Gujarati, in a callous attack on language and metaphor, which are the hallmarks of human civilization. Most disturbing about all this was the undeniable element of state complicity with the right-wing Hindu government of Gujarat, headed by Narendra Modi, not only standing away from the site of the carnage but actually facilitating this attempted genocide of Muslims.

The BJP government, by now firmly ensconced in New Delhi, did not dissolve the state government nor did it remove Narendra Modi from his post, both of which it could have readily done. It was busy in implementing its agenda of *Hinduttva*,[25] an important element of which

---

25. The ideology of Hindu supremacy and the belief that India belongs only to Hindus.

was rewriting the early history of India "often with a bizarre content" (Sainath 2004). School curricula were changed "without consulting the educational bodies that had earlier routinely consulted, such as the Central Advisory Board of Education" (Thapar cited in Gatade 2003, p. 10). Such revisionism was intended to (1) blur the boundaries between mythology, literature, and history; (2) demonize the British[26]; (3) "deny the contributions the Muslims have made to India" (*Economist*, May 22, 2004, p. 10); and (4) replace the well-established early Aryan invasion of India by the assertion that no such thing took place and these progenitors of North Indian Hindus had lived in India from time immemorial. Essentially the Hindu nationalist version

> divides Indian history into a Hindu period (1000 B.C. to A.D. 1200) and a Muslim period (A.D. 1200–1800) on the basis of the religion of some of the ruling dynasties. It brackets together Arabs, Turks, and Persians under the term "Muslims," even though that term is rarely used in contemporary sources before the 13th century. It uses the term "Hindu" as if it described a unified religious community, despite the fact that the term is not found in pre-Islamic sources. (It was first used by Arabs and later by others to refer to the inhabitants of the area near the river Sind or the Indus.) Basically, it is ahistorical view of the past in its denial of discontinuity and its assertion of essentialized categories. [van der Veer 1994, p. 152]

The Hindu nationalist portrayal of Indian history is actually a jump backward to the assumptions of the nineteenth-century colonial history, according to the preeminent scholar Romila Thapar. In her view,

> the colonial interpretation was carefully developed through the nineteenth century. By 1823, the *History of British India* written by James Mill

---

26. To be sure, the British did many harmful things to the Indian society during their nearly 100-year reign. However, this should not make one overlook their positive contributions, which include the construction of railroads and hill stations (mountain resorts), propagation of the English language, various judicial and administrative measures, Western attire, and the all-important game of Cricket. India's capital, New Delhi, with its majestic and sweeping boulevards and roundabouts, is almost exclusively built by the British. The nation's parliament meets in buildings constructed by the British, and its president, prime minister, and all other cabinet officers live in houses planned and built by the British.

was available and widely read. This was the hegemonic text in which Mill periodised Indian history into three periods: Hindu civilisation, Muslim civilisation, and the British period. . . . Mill argued that the Hindu civilisation was stagnant and backward, the Muslim only marginally better and the British colonial power an agency of progress because it could legis‑ late for improvement in India. In the Hinduttva version, this periodisation remains, only the colors have changed: the Hindu period is the golden age, the Muslim period, the black, dark age of tyranny and oppression, and the colonial period is a gray age of almost of marginal importance compared to the earlier two. [Lecture in February 2003 cited in Gatade 2003, p. 4]

Thapar (cited in Gatade 2003) emphasized that there was noth‑ ing new in the Hindu nationalist version of history except its aim to "bring about a new bonding by privileging the identity and origins of the majority community" (p. 27). The political capital gained out of denying the Aryan invasion was especially great. This so-called mod‑ ern viewpoint facilitated the denial of Aryan suppression of the darker skinned original inhabitants (*Dravids*) of the region. Moreover, it led to the obvious conclusion that the only Indians who had foreign roots were Muslims. They could therefore be declared to be not really Indians. The growth of Muslim labor migration to the Middle East further con‑ firmed their foreignness.

On commenting upon some of these developments under the BJP government, the British journalist Gwynne Dyer (2004) wrote:

The most spectacular recent manifestation of its Hindu-first, anti-minority policy was the massacre of Muslims in Gujarat in 2002, which had the tacit support of the BJP state government. More insidious for the long run was the deliberate attack on the education system. School textbooks have been systematically rewritten to represent a victimized and downtrod‑ den majority and to portray Muslims and Christians as somehow foreign and disloyal to the real, Hindu India. [p. A-19]

The veteran Indian journalist Kuldip Nayar (2004), who happens to be Hindu, wistfully acknowledges that "a preponderant number of Hindus have felt small even over the manner in which the BJP and other members of the *Sangh Parivar* have disfigured Hinduism, from its image of tolerance to fanaticism" (p. B-6). Clearly, both Hindus and Muslims of India have been harmed by the right-wing, religious nation‑

alism of Hindus. The ultimate conflict therefore seems to be not between Hindus and Muslims but between those who are fundamentalists and those are secular. Awareness of this creates the potential for fresh thinking in this realm. It sustains hope.

The Proverbial Silver Lining to the Cloud

One good outcome of the troika of Muslim narcissistic mortification (the *Babri Masjid* destruction, the politically driven rewriting of history, and the Gujarat riot) was that educated and liberal Muslims have began to organize themselves into a political voice of robust secularism. They are seeking to de-link Muslim societal concerns from religious orthodoxy and to mobilize the Muslim voting block by appealing to their politico-economic concerns rather than to their religious doctrines.

More importantly, there is evidence that the callous noose of Hindu fundamentalism has failed to strangulate the secular and democratic spirit of India. Its people, though poor and superstitious in Western eyes, are highly sophisticated when it comes to the power of their electoral vote. This democratic process, which removed the Congress Party's leader Indira Gandhi from national office after she had arrogantly assumed near dictatorial powers, has once again shown its strength. In a stunning reversal of fortune, the Indian electorate delivered a resounding defeat to the Hindu nationalist BJP government in May 2004, replacing it with a coalition government led by the secular Congress Party. And, within the first week of coming to power, the education ministry of this government, headed by Arjun Singh, announced that it would take immediate steps to recall the school textbooks distorted by the Hindu nationalist agenda.

Though immensely reassuring, this is only a first step. The path to resolve the Hindu–Muslim conflict and reduce anti-Muslim prejudices is a long one. It needs many types of interventions by both governmental and grass-roots organizations.

SUGGESTED REMEDIES

I will outline seven psychoanalytically informed social strategies aimed at ameliorating the Hindu–Muslim conflict in India. These measures pertain to the (1) educational, (2) cultural, (3) experiential, (4) economic, (5) political, (6) judicial, and (7) constitutional realms. I make these suggestions with humility and wish to enter two caveats at the outset. First, since the foundations of prejudice rest on ubiquitous childhood experiences, it is not possible to eliminate all such feelings; one can only hope to lessen their intensity. Second, while illustrations will be given here from the specific Hindu–Muslim context, some of these guidelines could possibly be applicable to other ethnic conflicts as well.

Educational Measures

While prejudice emanates from deep emotional roots going back to childhood, knowledge deficit and misinformation also play a role in its perpetuation and intensification. To combat this aspect of prejudice, educational measures must be set into motion. A multipronged approach is needed. Government agencies and nongovernmental organizations (NGOs), including those set up by progressive and secular Hindus and Muslims, should take it upon themselves to spread positive information about the minorities. Billboards with simple messages to such effect can go a long way in this regard. Imagine billboards in the predominantly Hindu areas of New Delhi, Bombay, and other similar parts of India declaring, "Many Muslims were against the partition of India," "Muslims fought hard for the independence of India," and "Muslims have greatly enriched Indian culture." And now imagine billboards in the high-density Muslim cities of Aligarh, Srinagar, and Hyderabad declaring, "Hindus have safeguarded the beauty of the Taj Mahal," "Hindus have a hand in India's having had three Muslim presidents," and "Hindus played an important role in postpartition India's being a secular nation." While certainly untested, it is my hypothesis that such billboards can have a powerful impact upon the consciousness of the masses.[27] Radio and television, especially in India where the central government has considerable say in the media's programming, can similarly broadcast antiprejudice messages.

---

27. The Indian government's family-planning campaign during the 1960s and 1970s certainly gained momentum from the "Hum do, Humare do" ("Two of us, two of ours") billboards scattered throughout India.

A scrutiny of what is being taught to schoolchildren might also be needed. Clearly, their textbooks need to incorporate both Hindu and Muslim figures who have contributed to the evolving history of the nation. Instruction along these lines during the formative years of childhood could have a major impact on the view Hindu and Muslim children will have of their counterparts as they grow up to become adult citizens of a secular country.

More importantly, the possibility of teaching children and adolescents about the nature of human prejudice should be considered. India might take the lead in the free world by introducing required courses in elementary and higher secondary education about the emotional forces that create and sustain people's hatred for their fellow beings. Such early sensitization, one hopes, would inoculate them against a future vulnerability to being exploited by religious politics, regardless of whether it is of Hindu or Muslim stripe. However, in contrast to what the BJP administration did, none of these changes should be made by government fiat and without detailed, critical, and thorough review by various academic bodies representing multiple disciplines and interests. It should be remembered that authoritarianism of the left is not the corrective to the authoritarianism of the right.

Cultural Measures

Another avenue to approach this matter is through Hindi movies. India is the largest producer of movies in the world and its people are avid watchers of these mostly caricatured and maudlin, song-laden family dramas. One particular genre among such movies goes by the curious title of "Muslim socials." They depict a colorful and seemingly positive, but nonetheless highly caricatured view of Indian Muslims. The era depicted is always that of princely states, never the contemporary one. The hero is invariably inclined to poetry and the heroine is a purdah-clad stunning beauty. There is also the required courtesan-cum-prostitute. These movies (e.g., *Chaudvin Ka Chand*, *Mere Mehboob*, *Palki*, *Bahu Begum*, *Pakeezah*, and *Mehboob Ki Mehndi*) are usually produced on a lavish scale and are quite popular among the masses, the majority of whom happen to be Hindus. Perhaps the idealization of Muslims by these movies is enjoyed on a conscious level as a defense against the doubt and suspicion toward them in the unconscious.

Actually, these movies are harmful since they perpetuate a stereotypic view of Muslims as merely given to matters of heart and leisure. Indeed, they also fuel the Muslims' retrospectively embellished nostalgia for their past days of royal glory; such idealization helps them deny their legacy of early atrocities toward Hindus. Either way, these movies perpetuate stereotyping of Muslims and thus potentially fuel prejudice toward them. Their production needs to be discouraged.[28]

Fascinatingly, even outside of this specific genre, when a Muslim character is shown in a Hindi movie, he is bearded, interested in *qawwali* (a sufi-derived form of Muslim devotional singing), and attired in a caricatured Muslim way. All this needs correction. Just the way political action is being taken in the United States to check the depiction of gratuitous violence in movies and on television, Indian social activists should also launch a campaign to have Muslims shown in movies as regular, working-class people like everybody else. Movies that have incidental, even minor, Muslims characters who behave and dress like ordinary people on the street should be given tax benefits by the government. Such depiction will subtly help erode the stereotyping mentioned above.

Another cultural avenue to reduce Hindu–Muslim friction is to encourage the production of plays and movies depicting friendly relations between them. These could be drawn from either their early history (imagine a movie or stage play on the life of Shah Jahan's son Dara Shikoh who translated *Upanashids* into Persian) or from some exceptional moments during recent times (for instance, Hindu and Muslims sheltering each other's relatives during the bloodshed associated with the partition of India). Witnessing such material, especially in the setting of a theater, can have powerful kindling effects and recharge submerged memories of good relations between the two groups.[29]

---

28. Actually such movies are being made less and less often these days. The reasons for this remain unclear. Could it be that the amount of societal aggression against Muslims is now so close to the surface that it can no longer be defended by such cinematographic fawning?

29. These ideas were mentioned to me by Joseph Montville during an informal conversation in 2000. For his important contributions in the realm of conflict resolution, see Montville 1987, 1991.

Experiential Measures

Closely parallel to the educational and cultural measures outlined above are methods of interventions that are experiential in nature. Two such measures readily come to mind. One pertains to creating opportunities for children, adolescents, and young adults of the two faiths to live with a family of the opposite faith. The Bombay-based liberal journalist Hamid Dalwai did succeed during the late 1960s in creating such an exchange program. Those Muslim and Hindu children who participated in it, and their host families, found the interaction immensely beneficial. This goes to show that there is no substitute for the knowledge of the other gained by the mutuality of living together on a day-to-day basis. The Kids for Peace sports camp in rural Connecticut hosting Israeli and Palestinian youngsters also confirms the value of such one-to-one human experience. Such programs need to be supported and popularized throughout India.[30]

Yet another study in this realm was conducted in a Israeli school. In a class exclusively made up of Jewish children, half were given an Arab identity for a period of a few days and then the situation was reversed so that the remaining half got to be "Arab" too. The results of this study (Rena Moses-Hrushovski, personal communication 1999) demonstrated a heightened sensitivity toward the feelings of the minority as a result of putting oneself in its shoes. Perhaps it is time for some Indian schools to attempt to undertake such experiential exercises.

Economic Measures

Frequently, it is a real or imagined threat to economic safety that leads a group to start scapegoating a religious or ethnic minority. The threat is exaggerated by the majority's leaders, who point fingers at the minority as lazy and unentitled devourers of scarce resources. Such threat to economic safety must be combated by legislative reforms whereby the

---

30. The importance of such civic bridges was also demonstrated in a study (Varshney 2002) comparing the positive Hindu–Muslim relations in Calicut with the frequently tense ones in Aligarh. About 90 percent of Hindu and Muslim families in Calicut reported that their children play together against a mere 42 percent in Aligarh!

need for viewing others with suspicion of thievery or parasitism would not arise, or at least stay within containable limits. Moreover, when and if extra provisions for a minority are democratically put into place, the government should make concerted efforts to educate the majority about the nature, reasons, and limits of such provisions. This would be akin to good parents' ensuring that an older sibling does not feel totally displaced by the arrival of a new baby. In the United States, a chronic source of irritation for white racists is the government's policy of affirmative action toward the African-American population. However, few white people know the details of the policy. And few white people appreciate the duration and extent of subjugation and abuse of blacks that has necessitated such reparation.

In the context of India, the mid-1990s outbreak of anti-Muslim violence all over the nation followed the release of the Mandal Commission Report (1990), which proposed that a proportion of federal jobs be reserved for ethnic minorities; curiously, the minority being offered the greatest protection was the lower caste Hindus! However, feeling suddenly threatened in their search for employment, the upwardly mobile, lower middle class Hindu youths were rendered vulnerable to finding scapegoats for their frustration. This vulnerability was exploited by right-wing Hindu leaders in order to fuel communal hatred. In light of all this, it is my sense that the economic reform needed to diminish ethnic prejudice should involve (1) improvements in the monetary status of the entire group, as well as (2) careful education to combat the view of protected minorities as pampered and overindulged.

Political Measures

From psychodynamic studies of leadership patterns (Post 1983, 1991, Post and Robins 1993, Robins 1986, Steinberg 1996, Volkan et al. 1998), it can be safely assumed that some character attributes in an individual headed toward a leadership position should be a cause for alarm. While "healthy narcissism" (Kernberg 1975) is a needed attribute in a leader, pathological degrees of self-absorption, especially when combined with paranoid tendencies, can impair the leader's decision making and render him or her prone to marked devaluation of others. The dreaded resurgence of inferiority feelings from within is then handled by attributing "badness" to others and creating ethnic targets of the consequent hatred.

At these moments the leader loses the adaptive elements. The means no longer serve the initial goals/ends. The pathologically paranoid leader projects hostility onto an enemy, likening this enemy to a cancer, or a disease. The leader selects a nation, group, a cultural entity, and/or a religious entity that has to be destroyed. The leader is forever obsessed with hatred and fear towards these entities. [Volkan et al. 1998, p. 155]

By instituting a system of checks and balances, such individuals could be prevented from ascending to positions of power. What exactly would constitute such a psychosocial filter and how effective—without acquiring fascist overtones itself—would it be, remains to be explored. Indeed, some might question whether this approach is practical at all. Yet psychoanalytically informed social interventions (e.g., consultations with political parties, disseminating pertinent information to significant NGOs, public lectures) might help create enough concern about potentially dangerous individuals to prevent them from acquiring much power. The sharp rejection of Richard Haider, the pro-Nazi leader, in 2000 by the Austrian public and government alike is a case in point here. If psychoanalytically informed social activism could achieve even this much, it would have done a great service.

Judicial Measures

While the actual deterrent value of retributive justice still needs study, democratic societies can hardly afford to look the other way when calculated efforts are made to hurt a minority group. Indeed, crimes emanating from racial or religious bigotry—hate crimes—need swift and condign punishment. Regardless of their social stature, individuals deemed responsible for inciting communal hatred and violence should be brought to justice. This might or might not deter others with similar plans, but it will certainly make the victimized group feel vindicated.[31] The latter's sense of full citizenship and the inalienable rights

---

31. Note in this connection the relief experienced by Jews when Nazi concentration camp officers are traced and brought to trial. Akin is the reaction of the African immigrant community in Germany to the harsh sentence against three skinheads handed down by a Berlin judge in connection with the murder of a worker from Mozambique (*Philadelphia Inquirer*, August 30, 2002).

that it bestows will be restored. And the secular conscience of the nation will be upheld, thus enhancing its esteem and democratic efficacy.

Within India's context, the indictment of Shiv Sena leader Bala Saheb Thackeray by the Bombay High Court was a shining example of this sort. By declaring the powerful head of the preeminent Hindu militant organization accountable for his role in the anti-Muslim carnage in Bombay, the Indian justice system injected a dose of confidence in the nation's commitment to secularism. Also when Thackeray was accused in 1995 of soliciting votes in the name of religion in contravention of existing laws, the Bombay High Court barred him from voting for six years as a punishment. In tragic contrast is the miscarriage (or should we say abortion?) of justice in the recent Gujarat riots. Clearly one hopes that courts in India will act in a fair, swift, and strict manner when dealing with anti-Muslim or anti-Hindu hate crimes.

Constitutional Measures

While the secular nature of India's constitution is to be applauded, its provision of a separate family law for Muslims is something that needs reconsideration. On the one hand, it lets them conduct the transactions of marriage, divorce, and inheritance in accordance with their religious dictates and therefore makes them feel secure about their identity. On the other hand, it separates them from the Hindu majority, which feels that Muslims are being pampered. This leads to friction between the two groups. Therefore, it might be worthwhile to reconsider such provisions. The disadvantage of Muslims' feeling deprived of erstwhile privileges and trampled upon in their religious freedom needs to be weighed against the societal damage done by the country's having two civil laws. To be sure, the entire issue needs to be revisited, debated, and researched in its constitutional, human rights, civic benefit, and legal aspects. It should be remembered that the country's criminal law for Hindus and Muslims is the same. And it should be registered that other secular democracies of the world (e.g., the United States) do not allow religious minorities to have separate family laws. Of course, lacking the historical complexity and cultural diversity of India, the Western democracies might have found such legal homogenization easier. This rationalization, however, should not be allowed to deter India's constitutional experts from courageously facing the possibility of changing course in regard to the civil laws of the nation. And Muslims of India should learn that to be truly equal with Hindus, they require two separate measures. On the one hand, they must be offered comparable socioeconomic opportunities. On the other hand, they must renounce the constitutional privileges not available to Hindus. Social dignity can be bestowed to only a certain extent. Mostly, it is an earned commodity.

CONCLUSION

After entering some caveats, I have highlighted the nodal points in the 1,300-year (700–2000 A.D.) history of the Hindu–Muslim coexistence in India. I have discussed the anti-Hindu feelings of Muslims and the anti-Muslim feelings of Hindus, highlighting their actual as well as retrospectively embellished roots in history. I have addressed the origins of the increased strife between the two communities in the contemporary politico-economic scenario of India, and have suggested seven psychoanalytically informed social strategies to combat such ethnic tension. I have spread my net wide, writing in a spirit of informed altruism, and have maintained a secular and psychoanalytic perspective throughout this chapter. However, it is not lost upon me that no matter what I say and what some others like me might express, the fundamentalist Hindu and Muslim forces against a kinder, more tolerant, interethnic stance are indeed powerful. Much governmental and nongovernmental intervention, concerted interdisciplinary research, and social activism on the part of both liberal Hindus and Muslims are needed to combat such forces. For my own humble contribution, a fitting conclusion comes from a couplet of the late Jigar Moradabadi (1896–1982), a renowned Urdu poet of India:

Unka jo kaam hai, voh ehl-e-siaysat jaanen
Mera paigham mohabbat hai, jahan tak pohnchey.[32]

---

32. An almost literal translation of the two lines would be "What the politicians and social engineers would do in the end, only they know/My message is one of love; let us see how far its reach turns out to be."

ACKNOWLEDGMENTS

I am thankful to many individuals who read earlier versions of this chapter and provided valuable input. Prominent among these are Anju Bhargava, Subhash Bhatia, Ira Brenner, Naresh Julka, Saida Koita, Harish Malhotra, Tarnjit Saini, Abu Salim, Hamida Salim, J. Anderson Thomson, Jr., and Vamik Volkan. I have incorporated many of their suggestions and the chapter is certainly enriched as a result.

REFERENCES

Adorno, J., and Frenkel-Brunswick, E. (1950). *The Authoritarian Personality*. New York: W.W. Norton.

Akhtar, J. N., ed. (1975). *Hindustan Hamara*, vols. I to IV. New Delhi: Hindustani Book Trust.

Akhtar, S. (1995). A third individuation: immigration, identity, and the psychoanalytic process. *Journal of the American Psychoanalytic Association* 43:1051–1084.

——— (1997). The psychodynamic dimension of terrorism. *Psychiatric Annals* 29:350–355.

——— (1999a). *Immigration and Identity: Turmoil, Treatment, and Transformation*. Northvale, NJ: Jason Aronson.

——— (1999b). The immigrant, the exile, and the experience of nostalgia. *Journal of Applied Psychoanalytic Studies* 1:123–130.

——— (2001). A note on the ontongenetic origins of prejudice. *Journal of the Indian Psychoanalytic Society* 55:7–13.

——— (2003). Dehumanization: origins, manifestations, and remedies. In *Violence or Dialogue? Psychoanalytic Reflections or Terror and Terrorism*, ed. S. Varvin and V. D. Volkan, pp. 131–145. London: International Psychoanalytic Association.

Akhtar, S., and Choi, L. (2004). When evening falls: the immigrant's encounter with middle and late age. *American Journal of Psychoanalysis* 64:183–191.

Bird, B. (1956). A consideration of the etiology of prejudice. *Journal of the American Psychoanalytic Association* 4:490–513.

Blum, H. P. (1995). Sanctified aggression, hate, and the alteration of standards and values. In *The Birth of Hatred: Developmental, Clinical, and Technical Aspects of Intense Aggression*, ed. S. Akhtar, S. Kramer, and H. Parens, pp. 15–38. Northvale, NJ: Jason Aronson.

Collins, L., and Lapierre, D. (1975). *Freedom at Midnight*. New York: Simon & Schuster.

Dyer, G. (2004). Sonia Gandhi's big mistake. *Philadelphia Inquirer*, May 21, p. A-19.

Encyclopedia of Asian History and Asian Society. (1988). New York: Asia Society.

Freud, S. (1918). The taboo of virginity. *Standard Edition* 11:191–208.

——— (1921). Group psychology and analysis of the ego. *Standard Edition* 18:67–144.

——— (1930). Civilization and its discontents. *Standard Edition* 21:59–145.

Gatade, S. (2003). Hating Romila Thapar, pp. 1–6. *Crosscurrents.org*.

Gay, P. (1988). *Freud: A Life for Our Times*. New York: W. W. Norton.

Gopal, S. (1991). *Anatomy of a Confrontation: The Babri Masjid–Ram Janmabhumi Issue*. New Delhi: Penguin.

Grinberg, L., and Grinberg, R. (1989). *Psychoanalytic Perspectives on Migration and Exile*. New Haven, CT: Yale University Press.

Hasan, M. (1991). Competing symbols and shared codes: intercommunity relations in modern India. In *Anatomy of a Confrontation: The Babri Masjid–Ram Janmabhumi Issue*, ed. S. Gopal, pp. 99–121. New Delhi: Penguin.

Huang, F., and Akhtar, S. (2005). Immigrant sex: the transport of affection and sensuality across cultures. *American Journal of Psychoanalysis* 64:179–188.

India Abroad. (2004). March 19, p. A-18.

Jafferlot, C. (1996). *The Hindu Nationalist: Movement in India*. New York: Columbia University Press.

Jagruthi, M. (2004). *Women and Communalism*. Bangalore: Jagruthi.

Kakar, S. (1996). *The Colors of Violence: Cultural Identities, Religion, and Conflict*. Chicago: University of Chicago Press.

Kernberg, O. F. (1975). *Borderline Conditions and Pathological Narcissism*. New York: Jason Aronson.

Loewenberg, P. (1995). *Fantasy and Reality in History*. Berkeley, CA: University of California Press.

Ludden, D. (1996). *Contesting the Nation: Religion, Community, and the Politics of Democracy of India*. Philadelphia: University of Pennsylvania Press.

Madhok, B. (1983). Persecuted or pampered? *Illustrated Weekly of India*, January 9, p. 31.

Mahler, M. S., Bergman, A., and Pine, F. (1975). *Psychological Birth of the Human Infant*. New York: Basic Books.

Mani, V. (1975). *Puranic Encyclopaedia*. Delhi: Motilal Banarsidass.

Manuel, P. (1996). Music, the media, and communal relations in North India, past and present. In *Contesting the Nation: Religion, Community, and the*

Politics of Democracy of India, ed. D. Ludden, pp. 119–128. Philadelphia: University of Pennsylvania Press.

Mead, W. R. (2004). India: slow motion fall into a U.S. embrace. *Los Angeles Times*, May 23, Part M, p. 2.

Mohan, S. (1997). *Awadh Under the Nawabs*. New Delhi: Manohar.

Montville, J. V. (1987). The arrow and the olive branch: a case for track II diplomacy. In *Conflict Resolution: Track II Diplomacy*, ed. J. W. McDonald, Jr. and D. B. Bendahmane, pp. 5–20. Washington, DC: U.S. Government Printing Office.

——— (1991). Psychoanalytic enlightenment and the greening of diplomacy. In *The Psychodynamics of International Relationships*, vol. 2, ed. V. D. Volkan, J. V. Montville, and D. A. Julius, pp. 177–192. Lexington, MA: Lexington Books.

Mukherjee, A. (1991). Colonialism and communalism. In *Anatomy of a Confrontation: The Babri Masjid–Ram Janmabhumi Issue*, ed. S. Gopal, pp. 164–178. New Delhi: Penguin.

Nayar, K. (2004). Defeat is a jigsaw puzzle—piece it together and you have an old story: arrogance. *The Indian Express*, May 18, p. B-7.

Oldenburg, V. T. (2001). *The Making of Colonial Lucknow: 1856–1877*. (The Lucknow Omnibus Edition). New Delhi: Oxford University Press.

Parens, H. (1999). Toward the prevention of prejudice. In *At the Threshold of the Millennium: A Selection of the Proceedings of the Conference*, vol. 2, pp. 131–141. Lima, Peru: Prom Peru.

Post, J. M. (1983). Woodrow Wilson re-examined. *Political Psychology* 4:289–306.

——— (1991). Saddam Hussein of Iraq. *Political Psychology* 12:279–289.

Post, J. M., and Robins, R. S. (1993). *When Illness Strikes the Leader*. New Haven, CT: Yale University Press.

Prasad, K., Chenoy, K. A. M., Singh, K., et al. (1993). *Report of the Inquiry Commission Submitted to the Citizen's Tribunal on Ayodhya*. New Delhi: Secretariat, Citizen's Tribunal on Ayodhya.

Radhakrishnan, S. (1967). *Recovery of Faith*. New Delhi: Orient Paperbacks.

——— (1975). *The Present Crisis of Faith*. New Delhi: Orient Paperbacks.

Robins, R. S. (1986). Paranoid ideation and charismatic leadership. *Psychohistory Review* 5:15–55.

Rudolph, S., and Rudolph, L. I. (1993). Modern hate. *The New Republic*, March 22, 1993, pp. 24–29.

Sainath, P. (2004). Mass media versus mass reality. *The Hindu*, May 4.

Sharar, A. H. (1920). *Lucknow: The Last Phase of an Oriental Culture*. (The Lucknow Omnibus Edition), trans. E. S. Harcourt and F. Hussain. New Delhi: Oxford University Press, 2001.

Sikand, Y. (2004). Hindu followers of a Muslim imam. *American Federation of Muslims of Indian Origin: News Brief* 14:6.

Spitz, R. (1965). *The First Year of Life.* New York: International Universities Press.

Steinberg, B. (1996). *Shame and Humiliation: Presidential Decision Making on Vietnam.* Montreal: McGill-Queen's University Press.

Sterba, R. (1947). Some psychological factors in Negro race hatred and in anti-Negro riots. *Psychoanalysis and the Social Sciences* 1:411–427.

Teja, J. S., and Akhtar, S. (1981). The psychosocial problems of FMGs with special reference to those in psychiatry. In *Foreign Medical Graduates in Psychiatry: Issues and Problems,* ed. R. S. Chen, pp. 312–338. New York: Human Sciences Press.

Tharoor, S. (2001). *Riot.* New Delhi: Penguin.

Thomson, J. A., Harris, M., and Volkan, V. D. (1993). *The Psychology of Western European Neo-Racism.* Charlottesville, VA: Center for the Study of Mind and Human Interaction.

van der Veer, P. (1994). *Religious Nationalism: Hindus and Muslims in India.* Berkeley, CA: University of California Press.

Varma, V. K., Akhtar, S., Kulhara, P. N., et al. (1973). Measurement of authoritarian traits in India. *Indian Journal of Psychiatry* 15:156–175.

Varshney, A. (2002). *Ethnic Conflict and Civic Life: Hindus and Muslims in India.* New Haven, CT: Yale University Press.

Volkan, V. D. (1988). *The Need to Have Enemies and Allies.* Northvale, NJ: Jason Aronson.

——— (1997). *Blood Ties: From Ethnic Conflict to Ethnic Terrorism.* New York: Farrar, Straus, and Giroux.

——— (2004). *Blind Trust: Large Groups and Their Leaders in Times of Crisis and Terror.* Charlottesville, VA: Pitchstone.

Volkan, V. D., Akhtar, S., Dorn, R. M., et al. (1998). The psychodynamics of leaders and decision making. *Mind and Human Interaction* 9:130–181.

Waelder, R. (1936). The principle of multiple function. *Psychoanalytic Quarterly* 5:45–62.

6

Bollywood and the Indian Unconscious

Salman Akhtar and Komal Choksi

> India is a country where there are many cultures, many languages, many subcultures, many states. Each have their own identity, their own culture, their own language. . . . In the same way, we have one more culture and one more ethos, and one more state—that of Hindi cinema which has its own traditions, its own culture and language.
>
> *Javed Akhtar (cited in Kabir 1999, p. 31)*

In one of its many bewildering juxtapositions, India is the source of some of the world's most sublime traditions and cultural forms as well as a kitschy and fantastical popular cinema. Its movies have exaggerated theatricality and extreme stylization. They privilege mise-en-scène over narrative in the interest of melodrama. Representing a cinema of excess, these films have been described as "glossy, semi-literate, and replete with stock situations" by *The Film Encyclopedia* (Katz 1994), packed with "exotica, vulgarity and absurdity" by the *Times of India* (Mohamed 1984), and a "gaudy, three-hour excess of wild melodrama" by *Time* magazine (Corliss 2002a). Pejoratively referred to as "formula" films, these movies have a remarkable homogeneity, each having romance, action, comedy, tragedy, musical numbers, and family drama, all rolled into one.[1] The driving force of these movies is high affect,

---

1. Each such movie has seven or eight songs. While the actors and actresses dance themselves, they are not required to sing. The function is performed by playback singers

achieved through lavish sets, highly choreographed dance sequences, hyperbolic dialogue, slapstick comedy, and lachrymose tragedy. The characters portrayed in them are stereotypical and hollow. Their narratives readily lapse into fantasy sequences, including song-and-dance numbers that operate in defiance of space, time, and logic.[2] These movies are manic departures from reality. There is a hallucinatory and dreamlike quality to them.

Equally incredible is the number of such movies made during a year. India is the world's largest producer of feature films, turning out an average of 800 movies annually in sixteen different languages; the production reached a record high of 1,013 in 2001 (U.K. Film Council Report on Indian Media 2002). Most of the movies in Hindi language come out of Bombay,[3] and the industry there is popularly known as "Bollywood." While Hindi movies make up only a quarter of the country's productions, they have the largest distribution both nationally and internationally[4] and collect the most revenues. Hindi popu-

---

who remain unseen on screen but who have become famous and legendary in their own right.

2. In a recent hit, *Kabhi Khushi Kabhie Gham* (2001), a three-minute song-and-dance sequence depicting the development of the hero's love for the heroine while in Chandni Chowk, a teeming bazaar in old Delhi, shows them cavorting among the pyramids in Egypt with the heroine going through a switch of ten saris.

3. In 2000, Bombay studios produced 240 films while films made in the four South Indian languages and Bengali numbered 500. Studios in Calcutta, Bangalore, Madras, and Hyderabad churn out these regional language productions. While having only a small national audience, these movies enjoy considerable popularity within their respective states. Indeed, in South India, fan adulation has reached unimaginable heights. Not only have these devoted fans helped cinematic megastars do spectacularly well in politics, but they have at times conferred a demigod status to them. Temples have been erected for the worship of several of these South Indian cinema stars, many of whom have made a career of depicting mythological gods on screen. In 1967, when the Tamilian megastar (and chief minister) M.G. Ramachandran, who had over 10,000 fan clubs devoted to him, was critically ill, 22 fans committed suicide by immolation, in hopes of appeasing divine forces and saving his life.

4. Hindi films are distributed to reach the 20 million nonresident Indians (NRIs) (as expatriates are referred to) in the U.S., U.K., and Canada. They are also exported to places as diverse as Australia, Hong Kong, Japan, the Caribbean, the Middle East, various countries of the former Soviet Union, Southeast Asia, and parts of Africa. From 1998, Bollywood movies have regularly made it to U.K. box office charts. Indeed, it is possible that Indian movies are the most watched movies in the world.

lar cinema has the broadest appeal and has found a way to traverse the cleavages of socioeconomic class, rural/urban divide, gender, religion, caste, and language that often rancorously split the country. In constant reciprocity with its traditions and arts, Hindi cinema has been a dominant, vital, and responsive element of Indian culture since the 1930s. "Bombay films consist virtually of a single genre which is especially conducive to the construction and reinforcement of an abiding myth, setting guidelines for social conduct" (Tremblay 1996, p. 295) and, one might add, themselves conforming to preexisting societal norms.

Popular cinema and its attendant fanfare have a ubiquitous presence in India. Public spaces are utterly colonized by its billboards and the air is full of its music. Film songs not only blare from every street corner shop, but are present at all social functions including weddings and religious services. Many recent TV shows have film-based programming (talk shows about films, film music shows, broadcast of films, etc.). With a daily average of 23 million people flocking to movie theaters (Rajadhyaksha and Willeman 1999), cinema-going is the major source of entertainment in India, and the country's popular music is synonymous with film songs. Indeed, it is the music that often determines the success of a film, as soundtracks are pre-released.

Commercial success being the near singular driving force behind all popular productions, directors and producers focus upon mastering a formula that works. Indeed, there is a fearful unwillingness to diverge from it. Indian moviemakers acknowledge this with hand-wringing wistfulness mixed with sly pride. Karan Johar, the writer and director of two recent blockbusters, *Kuch Kuch Hota Hai* (1998) and *Kabhi Khushi Kabhi Gham* (2001), says:

> We are restricted as Indian film makers. If I try to do something completely unusual, I know it won't be understood. We have to cater to the Indian Yuppie in New York and the man in rural Bihar. . . . The most difficult thing to do is to make a universally commercial Indian film. [Quoted in Kabir 2001, p. 7]

Indian filmgoers are not passive recipients of projected fantasies on the screen. They yell, sigh, scream, and in all sorts of other ways become the "real authors of the text in Hindi films" (Kakar 1989). Film viewing is an interactive experience and, as with everything else in the country, the theater itself is stratified and gendered. Seating is divided into front benches, lower stalls, upper stalls, and balcony, and each section is differently priced; in some smaller cities, one still can find separate seating areas for women. The audience in front benches and lower stalls is overwhelmingly male. This group tends to sing along, throw coins, catcall, recite dialogue along with the actors, offer suggestions to the characters on the screen, and show gleeful delight at dialogue with double entendres. It loudly cheers when the hero prevails over the villain and whistles when the heroine performs a seductive dance. Feverishly passionate about films, the audience is quick to render its critical verdict. Whether a movie will be a hit or a flop is usually determined by the second or third day of its release. The Indian audience is discerning, and only about eight movies become hits (by running for 25 consecutive weeks in a cinema hall) in a year and an even smaller percentage attain the status of superhit (by far exceeding the 25-week mark).

The 100 superhit films of the nearly 67,000 produced between 1931 (when sound came to the Indian screen) and 2000 (Varde 2001) have the collective stamp of approval of the unconscious of the Indian society. They reveal much about the evolving cultural and socioeconomic affairs in India (Tremblay 1996). These societal changes are accompanied by parallel intrapsychic processes in the Indian audience. And, the two registers seem to be in a dialectical relationship of cause and effect with each other. According to Nandy (1998),

> popular cinema represents the low-brow version of the values, ambition, and anxieties of Indians who are caught between two cultures, two lifestyles, and two visions of a desirable society [and studying it] is studying Indian modernity at its rawest, its crudities laid bare by the fate of traditions in contemporary life and arts. [p. 7]

The films of Indian popular cinema are in the end the story of the nation/family that has been broken and gets reunited into a whole by the time lights come on. Their deeper agenda consists of elucidating and healing the intrapsychic splits of their audience. To accomplish this, these movies keep repeating themes of which the audiences never tire. A cultural repetition compulsion seems to be in operation here. It is as if there are certain conflicts that the nation is collectively attempting to master with the help of these movies. These conflicts change with time and popular trends in cinema reflect these changes. The shifting content does not, however, affect the form of these movies; there is a "continuity amidst change" (Erikson 1950) here.

In this chapter, we trace, deconstruct, and hypothesize about the changes in the manner in which sexuality, gender roles, familial relationships, alcohol consumption, and foreign countries have been depicted through the various eras of Hindi popular cinema. Our aim, to paraphrase Freud's (1900) celebrated aphorism, is to find a royal road to the Indian unconscious.

SOME CAVEATS

First, we make no claims to be comprehensive. Indeed, we are aware that the material to be addressed is so large and complex that it is beyond our capability and the scope of this chapter to do justice to it. There are over 70,000 films to be dealt with and a comparably vast literature to cover. As a result, we have set our bar low and readily acknowledge the limited nature of our knowledge and coverage of this realm.

Second, our contribution is focused exclusively on the mainstream Hindi movies coming out of Bombay. We will not comment on the regional language movies made in other parts of the country, including those made by the universally acclaimed director Satyajit Ray. We will also not include the so-called art movies of Bombay. This genre, begun with *Bhuvan Shome* (1969), *Saara Akash* (1969), *Anubhav* (1971), and *Ankur* (1973), included many outstanding movies directed by Shyam Benegal, Govind Nihlani, and Mrinal Sen. These movies catered largely to the tastes of sophisticated and higher socioeconomic classes in the urban areas of the country. They did not embody the sentiments of India's masses, which are our main concern here.

Third, we will avoid speculation about the personal psychodynamics of individuals who have initiated major trends in Indian movies. We realize that such factors play a role, but we also are aware that a movie is the end result of many people's efforts, and its success and failure is determined by an even larger number of people. A moviemaker, like a poet, is "a community's daydreamer" (Arlow 1986), and his personal dynamic is pertinent only in tapping similar conflicts on a large-group level.

Finally, in dividing the 92-year history of Indian cinema into four eras—the era of mythological awe (1913–1946), the era of oedipal romance (1947–1972), the era of narcissistic rage (1973–1987), and the era of nostalgic defense (1988–present)—we run the risk of appearing simplistic. To counteract this, we wish to emphasize that we are aware that our chronological categories are not watertight. In each of these eras, movies have been made that did not fit the mold. Our compartmentalization is in the service of pursuing larger, more striking psychosocial trends and not isolated departures from them.

It is with these caveats that our contribution should be approached.

THE ERA OF MYTHOLOGICAL AWE (1913–1946)

Of the six forces that have shaped today's Indian popular cinema—the great Hindu epics, classical Indian theatre, *nautanki* (folk plays performed on makeshift street side stages), Parsi theatre, Hollywood, and MTV (Gokulsingh and Dissanayake 1998)—one can claim to be the true progenitor of the Indian movie industry. This is the famed Parsi theater of the nineteenth century, which itself was the product of diverse traditional cultural forces. Parsis (Zoroastrians of Persian origin) had settled in India around the turn of the 8th century A.D. Largely endogamous, cloistered, and more open to Western influences that other Indians, Parsis were a community given to nostalgia. Many of them went into selling musical instruments. Many others created plays that "blended realism and fantasy, music and dance, narrative and spectacle, earthy dialogue and ingenuity of stage presentation, integrating them within a dramatic discourse of melodrama (Gokulsingh and Dissanayake 1998, p. 94). These productions contained crude humor, melodious songs, and dazzling stagecraft.

> Many of the plays merged diverse influences from Persian lyric poetry, deploying themes of heroism and love legends, with local folk forms. . . . European opera was a big influence which migrated into regional state traditions. . . . The dominant genres of the Parsee [*sic*] theatre were the historical, the romantic melodrama and the mythological, with a major

influence being the seventeenth century Elizabethan theatre, especially via translations and adaptations of Shakespeare, a tradition that fed into film. [Rajadhyaksha and Willemen 1999, p. 17]

India's rich cinematic traditions developed, both thematically and aesthetically, in spite of and independent of colonial rule. Dhundiraj Govind ("Dadasaheb") Phalke (1870–1944) produced and directed the nation's first film, *Raja Harishchandra*, in 1913.[5] This movie revolved around the life of a noble king who faced many challenges and offered many sacrifices in his path of devotion to God. Phalke said that he was inspired to make a film on the life of the god Krishna after seeing the film *Life of Christ* in 1910. His oft-quoted moment of inspiration goes thus:

> While the *Life of Christ* was rolling fast before my physical eyes, I was mentally visualizing the gods, Shri Krishna, Shri Ramchandra, their Gokul and Ayodhaya. I was gripped by a strange spell. I bought another ticket and saw the film again. Could we, the sons of India, ever be able to see Indian images on the screen? [Quoted in Kabir 2001, p. 103]

With *Raja Harishchandra*, Phalke initiated the genre of mythological films, depicting the colorful and inspirational tales of Hindu gods and goddesses. He produced a number of such movies including *Satyavan Savitri* (1915), *Lanka Dahan* (1918), *Guru Dronacharya* (1923), *Janaki Swayamvar* (1926), *Bhakt Prahlad* (1926), *Hanuman Janam* (1927), and *Draupadi Vastraharan* (1928). Along with the closely related genre of devotional films, portraying Hindu singer-saints and their miracles (e.g., *Sant Namdev*, 1922), the mythologicals made by Phalke and others gained ascendancy through the 1920s. Phalke made many trips to England in order to sharpen his filmmaking skills. His focus, however, remained on Hindu religious themes, and most other filmmakers of the day emulated him.

---

5. *Pundalik* in 1912 was probably the first feature film, but it has traditionally been discounted as it was believed to be shot by an Englishman, and therefore not considered a true Indian production. Phalke marketed his movies as *Swadeshi* (of national origin) products, capitalizing on that day's anticolonial sentiment and pride in India's self-sufficiency.

Films based on stories from the *Mahabharata* and *Ramayana* were common, and a sense of piety prevailed on the celluloid screen. Women, particularly those of Indian descent, were rarely seen on screen, as acting was considered akin to prostitution. Female roles were at times played by male actors; Phalke's effeminate cook played the heroine's role in *Raja Harishchandra*. Western women or Indian women of Christian or Jewish faith were recruited for the purpose. Fascinatingly, such women often adopted Hindu names (Ruby Meyers became Sulochana, and Renee Smith became Seeta Devi, for instance) presumably for greater acceptance by the masses.

After nearly a thousand silent movies, sound came to Indian cinema. Music, song, and dance found their way to film from that very moment. Here we want to emphasize that an actor or actress bursting into song seems more artificial to the Western audience than it does to an Indian audience. The reasons for this are complex. To begin with, music constitutes an element of vocal expression in all areas of culture. "For Indian spectators the psychological distance between speech and song is considerably narrower than for Western spectators" (Beeman 1981, p. 83). No wonder that the masses, which were used to viewing traditional forms of drama with well-integrated music and dance, were delighted to see the same form preserved on the screen. Jan Nisar Akhtar (1962), in a foreword to his fellow lyricist Sahir Ludhianvi's collection of film songs, *Gaata Jaaye Banjara*, traced the antecedents of Hindi film songs back to the structure of ancient Indian plays and performance of epics in India's folk theater. Barnouw and Krishnaswamy (1963) have elaborated on this point:

> Corresponding to the *jatra* of Bengal and adjoining areas, other forms of musical folk drama persisted through the centuries in other parts of India. There were the *ojapali* of Assam, the *jashn* of Kashmir, the *kathakali* of Kerala, the *leela* of Orissa, the *swang* of Punjab. When a new Indian theatre began to develop in the 19th century, these folk drama forms exerted and immediate influence: a vast tradition of song and dance was available to the new theatre. When the sound film appeared, this same reservoir pressed strong upon it. . . . Into the new medium came the river of music, that had flowed through unbroken millennia of dramatic tradition. [pp. 67–68]

India's first sound film, *Alam Ara*, was produced and directed by Ardeshir Irani, a Parsi dealer of musical instruments. This movie was written by an Indian Jew, Joseph David, and an American by the name of Michael Denning was its sound recordist. This saga of a palace intrigue focused on the victorious return of Alam Ara, the daughter of an army chief who had been seduced and cast aside by the conniving queen. Released in 1931, this costume drama had seven songs; not much later a movie (*Indrasabha*, 1932) was released with an astounding seventy-one songs. The movement toward cinematic indulgences was clearly in full swing.

At the same time, there evolved a progressive commitment to make films that addressed social issues, including religious absolutism (*Amritmanthan*, 1934), feudal patriarchy (*Manmohan*, 1936), untouchability (*Achhut Kanya*, 1936), and Hindu–Muslim relations (*Padosi*, 1941). Director V. Shantaram was most notable for his reformist social films in which he critically approached feudal traditions. Along with other directors, he brought the neorealist style to depictions of the institutions of marriage, dowry, widow remarriage, casteism, and classism.

The movies of this era made only occasional reference to places beyond India's shores. Travel abroad, if at all hinted at, referred to England (*Vilayat Palat*, 1921), Japan, or Burma. During the 1930s to 1940s, however, the most exciting daredevil was a white woman, Fearless Nadia (actually, Mary Evans from Australia), who freely used violence to fight evil. Hindu women gradually braved societal pressures and began appearing in films, though such a professional choice was stigmatized until about the 1960s.

Indian popular cinema's most recurrent theme (the love triangle) and its most resonating character (the tragic hero) were born in *Devdas*[6] in 1935. The movie was based on Sharat Chandra Chatterjee's novel of the same name. In it, Devdas, the son of a landlord, falls in love with Parvati, who is the daughter of a poor neighboring family. Differences in social status thwart their desire to marry and Devdas is sent out of town to pursue higher studies while Parvati's family arranges her marriage to another man. When he comes to know of Parvati's impending marriage, the heartbroken Devdas finds solace in alcohol. He also begins to spend time in the company of the prostitute Chandramukhi,

---

6. Since its first screen adaptation, *Devdas* has been remade twice to huge success. The last, in 2002, also was fifth on U.K. box office charts in its first week of screening.

who falls in love with him. Though using her as an emotional crutch, Devdas rejects her as a lover. Devdas's life slowly falls apart. Parvati, hearing of his decline, comes to offer herself to him yet again. Devdas sends her back to her home but promises that he will come to see her at least once before his death. His drinking worsens with the passage of time. Finally, a weak and consumptive Devdas makes his way to her house, but Parvati's family refuses to let her out of the house. The love-lorn Devdas dies at her doorstep.

The reasons for *Devdas*'s becoming a hit are complex and fascinating. Its depiction of two lovers split apart owing to caste and class differences struck a deep chord in the audiences of a country where a majority of marriages are still arranged on such grounds. The Madonna–Prostitute split, pervasive at the oedipal bottom of the male psyche (Freud 1910, 1912), was also of great intuitive appeal to Indian men, who often hold deeply conflicted attitudes toward female sexuality. The "good" and nonsexual woman and the "bad" and sexual woman imagos were kept surgically apart in the form of the sari-clad, demure Parvati and the *Mujra* (seductive dance)-performing courtesan, Chandramukhi. The movie also provided ample extenuating circumstances for Devdas's heavy drinking; after all he was heartbroken and suffering the anguish of unrequited love. He did not deserve criticism for his excess and, by unconscious identification with him, neither did anyone in the audience who liked to drink. His visits to the prostitute were similarly justified. The audience could go along for a joyful ride without feeling any guilt whatsoever. Finally, the choice of Devdas's name was telling. Were he a true equal of Parvati (in Hindu mythology, the consort of god Shiva), he would be named Shiva or Shankar (another name for Shiva). Instead, he is named Devdas, which literally means "the slave or servant of God." He is thus subtly downgraded in generational status vis-à-vis Parvati. He is not the *Dev* (god) but *Devdas* (god's servant), a hint to his being her oedipal son. He longs for her but is not allowed by his conscience to consummate their relationship. Guilt is his earning, self-destruction his destiny.

In the decades following the release of *Devdas*, such doomed and tragic love found its way over and over again to the darkened cinema halls of India. A maudlin sentimentality became the favored idiom of popular cinema. The related theme of self-sacrifice in the name of pure, ideal love, fraternity, or family also provided a vehicle for such melodramas. The lost-and-found theme, in which family members are first separated by fate or villainy, then reunited, was also established, with 1943's *Kismet* (an enormously successful Indian film). In all these movies, the undercurrents were oedipal and the family romance (Freud 1909) fantasies rampant. This would take an even more significant place in the movies of the next era.

THE ERA OF OEDIPAL ROMANCE (1947–1972)

The 1950s are widely regarded as constituting the golden era in Indian cinematic history. Great directors such as Mehboob Khan, Guru Dutt, Bimal Roy, Raj Kapoor, and B. R. Chopra not only brought depth to the well-established cinematic theme of a love triangle but also addressed some new areas with vision and courage. Among the bold themes these directors addressed were single motherhood (*Mother India*), commercial disdain of meaningful literature (*Pyaasa*), land taxation (*Do Beegha Zamin*), adoption (*Sujata*), negligent fathers (*Awaara*), widow marriage (*Ek Hi Raasta*), illegitimate children (*Dhool Ka Phool*), and corrupt electoral practices (*Parakh*).

These bold departures notwithstanding, most films of the 1950s and 1960s stayed at the level of oedipal melodramas. They could be serious (e.g., *Daagh*, *Dil Apna Aur Preet Parai*, *Bheegee Raat*, and *Sangam*) or lighthearted (*Munimji*, *Junglee*, *Kashmir ki Kali*, and *Phir Wohi Dil Laaya Hoon*), but their essential thrust remained the same. Their story involved joint or extended families and the action revolved around a hero, a heroine, a villain, and a vamp. At times, a cruel mother-in-law and a comedian were thrown in as well. Essentially, the story went like this. The hero encountered the heroine and immediately fell in love. The heroine initially resisted but then gave in. She also fell in love. They wanted to marry each other but encountered difficulty in this aim. Problems that came in their way were invariably of external origin (e.g., her father would not give his blessing, there was a big socioeconomic difference in their status, or the family had already promised her hand to someone else) and never emanated from the internal ambivalence of the hero and heroine. Their love was straightforward and simple. At this point in the movie, the villain entered the scene. While he had a woman of his own, he nevertheless fell in love with the heroine. However, his love was not pure like the hero's love; it was sexual love. The heroine promptly rejected the villain's advances. Frustrated, he tried to abduct or rape the heroine.[7] The hero then rescued the heroine and they promptly got married. The movie dutifully ended right there.

The physical and psychological attributes of these characters revealed the oedipal foundations of these movies. The hero was a "good boy" type of man. He was clean-shaven, respected his parents, and had no vices. More significantly, he had no sexual life. His love was devoid of erotic desire even though his goal was immediate marriage. In other words, superego and social sanction for entry into the sexual phase of life were essential for him. In the same vein, the hero did not drink or smoke unless he was emotionally injured. Having thus paid off his harsh conscience, the hero could indulge in instinctual gratification. Moral masochism (Freud 1920) reigned supreme as the anguished hero drank alcohol and broke into a soulful song. The drunk-hero song would usually be a hit, and a large number of movies (e.g., *Sharabi, Pyar Ka Raasta, Main Nashe Mein Hoon, Dil Diya Dard Liya, Guide,* and *Yaqeen*) had such songs.

In contrast with this masochistic good-boy hero, the villain appeared to possess striking phallic attributes. He usually had a moustache, smoked cigarettes, drank alcohol, and made no secret of his enjoying sex. His accoutrements included a cigarette holder, a whip, and knee-length leather boots, and he often drove a car or rode a horse. Compared to the hero, the villain actually looked like more of a man. Indeed, he stood for the oedipal father, imposing authority, threatening castration, and violating mother's body at night.

This brings up the depiction of women in these movies. With a few exceptions, most movies of this era had two female characters. One was the heroine and the other the vamp. The heroine wore saris, adorned her forehead with a *bindi*, and was conservative in her approach to life. She was wholesome and virtuous and was forever ready to sacrifice self-interest at the altar of moral values and family cohesion. She suffered in silence. Stoicism was her ornament. While a huge number of movies (e.g., *Anpadh, Sharada, Biraj Bahu*) conveyed such sentiment, its essence was best captured in the title of the movie *Main Chup Rahoongi* which liter-

---

7. Movies became famous for having fantastic rape scenes, and certain actors (e.g., Manmohan, Ranjit) began to be called "rape masters."

ally means "I will remain quiet." Not surprisingly, such a woman hardly had any overt sexuality. The heroine of movies that appeared between 1950s and 1970s never bared her legs and never showed cleavage. Such restraint, however, could be overcome if God were on the audience's side, so to speak. Here we are referring to the scenes of pouring rain that drenched the sari-clad heroine and revealed her bare legs or the silhouette of her breasts; this clever ploy was frequently used in those days by Indian moviemakers, especially Raj Kapoor, to put sexually titillating scenes on the screen.

Outside of such divine relaxation of societal superego, female sexuality was the terrain of the vamp. She wore tight clothes, which frequently included leg-baring Western outfits. She smoked, drank, and danced in a highly sensual manner; audiences loved movies that had good scenes of this type. All in all, these movies maintained a firm compartmentalization of "good" and nonsexual as against "bad" and sexual women figures. As a result, the audience could retain its Madonna–Prostitute split and tolerate its ambivalent feelings toward maternal sexuality without consciously registering it as such. The heroine became the audience's mother of the day and the vamp their mother of the night. Even the names given to these characters conveyed this split; in the hugely successful *Shree 420*, for instance, the good woman is called Vidya (the Hindi word for education) and the bad woman is called Maya (the Hindi word for illusion). All this helped avoid intrapsychic conflict by keeping the two mental representations of women (and of the mother) apart.

Further support of such oedipal view of these movies comes from the fact that the rescue of the good woman from the evil, often lecherous, villain played a very important role in them. This transparently manifested the oedipal boy's desire to save his mother from father's amorous intrusions (Freud 1910, 1912). The predominantly male audience loved this rescue motif while vicariously enjoying the scenes in which the heroine was abducted and forcibly seduced by the villain. The fact that almost all these movies ended when the hero and heroine got married also upholds the oedipal hypothesis of their conceptual infrastructure. It was as if no one could tolerate the sexual consummation between the good-boy hero and the all-good maternal heroine. The intensified oedipal angst at the potential of such occurrence was often hidden by the last scene of the movie, which showed all the family members gathered as a group. Public cohesion worked as an ointment against the throbbing suspicion of what the hero and heroine would now do in private. The drama ended and it was time to go home.

The 1960s also saw the advent of the multistar romance movies (e.g., *Waqt*) with many love stories crisscrossing each other. While India's first color movie, *Jhansi Ki Raani*, was made in 1953, it was the 1960s that actually witnessed the demise of black-and-white movies. Initially, only the song and dance sequences would be shown in color while all the other scenes would be in black and white. Then color processing became widely available. Moviemakers began to depict stunning pastoral scenes as backdrops to romantic song and dance sequences. At first, they would shoot these sequences in the picturesque hills of Kashmir, Ootacumund, and Kodaikanal. Then they started taking their units abroad to look for visually unfamiliar, aesthetically striking, and colonially idealized backgrounds. Movies with titles like *Singapore* (1960), *Love in Tokyo* (1966), and *An Evening in Paris* (1967) showed spectacular terrain and reigned supreme in the minds of the masses. The hypnoid relief they provided from the daily hardship of life outside the theater was more than welcome. It was psychically lifesaving.

During these years, the modal family structure in India was that of the joint family in which many generations lived cooperatively under one roof. Children grew up with the constant company of grandparents, aunts, uncles, cousins, and—in middle and upper-middle-class families—the live-in domestic help. Such upbringing reduced separation anxiety (Mahler et al. 1975) and gave rise to a modal character that was full of trust and optimism. However, the crowded living quarters also led to greater "primal scene" (Freud 1918) exposure and frequent sighting of the opposite sex's genitalia. As a result, children grew up with heightened psychic bisexuality, intense oedipal fixations, and marked sexual anxiety. Not surprisingly, male impotence and female hysterical fits were the two most common conditions seen in psychiatric clinics in those days. It was the oedipal anxieties underlying them that found suppressive relief via the colorful extravaganzas mentioned above.

Other levels of concern also gave texture to these movies. The rivalries, intrigues, and interpersonal shenanigans of a joint family also found expression in a number of these movies (*Bhabhi*, *Ghunghat*, *Gharana*, *Chhoti Bahen*). Social and national events began to figure in the movies of this era, at times in an unconscious condensation with the private oedipal conflicts of the audience. This was, after all, the postindependence period. Patriotic feelings were abundant and nationalism was flying high. The departure of the British rulers had yielded a great sense of internal cohesion. This resulted in the heroes and heroines of the movies of this era being unmistakably Indian in their aesthetics and values. It also led to the ridicule of the characters who had returned from abroad, usually England. They were depicted as buffoons, and their Western mannerisms and attitudes were mercilessly mocked. By the end of the movie, though, such characters were reformed, having rediscovered their Indian traditions and sensibilities. Such a modernity–traditionalism dichotomy was another way of portraying the instinctual-moral dilemma that was central to these movies. It was all very noble, or so it seemed until the 1970s rolled in.

THE ERA OF NARCISSISTIC RAGE (1973–1987)

By the time a quarter century had passed since India's independence from the British, people began to lose the manic exaltation of their newfound nationalism. Their colonizers were no more around but societal ills persisted. There seemed little relief from hunger, poverty, overcrowding, and epidemics of life-threatening diseases. A sense that the nation's leaders had not delivered on their promises prevailed. Government no longer appeared credible and the nation was in a state of despair. The reigning affect of this era was smoldering anger, and the Gandhian principles of nonviolence that won India its independence were not reflected on the screen.

The renowned screenplay writer and lyricist Javed Akhtar, who, along with his writing partner, Salim Khan, created the angry young man protagonist of the 1970s movies, has significant insights to offer here. He links the changing face of the hero in Bollywood movies to the shifting sociopolitical scenario over the period of the 1940s through the 1970s. He notes that in

the forties, fifties, and sixties, the hero was the paragon of positive virtues. A feudal society where the joint family dominates is a strongly patriarchal society in which obedience and acceptance are virtue. . . . The halo over this submission is sacrifice, and sacrifice becomes a virtue in a society where exploitation is rampant. So you have a hero like Devdas in the 1930s, whose impact lasted into the 1950s. But gradually, with industrialization and a capitalist system, we emerged from feudal values—and winning became a virtue and the hero changed. So in the 1960s, we see a more positive hero, like Shammi Kapoor. We were optimistic, affluence was around the corner and better things were going to happen. . . . But they didn't. And that dream got shattered and created a kind of cynicism and anger. This led to a lack of trust in institutions, in systems, in law and order. And, the image of angry young man was the natural, logical result. [Quoted in Kabir 2001, pp. 43–44]

Such heroes found violence to be a necessary instrument to assure survival and have power. This motif led to the creation of some of the biggest blockbusters in the 1970s and 1980s. The trend was set by the 1973 movie *Zanjeer*, written by the Salim Khan–Javed Akhtar duo. With it the brooding vigilante Vijay, whose name literally meant "victory," was born. Amitabh Bachchan, a lanky and somewhat mysterious young man, played the role and achieved instant resurrection of his otherwise flailing film career. Indeed, he would go on to play the same—or, at least, very similar—role in an outstanding sixteen subsequent movies. Bachchan's[8] tall and gangly frame cast long shadows on Hindi films for the next two decades. Early Bachchan movies were also marked by significant depressive affect. Gloom, psychic desolation, and mournful privacy were his emotions. Romantic love was not at the forefront of his consciousness—vengeance was. This theme of the son who avenges the injustice done against himself and his mother by the father, presented in a light romantic manner by Raj Kapoor's *Awaara* (1955), found a new and fiery emotional intensity in the 1970s to 1980s films of Bachchan.

While previously the hero's aim was to possess the heroine, it was now to get even with the father and restore the lost omnipotence. The hero was propelled by narcissistic rage to heal the wound inflicted by the father who had either physically or emotionally abandoned him during childhood. The quest for revenge was also on the behalf of an

---

8. As a testimony to the hold of Indian popular cinema on British Asians—and also perhaps other citizens of the U.K.—Bachchan was voted actor of the millennium in a BBC news poll in 2000.

idealized mother or *Ma*, upon whom injustices had been heaped after the father's departure. *Ma*, who always silently suffered her fate, was the vehicle for her son's vendetta. At the heart of these intense dramas was the bond between the hero and his mother; her trials and tribulations drove him to take revenge on a cruel father and an unjust society. This seemingly oedipal material was not at all oedipal in meaning or intent. These movies lacked the hesitation of desire, the flickering allusion to primal scene, the seductive lure of female sexuality, and the pangs of erotic jealousy that are characteristic of oedipal phase conflicts. These movies were actually about narcissistic issues that lie parallel to (Kohut 1971) or deeper than (Kernberg 1975) oedipal configurations. Hurt of betrayal was their central motivation, mental pain (Akhtar 2000) their main affect, and revenge their ultimate reward.

Deewar (1975[9]) was the prime film of this genre and it catapulted Bachchan into megastardom. Here Vijay (played by Bachchan) is a dockworker and later smuggler in Bombay who has "*Mera baap chor hai*"

---

9. This was also the year of *Sholay*, the "curry western" starring Amitabh Bachchan that was India's biggest hit until 1994's *Hum Aapke Hain Koun . . . !* It played for five consecutive years at a Bombay theater. A cult favorite, this revenge plot is reminiscent of movies such as *The Magnificent Seven* (1960), *Butch Cassidy and the Sundance Kid* (1969), and *Once Upon a Time in the West* (1969). Thakur, a landlord/policeman, succeeds in capturing the dreaded *dacoit* (bandit) Gabbar Singh. Gabbar Singh retaliates by massacring Thakur's entire family except for his youngest daughter-in-law, who was away at the temple, and hacking off Thakur's arms. Thakur, bent on revenge, hires Veera and Jaidev (Bachchan) to hunt down Gabbar Singh. Veeru woos village belle Basanti while Jaidev engages in a muted romance with Radha, the widowed daughter-in-law. The kidnapping of Basanti by the *dacoits* leads to a confrontation with Gabbar Singh. Jaidev sacrifices his life, providing Veeru cover to rescue Basanti. Veeru comes back to kill Gabbar Singh, but Thakur insists on avenging his family's death. He kicks Gabbar Singh with his hob-nailed shoes and desists only when the police come to recapture the *dacoit*. Jaidev's death, as pointed out by Rajadhyaksha and Willemen (1999), "allowed the film to adhere to the Hindi cinema's norm that the widowed Radha may not remarry" (p. 426). This movie is a departure in that the primary bonds are of friendship and romantic love over family relations. Unusually, both the heroes and one heroine are shown without any family ties—expected for the villain and his crew, but not for the good characters. Also, in a regression from earlier films, not only is feudalism represented as a positive force and something to be protected, but the heroes, instead of being motivated by a personal sense of social justice, are mercenaries. In addition, the villain is pure evil, not driven by greed or a misguided set of values. He kills for the pleasure of it (such as killing Thakur's infant son).

("My father is a thief") tattooed on his arm. This was an allusion to his having been abandoned by his corrupt father during childhood. In one scene of the movie, as Vijay's mother berates him for the path he has chosen, he says, "*Maine jo kuch bi kiya, tera liye kiya*" ("Whatever I have done, it is for you"). In perhaps the most famous scene of the film, Vijay arranges a meeting with Ravi, his younger brother who is a police officer and whose life is wanted by the smugglers. Vijay fiercely questions Ravi: "Your principles, your ideals! Of what use are your ideals? These ideals! For the sake of which you're ready to stake your life! What have they done for you? A job that pays Rs. 400–500, a rented flat, a government jeep, two sets of uniforms? Look at where you are and where I am. We both come from this sidewalk but since then look at what you have achieved and at what I have achieved. I have buildings, property, a bank balance, a fine home, a car! What do you have?" Ravi looks Vijay squarely in the face and intones quietly, "*Mere paas ma hai*" ("I have Mother"), to which Vijay has no response. His embarrassed silence speaks volumes as to what *Deewar* and all other such movies are about. They are attempts to ameliorate a sense of inner void, a gaping hole in the platform of narcissism, that was ostensibly created by the father's betrayal and by the maternal depression that followed it. The allusion to disappointment with the nation's fathers and the subsequently suffering motherland is hard to miss here. Varde (2001) takes this point a step further by declaring that

> Vijay's agnostic rebellion and his final surrender to devoutness with an impassioned speech in front of Lord Shiva to save his beloved mother's life, seemed to echo the mood of anger and protest during [Mrs. Indira] Gandhi's dreaded emergency. [p. 95]

Such sociopolitical interpretations, however, do not overrule the possibility that some fuel to the raging fire could have been provided by intrapsychic conflicts emergent around these times. The typical family structure had changed around the 1960s from joint families to nuclear ones and migration from rural areas to the big cities was at its peak. More and more women had begun to work outside the confines of the home. The Indian child was being raised in a fashion similar to the Western one—abandoned by the greater extended family, left with babysitters of sorts, dealing with a preoccupied mother, hungry for affection, pseudo-independent, angry, and secretly blaming father for being responsible for the tense state of affairs. The ground for narcissistic rage (Kohut 1972) was set as this generation grew up as bona fide moviegoers. The movies of the 1970s gave voice to their anger.

These movies had a defiant and cocky tone. In sharp contrast to the 1950s and 1960s movies of restraint, the 1970s and 1980s offered movies of release. These films unleashed instinctual life with vengeance. Sexuality and aggression were portrayed relatively openly. The hero was cynical about authority figures. He drank without being propelled into it by tragedy. The heroine often wore short dresses, jeans, and so on that revealed her feminine curves. In many movies, the implication that the hero and heroine were having premarital sex was clear. In light of such changes, the drunk-hero song sequence and the stereotypical role of the vamp were hardly ever seen in movies after the late 1970s.

These movies—many of which starred Amitabh Bachchan—thus simultaneously expressed the societal rage at postindependence disillusionment and the individual rage of a generation that was increasingly being raised in tense, nuclear family environments with two working parents. Again and again, these movies repeated the theme of betrayal by authority, rage, and revenge. Three more examples should suffice.

Trishul (1987) was a blockbuster hit in its time, with the theme of vendetta and retribution within a family. The hero, once again named Vijay, is the illegitimate child of R. K. Gupta and Shanti. While Shanti is on her deathbed, Vijay learned how his father had spurned the pregnant Shanti to whom he was engaged in order to marry his millionaire boss's daughter. The angry young man is thus born and makes his way to Bombay to extract his revenge, in the form of his father's financial destruction.

In *Suhaag* (1979), the hero's mother's name is Durga, after the powerful mother goddess who is worshiped across the country. Her husband, Vikram, who is a gangster, refuses to acknowledge her or their twin sons after she gives birth to them. The twins are separated, with one, Amit, growing up a petty thief after having been raised by a criminal, and the other, Kishen, who was raised by the mother, becoming a policeman. Durga is steadfast in her devotion to her husband, waiting for the day when she will be accepted. As for Amit and Kishen, they are brought together by their shared desire to bring Vikram to justice, unaware that he is their father or that they are brothers. Kishen is blinded by Vikram and Amit adopts Kishen's role as a police inspector to carry on the quest. In the final scene, in which Vikram is finally cornered after his sons were in hot pursuit, everything is revealed, with the brothers discovering the real reason behind their bond with each other. Vikram, repentant and now the sacrificing father, donates his eyes to the son he blinded before heading off to prison a reformed man.

In *Shakti* (1982), Vijay is the son of Sheetal and Ashwini Kumar, an overscrupulous police officer and a stern father whose miscalculated adherence to his sublime civic values ends up traumatizing his son. After kidnapping Vijay, the gangster J. K. Verma places a call to Ashwini: "Are you interested in seeing that your son stay alive? His life is now in your hands." Vijay pleads with his father to save him, to which Ashwini responds, "Daddy won't let anything happen to you." Verma then says to Vijay, "We shall soon see how much your father loves you." However, in a bid to buy time, his father tells the gangster, "You may kill him. You may do what you wish with him, but I will not dishonor my obligations." Vijay overhears this before he escapes, and is left with the refrain of his father's words forever imprinted in his head, much as "Your father is a thief" was tattooed onto his skin in *Deewar*. Vijay's life is saved by K. D. Narang, a smuggler in whom he finds a father figure and for whom he later works, severing his relationship with his father. Vijay finds comfort in the parentless Roma, who becomes pregnant by him, leading to their marriage. Sheetal is eventually killed by Verma, the gangster who had kidnapped the young Vijay, and Vijay in turn by his father. As Vijay lies dying in his father's arms, felled by his bullet, Ashwini asks despairingly why did all this have to happen. Vijay responds that it had to, that through his life he had tried so hard to win his father's love, to no avail. Ashwini also declares his love for his son, thus ending the movie with Vijay having been accepted back into the fold of the family.

The second and third movies mentioned here—*Suhaag* and *Shakti*—had the betrayed and angry son theme but with a difference. The father was not entirely devalued. In *Suhaag*, he repented, reformed himself, and offered a grand reparation to his son. In *Shakti*, the audience was left in no doubt that the police officer father is a noble man. Indeed his wife, the hero's mother, chides the hero by saying, "Even if you die a hundred times and are reborn a hundred times, you still will not have your father's qualities." The introduction of the complexity that the hated father was not all bad was perhaps a bit taxing for an audience looking for pure and simple entertainment.

Shakti, which had the theme of infanticide rather than parricide,[10] was not a hit. In having the father kill the child, it clearly digressed too far from the audience's tolerable levels of anxiety and of conflict. Tang and Smith (1996) note that the major oedipal myth in India, captured in the story of Ganesha's birth, tilted toward infanticide rather than parricide. This is due to the particular child-rearing patterns in India, in which there is extended physical contact between mother and infant, compelling the father to righteously and forcefully reclaim the mother's body from the infant. Whether or not one agrees with these authors' interpretation—and, to be sure, there are many other ways of understanding the *Ganesha* fable—the fact is something about the movie's depiction of a father killing his son made the audience uneasy. The movie was only modestly successful. Perhaps other reasons, including the fact that the reign of the angry young man was anyway nearing its end, also played a role here.

Like its inception and meteoric rise to success, the decline and gradual disappearance of this type of hero also had both social and psychological causes. As the 1990s arrived, India had opened up its national

---

10. To the best of our knowledge, there are only two major Hindi movies depicting the murder of a grown child by an exasperated parent. The first is *Mother India* (1955) and the second *Shakti* (1982). In the former, a mother (played by Nargis) kills her son (played by Sunil Dutt) and in the latter, a father (played by Dilip Kumar) kills his son (played by Amitabh Bachchan).The former was a great success and the latter was not. Clearly, many other reasons accounted for this difference. One does wonder, though, if the audience found a mother's killing her child somehow less disagreeable than a father doing the same. After all, mother is the life giver and Indians have an enormous reverence toward mothers in general. Moreover, a child emotionally torturing the mother might have been found more deserving of this fate than a child similarly burdening the father. Or does the explanation lie in the fact that other aspects of the movie *Mother India* were so outstanding that they swept the audience off their feet and did not permit them to reflect deeply on the mother's murder of her son? It is also notable that in both these movies the offspring killed is male. The reasons for this are unclear. However, a suspicion does arise in the mind that showing the murder of a daughter might stir up too many repressed hostile wishes in a culture where the birth of a girl is still considered by many parents as a burden and where female infanticide is far from rare in certain areas.

economy to the world markets for capital investment, the Hindu nationalist movement was gaining strength, foreign travel was becoming easier, the television industry had begun booming, and the country's armed forces were getting better equipped with each passing day. In this context of renewed pride—and by virtue of sheer repetition—"the antihero became a caricature of himself and Indians grew tired of that image" (Javed Akhtar, quoted in Kabir 2001, p. 46).

THE ERA OF NOSTALGIC DEFENSE (1988–PRESENT)

While awe and reverence (1913–1947), desire and shy romance (1948–1972), and narcissistic rage and antiauthoritarian bravado (1973–1987) characterized the emotional and ideational texture of Indian movies in the three earlier eras, the period from 1988 to the present has been dominated by an aura of joy and playfulness. This trend was set by *Qayamat Se Qayamat Tak* (1988) and *Tezaab* (1988), which were soon followed by *Main Ne Pyar Kiya* (1989), *Ram Lakhan* (1989), *Tridev* (1989), and *Chandini* (1989). Together these movies brought back the elements of romance and music that had been put on the back burner by the intense and violent movies of the 1970s and mid-1980s. As a result, the flavor of the cinematic experience became entirely transformed.

Pyar, *prem*, *mohabbat*, and *ishq* (various Urdu and Hindi words for romantic love) now became the language of the day. Sensuality gained license. Salman Khan, the hero of *Main New Pyaar Kiya* (1989) and many hugely successful subsequent films, displayed "a penchant for showing off as much of his torso as possible (and thus) introduced a new kind of sexual, youthful hero to Indian cinema" (Kabir 2001, p. 50). As a counterpart to this, the typical heroine of the 1990s began to be younger and more conscious of her body. She began to dance graphically, at times even seeming to simulate sex. Scenes of the hero and heroine kissing each other, hitherto banished form the screen, began to appear in movies with increasing frequency. Such instinctual freedom also became evident in the fact that the new heroes (e.g., Salman Khan, Shah Rukh Khan, Aamir Khan, and Hritik Roshan) were younger, more athletic looking, and, without exception, great dancers themselves. The prominence of some choreographers (e.g., Farah Khan who was recently nominated for a Tony for her work on the Broadway musical *Bombay Dreams*) was also a testimony to the central importance dance sequences have, once again, acquired in the Hindi movies.

Besides such overt celebration of sensuality, the 1990s movies also depicted characters that were more financially affluent. More importantly, this was done casually and their monetary comfort was not rubbed in the audience's faces. These characters reflected a more affluent India; they drove cars, lived in nice bungalows, dated, had cell phones, and traveled everywhere by air. Going abroad to study or vacation (*Dil Waale Dulhaniya Le Jayeen Ge, Dil Chahta Hai*) was not a big deal for them. Of course, the foreign trips of these characters allowed the moviemakers to show exotic locales, which thrilled the common masses who had little access to these places otherwise. England, United States, and Canada were frequent sites to be shown, but Australia (*Dil Chahta Hai*), Egypt (*Kabhi Khushi Kabhi Gham*), Italy (*Hum dil de Chuke Sanam*), Kenya (*Khel*), Mauritius (*Arman*), and Switzerland (*Dil Waale Dulhaniya Le Jayeen*) also made their appearance on the screen.

All in all, there is a self-congratulatory air to these movies. There are love, money, sensual freedom, ease of travel, a cosmopolitan ambience, and an overall sense of relaxation to them. The impact of the globalization of the world culture is clearly evident. Indeed, it almost seems that these movies are more aimed to please the diaspora Indians or NRIs rather than the indigenous population. The fact is that the NRI market is huge and it exerts a powerful effect on the text and image preference of these movies. In the United States alone, Hindi films have become a $100 million industry and Bombay film stars regularly come over for live shows here, the likes of which are never seen in India. The Bollywood movie has indeed become a "universal symbol of subcontinental identity" (Sardar 1998).

It is precisely here that the pleasure of sonorous entertainment meets the pain of postimmigration dislocation, cultural unbelonging, and nostalgia. For the NRIs, watching Bollywood movies provides an opportunity to participate in the cultural politics of India in the present moment. This establishes a temporospatial continuity with their beloved homeland, even though such a homeland might be a place that is retrospectively idealized (by the first-generation NRIs), dimly remembered (by those who came here as children), or even pretty much unknown (by the generation born and raised here). The reunion none-theless gives psychic strength to the NRIs.[11] Harder to appreciate is the fact that the younger generations back home are themselves becoming alienated from Indian culture. Subject to globalization of styles and values, and growing up in a much more affluent and electronically so-phisticated and sexually relaxed society, with more and more broken homes, the newer generations are, in many ways, quite like their NRI brethren. They have become "emigrants without leaving home" (Kahn 1997), that is, foreigners in their own country. Srinivasan (2003) has designated such culturally alienated Indians in India as RNIs, resident non-Indians.

These two groups, the NRIs and the newly affluent young people of India, had two things in common: their superficial Westernization and their nostalgic longing for cultural roots. The former gave rise to hedonistic celebration of the present and the latter to a mournful ide-alization of the past. Both these affective strands were expressed in the movies of the last decade.

We have already commented upon the colorful excitement of these movies, and we now turn to the element of retrospective ideali-zation and nostalgia in them. A statement by the director Sanjay Leela Bhansali captures the spirit of glorification in these movies. Accord-ing to Bhansali, they have "good fathers, good uncles, good aunts, good families, good heroes, good heroines, and great songs" (quoted in Kabir 2001, p. 47). Besides such obvious manic defense (Klein 1935) in the realm of relationships, these movies are filled with good feelings about India traditions. Some of these traditions are truly past traditions and others are highly embellished versions of them. *Hum Aap Ke Hain Kaun!* (1994), the most commercially successful Indian movie ever made,[12] epitomizes this trend of retrospective idealization. Roundly dismissed

---

11. In fact, there is an emergent subgenre of movies focusing on the accul-turation conflicts of the NRIs and their foreign-born offspring. While *My Beautiful Laundrette* (1985), *Mississippi Masala* (1991), *Monsoon Wedding* (2001), and *Bend It Like Beckham* (2002) are the best known in this group of movies, the actual list of them is quite long indeed. Tummala-Narra and colleagues. (2005) have recently published a detailed and annotated filmography of this subgenre of interest to all Indians.

12. *Hum Aap Ke Hain Kaun!* is the highest grossing Bollywood film of all time, with sales of $63.8 million in the first year (*Guinness Book of World Records*, 2004).

by critics as nothing more than a three-hour wedding video, its success astonished everyone. There is little plot to it, no violence, no exotic locales, and the story is set entirely in two homes. It has a simple, linear narrative and no less than fourteen songs. It has been hailed by its supporters as the ultimate family film and is the story of two families that come together when they arrange the engagement of their respective son and daughter, Rajesh and Pooja. Rajesh's brother Prem and Pooja's sister Nisha fall in love. Their relationship blossoms and evolves as various family events unfold: their siblings' betrothal, engagement, *mehndi* (colorful henna paste used by women for decorative purposes on palms; most often used on the occasion of wedding), the wedding ceremony of their siblings, and the birth of a son to them. The families are hit by tragedy when Pooja unexpectedly dies, leaving behind a baby. Prem and Nisha sacrifice their love so that Nisha can marry Rajesh and be a mother to the baby. Fortunately, thanks to divine intervention, their love for each other is discovered by the families at the last moment, just as Nisha and Rajesh are about to marry. Nisha goes back to Prem and they get married.

Most of the film's action takes place either inside the home of the two families at the center of the film or immediately outside them, on sprawling lawns or around the swimming pools. The outside world of urban congestion, neighbors, or streets and public spaces is completely excluded from the film, thus creating a false, nostalgically fueled appearance of interpersonal cohesion (Juluri 1999). Everybody seems to love everybody else, and the institution of family is heavily idealized. To be sure, the NRIs facing separation from relatives back home and experiencing alienation from the offspring born abroad find all this very soothing.

Such family dramas have an ill-concealed reformist agenda and even a didactic attitude. In an ironic comeback of sorts, Amitabh Bachchan, who played the angry young man in the 1970s, appears in the role of the mortally disappointed and wounded father, sermonizing the wayward, prodigal son in two recent movies. He seems to have moved "from playing the role of the quiet, well-behaved but effete hero, in films that were but minor successes, to his triumphant portrayals of angry, violent vigilantes functioning at the margins of society" (Nandy 1998, p. 9) and from there to the role of an elder patriarch whose younger generations are leaving him behind. The pain of this last-mentioned character is shared by those Indians whose children have become RNIs and by those NRIs who experience a great acculturation gap (Prathikanti 1997) between them and their foreign-born children.

No wonder the recent *Kabhi Khushi Kabhi Gham* was extensively marketed with the tagline, "It's all about loving your parents." This three-and-a-half-hour extravaganza on the dynamics of the three-generation, fabulously wealthy Raichand family, headed by Yashovardhan (Bachchan), the indisputable patriarch, and his dutiful wife Nandini, is mawkishly sentimental and out to revive patriarchy as if it were on its deathbed. The exhortation, repeated at strategic dramatic moments, is "If you want to be someone, close your eyes and think of your parents; you will cross all hurdles and victory will be yours." Against a background of lavish sets, palatial homes, fancy cars, a personal helicopter, and numerous larger-than-life photographs of various configurations of the family, solemn vows of such sort are repeatedly extracted from family members by other family members. Most of the story is told in a lengthy flashback to the younger son, Roshan, who has no idea that his elder brother, Rahul, had been banished from the home by their father when he dared to marry the woman of his choice rather than the socially more suitable bride that the father had in mind for Rahul. This Rahul dared to do early in the film, after Yash extracted a vow from him: "Never take a step in life that will bring shame to the family name or prestige—vow to me that you will follow the traditions of the family," invoking his own father's words to him. Nine years later, Roshan reunites the family and amidst many tears, Raichand accepts Rahul, his wife, and child, back into the fold of the family.

Kabhi Khushi Kabhi Gham succeeded in allaying the anxieties over family background felt by both the Indians in India and the NRIs. Perhaps underneath such family breakdown anxieties were also the loss of caste, regional, and tribal identities in India with more and more movement and marriage across such divisions. The need for a reinvigorated family was great, and *Kabhi Khushi Kabhi Gham* filled it. Paradoxically, however, by this very rescue effort, the movie validated the existence of a problem. There was a dread, as if Indians—now heavily engaged in the global market of ideas—were losing a sense of identity. Who were they? Where was their home? Who would take care of them?

Such anxieties were sharply voiced in *Baghban*, a major hit movie of 2004. This was a family melodrama ("Can you depend on your family?" being its tagline), about a retirement-age couple, Raj (Bachchan, again) and Pooja. Pains are taken to show how this deeply loving couple is looking forward to the day when Raj, a bank manager, will retire and they will have time for each other. They have four sons, three of whom are married, and two grandchildren. The young ones visit regularly from out of town, on occasions such as Raj's birthday and Holi (the Hindi festival of colors), both celebrated with much fanfare and the mandatory song and dance routines. Raj sees himself as a gardener (*baghban*) who nurtures and protects a sapling with the hope that it will blossom and provide for him when he is in need. Raj retires, and he and Pooja, eager to now spend time with their children, arrange a family meeting to ask them to collectively decide with whom they will live. As none of the four is interested in taking on the responsibility, they arrive at a compromise. The elder two children will take one parent each for six months, after which it will be the turn of the younger two. Raj and Pooja reluctantly agree, and spend six miserable months separated from each other and suffering their children's ill-treatment and disrespect. Raj and Pooja finally reunite, but their children show no repentance until Raj suddenly achieves enormous fame and fortune with a book he writes about his experiences with his children and the forced separation from his wife. In the last scene, Raj launches a resounding diatribe, denouncing the values of the younger generation, which does not cherish and respect the bonds between parents and children. His children then disingenuously seek forgiveness, which, unusually for a Hindi movie, is not granted by Raj, and the film ends with the family split apart. Thus while in most movies it is the patriarch who must repent for the withholding of his love, here it is the stone-hearted children of the benign, loving father who have denied him his role as a patriarch and who must atone.

All in all, it seems that the early intoxicated pleasure of *Qayamat Se Qayamat Tak*, *Maine Pyar Kiya*, and *Dil Wale Dulhaniya Le Jayenge* has given way to the desperate and clinging idealization of *Hum Aap Ke Hain Kaun* and *Kabhi Khushi Kabhi Gham*, and this, in turn, has been replaced by the brooding sadness of *Baghban*. Glorification of family values has run its course, it seems. The sociopolitical counterpart to this is the resounding defeat of the Hindu nationalist party, running on an "India shining" slogan, in the recent national elections. On the level of family, the increasing number of divorces also has rendered a continuing idealization of the family unit difficult. Cracks in the narcissistic defense (on both familial and national levels) are showing. Sadness is seeping in. How all this will affect the movies of the next decade remains an open question. Are we headed for an era of melancholy?

BOLLYWOOD PSYCHOPOLITICS

Having surveyed the evolution of Hindi movies over the last ninety-two years, we now move on to a potpourri of issues involving the Bombay film industry. Consideration of them can shed further light on important political processes and large-group psychology involving Hindi films.

The Hollywood Connection

To begin with, the term *Bollywood* (which links the Bombay film industry with Hollywood) is itself significant. It started appearing in the press only during the last decade and shows the continued hankering after Western linkages on the part of a colonized people. The fact that this term appeared on the scene when the NRIs in the United Kingdom, United States, and Canada were becoming a matter of interest to Indian moviemakers, however, suggests that the term *Bollywood* is a lexical bridge across the chasm of migration.

Beside this verbal play, there are other connections between the Bombay film industry and Hollywood. Some Hindi film stars (e.g., Shabana Azmi, Om Puri, Amrish Puri, Kabir Bedi) have acted in Hollywood movies, but by and large this has been a limited phenomenon. Official accolades from Hollywood have also been few and far between. Only two Hindi movies have received a nomination for the best foreign-language film category of the Academy Awards. These were *Mother India* (1955) and *Lagaan* (2001). Interestingly, both these movies were long, lavish, melodramatic, and set in rural backgrounds. Perhaps Hollywood prefers a rural vision of India. If correct, this is no different from the generally biased attitude of all media in the West toward the portrayal of India. This, however, has not precluded Hindi filmmakers from purloining Hollywood movie plots. Nayar (1997, 2003) has provided a detailed analysis of the extent of such pilfering and the lawsuits that have been brought against Indian film companies in this connection.

Political Movies

Political agendas have occasionally given content to Hindi movies. Matters that have invited such forays include Hindu–Muslim relations (*Padosi*, 1941; *Dharamputra*, 1961; *Bombay*, 1995), partition of India (*Nastik*, 1954; *Garam Hawa*, 1973; *Pinjar*, 2004), land taxation (*Do Beegah Zamin*, 1953), factory workers' wages (*Paigham*, 1959), the Indo-Chinese War (*Haqeeqat*, 1964), Indo-Pakistan conflicts (*LOC*, 2003; *Lakshya*, 2004) and the acquisition of near dictatorial powers by Indira Gandhi (*Aandhi*, 1975). However, these movies are exceptions. In general, Hindi movies have stayed away from political themes. Perhaps the audience, already overwhelmed by problems of daily living, is looking for escapist entertainment and not thought-provoking questions. The cinematic lack of interest in politics could also be related to the moviemakers' wish to avoid polarization of the audience into different camps; after all, Hindi movies are an all-Indian phenomenon thriving on the homogenization of mentality. Moreover, people in India are publicly quite vocal about political matters, which, as a result, are not repressed and do not need disguised presentations.

Depiction of Minorities

Most characters in Hindi movies are Hindus. This is understandable in light of the fact that Hindus constitute 80 percent of the nation's population. Some movies bend over backward to present various ethnicities together, but such fare turns out to be rather contrived; an air of caricature surrounds the depiction of minorities. Sikhs are made to appear silly, Parsis esoteric, and Christians overanglicized.[13] Muslims are also

---

13. Exceptions to this rule certainly exist; the movies *Ghadar* (2001), *Pestonjee* (1987), *Memdidi* (1964), and *Pinjar* (2004) offered favorable portrayals of Sikhs, Parsis, Christians, and Muslims, respectively.

presented in a stereotypical ways. Indeed, there was a genre of Muslim "socials" (now passé[14]) that included films like *Chaudhvin Ka Chand* (1961), *Mere Mehboob* (1963), and *Pakeezah* (1971). These movies depicted Muslim aristocracy in a highly stylized and opulent manner. While entertaining, they were socially harmful in the long run because they perpetuated a stereotypically view of Muslims as lazy, hedonistic, and given to matters of luxury and leisure.

The Significance of Names

In a medium that thrives on glossy surfaces, the names of people and things often reveal deeper group dynamics. For instance, political concerns underlie the practice of referring to all Bombay films as Hindi films. The majority of these movies are actually in Urdu or at least in a mixed Hindi–Urdu language. Their dialogue, their songs, and even their titles (from *Talaaq* to *Mere Sanam*, from *Mughal-e-Azam* to *Masoom*, from *Aakhri Khat* to *Lamhe*, and from *Taqdeer* to *Namak Haram*) are mostly in Urdu. Yet hardly any movie is called an Urdu movie. This has less to do with Urdu's Muslim connections and more with the fact that Hindi is a national language and Urdu is a regional language. Calling a movie an Urdu movie would deprive it of the chance to compete for national awards and might even subject it to different taxation regulations.

Names of film actors and actresses also reflect the psychological concerns of the masses. In the early days, when Hindu women did not appear on screen, Jewish and Christian women took on Hindu names to become popular as heroines. Many Muslim actors and actresses did the same. Yusuf Khan, Zakaria Ali Khan, Hamid Ali Khan, and Abbas

---

14. Another type of movie to have become extinct had a child as the main character. A number of such movies (*Boot Polish*, 1954; *Jagriti*, 1954; *Munna*, 1954; *Hum Panchhi Ek Daal Ke*, 1957; and *Zamin Ke Taare*, 1960) were released in the 1950s and 1960s. Child stars like Master Rumi, Baby Naaz, Baby Farida, Roop Kumar (actually Daisy Irani), and Honey Irani (now a highly acclaimed writer and filmmaker) were widely known. However, during the era of narcissistic rage (1973–1987) and the era of nostalgic defense (1988–present), there are no such stars, and the number of child-based movies has dropped. The occasional films portraying children (e.g., *Masoom*, *Rahul*) are not child-based movies in the proper sense. It seems that both the angry and happy characters of the last two eras have been so self-absorbed as to become delinked from the inner child self.

Khan became Dilip Kumar, Jayant, Ajit, and Sunjay, respectively, and Mahjabeen Ara and Mumtaz Jahan became Meena Kumari and Madhubla, respectively. Hindus, on their part, also played with their names. They often dropped their last names so that their caste or regional origins would not be identified. Ashok Kumar Gangulee, Raj Kumar Kohli, and Dharmendra Deol thus restricted themselves to Ashok Kumar, Raj Kumar, and simply Dharmendra. This tendency was not limited to those on the screen. Among the music directors, Ramchandra Chitalkar became C. Ramchandra, Arjun Churmalani became C. Arjun, and Roshan Lal Malhotra became simply Roshan. However, as the movie industry advanced and as entry into the profession became less stigmatized, regional last names of Hindus (e.g., Khanna, Matondkar) began to appear among actors and actresses, and Muslims (e.g., Naseeruddin Shah, Shah Rukh Khan, Saif Ali Khan, Aamir Khan, Salman Khan) stopped taking on Hindu names. False homogenization was beginning to give way to authenticity.

Regardless of their religious affiliation, actors who frequently played the role of villains kept one-word names (e.g., Pran, Ajit, Jeevan, Habib, Shetty, Ranjit) in contrast with the usual two-word names (e.g., Raj Kapoor, Ashok Kumar, Sunil Dutt) of those who played heroes. The same was true when it came to vamps (e.g., Helen, Cucko, Bindu, Nilofer, Faryal) and heroines (e.g., Mala Sinha, Waheeda Rehman, and Shabana Azmi). It is also true of those who exclusively played comic roles (e.g., Bhagwan, Gope, Sheikh, Mehmood, Mukri, Asrani, Paintal, and Polson[15]). This was because the actors and actresses playing unsavory characters perhaps felt a greater need to hide their communal origins. At a deeper level, it also signified a contra-oedipal defiance of affiliation at large.

Religion and Secularism

The attitude of Hindi films toward religion has been a fundamentally accepting one. Movies that are manifestly about religious epics and characters (e.g., *Sampoorn Ramayana*, *Jai Santoshi Maat*, and *Khuda Ki*

---

15. Exceptions in this regard include villains (e.g., N. A. Ansari and Prem Chopra), vamps (e.g., Kuldip Kaur, and Aruna Irani), and comedians (e.g., Johnny Walker and Rajinder Nath) with two-word names.

Shaan) aside, all movies treat religious beliefs with respect and credulousness. A tear rolling down a *Murti's* (religious idol) cheek and a flower that drops from the *Murti's* hands on the temple floor at opportune moments are taken to be divine signals of unacceptability of an intended action or God's blessing, respectively. Such accepting attitude is extended to all religions of the land. Scenes of Muslim mosques and shrines as well as Christian churches are treated with comparable dignity and their sacredness remains unquestioned. In the same vein, whenever a character is shown to be overtly agnostic or atheistic, sooner or later he sees the error of his ways and returns to the ever-comforting fold of religion. Indian movies, like Indian people, are fundamentally God-loving.

The fact that all religions of the land receive equally respectful treatment in the movies is also reflected in the completely smooth and harmonious mixing of people of different religious faiths in the profession itself. Hindus, Muslims, Sikhs, Christians, Parsis, and Jews all work in a remarkable spirit of collaboration. It seems that what the Greeks had intended to achieve by establishing the Olympic Games, namely a world of equality and harmony, has been mastered by the Bollywood community. This is no mean achievement in a nation of great religious, ethnic, linguistic, and cultural diversity. The old adage that art can inform society better than science or politics has been proven to be correct after all!

CODA

In this chapter we have offered an overview of Hindi movies and the psychopolitical undercurrents in Indian society that sustain them and, in turn, are sustained by them. What remains most impressive is the mesmerizing power these movies have over the nation's masses. The reasons for this remain unclear, and unanswered questions abound in the realm. For instance, could it be that these movies have such a hold because they embody, express, and seek to resolve the psychosocial conflicts of the modal audience? Or is it possible that watching so many movies itself constitutes an addictive defense against the hardships of life in India? Does the celluloid screen simply buttress the "waking screen" (Pacella 1980) of the audience or entirely replace it? Could it be that movies in India represent a secular religion for a people who seem to have an intrinsic yearning for worship? Could going to the movies be a form of a *darshan* (Hindi word for catching the sight of revered gurus or religious icons) for a population that, in the words of Chauncey Gardiner,[16] "likes to watch"?

REFERENCES

Akhtar, J. N. (1962). Foreword. In *Gaata Jaaye Banjara*, ed. S. Ludhianvi. New Delhi: Punjabi Pustak Bhandar.

Akhtar, S. (2000). Mental pain and the cultural ointment of poetry. *International Journal of Psycho-Analysis* 81:229–243.

Arlow, J. A. (1986). The poet as prophet: a psychoanalytic perspective. *Psychoanalytic Quarterly* 55:53–68.

Barnouw, E., and Krishnaswamy, S. (1963). *Indian Film*. New York: Columbia University Press.

Beeman, W. O. (1981). The use of music in popular film: East and West. *India International Centre Quarterly* 8:77–87.

Corliss, R. (2002a). Going Bollywood. *Time*, July 22, p. 4.

——— (2002b). Love and death in Bollywood. *Time Europe*, December 30, pp. 26–27.

Erikson, E. H. (1950). *Childhood and Society*. New York: Norton.

Freud, S. (1900). The interpretation of dreams. *Standard Edition* 4/5:1–626.

——— (1909). Family romances. *Standard Edition* 9:237–241.

——— (1910). A special type of object choice made by men. *Standard Edition* 11:163–175.

——— (1912). On the universal tendency to debasement in sphere of love. *Standard Edition* 11:178–190.

——— (1918). From the history of an infantile neurosis. *Standard Edition* 17:3–23.

——— (1920). Beyond the pleasure principle. *Standard Edition* 18:7–64.

Gokulsingh, K. M., and Dissanayake, W. (1998). *Indian Popular Cinema. A Narrative of Cultural Change*. Staffordshire, England: Trentham.

Juluri, V. (1999). Global weds local: the reception of *Hum Aapke Hain Kaun! European Journal of Cultural Studies* 2:231–248.

---

16. This was the television-addicted protagonist of the 1979 movie *Being There*, starring Peter Sellers.

Kabir, N. M. (1999). *Talking Films: Conversations on Hindi Cinema with Javed Akhtar.* New Delhi: Oxford University Press.

——— (2001). *Bollywood: The Indian Cinema Story.* London: Channel Four Books.

Kakar, S. (1989). *Intimate Relations. Exploring Indian Sexuality.* New Delhi: Penguin.

Kalin, C. (1997). Emigration without leaving home. In *Immigrant Experiences: Personal Narrative and Psychological Analysis,* ed. P. H. Olovity and C. Kahn, pp. 255–273. Cranbury, NJ: Associated University Press.

Katz, E. (1994). *The Film Encyclopedia.* New York: HarperCollins.

Kernberg, O. F. (1975). *Borderline Conditions and Pathological Narcissism.* New York: Jason Aronson.

Klein, M. (1935). A contribution to the psycho-genesis of manic depressive states. In *Love, Guilt and Reparation and Other Works 1921–1945,* pp. 262–289. New York: Free Press, 1975.

Kohut, H. (1971). *Analysis of the Self.* New York: International Universities Press.

——— (1972). Thoughts on narcissism and narcissistic rage. *Psychoanalytic Study of the Child* 27:360–400. New Haven, CT: Yale University Press.

Mahler, M. A., Pine, F., and Bergman, A. (1975). *The Psychological Birth of the Human Infant.* New York: Basic Books.

Mohamed, K. (1984). *Times of India,* January 8.

Nandy, A. (1995). An intelligent critic's guide to Indian cinema. In *The Savage Freud and Other Essays on Possible and Retrievable Selves,* ed. A. Nandy, pp. 196–236. New Delhi: Oxford University Press.

——— (1998). Indian popular cinema as a slum's eye view of politics. In *The Secret Politics of Our Desires. Innocence, Culpability and Indian Popular Cinema,* ed. A. Nandy, pp. 1–18. New Delhi: Oxford University Press.

Nayar, S. J. (1997). The values of fantasy: Indian popular cinema through Western scripts. *Journal of Popular Culture* 31:73–90.

——— (2003). Dreams, dharma and Mrs. Doubtfire. Exploring Hindi popular cinema via its chutneyed Western scripts. *Journal of Popular Film and Television* 31:73–82.

Pacella, B. (1980). The primal matrix configuration. In *Rapprochement: The Critical Subphase of Separation-Individuation,* ed. R. F. Lax, S. Bach, and A. J. Burland, pp. 117–133. New York: Jason Aronson.

Prathikanti, S. (1997). East Indian American families. In *Working with Asian Americans: A Guide for Clinicians,* ed. E. Lee, pp. 79–100. New York: Guilford.

Rajadhyaksha, A., and Willemen, P. (1999). *Encyclopedia of Indian Cinema.* London & New Delhi: British Film Institute and Oxford University Press.

Sardar, Z. (1998). Dilip Kumar made me do it. In *The Secret Politics of Our Desires. Innocence, Culpability and Indian Popular Cinema*, ed. A. Nandy, pp. 19–91. New Delhi: Oxford University Press.

Srinivasan, R. (2003). Patriot games and resident non-Indians. May 22, 2003 posting. www.rediff.com.

Tang, N. M., and Smith, B. L. (1996). The eternal triangle across cultures: Oedipus, Hsueh, Ganesh. *Psychoanalytic Study of the Child* 51:562–579.

Tremblay, R. C. (1996). Representation and reflection of self and society in the Bombay cinema. *Contemporary South Asia* 5:295–308.

Tummala-Narra, P., Bewtra, A., and Akhtar, S. (2005, in press). The celluloid Ganges: an annotated filmography of the Indian diaspora. *International Journal of Applied Psychoanalytic Studies*, vol. 2, no. 3.

Varde, A. (2001). *The Hundred Greatest Films of All Time*. Bombay: Magna.

BODY

7

The Cloistered Passion of Radha and Krishna

Sudhir Kakar and John Munder Ross

> Two birds of beautiful plumage, comrades,
> Inseparable, live on the selfsame tree.
> One bird eats the fruit of pleasure and pain;
> The other looks on without eating.
>
> *Shvetashvatara Upanishad* (IV.6)

A psychoanalytic patient, a passionate man of twenty-four, found himself avoiding more and more the pleasure of intercourse with his girlfriend. Yet another of his symptoms was his inability to weep, much to his consternation, denting his image of himself as a romantic.

A dream brought to light one level of his terror, and desire. In it the patient dived with other children into a great gulf. He emerged as if uncertain of his body—of what lay below the neck—and found himself crossing his old school's soccer field, making his way not to the boy's but rather to the girl's changing room. In his associations he talked of the eerie feeling that, with penetration, he was welded to his lover, as if their pubic hair were somehow squashed, almost glued together. Her breasts, so delightful in their spongy roundness, seemed to seep into his chest and become his own. Upon climaxing he felt in an almost altered state of consciousness, that he was taking in her moistened vagina with his penis and found himself fighting off unnamed fears, becoming chilled and anxious. All of a sudden he remarked on his inadvertent refusal to weep, equating the watering of his eyes with the lubrication of a woman's genitals.

The analysand at last discovered and voiced what seemed his most secret of wishes. He wanted to be as beautiful and bountiful as his lover; he wished to be a woman. Tasting the illusion, satisfying this surprising desire in the safety of the analytic space, he wondered whether he would reemerge from a woman as a man—ambitious, powerful, and rich.

After a pause the patient comforted himself with thoughts about the ubiquity of what had seemed an altogether idiosyncratic perversity. Perhaps his analyst "knew" women in much the same way as he did. Had not the self-revelatory hero of Janet Malcolm's *The Impossible Profession*, the dreamy workmanlike amalgam portrayed by her as the typical psychoanalyst, confessed the source of his failure to speak or write more? To do so, the hero of the book lamented, would be to symbolically fulfill a treasured but shameful wish—to parade before the gaze of others as a beautiful woman, and this before analysts who saw into people's souls.

Another patient, in imitating an illicit love affair with the wife of a businessman for whom he worked, had crossed daunting social barriers of caste and class. The couple had secretly met on three occasions but had not yet become sexually intimate. An illness was preceded by a dream about the long-desired moment of consummation. In it, as the would-be lovers finally embrace, he discovers to his excited horror that the woman has grown a penis that is rubbing against the wet lips of his newly formed vagina in a welter of unknown but exquisite sensations. Soon he felt strange changes taking place in his body: parts of it becoming soft and delicate like a woman's while others became even stronger and muscular. His terror began mounting when he began having visions of Hindu gods and goddesses—Shiva and Parvati, Krishna and Radha, Rama and Sita—in amorous embrace. The sensations and feelings of the gods and goddesses in intercourse, he felt, were being manifested in his own person, succeeding each other with a frightening rapidity.

It is some secrets of these patients—and of many normal others—that we now address in the paradigmatic love story of Hindu India. For an Indian—or, more exactly, a Hindu—the love of Radha, the beautiful cowherdess who later became a goddess for some cults, and Krishna, the youthful dark god who is the object of widespread devotion, is less a story remembered than a random succession of episodes seen and heard, sung and danced. Over the centuries their liaison has been portrayed in thousands of exquisite miniature paintings that have fixed the lovers in separation and union, longing and abandonment. The story is heard whenever we listen to the great vocalists of Indian classical music—from Kumara Gandharva to Jasraj—sing the devotional songs of medieval saints who in their poems sometimes watch and at other times participate in the lovemaking as Krishna's beloved. The story grips our imagination every time we behold the animated expressions, flashing eyes, and sinuous movements of an Indian dancer who (as Radha) dances her anger at Krishna's infidelities or (as Krishna) begs forgiveness for his impetuous dalliance. The affair is re-created each time a Krishna devotee participates in the communal singing of an episode from the story in a temple, and especially when he or she, possessed by the spirit of one of the lovers, feels impelled to get up and ecstatically dance the god or his beloved.

The Radha–Krishna legend, then, is not a narrative in the sense of an orderly progression whose protagonists have a shared past and are progressing toward a tragic or happy future. It is more an evocation and elaboration of the here-and-now of passion, an attempt to capture the exciting, fleeting moments of the senses and the baffling ways in which pleasures and pains are felt before the retrospective recollection, which, in trying to regain a lost control over emotional life, edits away love's inevitable confusions. It is not tragic but tender, and, ultimately, cheerful.

The sybaritic tenderness enveloping the cameos of the lovers is striking. A long line of bards and balladeers, most of them indebted to the twelfth-century Sanskrit poet Jayadeva, who decisively shaped the legend's outlines, have often described the setting of their meetings. A Hindu needs only to close his eyes and remember to see Vrindavan, an Indian garden of Eden, spring into existence. In the perpetual sunshine of the myth, distinct from the mists of history, a forest thicket of the banks of the river Yamuna awakens to life on a tropical spring day. The mustard fields at the edge of the forest, with their thick carpet of dazzling yellow flowers, stretch far into the distance. The air is redolent with the perfume of the pollen shaken loose from newly blossomed jasmine and bunches of flame-colored mimosa flowers hanging round and heavy from the trees. The ears are awash with the humming of bees, the cries of cuckoos, and the distant tinkling of bells on the necks of grazing cattle. The call of Krishna's flute comes floating through the forest thicket, further agitating the already unquiet senses, making for an inner uprising and an alien invasion. The story, aiming to fix the essence of youthful ardor, has an amorous rather than geographical landscape as its location; its setting is neither social nor historical but sensuous.

In the falling dusk, Nanda, Krishna's foster father and the chief of a community of cowherds, asks Radha to escort Krishna home through the forest. On the way, in a grove, their "secret passion triumphs." Radha's thoughts come to be absorbed by Krishna, who, however, is unfaithful to her as he sports with other cowherdesses—hugging one, kissing another, and caressing yet another dark beauty.

> When he quickens all things to create bliss in the world
> His soft black sinuous lotus limbs
> Begin the festival of love
> And beautiful cowherd girls wildly
> Wind him in their bodies.
> Friend, in spring young Hari [Krishna] plays
> Like erotic mood incarnate.[1]

Radha is jealous as she imagines the "vines of his great throbbing arms circle a thousand cowherdesses." But more than that, she is infused with all the confusing emotions of a proud, intense woman who feels deserted by her lover.

> My heart values his vulgar ways,
> Refuses to admit my rage,
> Feels strangely elated,
> And keeps denying his guilt.
> When he steals away without me
> To indulge his craving
> For more young women,
> My perverse heart
> Only wants Krishna back
> What can I do?

---

1. The verses from the *Gitagovinda* quoted here are taken from the scholarly yet intensely lyrical translation by Barbara Stoler Miller (1977).

Solitary grief and images of love betrayed and passion lost, re-created in reverie, alternate and reinforce each other but seem somehow benign.

My eyes close languidly as I feel
The flesh quiver on his cheek,
My body is moist with sweat; he is
Shaking from the wine of lust.
Friend, bring Kesi's sublime tormentor to revel with me!
I've gone mad waiting for his fickle love to change.

The power of Radha's yearning works a change in Krishna. Of all the *gopis* (cowherdesses), interchangeable suppliers of pleasure and feelings of conquest, Radha begins to stand out in Krishna's mind as someone special who is desired in her uniqueness. In Maurice Valency's formulation, from the heroic lover for whom no woman is exceptional and who simply desires a variety of amatory dalliances, Krishna becomes the romantic lover impelled toward a single irreplaceable mistress (Valency 1958). The unheeding pursuit of pleasure, a bewildered Krishna discovers, had been brought to a halt by pleasure's worst enemies—memory and attachment.

Her joyful responses to my touch,
Trembling liquid movement of her eyes,
Fragrance from her lotus mouth,
A sweet ambiguous stream of words,
Nectar from her red berry lips—
Even when the sensuous objects are gone,
My mind holds on to her in a trance.
How does the wound of her desertion deepen?

Having been the god who strove to please himself alone, Krishna has become a man for whom the partner's well-being assumes an importance easily the equal of his own. He discovers that he would rather serve and adore than vanquish and demand. As a tale of love this transformative moment from desire's sensations to love's adoration gives the story of Radha and Krishna its singular impact.

It is a remarkable coincidence that three of the world's best-known works of romantic love that occupy pivotal positions in their respective cultures—Beroul's Tristan and Isolde in Europe, Nizami's Layla and

Majnun in the Islamic world, and Jayadeva's Gitagovinda in India—
were all produced roughly at the same time: in the twelfth century.
Whether this represents happenstance, coincidence, or springs from
sociohistorical trends coalescing across the globe is beyond our scope
in this more life historical endeavor. However, it is striking that the
poetry of passion should predate and possibly prefigure important
cultural-historical changes in Europe, India, and the Middle East. It is
as if the unfolding discovery of each other portrayed in the love story
sheds light on what is fundamental to the human spirit.

To continue the story: hearing of Krishna's remorse and of his attachment to her, Radha, dressed and ornamented for love, awaits Krishna
at their trysting place in the forest. She lingers in vain for Krishna does
not come. Radha is consumed by jealousy as she imagines him engaged
in an amorous encounter with a rival. When Krishna finally does appear, Radha spurns him angrily:

> Dark from kissing her kohl-blackened eyes
> At dawn your lips match your body's colour, Krishna
> Damn you Madhava! Go! Kesava leave me!
> Don't plead your lies with me!
> Go after her, Krishna!
> She will ease your despair.

But, in separation, Radha and Krishna long for each other with a
mounting sense of desolation. Eventually, Radha's friend persuades her
to abandon her modesty and pride and go to her lover.

> Your full hips and breasts are heavy to bear.
> Approach with anklets ringing!
> Their sound inspires lingering feet.
> Run with the gait of a wild goose!
> Madhu's tormentor
> Is faithful to you, fool.
> Follow him. Radhika!

In the full throes of a sexual excitement—when even her "modesty left in shame"—Radha rushes to meet an equally ardent (and repentant) lover. Krishna sings:

Throbbing breasts aching for love's embrace are hard to touch.
Rest these vessels on my chest!
Queen love's burning fire!
Narayana [Krishna] is faithful now. Love me Radhika!
Offer your lips' nectar to revive a dying slave, Radha!
This obsessed mind and listless body burn in love's desolation,
Narayana is faithful now. Love me, Radhika!

Once the ecstatic lovemaking has subsided momentarily in an orgasmic release, a playful Radha asks Krishna to rearrange her clothes and her tousled hair:

Paint a leaf on my breasts!
Put colour on my cheeks!
Lay a girdle on my hips!
Twine my heavy braid with flowers!
Fix rows of bangles on my hands
And jewelled anklets on my feet!
Her yellow-robed lover
Did what Radha said.

Jayadeva, legend has it, hesitant to commit sacrilege by having the god touch Radha's feet—the usual sign of a submissive lower status—was unable to pen the last lines and went out to bathe; when he returned the found that Krishna himself had completed the verse in his absence!

The fascination of Jayadeva's creation is, of course, also due to its musical form. Jayadeva set each canto of the love poem to a different musical mode (*raga*) and rhythm (*tala*). It is a work that succeeding generations have regarded a marvel of music as much as of language and meaning. And music, we know, that fine-tuned language of the senses, best captures the Dionysian—or rather, in our context, the Krishnanian—spirit and sensual spontaneity of the erotic. The great Persian poet Rumi has aptly described the house of love as having doors and roof made of music, melodies, and poetry. The sensibilities and pulse of lovers, and of others with either the potential for love or its haunting memory, can be reproduced in music with greater fidelity than in words since there is a direct rather than signified correspondence between musical forms and the forms of emotional life. Love is not *about* something: it *is*. Jayadeva seems to have intuitively known that the sensual word is too heavy and too dense to be sustained by speech; only music can express it.

The story of Radha and Krishna, as it has come down to us today, differs from Jayadeva's version in only one significant respect. Jayadeva merely hints at the illicit nature of their love when he has an older Radha change from young Krishna's protective escort to become his lover, thereby also defying the authority and instructions of the chief of cowherds:

> "Clouds thicken the sky.
> Tamala trees darken the forest.
> The night frightens him.
> Radha, you take him home!"
> They leave at Nanda's order,
> Passing trees in thickets on the way,
> Until secret passions of Radha and Madhava
> Triumph on the Jamuna riverbank.

Later poets, notably Vidyapati, who tend to focus more on Radha and her love than on Krishna, gave the illicit in the story a more concrete cast and a specific content. Radha is another man's wife and her liaison with Krishna, whatever its meaning in mystical allegory, is plainly adulterous in human terms. Radha is certainly not a paragon of womanly virtues detailed in Hindu texts, nor does she come close to any of the good or bad mother-goddesses of Indian mythology and religion.

She is a more sophisticated character, more rounded and complex than a toddler's (or a Majnun's) dichotomous imagery would allow for. Radha is, indeed, a figure of the imagination of the boy just as he begins to discover his and his mother's sexuality. Rivals have just begun to enter the scene and have not yet been re-created as internal inhibitions, jaundicing any delight in the mother's eroticism. There is an unobstructed joy to the sensuality of this all-too-brief era, a lack of self-consciousness about experimenting with its variations. In her passionate craving for sexual union with her lover and in her desperate suffering in his absence, Radha is simply the personification of *mahabhava*, a "great feeling" that is heedless of social proprieties and unbounded by conventions.

Before continuing in our own interpretation of the *mahabhava* of the legend, we must first briefly locate the love of Radha and Krishna in its cultural-historical context. As various scholars have pointed out, many different Indian traditions—religious and erotic, classical literary, and folk—have converged and coalesced in the poetical renditions of the myth, especially Jayadeva's Geetagovinda, to give that particular work an allure that extends over large parts of the subcontinent (Siegel 1978).

In India passion love first appeared in the court poetry and drama of the so-called classical period of Hindu civilization, spanning the first few centuries of the Christian era. Earlier, in the epics of Mahabharata and Ramayana, love was usually a matter of straightforward desire and its gratification (for a discussion of erotic love in ancient India see De 1959, Meyer 1930). This was especially so for the man, for whom a woman was an instrument of pleasure and an object of the senses (*indriyartha*)—one physical need among many others. There is an idealization of marriage in the epics, yes, but chiefly as a social and religious act. The obligation of conjugal love and the virtue of chastity within marriage were primarily demanded of the wife, while few limits were set on a husband who lived under and looked up at a licentious heaven teeming with lusty gods and "heavenly" whores—otherworldly and utterly desirable at once, and most eager to give and take pleasure. Their Hindu pantheon is not unlike the Greeks' Olympus where gods and goddesses sport and politic with a welcome absence of moralistic subterfuge.

The Buddhist domination of Indian society that followed brought with it Buddhism's somber view of life, in which the god of love was identified with Mara or Death. The new cosmology it imposed was not particularly conducive to developing a literature of passionate love. Nor did love enter through the backdoor of erotic mysticism. In the Therigatha, or psalms of notable sisters of the Buddhist order, marked by dutiful daughterly sentiments toward the Buddha, there is none of the eroticism of their medieval Christian counterparts who in their passionate outpourings conceived of Christ as a youthful bridegroom.

All this seems to have changed radically with the dawn of the classical period that spanned the first six to seven centuries of the present era. In the poetry and drama flourishing at the courts, love became a predominant theme, indeed one overshadowing every other sentiment. It is a love that is both deeply sensual and molded by mutual passion. The woman is as ardent as the man and initiates the wooing quite as often. Masculinity is not equated with seduction and conquest. Indeed the surviving poems of the few women poets show them to be even freer in their expression than their male counterparts.

Yet, though one's ego or self is not at stake, the verse depicts an eroticism that is narcissistic in spirit, more hedonist than impassioned. The Sanskrit poems and dramas are characterized by a playful enjoyment of love's ambiguities, a delighted savoring of its pleasures and a consummately refined suffering of its sorrows. Spontaneity, fervid abandon, and exaltation are generally absent from this poetry. Apart from one or two notable exceptions, the rendering of love is on a miniature scale, corresponding to the paintings for which the culture is known. Short stanzas seek to freeze one or another of love's emotions; they are cameos yielding glimpses into arresting erotic moments. What is considered important—and this is the core of the Indian theory of aesthetics—is to capture the *rasa*, literally, "flavor" or "essence" or the mood, of a particular passionate instant, which can then be relished by the poetically cultivated connoisseur. The intensity of the mood is not enhanced through psychological depth but by the accumulation of sensuous detail.

Blurring the boundaries between internal feeling and external sensation, the poet seldom treats love as something ethereal or lifts from it a sentiment to be evaluated. Rather it is equated with a definite sensation or a feeling in its concrete bodily manifestation. As Barbara Miller remarks in relation to the Gitagovinda:

> Passion is made palpable through the sensuous descriptions of movements and physical forms. Seasonal changes in nature and bodily signs of inner feelings are colored richly to create a dense atmosphere of passion. [Miller 1977]

The emphasis, replete with developmental resources in the early genital stage and its revival in pubescence, is on sexual self-discovery. The other is a source of excitement and delight, enlivening the senses and the body with her image and aura. This other is to be explored thoroughly, in enormous detail, and therefore she is not quickly abandoned. Yet her inner life or her past and future are not subjects of the entrancement; the impulse is not one of fierce monogamy.

For most modern readers who have an affinity for the personal and the subjective, the emphasis of classical Indian literature on love as a depersonalized voluptuous state, while delighting the senses, does not touch the heart. For those whose sensibility has been molded by romanticism and individualism it is difficult to identify with the impersonal protagonists of Sanskrit and Tamil love poems. These are not a particular man or woman but man and woman as such—provided he is handsome, she beautiful, and both young. The face of the heroine, for instance, is always like a moon or lotus flower, eyes like waterlilies or those of a fawn. She always stoops slightly from the weight of her full breasts, improbable fleshy flowers of rounded perfection that do not even admit a blade of grass between them. The waist is slim, with three folds, the thighs round and plump, like the trunk of an elephant or a banana tree. The navel is deep, the hips heavy. These lyrical yet conventional descriptions of body parts seem to operate like collective fetishes, culturally approved cues for the individual to allow himself to indulge erotic excitement without the risk of surrender or merger.

Now, a facet of the beloved woman's beauty is certainly impersonal in the sense that it is nature's gift, especially to youth, and its minimal presence is necessary for the glance to become a gaze, for the poet to wax lyrical. As Auden remarks, "A girl who weighs two hundred pounds and a woman of eighty may both have beautiful faces in the personal sense, but men do not fall in love with them" (Auden 1973, p. 67). For our tastes, however, the part played by impersonal beauty is receding in favor of a personal beauty that is more an individual than a natural or cultural creation. To borrow from the Brontës, "Beauty lies in the eye of the beholder," whose scrutiny sees in lustrous eyes windows to the soul and reflections of the whole. The lust evoked by looking at a woman in parts—and at the parts of a woman, as in most traditional Indian poetry—is for a mature modern man no longer solely determined by her conformity to a uniform cultural model. Rather it also resides in a feeling for her uniqueness in which even her flaws are cherished. It is now the fleeting yet characteristic trivialities—the narrowing of her eyes in a quizzical smile, the nibbling of the fleshy part of the lower lip when engrossed in thought—that fascinate and enthral the lover, the flash of aesthetic admiration superseded by the wave of adoration. In the verses of Shakespeare's great sonnet:

> My mistress' eyes are nothing like the sun;
> . . .
> My mistress, when she walks, treads on the ground.
> And yet, by heaven, I think my love as rare
> As any she belied with false compare. [Shakespeare, Sonnet 130]

A woman is a woman not out of her predictable construction but because she is herself, her limbs and features moved by her destined femininity. Appreciating her individuality goes hand in hand with what Jung, and later Mahler, termed the lover's individuation. Its attainment, relatively speaking, is a developmental milestone that brings to a close the early dyadic struggles of infancy and introduces the growing child to a world of whole objects or person, each with his or her complex attributes. Loving these people, a child or the adult proceeds beyond the self and its sensations for their own reflexive sake. To do otherwise, to reify sybaritics, is to deny the regressive and progressive thrusts of genuine passion.

Indian poetry becomes inaccessible, even boring, when its early freshness begins to wilt under scholastic dictates, which become more and more compelling in the later centuries. Not unlike the cataloging efforts of modern sexologists, Sanskrit poetics and "erotics" began to define, analyze, and categorize the many moods and situations of love. Lovers—men and women—were stereotyped according to the ways they approached and reacted to love. They were further divided and subdivided according to rank, character, and circumstances, as well as by the different shades of their feelings and gestures. An initial revolutionary aesthetic fervor gave way to the bureaucratization of beauty. With its insistence on the appropriate combination of types, feelings, and situations, the scholastic steamroller gained momentum and, in its way, crushed the creative expression of passionate love as effectively as epic indifference or Buddhist disapproval.

From the sixth century onward, first in the south and then in the north, another auspicious shift took place that led to a reemergence of passionate love. As with most things Indian, the change originated in the religious sphere but then expanded to influence Hindu culture and sensibility in such a profound way that its reverberations are still felt today. Scholars have called the shift *bhakti*, the rise of devotional religions in rebellion against the petrification of contemporary Hindu practice. Drawing on conventions of the classical literature of love and using an existing pan-Indian stock of symbols and figures of speech, the *bhakti* poets nonetheless strive for spontaneous, direct, personal expression of feeling rather than a rarified cultivation of aesthetic effect and the emotion recollected preferred by Sanskrit poets (Ramanujan 1981).

Although linked to the heroine and hero of classical love poetry in many ways, the figures of Radha and Krishna are primarily products of the *bhakti* movement, whose principal mood has always been erotic. Here the culture has imprinted its particular stamp upon the sensual experience—in contrast to much Western poetry of sexual mysticism—though Radha and Krishna are not figures of erotic allegory. *Bhakti* extols possessing and being possessed by the god. For it sexual love is where the fullest possession, the "closest touch of all," takes place. With this the creators and audiences of *bhakti* poetry seek to project themselves into Radha's love for Krishna through poems that recount all its passionate phases. *Bhakti* is preeminently feminine in its orientation, and the erotic love for Krishna (or Shiva as the case may be) is envisioned entirely from the woman's viewpoint, or at least from her position as imagined by the man. The male devotees, saints, and poets must all adopt a feminine posture and persona to re-create Radha's responses in themselves. Radha's passionate love for Krishna, raised to its highest intensity, is not an allegory for religious passion but *is* religious passion (Ramanujan 1981, Siegal 1978). Jayadeva thus does not need to make a distinction or choose between the religious and the erotic when he introduces the subject matter of his poem by saying:

If remembering Hari [Krishna] enriches your heart,
If his arts of seduction arouse you,
Listen to Jayadeva's speech
In these sweet soft lyrical songs.

Befitting his status as the *adi-guru* (first teacher) of Radha–Krishna cults, Jayadeva knows that the enrichment of the heart and the arousal of senses belong together. Moreover, this coincidence of knowledge and feeling is intimately tied to an illusion, or at least a crossing over, of genders.

The augmentation of passion, or, more specifically, the heightening of sexual excitement, is then the great feeling, the *mahabhava*, that pervades the Radha–Krishna legend. Radha incarnates a state of permanent amorous tension, a here-and-now of desire that carries within itself a future expectation of pleasurable release but . . . oh, not yet! Her concern is not with "lineaments of gratified desire" but with their anticipation. Radha personifies an enduring arousal that does not seek orgasmic resolution, an embodiment of ideals elsewhere put into Tantric practices. Hers is an effort to reach the very essence of eroticism. As she herself says in one of Vidyapati's songs:

> Through all the ages he [Krishna] has been clasped
> To my breast,
> Yet my desire never abates.
> I have seen subtle people sink in passion
> But none came so close to the heart of the fire. [Translated by Dimock
> and Levertov 1967]

In her interviews with the temple dancers of Orissa, the anthropologist Frederique Marglin highlighted the fact that when these women talk of the love (*prema*) of Radha and other cowherdesses, they do not mean a chaste, platonic love. Rather they refer specifically to the fantasy—conscious in this case but unconscious in many others—of unending and sustained sexual excitement (Marglin 1982). The absence of *kama* or lust in Radha's love for Krishna does not mean an absence of desire, but simply of orgasm. The dancers, who seek to enact for themselves the tension and intensity of the mythical cowherdesses, explicate the distinction by stating that one of Krishna's names is *Acyuta*, "the one whose seed does not fall." Marglin writes:

> What is the meaning of Krishna's retention of his seed? My informant delineated several levels of meaning. First, there is the testimony of everyday experience, in which sexual pleasure is only momentary. After orgasm the pleasurable erotic tension is gone; in such a manner one attains only temporary pleasure or happiness (*khyanika sukha*). Furthermore, by ejaculating one loses one's strength and becomes old. In this world, the world of *samsara*, pleasure is brief and one begets children, whereas in

the divine play of Krishna there is continuous (*nitya*) pleasure and no children. The *gopis* are not impregnated. . . . The shedding of the seed has ulterior consequences, i.e., a birth. Krishna's erotic dalliances with the gopis has no ulterior purpose or consequence. It exists for itself, in itself. [Marglin 1982]

It is indeed a dwelling in the immediacy of excitement, a locking in of body and mind in total involvement.

Using classical conventions in which sexual excitement is denoted by certain bodily manifestations such as sweating and the bristling of hair (the mention of sexual organs and genital sensations were always crude and unacceptable), poem after poem seeks to convey the *rasa* of Radha's arousal. In giving central place to the body in the depiction of erotic passions—which are, after all, ideas that the mind would not entertain unless it were united to the body and dependent on it for its survival—the *bhakti* poets seem to intuitively recognize and affirm the truth of Auden's assertion that "Our bodies cannot love: / But, without one / what works of love could we do" (Auden 1973, p. 536). In Radha's excitement, produced by the anticipation of intercourse,

> She bristles with pain, sucks in breath
> Cries, shudders, gasps,
> Broods deep, reels, stammers,
> Falls, raises herself, then faints.
> When fevers of passion rage so high,
> A frail girl may live by your charm. [Miller 1977, p. 89][2]

While in the sensuous fervor of foreplay,

> There was a shudder in her whispering voice.
> She was shy to frame her words.
> What has happened tonight to lovely Radha?
> Now she consents, now she is afraid.
> When asked for love, she closes up her eyes
> Eager to reach the ocean of desire.
> He begs her for a kiss.
> She turns her mouth away

---

2. See also the poems in Dimock and Levertov 1967, pp. 7 and 11.

And then, like a night lily, the moon seized her
She felt his touch startling her girdle.
She knew her love treasure was being robbed.
With her dress she covered up her breasts.
The treasure was left uncovered. [Bhattacharya 1963, p. 41]

At first perusal the large number of Radha–Krishna poems that describe the near harrowing effects of their separation on Radha do not seem to support the contention that sexual excitement is the central emotion and its generation their chief object. Much of the content of the separation poems, however, consists of Radha's recollections of their erotic pleasure—an effort to retain expectancy through reminiscence. Further, in romantic literature around the world, the division of lovers has been a well-known device for whetting erotic hunger. In life, as in art, turnings in the path of love's fulfillment have always been found necessary to swell the libidinal tide. Separateness and union are not different categories of love, as the convention of Indian poetics would have it, but are merely different phases of the cycle of love, both intimately connected through the workings of desire. The lover's and the poet's dwelling on apartness represents his or her renouncing a possession that would deflate desire. Erotic passion, in de Rougemont's (1963) anthropomorphic formulation, always invents distance in order to exult itself more completely. Below the surface sadness lies the lover's *need* to create impediments to the enjoyment of their love, to *deliciously* postpone delight, to suspend ecstasy in time, make it all last forever.

Sexual excitement is also a mental state, the product of those fantasies wherein, as Robert Stoller (1979) has pointed out, one oscillates between an anticipation of danger and the expectation of replacing danger with pleasure. The major fantasies, largely unconscious, which are reflected in the trembling attraction of Radha's love for Krishna, are decisively formed and colored by the theme of a forbidden crossing of boundaries.

First, in the pervasive presence of the adulterous in the narrative there is an illicit transgression of moral limits. Second, in striving to entertain the erotic feelings and sensations of the other sex, a lover would violate his primal sexual demarcation as a male. Furthermore, the arousal provoked by these fantasies is both preserved and brought to a pitch by the stealth and secrecy in which the crossing of such bounds takes place.

The most obvious manifestation of the illicit, involving the crossing of boundaries set by social mores and norms, is found in the adulterous and later accounts that saddle Radha with a husband, throwing in a mother-in-law for good measure. These persistently underline the adulterous nature of her love for Krishna. There was, of course, much theological uneasiness regarding this circumstance. Some commentators went to great lengths to explain why, since Krishna is god, he could not have actually coveted the wife of another. Others strained to prove the contrary, explaining that precisely because Krishna is god he is not bound by normal human restrictions. In the end, and perhaps inevitably, the community's quest for pleasure triumphed over its theological scruples in firmly demanding that the mythical lovers be accepted as unambiguously adulterous.

The identification of the adulterous with the thrilling and romantic is common enough in the Western literary tradition, evident in the etiquette of Aquitaine and the novels of our own day. But in the Indian context the link is possessed of a special resonance since there the dichotomy between the conjugal and the adulterous had remained sharp and charged with tension over many centuries.[3]

In the ritual sphere the god and goddess of sexual love have always been segregated from deities who preside over marriage and fertility. Even today in India the so-called love marriage, almost a contradiction in terms and the subject of much excited gossip when it occurs, is mostly met with in the fantastical world of movies and is generally deemed a daring Western import of the urbanized and presumably licentious upper classes.

As far as legalities are concerned both the conventions and the laws about adultery have been and remain extremely strict. The epics considered adultery as one of the five great sins for which there is no atonement—the others are the murder of a Brahmin, the slaying of a cow, unbelief, and living off a woman—and warned against its frightful consequences:

> In all castes a man must never approach the wife of another. For there is nought in the world which so shortens life as that the man on earth should

---

3. The third-century Tamil epic of *Shilappadikaram* (The Ankle Bracelet) (Adigal 1965) is perhaps the earliest illustration of the separate but equal attraction of the adulterous and the conjugal for the Indian man.

visit the wife of another. As many pores as are on women's bodies, so many years will he sit in hell. . . . He that touches another man's wife is born as a wolf, as a dog, as a jackal, then born as a vulture, a snake, a heron, as also a crane. [*Mahabharata*, XIII, 104.20ff, cited in Meyer 1930, pp. 246–247][4]

In mythology, too, the adulterous woman at least, rarely escapes the consequences of her actions. Ahilya, the wife of a sage, who was more a victim of Indra's (the king of the gods) lechery and less an enthusiastic participant in their short-lived revel, paid dearly for her unwitting lapse. Parshuram, commanded by his father, killed his own mother, who, when out bathing, caught sight of a handsome king sporting with his wives and was "unfaithful in her heart." Even today we know from clinical practice that in most sections of Indian society adultery is rarely a matter of casual, commonplace liaison. Its mere contemplation is a momentous psychological event for a woman, provoking moral dread.

In contrast the poets and literati of the classical period, who have exercised a great influence on subsequent cultural attitudes and sentiments, at least of the upper castes, generally scorned the Hindu marriage as a preeminently social and religious duty. They saw in marriage a deadly foe of the great feeling to which they—as indeed most poets— have always aspired. In writing with nostalgia of scenes of love unhampered by matrimony, or in lamenting the disappearance of love with marriage, the poet's scorn of conjugal love was unremitting.

Where the moon is not inveighed against
And no sweet words of the messenger are heard
Where speech is not choked with tears
And the body grows not thin;
But where one sleeps in one's own house
With he who owns subservient to one's wish;
Can this routine of household sex,
This wretched thing, deserve the name of love? [Ingalls 1965, p. 256]

The poets, then, and especially the females of this artistic species— Vidya and Bhavakadevi, for example—idealized the rapture of the il-

---

4. See also *The Laws of Manu*, XII, 165.63ff.

licit liaison (Merwin and Masson 1977). In counterpoint to the damnation heaped upon her in religious and legal texts, the adulteress was assured of the poet's admiration.

In the poetic and dramatic conventions, for instance, there are three kinds of women: the courtesan (*veshya*), the wife (*svakiya*), and the other woman (*parakiya*). The other woman is further subdivided into two kinds: the unmarried young girl (*kanyaka*) and the married woman (*parodha*). In an obvious oedipal allusion, it is the *parodha*, the other man's wife, who best embodies the principle of eros (since, risking much, she has the most to lose) and is therefore considered the most desirable lover. As one Sanskrit poet writes:

So there are
women who attract
with their loose ways
prostitutes
and there is the deep shyness
of one's own wife
the most beautiful and most
graceful showing
her love
opening flower
but who in this world can
fill one with joy
like another man's wife
loving with naked breast.

In contrast to classical poets who stressed the frank elation, the incomparable joy of loving another man's wife, the *bhakti* cults gave more exalted reasons for making Radha an adulterous *parakiya*. For them the adulterous was symbolic of the sacred, the overwhelming moment that denies world and society, transcending the profanity of everyday convention, as it forges an unconditional (and unruly) relationship with god as the lover. Stirring our sense of the essential instabilities and disorderliness of passionate love, Radha would sing:

At the first note of his flute
down came the lion gate of
reverence for elders,
down came the door of *dharma*,

my guarded treasure of modesty was lost,
I was thrust to the ground as if by
a thunderbolt.
Ah, yes, his dark body
poised in the *tribhanga* pose
shot the arrow that pierced me;
no more honour, my family
lost to me,
my home at Vraja
lost to me.
Only my life is left—and my life too
is only a breath that is leaving me. [Dimock and Levertov 1967, p. 28]

In imparting adulterous love elements of the divine, the *bhakti* poets went even further than the troubadours of medieval Europe who had equated it with true love. In the legendary decision taken at the so-called Court of Love in Champagne in 1174 it was maintained:

We declare and affirm, agreeably to the general opinion of those present, that love cannot exercise its powers on married people. The following reason is proof of the fact; lovers grant everything, mutually and gratuitously, without being constrained by any motive of necessity. Married people, on the contrary, are compelled as a duty to submit to one another's wishes, and not to refuse anything to one another. For this reason, it is evident that love cannot exercise its powers on married people. [Capellanus 1941, Book 1, Chapter 6, Seventh Dialogue]

Both the Indian sanctification and the European romanticization of extramarital love distract attention from its real fascination: its obviation of many factors that promote sexual anxiety and consequently inhibit desire. The structure of the adulterous, so far removed from the mundane, the long-term "dream of safety" and dependability of the conjugal relationship, may not be so easily subject to the steady erosion wrought by oedipal taboos, which, in a marriage, often come to attach themselves to the partner. In other words, lacking in defensiveness, the adulterous relationship is relatively free of those instances of impotency or frigidity in marriage that involve a transference to the spouse of unconscious sexual attitudes and prohibitions entertained earlier toward the parent of the opposite sex. Freed of inner taboos the adulterous situation yet partakes of its delightful excitement, with the betrayed spouse serving as an outside impediment, both regulating erotic intensity and, insofar as he or she is an obstacle, enhancing it. Reliving the thrills of oedipal fantasy, the adulterous lover does not confront the parent's image or injunctions in the person to whom he or she makes love. In this adventure taboos have been cast by the wayside and are not everyday matters.

In the Indian case there is an additional consideration. The hierarchical dictates of the family call for male supremacy within marriage. The adulterous, in contrast, is free of all distinctions of relative status between man and woman. Radha can address Krishna as *"tu chora"* ("You thief!"), which would be unthinkable for a wife, who is constrained to use the most respectful form of second person address when speaking to her husband—a proscription that is hardly conducive to sexual abandon in the master's bedroom. Furthermore, the clandestine life of the adulterous is composed of snatches of stolen time, rather than long periods of coexistence. This mitigates demands for intimacy on levels other than the sexual. The body, shackled by social and moral restraints and enmeshed in a web of unconscious expectations and attitudes from the past, glimpses in the adulterous a promise of newfound emancipation and expansiveness. Therein it is liberated by the spontaneous, vivid, if transient, encounter.

Besides the adulterous overthrow of social convention, indeed facilitated by this very circumstance, the crossing of individual sexual boundaries provides the other major source of erotic excitement in the artistic treatment of Radha and Krishna. We are either men or women, after all. We have known this to be an intractable fact of life since we were two and a half years of age when our core gender identity becomes fixed. Thereafter we grow up in an established social milieu that affixes to gender sex roles that seem to emanate from our bodies, our penises and wombs, and all those secondary sexual characteristics that go along with them. Can all this be changed, should it—when it is the distinctions of sex that impel and permit man and woman to come together? To these questions the Indian love poetry and art respond with a resounding yes. And they do this within an elaborate mythological tradition rather unknown to the West, whose deities have always tended to be more prosaically human than otherwise.

In painting, the depiction of this crossing ranges from the portrayal of the lovers in the traditional Orissa school, where they appear as one androgynous entity, to some of the paintings from the Himalayan foothills where Radha and Krishna are dressed in each other's clothes, or Radha is seen taking the more active masculine role in coitus. In poetry, Sur Das would speak in Radha's voice:

> You become Radha and I will become Madhava, truly Madhava; this is the reversal which I shall produce. I shall braid your hair and will put [your] crown upon my head. Sur Das says: Thus the Lord becomes Radha and Radha the son of Nanda. [Spink 1971, p. 88]

The inversion of sexual roles is all the more striking in the depiction of their intercourse. The poet Chandi Das praises as beautiful "the deliberate, sensuous union of the two / the girl playing this time the active role / riding her lover's outstretched body in delight" (Dimock and Levertov 1967, p. 56), while Jayadeva gives voice to what are normally regarded as feminine masochistic sexual wishes when he has Krishna sing:

> Punish me, lovely fool!
> Bite me with your cruel teeth!
> Chain me with your creeper arms!
> Crush me with your hard breasts!
> Angry goddess, don't weaken with joy!
> Let Love's despised arrows
> Pierce me to sap my life's power! [Miller 1977, p. 113]

It was only under the influence of nineteenth-century Western phallocentricity, one of the dubious intellectual blessings of British colonial rule, that many educated Indians would become uneasy with this accentuation of femininity in a culture hero. The great Bengali writer Bankim Chandra Chatterji, the proponent of a virile nationalism, would write of the Gitagovinda:

> From the beginning to the end, it does not contain a single expression of manly feelings—of womanly feelings there is a great deal—or a single elevated sentiment. . . . I do not deny his [Jayadeva's] high poetical merits in a certain sense of exquisite imagery, tender feeling, and unrivalled

powers of expression, but that does not make him less the poet of an effeminate and sensual race. [Quoted in Miller 1995, p. 25]

In the *bhakti* cults, where the worshiper must create an erotic relationship with Krishna, the transcendence of boundaries of gender becomes imperative for the male devotee, who endeavors to become as a woman in relation to the Lord. In his case the violation of the biblical injunction "The woman shall not wear that which pertaineth unto a man, neither shall a man put on a woman's garments" is far from being an "abomination unto the Lord thy God." In *bhakti* Krishna not only demands such a willing reversal from his male worshipers but is himself the compelling exemplar. Consequently, tales of Indian saints who have succeeded in feminizing themselves are legion. To give only two illustrations: the fifteenth-century Gujarati saint Narsi Mehta writes,

> I took the hand of that lover of *gopis* [Krishna] in loving converse. . . . I forgot all else. Even my manhood left me. I began to sing and dance like a woman. My body seemed to change and I become one of the *gopis*. I acted as go-between like a woman, and began to lecture Radha for being too proud. . . . At such times I experienced moments of incomparable sweetness and joy. [Alston 1980, pp. 24–25]

A. K. Ramanujan tells us that the voice of the Tamil saint-poet Nammalvar, who wrote 370 poems on the theme of love, was always that of a woman: Krishna's beloved, the girlfriend who consoles and counsels, or "the mother who restrains her and despairs over her daughter's lovesick fantasies" (Ramanujan 1981, p. 154). Nammalvar's love poems alternated with other subjects and a thirteenth-century commentary explained these shifts: "In knowledge, his own words; in love, a woman's words" (p. 154). A legend has it that Amaru, one of the earliest and greatest Sanskrit poets of love, was the hundred and first incarnation of a soul that had previously occupied the bodies of a hundred women.

Narsi Mehta, Nammalvar, and countless other unknown devotees of the Radha–Krishna cults, bear testimony to the primal yearning of men, ensheathed and isolated by their phallic masculinity, to yield their heroic trappings and delight in womanliness, woman's and their own. These universal wishes are distinct from the pathological cases where similar fantasies and feminine behavior might well be a manifestation of homosexual libido, a retreat from phallic masculinity into anal eroti-cism. In other words some of the devotees may indeed be closer to Freud's (1911) history of the paranoid Schreber, the psychotic German judge who was convinced that he was being transformed into a woman in order to become God's wife and give birth to a whole new race of men. Like Schreber, these devotees too may be defending against their fear and unconscious belief that they have been emasculated and con-soling themselves with femininity as a compensation.

Yet for most of the worshipers and the saints, as for the rest of us, the wish to be a woman is not a later distortion of phallic strivings but rather another legacy from our prehistoric experience with our mothers. Indeed this ambisexuality, the play of masculine and femi-nine, probably represents the acme, the climax of preoedipal devel-opment before castration anxiety and guilt enter to limit and dull the sexual quest.

The mother has figured early on as the omnipotent force of a pa-rental universe, making things, including fathers and other males, ma-terialize as if at will. It is she whose breast and magic touch have long ago soothed the savage instinctual imperatives, she whose fecund womb seemed the very fount of life. Such maternal and feminine powers are earthly yet mysterious and transcendent, undiminished by the utter sensuousness in which they are manifest. As the little boy grows toward manhood and assumes his predestined masculine role in society, he may come to exaggerate the brittle and rather obvious puissant attributes of the phallus and disparage those who do not possess it. Notwithstand-ing what has been termed his masculine protest, what he does not have gnaws at a boy, at a man. In the veil of night, or in the veil drawn over consciousness in the ecstasy of religious possession, he would gratefully surrender his penis to the vagina and the woman who possesses it—that is, so long as he does not lose it forever.

Krishna's erotic homage to Radha conveys something of the ach-ing quality of the man's fantasy of surrender at the height of sexual ex-citement. He longs to be smothered and penetrated by the woman's breasts as he himself willingly shrinks in his mind's eye. Every genital fiber is attuned to the welcoming wetness his eyes cannot see or know from within, straining even as he finally expels his seed from his self, an emis-sary journeying deep into the lover's internal dark continent, still forbid-den to him. The thrusting penis, man realizes once again, can never take or hold the woman. It merely enters her territory and touches her portals, only to shrivel and all too rapidly to be withdrawn. Did it not provide a recurrent bridge to her, man would gladly cede his crude organ and castrate himself to be one with the beloved—at least for a moment of bliss. The secret of men, gods included, to borrow from Bruno Bettelheim, is that they want to be that which they cannot have: woman.

The profusion of the imagery of darkness and night—in the meetings of Radha–Krishna—as indeed in the trysts of Romeo and Juliet and of Layla and Majnun (or, for that matter, Tristan and Isolde)—underscores the secret nature of these fantasmagoria and illusions of the soul. The paintings show Radha and Krishna surrounded by darkness while they themselves are lit by a sullen glare from the sky. They portray the lovers enclosed in a triangle of inky night while around them the rest of Vrindavan's inhabitants unconcernedly go about the day's tasks. These are visual metaphors for a sensualism that is simultaneously hidden from the world and from the lovers' awareness. For Radha, as for Juliet, night and darkness are excitement's protectors, silence and secrecy its friends. Shrill disturbances to these servants of nature's erotic cycle are to be avoided: "Leave your noisy anklets! They clang like traitors in love's play/Go to the darkened thicket, friend! Hide in a cloak of night!" (Miller 1977, p. 92). In a Basholi painting from *Rasmanjari* the text describes the seated lovers thus: "Fear of detection does not permit the eager lovers' gaze to meet. Scared of the jingling sound of armlets they desist from embracing. They kiss each others' lips without the contact of teeth. Their union is hushed too" (Randhawa and Bambri 1981, p. 99). Many other portraits of Radha reveal that it is not only other people who must remain unaware of her sexual arousal. Radha, too, when in a state where "love's deep fantasies/struggle with her modesty" (Miller 1977, p. 122), would fain ignorance of her true condition, as if it were a secret another part of her self must not admit to knowing. It is given to the poet to perceive correctly her struggle.

Words of protest filled with passion
Gestures of resistance lacking force,
Frowns transmuted into smiles,
Crying dry of tears—friend,

Though Radha seeks to hide her feelings
Each attempt betray's her heart's
Deep love for demon Mura's slayer. [Quoted in Wulff 1982, p. 39]

Identifying with Radha's pounding breast as she steals out at night to meet Krishna, other poets graphically describe her fear while merely hinting at the suppressed thrill of her sortie, her arousal sharpened by the threat of discovery. They give us images of storm, writhing snakes, scratched and burning feet.

O Madhava, how shall I tell you of my terror?
I could not describe my coming here
If I had a million tongues.
When I left my room and saw the darkness
I trembled:
I could not see the path,
There were snakes that writhed round my ankles!

I was alone, a woman; the night was so dark,
The forest so dense and gloomy,
And l had so far to go.
The rain was pouring down—
Which path should I take?
My feet were muddy
And burning where thorns had scratched them.
But I had the hope of seeing you,
None of it mattered,
And now my terror seems far away . . .
When the sound of your flute reaches my ears
It compels me to leave my home, my friends,
It draws me in the dark toward you. [Dimock and Levertov 1967, p. 21]

We imagine that on hearing Radha's plaint, Krishna, whose gaze into the recesses of the human heart is as penetrating as it is compassionate, smiled to himself in the dark. He would have surely known that the strains of his flute, like that of Pan's before him, are the perennial and irresistible call of the human senses caught up in the throes of love.

And what do darkness and night mean to Krishna as he passively offers himself to Radha's embraces? Here, too, only under the cloak of night does the Lord reveal the deepest secret of man—that he, too, would be a woman. In the night, in the jungle, visual and discrete modes of perception are replaced by the tactile, the visceral, and the more synesthetic forms of cognizance. Representations of the self and beloved fade and innermost sensate experience comes to the fore. As the illusion of bodies fused, hermaphroditic, it fostered, the fantasies around womanliness and sexual excitement feed each other, and Krishna "knows" Radha not with the eye but with the flesh.

Night's curtains never completely part in this gentler story, whose protagonist, moreover, is a god able to withstand and transcend such protean changes. Hence the lovers survive, and tragedy is averted. Undiscovered, they remain unseen by the eyes of inner vigilance—by castration terror, by ambivalence, or, worst of all, by guilt.

REFERENCES

Adigal, I. (1965). *Shilapaddikaram* (The Ankle Bracelet), trans. A. Danielou. New York: New Directions.

Aiston, A. J. (1980). *The Devotional Poems of Mirabai*. Delhi: Motilal Banarasidass.

Auden, W. H. (1973). *Forewords and Afterwords*. London: Faber.

Bhattacharya, D. (1963). *Love Songs of Vidyapati*. London: George Allen and Unwin.

Capellanus, A. (1941). *The Art of Courtly Love*, trans. J. J. Parry. New York: Columbia University Press.

De, S. K. (1959). *Ancient Indian Erotics and Erotic Literature*. Calcutta: Firma K. L. Mukhopadhyaya.

De Rougemont, D. (1963). *The Myths of Love*. London: Faber and Faber.

Dimock, E. C., and Levertov, D. (1967). *In Praise of Krishna: Songs from Bengali*. New York: Anchor.

Freud, S. (1911). Psychoanalytic notes upon an autobiographical account of a case of paranoia. *Standard Edition* 12:3–82.

Ingalls, H. H. (1965). *An Anthology of Sanskrit Court Poetry*. Cambridge, MA: Harvard University Press.

Marglin, M. (1982). Types of sexual union and their implicit meanings. In *The Divine Consort*, ed. J. S. Hawley and D. M. Wulff, pp. 305–307. Berkeley, CA: Religious Studies Series.

Merwin, W. S., and Masson, J. M. (1977). *Sanskrit Love Poetry*. New York: Columbia University Press.

Meyer, J. J. (1930). *Sexual Life in Ancient India*. New York: E. P. Dutton.

Miller, B. (1982). The divine duality of Radha and Krishna. In *The Divine Consort*, ed. J. S. Hawley and D. M. Wulff, pp. 22–31. Berkeley, CA: Religious Studies Series.

Miller, B. S. (1977). *Love Song of the Dark Lord: Jayadeva's Gitagovinda*. New York: Columbia University Press.

Ramanujan, A. K. (1981). *Hymns for the Drowning*. Princeton: Princeton University Press.

Randhawa, M. S., and Bambri, S. D. (1981). Basholi paintings of Bhanudatta's Rasamanjari. *Roop Lekha* 36:99.

Siegel, L. (1978). *Sacred and Profane Dimensions of Love in Indian Tradition*. Delhi: Oxford University Press.

Spink, W. M. (1971). *Krishnamandala*. Ann Arbor, MI: Center for South and South East Asian Studies.

Stoller, R. (1979). *Sexual Excitement*. New York: Pantheon.

Valency, M. (1958). *In Praise of Love*. New York: Macmillan.

Wulff, D. M. (1982). A Sanskrit portrait: Radha in the plays of Rupa Gosvami. In *The Divine Consort*, ed. J. S. Hawley and D. M. Wulff, p. 39. Berkeley, CA: Religious Studies Series.

8

Sita-Shakti @ Cultural Collision: Issues in the Psychotherapy of Diaspora Indian Women

Jaswant Guzder And Meenakshi Krishna

"If it were not for the family name, straight away I would take you to the mental home," he mumbled. As the years passed, he found he understood her less and less instead of more and more.

Kiran Desai (1998)

India has an unbroken tradition of the *Devi* (Mother Goddess) culture for over 5000 years, and we explore some of the mythic resonances and paradigms of Indian feminine identity using clinical narratives from psychotherapy with diaspora women of Indian origin. It is impossible to generalize the created individual solutions that arise out of this internal transforming, integrating, translating, and transcending occurring within the immigration experience of cultural hybridization or the "in-between realities" of a "third space" (Bhabha 1990, 1994). These emotional shifts, in which the parameters of specific historical moments are embodied, scattered, and regrouped into new points of becoming (Braziel and Mannur 2003), involve a collision of values, set off by pulling up roots and relocation, and the intersection of the Subcontinent psyche meeting Judeo-Christian traditions and individualistic milieus of the West. Therapeutic discourse of these immigrants includes themes about the discordance created by dislocation, immigration, and modernity, factoring in intergenerational issues, colonization, decolonization, history, and cultural specificity.

The Indian feminine is shaped within a gendered hierachy of extended family life, consciously preoccupied with purity, restraint, and honor, while implicitly influenced by a historic, religious, and mythic collective memory. The Indian woman, "revered as an idea and oppressed in the reality" (Nandy 1995, p. 35), is located within a rich hagiography, in a syncretic context of Hinduism, Jainism, Islam, Buddhism, Sikhism, Zoroastrianism, Christianity, and other tribal cultures. Indian patriarchy essentially differs historically and imaginatively from European patriarchy, and influenced the Mugal Islamic culture as it evolved in India (Guha 1989, Pandey 1989). While modernity has shifted part of India's reality to scientific, technological, and urban agendas, the family is the essence of Indian life, with its interdependent and cohesive support as reflected in the strong loyalties and continuity of contact, caring, and reciprocity throughout the life cycle. Extended family life reinforces priorities on the care of its youth and elderly, respect for its elders, sanctifying of householder duties, holding fast to religious traditions, and taking care to influence or arrange marriages that provide continuity and suit the needs of their children and the family. Ancient and dynamic realities coexist in modernity, as motherhood remains the central identity of the Indian woman, even though contemporary Indian women have become prominent politicians, Bollywood stars, astronauts, activists, artists, businesswomen, and scientists.

Second- or third-generation immigrants may have a completely different appreciation of parental cultural parameters (Adams 1996, Niranjana 2001, Obeyesekere 1981, Ram 2002, Rayaprol 1997) blending their mother-tongue mythologies with local or global cultural myths or folk or fairy tales to create another experiential category. Gendered hierarchy, issues of power, the inequalities of caste, recent communal violence (Davar 1999, Thapan 1997), and poverty are contemporary social preoccupations of the subcontinent, whereas identity, racism, and culture change are predominant issues of Indians in the diaspora.

The postcolonial discourse informed by current studies of race, gender, subaltern histories, anthropology, sociology, as well as influences of contemporary expression in cinema, literature, and theater, challenges psychotherapists to "mind the gap" of imaginations arising from different worlds, and to deal with the countertransference possibilities implicit within the diaspora (Adams 1996, Bhabha 1990, 1994, Fanon 1967, Fernando 2003, Hall 2003, Ho 1992, Ponterotto et al. 2001, Ravindran, 1992, Sue and Sue 1999). The psychoanalytic premise of neutrality assumes an empathic listening adjusting to the slippery shifts of Otherness. In countertransference, the therapist tolerates the ambiguous "not knowing" of being part of a transitional phenomenon or process with their patients. This territory is a moral thicket of how judgments are posed across the boundaries of cultural difference (Adams 1996, Taylor 1992) since ideas of individual autonomy, freedom, equality, social justice, and human rights appear to have various meanings as they are translated from one civilization to another (Geertz 1993, Huntington 1997, Ignatieff 2001, Said 2002), particularly for women whose issues are often invisible in mainstream discourse dominated by male perspectives and agendas.

Hedge (1998) and others point out that most research assumes to speak for both genders on the assumption that women and men have similar immigration experience, "inevitably the specificities of immigrant women's lived realities are rendered invisible" (Ram 2002, p. 26). "Imagined homelands," as Rushdie (1991) called them, are internally constructed by immigrants, refugees, exiles, or marginals, surviving and remembering while externally negotiating successful adaptation or assimilation (Said 1978). The Orientalism gaze of the West formulated by Said (1978) often reinforces cultural stereotypes of projected primitive or historically negative stereotypes. As Khan (2002) has commented on Islamic women (and as can be generalized to Subcontinent women), "they find devaluation and apprehension in the West (Orientalism), and mechanisms for their control in (Subcontinent cultures) Islam" (p. 3).

DIASPORA SPACES AND PSYCHOTHERAPY

The concepts of transitional phenomena and processes, as described by Winnicott (1966) or for groups by Bridger and his colleagues (Amado and Ambrose 1994), could serve as helpful models for framing the continuous shifting dynamics of women's identity in the diasporic space. In addition, the conceptualization of the third individuation (Akhtar 1995) addresses cultural identity within the frame of an individuation process. The unconscious processes surfacing in the individual and the group are activated in those left behind as well as in members of the host cultures and the immigrant herself (Grinberg and Grinberg 1989), leading to a collision of reality and fantasy, ambivalences and reparations. This unconscious and conscious reassembly of identity results in resilient, creative outcomes or at times derailment in varying degrees into lifelong mourning that might be influenced or exacerbated by external and internal factors. Psychotherapy may offer a space to work with meaning and values, systemic conflict, dislocation, or trauma, complicated by the cultural change process that is experienced as a lifelong transitional phenomenon and requires a particular empathy in building of therapeutic alliance (Adams 1996, Thomas 2002).

The ambivalence of belonging and disengagement, wanting to return and wanting to stay, along with the myriad ambiguities of living in two houses and two cultures (Falicov 2002), implies that assumptions and generalizations cannot be made, but also diagnostic issues can be problematic when cultural agendas are unclear. In addition, research in community studies of visible minority women indicates trends of underutilization of mental health services (Crenshaw 2003) complicated by issues of language, alternate cultural-mythic worlds, stigma, and difficulty accessing appropriate help (Fernando 2003, Khan 2002, Kim 2002, Ponterotto et al. 2001, Sue and Sue 1999). Multiple and complex intergroup negotiations make it impossible to generalize psychoanalytic intervention strategies even within India (Davar 1999). Since immigration is yet another parallel agenda in a lifelong process of individuation, a multifocal approach is necessary when working with women in the Indian diaspora (Kirmayer et al. 2003, Niranjana 2001, Rayaprol 1997).

Indian women need a therapist to acknowledge cultural parameters outside the usual Eurocentric or North American grids (Derrida 1998) as they grapple with a personal identity rooted in both their maternal identifications and collective feminine identifications of their ethnic and host communities, while individuating in multicultural spaces. A psychotherapy process grounded in the lived experience of the subject, rather than the premise of neutrality, can provide such women with empathic holding, and increased awareness of personal narrative as they work through repetitions, trauma, and individuation dilemmas. To a traditional culture that carefully silences and separates hierarchical spaces defining power and agency, psychotherapy risks being viewed as a subversive project that facilitates alternate individualistic choices in a group-oriented cultural space. Silencing for the sake of *izzat* (honor, family name, social persona of the family unit) or avoiding distressing rupture of families results in not reporting or verbalizing one's concerns (Crenshaw 2003). This silence has congruence with an ego ideal influenced by many mythic heroines whose strength of character positively models endurance, humility, anonymity, silence, or self-sacrificing qualities. It is therefore quite an accomplishment for many Asian women to seek social services.

Second-generation women socialized in Europe and North America may be more inclined through their socialization in school and university to seek psychological services and individual psychotherapy. First-generation immigrants and family elders often find their support during situations of psychological distress among the circle of familial networks, women friends, religious rituals, and meditative practices. They tend to seek therapy only in crisis or serious distress and might have a strong privacy ethic. Indian women may have successfully found support and mediation of conflict within their traditional social networks created in their new countries (Rayaprol 1997). The community endorses a strong mandate of protective idealism of womens rights, validating and supporting the high achievement of their women (Naidoo 1992) but having difficulty with open discourse or support on such issues as abused women, epilepsy, or mental illness.

Case 1

Ranjana was a first-generation Hindu girl living in America. She was a self-proclaimed agnostic and radical feminist who usually wore jeans. She reported in therapy that she liked visiting the local South Indian temple in a sari ("it makes me feel so normal"), as it served as a symbolic substitute for visiting her family in India. Mixing with extended families and people of different generations in the temple was a satisfying return to a maternal *temenos* (Greek for sacred spaces), though too much time among her family or the Indian community "suffocated" her. She also revealed her interest in a separate world of lesbian groups. She was ambivalent and uncomfortable when on one occasion she saw her Indian-origin therapist in Indian clothes. She had consciously sought a therapist who could be "both near and far" from her own mother. She felt she had to keep her therapy a secret from her family, and had sought therapy to support identity shifts that differentiated her from her traditional mother. During her therapy, themes of longing for the extended family and reconciliation by refueling remained important, and each symbolic event that occurred marked in some way a separation from her maternal and familial identity. The transference mother embodied and identified with the host society (wearing Western clothes, promoting verbalization of sexual and identity issues) was split, fragmented, and held in the maternal transference as good (holding, a homeland like the temple) and bad (shaming, disapproving of her autonomy or hybrid identity).

Purity, asceticism, and apprehension of the uncontained feminine remain variables in a social context of gendered hierarchy (Thapan 1997) where many decisions are unilaterally made by males or elders. Nonetheless, women need to be seen as agents, even in moments of being "intimately, viciously oppressed" and even when appearing "to be passive," "acted upon," and "always a victim" (Frankenberg and Mani 1993). Women's identities evolve with culturally mapped life-cycle agendas (Kakar 1978), within the intergenerational life of extended family, caste, and community, including a bond of blood, reincarnation, history, and language. A woman's identity may shift with the deaths of her parents, elders, or siblings even in midlife, when roles and duties are displaced in traditional families by lost members, or issues arise out of caring for the elderly, accommodating the marriages of her children, and enduring widowhood. An important parallel thread of religious life provides the neutral spaces and cherished ideals connected with *dhyana* (meditation), *seva* (compassionate service), *sadhana* (mystical path), and *moksha* (renunciation and detachment). The last mentioned is usually attained through spiritual practices, seeking a guru, spending time in ashrams, or following ritual and spiritual practices.

While ethnocentric psychological literature embraces individual rights and Western development or social norms as universal aims, cultural relativists would argue that gender equality, individual rights, and personal choice sit uneasily alongside a highly elaborate moral order in the East, which cherishes self-development, self-control, loyalty, and duty to the extended family (*dharma*) or others (*seva*). From a study of successful California Sikh immigrants, Margaret Gibson (1988) reported a calculated immigrant strategy of "accommodation without assimilation," which allows such communities to remain within both moral orders, implying a bicultural persona or competence. Therapist countertransference is, at times, stirred by the dialectics of these bicultural aims and adaptations (Adams 1996, Davar 1999, Lane 1998, Orbach 1999, Thomas 2002).

With selective immigration screening to Europe and North America, the waves of Indian immigrants after the 1960s, in contrast to earlier immigrations (some as indentured labor or without citizenship rights), were more likely to be well adapted in the West as "the model minority," building positive supports of social networks within their communities (Rayaprol 1997), unless they were geographically isolated. These women are more likely to be participants in religious or community activities (Rayaprol 1997) and are actively engaged in socializing their children to hold Indian values, with concerns diverging from male experiences of marriage and family. Urban middle class Indians, for example, have traditional gender ideology with regard to marriage and family but are egalitarian with regard to education and careers of women (Liddle and Joshi 1986, Naidoo 1992), facilatating access to successful career and educational goals among urban diaspora Indian women. Nussbaum (2000), after years of cross-cultural work, suggested that women universally desire independence and economic self-sufficiency, but the possibilities of agency for these aims are shaped by the different life-span concerns in which women find themselves involved.

MYTHIC PARADIGMS AND GENDERED HIERARCHIES

Whereas the Olympian gods dislodged the ancient Minoan earth goddess, the long tradition of the *Devi* or Mother Goddess in her multiple forms such as *Durga* (reverently and affectionately called *Ma* in Bengal), *Kali, Parvati, Maha-devi* (Doniger 1999, Kakar 1989) continues as a living part of the culture. The imagery of the phallic-maternal *Adi-Shakti, Ardhi-Narishwara* (*Shiva* as half-man and half-woman) and the principle of

Purush-Prakruti (nature as inert until activated by female energy) point to a fluidity and integration of masculine and feminine identifications (Kakar 1989) remaining alive in the oral traditions and visual cultural imagery of India. While the Indian patriarchy provides a social framework invested with masculine superiority and voice, the maternal-feminine identifications remain the psychic bedrock, surfacing readily in case histories of male analysands (Kakar 1989, Roland 1990). Mythic idealized feminine identifications culturally resonate with pervasive values such as obedience, deference, self-sacrifice for the family or group, a capacity to work well within hierarchies, receptivity (Roland 1990), and deference to patriarchy reflected in mythic paradigms of self-sacrifice by sons for fathers (Kakar 1989, Obeyesekere 1990) or daughters for husbands or fathers.

The birth of a son remains embedded as the highest achievement of a woman in these traditional patriarchal systems, which then reinforce a woman's identity, status, and familial roles. Religion, community, caste, and economic class continue to define a woman's role, realities, and possibilities, though with wide variation of opportunities and value systems between communities. In any case, unconscious implications of a long affiliation with maternal socialization within extended families prepare males later in life to both contain and support women within the boundaries of familial hierarchy. While the daughter prepares in her developmental passages to separate with marriage, the son traditionally remains in lifelong affiliation close to his mother, as idealized and modeled in the mythic divine devotion of Ganesh for his mother Parvati. "The boy never loses his mother" (Roland 1996, p. 136).

Nonetheless, in aspects of social power, mythology, and iconography, women are often precariously positioned, holding projections as idealized, highly venerated (e.g., *Devi*, ideal mother), impure (e.g., menstruating, polluting, unclean), transgressive (e.g., mad or bad), and intrusive (e.g., seductive, restless eroticism, engulfing) intentions. These emerging split projections of the feminine are reflected in such feminine mythic themes as devoted Sita (generative, pure, creative) versus awesome Shakti (uncontainable, feminine, transgressive, dangerous, or phallic). Lack of feminine restraint or containment is alternatively seen as powerful, erotic, or dangerous, or associated with bad or mad projections onto women. Diaspora women may be more likely to move out of traditional ideals, and may be seen as inappropriately unrestrained, imbalanced, potentially able to destabilize the social order, or as deeply suspect in their intentions or values. In this context, female asceticism, as described in case studies of Obeyesekere (1990), may be an option that transforms the oppressive demands of heterosexuality into the power to heal themselves (Das 1989) and reduces projections by moving into the androgynous areas of religious identities. Possession states or dissociative states in women could be viewed, in situations of social oppression, as an acting out of repossessing female body rather than formulated only "as evidence of infantile sexuality and hysteria" (Davar 1999, p. 185). The immigrant girl may successfully move in and out of both Indian and Western contexts with crises at times marking her autonomy from the family in matters of marital or life choices.

Procreative powers are embodied as the mythic purview of the earth mother and the feminine, as in the classical Ganesh myth, where Parvati creates a son from a pile of earth without need of her consort Shiva. Women are both revered for mothering and blamed for infertility; thus, approbation for the lack of a son reinforces the mythic projections idealizing the potency of fathers and sons (Carstairs 1957, Guzder and Krishna 1991, Kakar 1989, Obeyesekere 1990). Pluralism and contradictory repertoires of the Indian mythic world are congruent with India's capacity to maintain contradictory theories, from among which the appropriate one for dealing with each problem is selected as it arises, as Morris Carstairs (1957) said "In the village, no statement, and no narrative was ever felt to be entirely right or wrong, and so none was disgarded" (Doniger 1999, p. 6).

Sexuality in adolescent Indians traditionally is not experienced as liberating, though Indian childhood often is indulgent and sensuous. Young girls may have an indulgent, nuturing, or very affectionate bond with their fathers, while the relationship of the husband–wife dyad may be more reserved. Adolescent girls are not encouraged to prematurely seek autonomy outside the family. Pubescent sexuality traditionally marks a life stage associated with more serious obligations and preparing for the duties of marriage (Roland 1996), with families more focused on anticipating marriages or completing educational goals prior to marriage. Young women strive to maintain an appropriate social persona of purity and honorable conduct outside the family before marriage, as if "a woman's body has a thousand eyes upon it" (Roland 1990,

p. 139). As one young woman commented, "When I was at Harvard I wanted respect, but back here at home I seek approval."

A woman internalizes the ego-ideal of her mother, her body (Douglas 1966), and conduct embodying familial honor (versus pollution or transgression), fearing impingements of gossip or criticism that are reinforced by parental warnings. While within fantasy or within the space of the extended family she might practice or play as a sensuous feminine self, within the circle of male relatives, especially maternal uncles or cousins, she has more boundaries. In public spaces she uses varying degrees of actual or symbolic self-imposed "purdah," providing her with protection from outside or unwanted influences and harassment, with the cost of restricting her in public spaces (Viswanath 1997). The female as the embodiment of *izzat* (familial honor or face) must manage these developmental issues, in marked contrast to her adolescent brothers or peers in the West, for example, who are less adamantly constrained by their superego or family. In the diaspora, second- and third-generation women may have more in common in their families with the Mahabharata heroine Draupadi, who implicitly holds traditional socialization but explicitly asserts gender equality, assertiveness, autonomy, and a strong voice of her own. There are indeed many examples of daughters who are chosen by fathers for leadership roles (including Indira Gandhi by her father Pandit Nehru), and groomed to be assertive and dutiful with their blessing,

Case 2

> Tara, a second-generation, Indian-origin university student, growing up in an isolated community in Alberta, Canada, came to therapy relating a distressing incident. Tara's father forbade her to wear jeans on a family outing when all her female relatives wore ethnic suits (*salwar khameez*), on the grounds of family shame, even though she protested that her legs were fully covered. Her paternal grandmother came to her rescue and overruled her son, Tara's father, when his wife was also brushed aside. Tara was conscious of her individuation process in trying to confront her father, disengage from the family, and identify with her Canadian peers. Her father remained vulnerable to group shame (other men would look at her), though he encouraged her assertiveness as the family spokes-

person, calling her his "'wonderful son." She had felt her father had "loved me too much" (more than he loved her mother) and now felt in young adulthood that father discouraged her assertiveness in areas ascribed as autonomous or sexual, which he interpreted in exhibitionistic and transgressive acts. In prepubescence, she had played at being the only son among daughters, estranged from her mother, and suppressing incestuous feelings in her role as the father's confidante. In adolescence, as she experienced her sexuality more ambivalently, she described the parental possession of her body as oppressive. At 14, she had self-destructive urges and had started to cut herself in hidden parts of her body. Her positive relationship with her paternal grandmother, who lived with the family, allowed her some leeway in family negotiations, and the elder matriarch became the family mediator in a familial culture of male hierarchy.

Older women are in a different life-cycle stage, caring for aging elders, facilitating communication within the extended family, facilitating the separation stages of their children into peer or immigrant cultures, adjusting to cross-cultural marriages of their children, or dealing with death or loss of home-country relations. While menopause appears so threatening to Western women, for Indian women it is generally a better time in their lives, as they attain more esteem with age, unless there is divorce or untimely spousal death (widowhood is often stigmatized). It also may be a more spiritual time, marked bodily with the return of ritual purity (nonmenstruating). Older immigrant women may feel they are disempowered, disappointed, or not heard in the immigrant cultural spaces that promote egalitarian and democratic familial values, romantic ideals, youth, and individualism, while familial interdependence, reciprocity, hierarachy, and respect accrued by aging wisdom are less valued. While an extended-family daughter remains identified with the family group of mothers or *ek hi* of family unity (Kurtz 1992), she is preparing to shift her loyalties to her husband's family with marriage, and later as a mother, mother-in-law, and grandmother she will accrue higher status as a matriarch. In immigration situations the younger women will be more conversant with the new cultural spaces. The elder woman will (metaphorically or in reality) remain behind, dislodged from her final attainment of traditional role unless she also

shifts her competence. Sometimes to her psychic detriment immigration may reactivate early marital trauma of being sent to the stranger's
home after an arranged marriage and encountering difficulties. Many
older women move into employment or careers for reasons of family
survival or income for the first time with immigration. They will have
assembled a new map with a shift far more profound than the second-
or third-generation daughters who are socialized in host cultural milieus
from childhood. The shift of familial dynamics for husbands and fathers,
especially those who are not able to be providers or are less successful
financially, will effect the dynamics of these women, depending on the
characters of the players.

Davar (1999) gives a pointed commentary of the pathologizing of
women and victimicizing them for a sexuality defined by social factors
in a male hierarchy. She suggests that many analytic case studies focus
on high-caste Hindus without acknowledging other diverse Indian backgrounds and leave out women's experiences of their bodies, ignoring the
widespread disempowerment of women. She underlines this with case
history examples of good outcomes described by male analysands (e.g.,
taking a third wife to have a son and thus please his parents, or regain-
ing the sexual vitality of a relationship with mistress), as leaving aside
consideration of "the fate of invisible women in these clinical narratives [who] are trapped between Hindu constructions of womanhood
and that of cure" (Davar 1999, p. 188). Entanglements of mothers with
their sons and the traditional significant power of the mother-in-law
in the joint family system are often reduced by immigration realities.
A couple may solve a familial impasse by creating nuclear units, or a
woman may achieve some autonomy through diaspora options or identifications. The daughter's positive maternal identification is not problematic in this context if her treasured position as a dutiful wife or
daughter remains, but a negative identification or hybridization agendas could later undermine her capacity to hold her hierarchical duties,
leading to her exclusion or placing her in a fragile social position. There
are strong normalization and homeostatic forces in stable and functional
extended families to protect male esteem, even if the male is alcoholic,
violent, mentally ill, and incompetent, or impaired, while the role of
women as nurturing familial cohesion continues.

The psychoanalytic literature continues to overlook, dismiss, or
misinterpret evidence of the fundamental psychological importance of

nonnuclear family relatives in non-Western societies, by focusing more on a nuclear triadic universe in childhood to accomplish differentiation from the mother, not acknowledging the discourse of ethnographic studies (Kurtz 1992, Trawick 1990) or family therapy literature (Bowen 1978, Selvini 1988). This descriptive relational map offers access to a significant, rich, and highly invested object universe normative in Indian childhood.

In addition, while householder duties, nurturing, and generativity are essential to the marital alliance, the possible balance of differentiating from extended families by asceticism, voluntary sacrifice, renunciation, and *moksha* are all typical maps quite different from the usual Western paradigms of separation-individuation from family, and often evolve in a context of a spacious marital bond (Kakar 1978). The strength of the Indian family is its capacity to sustain commitment, close affiliation, and nurturing within networks grounded in a maternal-feminine essence.

Shame (*sharm*) and agency are negotiated around the socially constructed bodies of women. These constructions have been experienced by women as both oppressive (limiting her options) and securing (holding her within a familial matrix). Women's poetry, songs, and oral traditions have transmitted Indian women's ideas about these social predicaments over centuries where women expressed change in social activism and spiritual retreat; for example, Mira and Janabhai (Tharu and Lalita 1991) are among the female saints who abandoned oppressive families and became spiritual wanderers.

Shame is the primary regulating modality in the discourse that molds the socialization of girls, implicit in the ways they are taught to sit and to talk, and the multiple messages they receive from their family and community (Thapan 1997). The careful familial and group management of women's sexuality assists in maintaining *izzat* (honor) and therefore maintaining the best possible marriage arrangements by parents. Shame is prominent in femininist discourse (Khan 2002, Viswanath 1997) especially around the premises of *izzat* and honor killing occurring at home and post immigration. Reversing shame strategies, women's groups have resisted alcoholism, wife beating, and dowry in public campaigns that humiliate perpetrators in a group context (Kumar 1993) and have made efforts to reverse shame and silencing by seeking male support for freer and more secure public movement of women, and group voices to promote support of sexual expression without taboo or patriarchal retaliation. Feminist discourse in India until recently was a critique of patriarchal control over women (Kumar 1993, Thapan 1997), while now desire and the body, relating to issues of sexuality, violence, legal representation, pornography, and lesbian issues, are more evident. Currently issues of concern include vulnerable daughters in view of feticide, infanticide, child marriage, education, dowry, domestic abuse, rejection after intermarriage, bride burning (Kumar 1993), as well as proactive efforts for issues of widows, promoting birth control, legal rights of married or divorced women for custody or alimony, as well as marginalized and prostituting women who have often been sold or kidnapped. The rise of AIDS and sexually transmitted diseases reflects the prevalence of extramarital sexuality, which is more accepted for men and leaves traditional women vulnerable. In addition, with decades of positive and active entry of Indian women into sociopolitical, artistic, and work domains, there is a broadening discourse on women's lived experience of agency. Sexuality, desire, lesbianism, renunciation of life options, and managing shame are seen as directly linked to traditional feminine socialization and identity formation (Thapan 1997).

HYBRIDIZATION AND TRANSGRESSION

Hybridization of culture expressed in areas of sexuality and autonomy often systemically provokes concern or conflict. As a result, families make efforts at containment, exclusion from the group, or silencing of woman, as strategic gestures to resolve, deflect, or avoid confrontation with more powerful group members. Hybridization might be on a spectrum ranging from threatening (equated with killing a traditional paradigm and assaulting a homeostatic system) to creative. As an assimilation process, we see this reflected in diaspora community work, theater, dance, media, film, writing, and art. As immigrant women create hybrid identities and rework ego ideals or archetypes, they may be seen as evolving or redefining Indian feminine ideals. Transgressive acts of girls dating without parental consent might propel the family into uncharted territory of increased flexibility, new identities, and intermarriage of their children, but on occasion has resulted in severe reprimands or even the murder of girls for violation of *izzat*.

There are no valid generalizations on hybrid identity. Diaspora Indians, for example, constitute 45 percent of Trinidad's population, and their women absorbed African cultural influences in a biracial postcolonial context to become assertively modern and sexually liberated, in a unique idiom, diverging from historical connections with Gandhi, Indian nationalism, and the issues of indentured labor (Niranjana 2001). Diaspora Indians from the Caribbean have their own familial paradigm of proper traditional ways and chutey-soca culture, a creolization of Indian and calypso influences. Immigration to North America is another horizontal path in a line of evolving cultural identity for women of Indian origin.

In an ethnographic study using a Pittsburgh Hindu temple as the site of transitional experience for a "deterritorialized" conservative and highly successful community, Rayaprol (1997), looking at renegotiation of gender roles with immigrant agendas, does not see these women as oppressed but rather as resilient and strong. They have created a validating women-centered life in the temple focusing on youth, education, and ritual. These American career women were assimilated high achievers, but their cultural life was closer to values of elite or privileged Indian women. Their main concerns anticipated the separation and individuation of their children, addressing that gap between themselves and their second-generation children by holding a cultural space for their community. In addition to religious networks, American and British South Asian women's groups in many urban communities are often secular and united around broader social concerns, taking on supportive roles with refugee and less established immigrant woman from mixed ethnicities, who are dealing with initial immigration or refugee realties, legal issues, single parenting, language fluency, racism, domestic violence, or sexual abuse issues.

Case 3

Anuradha was a married, 59-year-old, first-generation Hindu woman immigrant who had three college-aged children. She felt she had been a good mother and was able to maintain a positive social persona through her temple activities. She was referred for therapy with her husband, who had challenged her psychiatrist on medication management. Though Anuradha had been hospitalized several times for affective disorder, he would not recognize her mental illness, stating she was a "bad and lazy wife." Anuradha was overwhelmed by his criticism and either was silent or dissociated in years of marital therapy. After this fiasco, she sought individual therapy because she feared a relapse, could not tolerate her husband's verbal abuse, felt her children were affected by seeing her as a victim of domestic verbal abuse, and was paralyzed by the possibility of a divorce. Therapeutic work involved examining her anxiety about absorbing the accusation of being a bad wife and her loss of voice. Eventually she was able to attribute some of her vulnerability to the resurfacing of her childhood trauma around the divorce of her own parents when she was 10 years old. She had chosen "not to take sides," taking the place of the "bad wife" (her mother) and remaining with her father. Repressed memories of sexual abuse perpetrated by a family servant and repressed memories of parental extramarital affairs surfaced. Her own marriage in late adolescence was another traumatic identity rupture, when she was sent away to Britain (then moving later to America) after an arranged marriage, and continued in her pattern of respecting and serving her husband, treating him like her father. She often uses art therapy or meditation as healing solutions for her fragile imbalances. Through therapy she started to put limits on her husband's rage attacks and address proactive care of herself. The idea of divorce still threatened to tear apart her social identity, but she began to work on differentiation and earning an independent income, with decreasing anxiety about separating. Her need to marry her children off from what she still felt to be a good home was a motivation for staying married and dealing with her conflicts around being a "good woman." She was able to see that her maternal deprivation had significantly motivated her devotion and absorption in her own children. She felt depleted as they grew up and moved away from home. Holding onto a Sita ideal of womanhood in a dyad with her husband in the West was untenable without extended family mediators or a supportive social network. Connecting by email and visits with receptive extended family members, validation of childhood memories, differentiating from parental objects, and strengthening her temple network increased her motivation to assert herself. She felt her new hybrid identity brought her strength (identifying with her daughters), and after years of therapy she was able to contemplate "finally moving west" by applying for a passport.

The diversity of lost and rediscovered histories with women's voices, recording their thoughts, politics, imagination, and lived experience, are part of the contemporary genre of writing that bears witness to the silence of previous generations of women's experience. These writings have informed us historically that there is no monolithic theory but rather various realities. The impact of works such as Ismat Chughtai's (1990) writing a lesbian love affair, a short story in the 1940s that led to her arrest for writing subversive literature, is part of that legacy. The Indian diaspora voices give accounts of cultural hybridization, dislocation, dissociation, and transitional experiences through a host of writers including Bharati Mukherjee, Jhumpa Lahiri, Zadie Smith, Anita Rau Badami, Shani Mootoo, and Shauna Singh Baldwin. These writings are preoccupied with repossessing female voices, experiences, and bodies after generationally experiencing silence or at times the absence of possibilities. Fitting the ideals that patriarchy defines is delegated to mothers, though again many mothers support nontraditional choices for their daughters.

While research studies validate the importance of gender role conflicts in Western suicidal adolescent girl cohorts (Pinhas et al. 2002), the underpinnings of role conflicts and cultural maps may vary in their impact on dynamic psychotherapy work with immigrant women. Psychologically this process of negotiating Eastern and Western gaze relates to "the recognition of a split-space of enunciation" and the "articulation of cultural hybridity," which Homi Bhabha (1994, p. 173) relates to living in "the third space" of the hybrid.

COUNTERTRANSFERENCE BETWEEN WORLDS

Cultural hybridization raises countertransference agendas in therapy in complex ways (Bronstein 1986, Reid 1993, Richardson and Molinaro 1996, Solomon 1992), whether with therapists working with ethinically matching or diverse backgrounds from their clients, affecting dynamics, split identities, personas, and race, gender, and cultural motifs. Franz

Fanon (1967) was the first psychiatrist to underline the complex splits of persona related to cultural otherness for visible minorities in white societies. After Fanon's seminal works on race countertransference, there was an increasing exploration using psychoanalytic reference points (Adams 1996, Holmes 1992, Kareem and Littlewood 1992, Lane 1998, Nandy 1995, Sue and Sue 1999, Young-Bruehel 1996). Using culturally congruent metaphors, respecting and empathizing with different frames of reference and values are essential to this therapeutic work (Lau 1995). Said's (1978) thesis of Orientalism is particularly relevant to the treatment of diaspora women. He suggests that these projections (of Orientalism) on cultural Others in the colonial context of the East and West, while deeply embedded as social, institutional, and unconscious elements of a multicultural society, remain largely denied in explicit dialogue (Imhasly-Gandhy 2001, Khan 2002). Spivak (1988) suggests in this context, for example, that the British colonial ideology once justified itself as a project of white men "saving brown women from brown men." Though persona reflects the individual strengths, weaknesses, vices, and virtues, it also very much represents the culture and society to which the individual belongs, along with the shadow side of that society (Fernando 2003, Obeyesekere 1990). When groups are excluded from the structure of power and privilege within a society, the damage wreaked on the psyche and soul of the excluded group is brought to the therapist (Hopcke 1995), an issue that effects diaspora women within their natal and host societies.

Case 4

> Rani, an 18-year-old, suicidal and distressed single second-generation immigrant Indian-origin woman, was seen in consultation with two Indian-origin therapists (one of whom had actually grown up in the Caribbean Islands). She had been referred by her therapist, who had difficulty understanding her issues. Rani voiced her apprehension that one of the therapists might know her community or be "too close" to her mother's community, which she felt projected significant stigma onto mentally ill women. She was intrigued by the other therapist of Caribbean origin, who looked like her and had a Hindu name, but didn't know any maternal Indian languages. She proposed to have her therapy with the Caribbean-origin thera-

pist who would understand being a visible minority but would not be "too close." She reflected later that many affects seemed deeply embedded and accessible in her language but were too threatening to reexperience in therapy, and a second language (English) gave her space to think differently with more detachment from family issues. Her ability and entitlement to speak openly was associated with the host culture spaces or language. She feared being judged by traditional ideals (parental and group transference issues), stating that her fear of intrusion, criticism, or risk of community disclosure was lessened with her new therapist, who also understood the cultural maps of her family. She had kept many secrets from her parents, particularly around her sexual adventures, and had been very self-destructive with her body prior to entering therapy, with episodic life-threatening anorexia, an abortion, and self-mutilating behaviors not evident to her family members. She was able to establish a positive therapeutic alliance in long-term therapy. Later her self-destructive acts abated, her parents stopped pressuring her to return for marriage to the village, and she chose an Indian-origin partner in America after completing her studies. She never disclosed her sexual adventures to her family of origin, and terminated her therapy a few times, only to resume later, refueling with her therapist as new individuation conflicts arose. Her therapist as a "hybrid woman" accompanied this young woman as a transitional person who was competent in the Canadian milieu but who respected traditional life from a marginal position.

Narratives, whether clinical or literary, may inform us of the predicament of women. Ethnographic studies also help in tracing the explicating facets of the internal dynamics of institutional and religious influences (Rayaprol 1997), and contribute to our understanding community population samples showing underutilization of mental health services by Asian minorities. Psychoanalytic therapy appears to have had limited congruence with Indian milieus in the past, and immigrants often report disappointing encounters with Western therapists. If the immigrant woman is overidentified with the host culture, then the ethnic identity may be suppressed, repressed, or pushed aside, though it may be these identifications that are at the core of her inner world. Surviving the host culture agendas of adaptation may necessitate a split of worlds (peers and home). Therapists may be chosen by these women as allies to resolve or maintain these splits. These repressed identifications may indeed surface later in life, with losses, traumas, rejection, or distress in the adopted homeland or emerging in seemingly self-destructive acts that sabotage achievements in the host society. These dynamics might be related to unconscious processes such as attempts to reassert the true self (including familial identifications), expose ambivalence associated with breaking with the control of the familial "other" world, or erupt in bodily distress such as anorexia or self-mutilation.

Madness like gender is socially constructed as Foucault (1988), Das (1989), Spivak (1988), Davar (1999), Seshadri-Crooks (1994), and others have elaborated, while stigma or prejudice, as Obeyesekere (1981, 1990) suggests, reaches into the deeper fears of social groups. Traditional Indian systems in fact offer a complex manner of intervention, spirituality, and methods of healing or rebalancing disturbed individuals. Popular wisdom cautions about imbalances from excess of grief, pride (*sir jhuk gaya, sir phir gaya*), or negative emotions. As elaborated in the ancient Tamil text of Tiruvalluvar, "envy, greed, wrath and harsh words—these are to be avoided in domestic life especially by women." "A good wife is a boon to the house, the good children its jewel" (Tiruvalluvar 1990). In this context, speaking to outsiders in psychoanalytical psychotherapy sometimes presents resistances based on shame or fear, crossing a taboo of connectedness to the family circle. Cultural spaces indicate why to talk, how to talk, when to talk, and what to talk about (Bruner 1996, Fiske 1996, Kim 2002, Lau 1995, Shore 1996).

Case 5

Begum, a socially isolated, educated, first-generation Bangladeshi woman, who had five children ranging from age 4 to adolescence, suffered from a psychotic illness after her immigration. She was seen in consultation along with her family, as the clinic she attended for the previous five years was concerned that her husband wanted to abandon her in her native village. They felt frustrated with the patient and sought a cultural formulation of their countertransference feelings. It emerged during the first interview that she had always been heard through her husband as translator (outsider translation is essential to hearing her voice), had many side effects from elevated levels of neuroleptics, and was unable to manage her older children, who were ashamed of her. The clinic was unaware that the oldest child had in fact been expelled from school and was affiliated with street gangs, as he was often unsupervised from a young age. Begum was unaware of concerns about her children other than the lack of respect from her older children. She was inappropriately disengaged as a parent and left her home in a chaotic state. She knew that her husband had a mistress (with whom he had a child), who was treated as a favorite aunt by the children. She appreciated the help of the mistress who was much more functional and assimilated into the Canadian milieu and therefore able to help both the children and husband with assimilation and school-related issues. While the clinic was aware of neglect issues, they had never explored the issues of attachment or understood Begum's position in her family. They had been sympathetic mainly toward her husband, who was burdened by a chronically ill, psychotic wife and "fed up" with her inability to fulfill her familial duties. He negotiated plans for her return to the Subcontinent, through her oldest living male relation, a brother living in the Persian Gulf, without consulting her. When this plan was explored in the session, she was clear she wanted a Canadian passport. "Don't dump me without a passport." She understood she could not return without papers, and said she would miss her children if she was sent away. The clinic then advocated for the father's trying to return to work, for helping the neglected children, and for the patient by undertaking the task of getting her passport. Her husband offered her the youngest child, the 4-year-old, who was still limited in language skills and understimulated, having spent most of her time with a psychotic mother. A compromise was reached, to allow Begum to get a passport, to delay the child's departure, and to send her to a day-care center in Canada. The Indian-origin mistress was included in subsequent meetings to negotiate family issues, and she brought up her own issues of being pressured by her family to marry or to leave her child with her family in a village on the Subcontinent. The patient suffered from paranoid feeling and was reluctant to talk to anyone, as no one had listened to her despite many years of hospitalization. Language and systemic issues compounded the therapists' attempts to lessen her disorienting and dislocating experiences.

For women with a psychotic illness, the additional disorientation of language and alienation can be overwhelming and permanently disturb attachments with children (Penfold and Walker 1984). There had been concerns raised in the literature that these women may be more often committed or treated inappropriately with electroshock therapy or large amounts of neuroleptics (Burck and Speed 1995, Fernando 2003, Lau 1995, Penfold and Walker 1984). Efforts to understand and not assume parameters of the psychosocial context of these women is essential to intervention planning. Bowen (1978) described a "societal projection process" where the benefactors of family systems define others as inferior or incompetent in order to relieve their own anxiety and uncertainty. This leaves the therapists in danger of becoming over-sympathetic to the power relations in the family, placing inferior members in one-down positions, and "either keep them there or get angry with them" (Ratna and Wheeler 1995, p. 139). Countertransference needs to be informed on systemic, intrapsychic, and social levels.

CONCLUSION

The diaspora experience is about an "unsettling, recombination, hybridization, cut and mix" (Hall 2003) marked by a deep ambivalence of identification and desire, and a journey with no map. Women of Indian origin weave identities from an imaginary idea of India (Khilnani 1997, Raine 1991, Suleri 1992) with mythic influences rooted in maternal-feminine identifications resonating with a mother goddess as psychic bedrock, a social system influenced by religious diversity, unsettling recombinations acquired in global immigration, and the alternate paradigms of individuation arising from global spaces. The relationship of past self to present self is full of diverse choices, mediated intrapsychically by memory, fantasy, and desire, with representations altered by the influences of technologies, the arts, and globalization. These predicaments contribute to a fertile ground either for precipitating crises that will drive a renewal to build identity, to faciliatate individuating anew, and to encourage enrichment, or for precipitating what Bion (1967) calls catastrophic shifts (Grinberg and Grinberg 1989).

The sensitive facilitation of interfamilial communications and relationships remains a key part of psychoanalytic psychotherapy of diaspora Indian-origin women influenced by the gaze from West and East as the self becomes a kaleidoscope of experiences (Ponterotto et al. 2001, Solomon 1992). Despite the rich iconography and metaphoric plays on gender change and androgyny (Doniger 1999, Kakar 1989, Roland 1990), traditional and contemporary Indian society is homophobic, so therapy may also allow exploration of sexuality that is taboo in the homeland object or group world, though not in the diaspora. Therapeutic interfaces and interactions need to be referenced by dimensions of Subcontinent realities pertaining to class, gender, sexuality, ethnicity, and nationality. They must also be vigilant for the potential of "epistemic violence" (Spivak 1995), that is, culturally imposed destruction of psychological links. Imaginative empathy remains essential in the therapeutic relationship.

We have tried to promote a multifocal approach to providing therapy to women of Indian origin, and suggested that therapy may continue on a long-term intermittent basis. Patients do not need to adhere unquestioningly to the beliefs and values of the Indian traditional family or community group, and can come to own their own mind and voice. At the same time, they do not have to identify with the host culture and its values, but may affirm their various personas in a coherent and strategic bicultural mind set.

Given that much of the lived experience of the traditional feminine was anonymous and "inside the *haveli*" (a traditional feudal home) (Mehta 1977) or within the important roles of family rituals and nurturing, then shifting into an autonomous choice and individualism is both a radical departure and an intragenerational process that searches for multidirectional and heterogeneous modes of representation. The psychological agendas of joint family life, and malevolent, painful realities of middle class dowry death or pressures promoting female feticide in India, cannot be reduced to symbolic, imaginary, or cultural representations. Depressions, possession states, hysteria, and dissociation need to be situated in larger regulatory sociopolitical processes (Davar 1999) that constrain women's voices and agency.

Immigration mixes the possibilities of maintaining traditional motifs, bicultural competence, autonomy, intermarriage, assimilation, and creolization. Immigration is about the clash of Old World nostalgia and the casual breaking of deeply held taboos. While children in the diaspora may have entirely different perceptions of India from their parents, these unresolvable experiential jumps are part of the concerns of families and individuating children. Some women who cross a centuries-old silent boundary to verbalize about conflict outside the family may seek psychotherapeutic help. Psychotherapy can be viewed from an Eastern gaze as a subversive activity or as a healing opportunity to negotiate journeys on "the swinging bridge" (Espinet 2003, Tagore 2002) of immigration. Identity, race, and countertransference are the most significant issues in psychotherapy with Indian diaspora women.

REFERENCES

Adams, M. V. (1996). *The Multicultural Imagination*. London: Routledge.

Akhtar, S. (1995). The third individuation: immigration, identity, and the psychoanalytic process. *Journal of the American Psychoanalytic Association* 43:1051–1084.

Amado, G., and Ambrose, A. (1994). *Introduction to Transitional Thinking*. London: Karnac.

Bhabha, H., ed. (1990). *Nation and Narration*. London: Routledge.

––––––– (1994). *The Location of Culture*. London: Routledge.

Bhattacharyya, G. (1998). *Tales of Dark Skinned Women: Race, Gender and Global Culture*. London: UCL Press.

Bion, W. R. (1967). *Second Thoughts: Selected Papers in Psychoanalysis*. London: Heinemann.

Bowen, M. (1978). *Family Therapy in Clinical Practice*. New York: Jason Aronson.

Braziel, J., and Mannur, A. (2003). *Theorizing Diaspora*. Oxford: Blackwell.

Bronstein, P. (1986). Self disclosure, paranoia and unaware racism: another look at the black client and the white therapist. *American Psychologist* 41:225–226.

Bruner, J. S. (1996). *The Culture of Education*. Cambridge: Harvard University Press.

Burck, C., and Speed, B. (1995). *Gender, Power and Relationships*. London: Routledge.

Carstairs, G. M. (1957). *The Twice Born: A Study of a Community of High-Caste Hindus*. Bloomington: Indiana University Press.

Chughtai, I. (1990). *The Quilt and Other Stories.* New Delhi: Kali.

Crenshaw, K. (2003). Mapping the margins: intersectionally, identity politics, and violence against women of colour. In *Identities, Race, Class, Gender, and Nationality,* ed. L. M. Alcoff and E. Mendieta, pp.357–383. Oxford: Blackwell.

Das, V. (1989). Subaltern as perspective. In *Subaltern Studies VI,* ed. R. Guha, pp. 310–324. New Delhi: Oxford University Press.

Davar, B. V. (1999). Indian psychoanalysis, patriarchy, and Hinduism. *Anthropology and Medicine* 6:173–194.

Derrida, J. (1998). Geopsychoanalysis and the rest of the world. In *The Psychoanalysis of Race,* ed. C. Lane, trans. D. Nicholson-Smith, pp. 65–95. New York: Columbia University Press.

Desai, K. (1998). *Hullabaloo in Guava Orchard.* New Delhi: Viking-Penguin.

Doniger, W. (1999). *Splitting the Difference: Gender and Myth in Ancient Greece and India.* New Delhi: Oxford University Press.

Douglas, M. (1966). *Purity and Danger: An Analysis of the Concepts of Pollution and Taboo.* London: Routledge & Kegan Paul.

Espinet, R. (2003). *The Swinging Bridge.* Toronto: Harper Flamingo.

Falicov, C. J. (2002). Foreword. In *Therapeutic Care for Refugees, No Place Like Home,* ed. K. Papadoupoulos Renos, pp. i–vii. London: Karnac.

Fanon, F. (1967). *Black Skins, White Masks.* New York: Grove Weidenfeld.

Fernando, S. (2003). *Cultural Diversity, Mental Health and Psychiatry.* London: Routledge.

Fiske, A. P. (1996). The cultured mind: why psyches depend on cultures. Review of Philip K. Bock, *Philosophical Anthropology. Contemporary Psychology* 41:929–930.

Foucault, M. (1988). *Politics, Philosophy and Culture: Interviews and Other Writings 1977–1984.* New York: Routledge.

Frankenberg, R., and Mani, L. (1993). Cross-currents, cross-talks: race, postcoloniality and politics of action. In *Displacement, Diaspora, and Geographies of Identity,* ed. T. Swedenberg and S. Lavie, pp. 292–310. Durham, NC: Duke University Press.

Geertz, C. (1993). *The Interpretation of Culture.* London: HarperCollins.

Gibson, M. (1988). Accommodation without assimilation: Punjabi Sikh immigrants in American high schools. In *The Anthropology of Contemporary Issues Series.* Ithaca, NY: Cornell University Press.

Grinberg L., and Grinberg, R. (1989). *Psychoanalytic Perspectives on Migration and Exile.* New Haven, CT: Yale University Press.

Guha, R., ed. (1989). *Subaltern Series: Writings on South Asian History and Society,* vols. 1 to 6. New Delhi: Oxford University Press.

Guzder, J., and Krishna, M. (1991). Sita-shakti: cultural paradigms for Indian women. *Transcultured Psychiatric Research Review* 28:257–301.

Hall, S. (2003). New ethnicities. In *Identities, Race, Class, Gender, and Nationality*, ed. L. M. Alcoff and E. Mendieta, pp. 90–95. London: Blackwell.

Hedge, R. S. (1998). Swinging the trapeze: the negotiation of identity amongst Asian Indian immigrant women in the United States. In *Communication and Identity Across Cultures*, ed. D. V. Tanno and A. Gonzalez, pp. 34–55. Thousand Oaks, CA: Sage.

Ho, K. M. (1992). *Minority Children and Adolescents in Therapy*. New Delhi: Sage.

Holmes, D. E. (1992). Race and transference in psychoanalysis and psychotherapy. *International Journal of Psycho-Analysis* 73:1–11.

Hopcke, R. H. (1995). *Persona: Where Sacred Meets Profane*. London: Random House.

Huntington, S. (1997). *The Clash of Civilizations: Remaking the World Order*. New York: Touchstone.

Ignatieff, M. (2001). *Human Rights, Politics and Idolatry*, ed. A. Gutman. Princeton, NJ: Princeton University Press.

Imhasly-Gandhy, R. (2001). *The Psychology of Love: Wisdom of Indian Mythology*. Mumbai, India: Namita Gokhale Editions, Roli Books.

Kakar, S. (1978). *The Inner World: A Psychoanalytic Study of Indian Childhood and Society in India*. New Delhi: Oxford University Press.

——— (1989). The maternal-feminine in Indian psychoanalysis. *International Review of Psycho-Analysis* 16(3):355–365.

——— (1997). *Culture and the Psyche*. New Delhi: Oxford University Press.

Kareem, J., and Littlewood, R. (1992). *Intercultural Therapy*. Oxford: Blackwell.

Khan, S. (2002). *Aversion and Desire: Negotiating Muslim Feminine Identity in the Diaspora*. Toronto: Women's Press.

Khilnani, S. (1997). *The Idea of India*. New York: Farrar.

Kim, H. S. (2002). Freedom of speech and freedom of silence: an analysis of talking as a cultural practice. In *Engaging Cultural Differences: The Multicultural Challenge in Liberal Democracies*, ed. R. Schweder, M. Minow, and H. R. Markus, pp. 432–452. New York: Sage.

Kirmayer, L. J., Groleau, D., Guzder, J., et al. (2003). Cultural consultation: a model of mental health service for multicultural societies. *Canadian Journal of Psychiatry* 48:145–153.

Kumar, R. (1993). *The History of Doing*. New Delhi: Kali for Women.

Kurtz, S. (1992). *All the Mothers Are One*. New York: Columbia University Press.

Lahiri, J. (1999). *Interpreter of Maladies*. Boston: Houghton Mifflin.

Lane, C. (1998). *The Psychoanalysis of Race*. New York: Columbia University Press.

Lau, A. (1995). Gender, power and relationships: ethno-cultural and religious issues. In *Gender, Power, and Relationships*, ed. C. Burck and B. Speed. London: Routledge.

Liddle, J., and Joshi, R. (1986). *Daughters of Independence: Gender, Caste, and Class in India*. London: Zed.

Mehta, R. (1977). *Inside the Haveli*. New Delhi: Penguin.

Mukherjee, B. (1993). *The Holder of the World*. New York: Knopf.

Naidoo, J. (1992). Between East and West: reflections on Asian East Indian women in Canada. In *South Asian Canadians: Current Issues in the Politics of Culture*, ed. R. Ghosh and R. Kunango, pp. 81–90. New Delhi: Shastri Indo-Canadian Institute.

Nandy, A. (1995). *The Savage Freud*. New Delhi: Oxford University Press.

Niranjana, T. (2001). "Left to the imagination": Indian nationalisms and female sexuality in Trinidad. In *Alternative Modernities*, ed. D. P. Gaonkar. Durham, NC: Duke University Press.

Nussbaum, M. (2000). Women and work: the capabilities approach. *The Little Magazine* 1:26–27.

Obeyesekere, G. (1981). *Medusa's Hair: An Essay on Personal Symbols and Religious Experiences*. Chicago: University of Chicago Press.

————— (1990). *The Work of Culture: Symbolic Transformation in Psychoanalysis and Anthropology*. Chicago: University of Chicago Press.

Orbach, S. (1999). *The Impossibility of Sex*. London: Penguin.

Pandey G. (1989). The colonial construction of "communalism": British writings on Benares in the nineteenth century. In *Subaltern Series*, vol. 6, ed. R. Guha, pp. 132–168. New Delhi: Oxford University Press.

Penfold, P. S., and Walker, G. A. (1984). *Women and the Psychiatric Paradox*. London: Oxford University Press.

Pinhas, L., Weaver, H., Bryden, P., et al. (2002). Gender-role conflict and suicidal behaviour in adolescent girls. *Canadian Journal of Psychiatry* 47:473–475.

Ponterotto, J. G., Casas, J. M., Suzuki, L. A., and Alexander, C. M. (2001). *Handbook of Multicultural Counselling*, 2nd ed. Springfield, IL: Charles C Thomas.

Raine, K. (1991). *India from Afar*. New York: George Braziller.

Ram, A. (2002). Framing the feminine; diasporic readings of gender in popular Indian cinema. *Women's Studies in Communication* 25(1):25–52.

Ratna, L., and Wheeler, M. (1995). Race and gender issues in adult psychiatry. In *Gender, Power and Relationships*, ed. C. Burck and B. Speed, pp. 136–152. London: Routledge.

Ravindran, K. (1992). Towards a feminist psychoanalytic paradigm. *Indian Journal of Social Work* 53(3):411–428.

Rayaprol, A. (1997). *Negotiating Identities: Women in the Indian Diaspora*. New Delhi: Oxford University Press.

Reid, P. (1993). Poor women in psychological research: shut up and shut out. *Psychology of Women Quarterly* 17:133–150.

Richardson, T. Q., and Molinaro, K. L. (1996). White counsellor self-awareness: a prerequisite for multicultural competence. *Journal of Counselling and Development* 74(3):239–242.

Roland, A. (1990). *In Search of Self in India and Japan*. Princeton, NJ: Princeton University Press.

——— (1996). *Cultural Pluralism and Psychoanalysis*. New York: Routledge.

Rushdie, S. (1991). *Imaginary Homelands: Essays and Criticism 1981–1991*. London: Granta.

Said, E. (1978). *Orientalism*. New York: Routledge.

——— (2002). *Power, Politics and Culture: Interviews with Edward Said*. New York: Vintage.

Selvini, M. (1988). *The Work of Mara Selvini Palazzoli*, ed. M. Selvini. London: Aronson.

Seshadri-Crooks, K. (1994). The primitive as analyst: post colonial feminism's access to psychoanalysis. *Cultural Critique* 28:175–215.

Shore, B. (1996). *Culture in Mind*. New York: Oxford University Press.

Sidoli, M. (2000). *When the Body Speaks: The Archetypes in the Body*. London: Routledge.

Smith, Z. (2000). *White Teeth*. London: Hamish Hamilton.

Solomon, A. (1992). Clinical diagnosis amongst diverse populations: a multicultural perspective. *Families and Society* 73(6):371–377.

Spivak, G. C. (1988). *In Other Worlds: Essays in Cultural Politics*. New York: Routledge.

———. (1995). *Imaginary Maps: Three Stories by Mahasweta Deir*. New York: Routledge.

Sue, D. W., and Sue, D. (1999). *Counselling the Culturally Different: Theory and Practice*, 3rd ed. New York: Wiley.

Suleri, S. (1992). Woman skin deep: feminism and the post colonial condition. *Critical Inquiry* 18:756–769.

Tagore, P. (2002). The Shapes of Silence: Contemporary Women's Fiction and the Practices of Bearing Witness. Unpublished PhD thesis, Faculty of Arts, McGill University.

Taylor, C. (1992). *Multiculturism and the Politics of Recognition*. Princeton, NJ: Princeton University Press.

Thapan, M. (1997). *Embodiment: Essays on Gender and Identity*. Calcutta: Oxford University Press.

Tharu, S., and Lalita, K. (1991). *Women Writing in India: 600 B.C. to the Present*, vols. 1 and 2. New York: Feminist Press City University.

Thomas, L. (2002). Ethnic sameness and difference in family and systemic therapy. In *Exploring the Unsaid*, ed. B. Mason and A. Sawyer, pp. 49–68. London: Karnac.

Tiruvalluvar (1990). *The Kural*, trans. P. S. Sundaram. New Delhi: Penguin.

Trawick, M. (1990). *Notes on Love in a Tamil Family*. Berkeley, CA: University of California Press.

Viswanath, K. (1997). Shame and control: sexuality and power in feminist discourse in India. In *Embodiment: Essays on Gender and Identity*, ed. M. Thapan, pp. 313–337. New Delhi: Oxford University Press.

Winnicott, D. W. (1966). The location of cultural experience. *International Journal of Psycho-Analysis* 48:368–372.

Young-Bruehel, A. (1996). *The Anatomy of Prejudices*. Cambridge, MA: Harvard University Press.

9

Psychic Bisexuality, Male Homosexuality, Plural Oedipus Complex, and Hinduism

Bhaskar Sripada

And the hushed battlefield of our epic is my brown, bisexual body, which even you, who made it, cannot accept.

Minal Hajratwala (1995)

Both psychoanalysis and Hinduism subscribe to the value of depth psychology. Both propose that a proper understanding of reality starts at a manifest level but sooner or later goes into a deeper, latent content. In psychoanalysis, this constitutes the link between the conscious and unconscious systems of the mind. In Hinduism, the notion of *Maya* (illusory aspects of external reality) demands a deeper understanding of life. Applied to matters of sexuality, both psychoanalysis and Hinduism uphold the fundamentally bisexual nature of human beings. Psychoanalysis evolves it from ontogenetic development and Hinduism from a divine and mythical perspective. The desirability of assimilating such bisexual attributes at the deepest level of subjectivity, while recognizing one's given male or female sex, is also a feature of both psychoanalysis and Hinduism.

However, there is a remarkable difference in the degree to which the two can accommodate ideological relativism. Freud's ideas developed in a Western milieu of Judeo-Christian monotheism, a bivalent

Aristotelian organization of thought, and isolated identity formation. Like Occam's razor, which seeks to find pure concepts that are indispensable on the basis of parsimony, various psychoanalytic schools (instinctual, ego psychological, relational, and self psychological) make exclusive claims on true psychic understanding. Attempts to seek accommodation among these competing schools have not captured any lasting denominational following. Exclusivity dominates the field. In contrast, Hindu religion is guided by plural but complementary beliefs and perspectives. For example, the Rig Veda (I.64.46), Hinduism's most ancient scripture, says: "*Ekam sat vipraha bahudha vadanti*" ("Truth is One; the wise call it by many names"). In the realm of beliefs, all Hindus recognize the main gods, Brahma (representing creation), Vishnu (representing preservation), and Shiva (representing destruction). Unlike the West where God is quintessential and actual, gods from a Hindu perspective are projections of human psychology. Each adherent may extol the virtues of the god of his or her choice but still consider the other deities as gods. Regardless of which god an adherent subscribes to, the three main gods are believed to be pluripotent. It is impossible to consider one of these gods without needing to account for the other two gods. A Hindu may choose any one of them (Brahma, Vishnu, or Shiva) or their tripartite composite of them (*Trimurthy* is a combination of Brahma, Vishnu, and Shiva), or none of them and be agnostic. Hinduism is based on pluralism of faith (polytheism, agnosticism, and atheism) and philosophical perspectivism of *Darsana* (i.e., complementary viewing of reality from different perspectives). Hindu thought favors dimensional thinking (the notion of greater or lesser degrees, which is different from the categorical, yes-or-no mode of Judeo-Christian and Islamic traditions) and readily accommodates multiple identities of the self and object, including the ones in the divine realm.

In this chapter, I will make a case that Western psychoanalytic views on sexuality generally tend to be categorical (thus classifying a person as heterosexual, homosexual, bisexual, or asexual) while the Hindu orientation classifies all people as partly heterosexual, partly homosexual, partly bisexual, and partly asexual. My contribution supports this Hindu argument without losing a conceptual anchor in psychoanalysis. Consequently, I will also formulate a plural oedipal framework in which instinctual, relational, and narcissistic elements of the personality are linked, without universal primacy being assigned to any of the elements. The cross-fertilization between psychoanalysis and Hinduism that this chapter seeks will be most evident in my amalgamation of psychoanalytic oedipal theory and Hindu pluralism.

PSYCHOANALYTIC VIEWS ON HOMOSEXUALITY

Freud (1933) held that psychic bisexuality was a bedrock phenomenon; but he also held that masculinity was the natural state. In contrast to Freud's assumption of the primacy of masculinity, Greenson (1967) noted that the boy's initial identification is with the mother. Subsequent development involves his dis-identifying with the mother. It is only after this has been accomplished that a boy can acquire a masculine identification with the father. Stoller (1968) indicates that this initial feminine identification and the need to break free from it often leads the boy to effeminacy or defensive hypermasculinity. However, it was not the boy's maternal identification but his narcissism—and the object choices emanating from it—that was at the center of Freud's (1914) discussion of homosexual love.

Preoedipal Development and Separation-Individuation

Socarides (1968) initially described exclusive homosexuality as a pathology related to unresolved preoedipal conflicts. The preoedipal stage of development represents a time when the child does not realize or acknowledge the significance of the parental relationship. Influenced by Mahler's (Mahler et al. 1975) developmental observations on the relationship between a growing child and his mother, Socarides (1978) came to understand exclusive homosexuality as a preoedipal fixation and hence a pathological outcome. His view was that the homosexual has not adequately worked through the developmental tasks relating to separation-individuation and therefore fears reengulfment by all other subsequent women. He fears them and avoids encountering their sexual desire.

Oedipal Origins

Highlighting a point that Socarides (1968) had also conceded, Meissner (1993) suggests that not all homosexuality is preoedipally derived. In many instances, the underlying mechanism is a defensive flight from castration anxiety of oedipal origin. Meissner contrasted the oedipal configuration of the heterosexual with that of the homosexual. In the heterosexual, the opposite-sex parent is loved and the same-sex parent is feared, whereas in the homosexual, the opposite-sex parent is feared and the same-sex parent is loved. The sight of the female genital is avoided since it stirs up the dread of castration. Ovessey (1969) also viewed homosexuality as emanating from this neurotic conflict. This homosexual avoidance of females often emanates from a vagina dentata fantasy or from the fear of a rivalrous father since the woman becomes linked with the oedipal mother imago in the mind.

Adolescence and Homosexuality

Blos (1962) clarifies three preconditions in adolescence that favor the channeling of genital sexuality into a homosexual object choice: (1) fear of the vagina as a castrating, devouring organ linked to projected oral sadism; (2) the boy's continued identification with the mother, which is exacerbated when the mother is inconsistent and frustrating; and (3) an oedipal inhibition based on unconsciously equating all females with the mother, who is after all the father's prerogative.

Object Relations

The Committee on Medical Psychoanalysis under Bieber (Bieber et al. 1962) found that homosexual and heterosexual patients varied in their family makeup. They concluded that the configuration of close, binding mothers and hostile or detached fathers caused homosexuality. Friedman (2002), however, states that such a specific family pattern in homosexual families has not been validated. At the same time, Friedman (1988) acknowledged that gay men more often than heterosexual men describe difficulties with their fathers during development. Freud (1920) stated that homosexual men experience a specially strong fixation on their mothers, and he claimed (1910) that Leonardo da Vinci's homosexuality constituted identification with his mother. Drescher (2002) wondered whether the cultural stereotype of a homosexual as a "mama's boy" had its origins in the society's unconscious knowledge of this dynamic.

Bollas (1992), while acknowledging that not all mothers of homosexuals are domineering, relies on a combination of maternal, paternal,
and anxiety factors in understanding homosexuality. He states that
mothers of homosexuals are different because they seem to offer reli-
able refuge from an otherwise anxiety-provoking world, often supply-
ing love and affection unavailable from a distant or remote father.

Narcissism

Extending Freud's (1914) notion about narcissistic object choices,
Isay and Friedman (1986) suggest that homosexuality may be considered "a specific form of narcissism" (p. 195). However, they emphasize
that this should not be taken as evidence of *pathological* narcissism.
Tolpin (2002) states that sexuality, gay or straight, may be part of the
healthy "forward edge" of self-development, or part of the trailing edge
of pathology. In an analysis with transference of the forward-edge kind,
the analyst is experienced unconsciously as mirroring, idealizing, and
as an alter selfobject.

Evolutionary, Hereditary, and Biological Factors

Biological factors also have significant impact on gender identity
and sexual object choice. Kolodny et al. (1971) reported higher serum
testosterone in heterosexual than in homosexual men. Differences between the hypothalamic structures of homosexual and heterosexual men
have also been identified (LeVay 1991). However, Friedman (2002) compared the blood levels of sexual hormones in socially well-adjusted men
of homo- and heterosexual orientation and concluded there is no basis
for regarding homosexuality to be pathological. A similar stance is taken
by Schafer (2002). He states that Freud, operating within the Darwinian evolutionary ethic and the norms of his times, developed two biased notions concerning homosexuality: (1) that homosexuality was a
perversion, and (2) that it was a manifestation of arrested development.
Schafer states,

> Viewing the individual as the carrier of the reproductive organs and sub-
> stances designed to guarantee the survival of the species, he [Freud] rea-
> soned that it was essential that there be successful transmission of the

germplasm from generation to generation. It followed that psychosexual development should culminate in genital, heterosexual, reproductive sexuality. . . . Freud continued to consider the procreative endpoint the only one that was complete and natural. [pp. 29–30]

Schafer (2002) states that Freud "seemed not to notice that he was leaping from biological norms to moral judgments when he assumed that development *ought to* culminate in reproductivity" (p. 30). Idealizing procreation, Freud and other early analysts, especially Rado (1940), regarded men who diverged from the procreative norm as developmentally stunted.

Countertransference Biases

Freud stated that "normal people have a certain homosexual component and a very strong heterosexual component" (cited in Wortis 1954, pp. 99–100). He (1920) remarked that homosexuality is a complex phenomenon with many permutations of three relatively independent characteristics: (1) physical sexual character, (2) mental sexual character, and (3) object choice. There he also stressed that a considerable measure of latent homosexuality can be detected in all normal people.

Several psychoanalysts have held that homosexuality is a pathological condition. Bergler (1957, p. 79) held that "there are no healthy homosexuals." Socarides (1978, pp. 54–55) held that "all homosexuals suffer from psychic masochism." Anna Freud (1973) stated that homosexuality is an abnormality. This can lead to a prejudiced technical stance. Stoller (1968) noted that a homosexual patient complained that Stoller was putting pressure on the patient and not understanding that the patient was truly a homosexual. He acknowledges that the patient's view was not delusional. "It may well have been based on his realization that I really did have wishes that he could become heterosexual. . . . [It is my] bias that in our world heterosexuality still has greater potential for pleasure and happiness" (pp. 161–162).

In sharp contrast is Isay's (1993) idea that homosexuals can live well adjusted, productive lives with gratifying and stable love relationships. He disagrees with the view generally held by psychoanalysts until the late 1980s that homosexuality is pathological and only heterosexuality is normal. This he considers to be a theoretical and cultural bias on the part of the analyst, one that propels a desire to change the sexual orientation of the homosexual patient.

PERSPECTIVES OF HINDUISM

Purusarthas refers to the aims of life according to Hinduism (Radhakrishnan 1969). The chief aim of man is self development and self-realization. *Moksha* is the goal to find the real self, to exceed his apparent, outward self. *Kama* is the goal of attaining enjoyment through the medium of emotions, feelings, and desires. *Artha* is the goal of obtaining wealth and material well-being. *Dharma* is the goal of living life by the rule according to right practice. *Dharma* clarifies that while our life is in the first instance for our own satisfaction, it is more essentially for the community and most of all for the universal self that is in each of us and in all beings. Here we may note that there is a clear understanding of the existence of differences between the real self (which is to be found) and the apparent self (which is imaginary and illusory).

Ardhanarishvara, the Androgynous Form of Shiva

Among the many instances of gods with an androgynous character, *Ardhanarishvara,* the single, united, and half-male–half-female form of the god Shiva, is the most prominent one. Its right side is male and left side female.

> It represents the culmination of all male and all female forms. From the union of the male and female energies lust arises, and hence this form of Shiva symbolizes lust (*Kama*). Ardhanari carries out the creative process and begets Skanda [a son]. . . . Thus, Ardhanari conducts the mind beyond objective experience in a symbolic realm where duality is left behind. [Stutley and Stutley 1917, p. 18]

Danielou (1987) states that the androgynous aspect of *Ardhanarishvara* is the "life principle, the origin of the species" (p. 112). He (1984) emphasizes that "primordial divinity is essentially bisexual. The division of this principle into two opposing poles [duality] which give life to the world is merely apparent. . . . All degrees of bisexuality appear in the various aspects of the god" (pp. 63–65). Subramuniyaswami (2002) also views *Ardhanarishvara* as representing "pure consciousness," adding that any mediator who balances the masculine and the feminine sides through yoga or other exercises becomes fully self-realized like Shiva.

From a psychoanalytic perspective, *Ardhanarishvara* indicates the essence of Freud's (1905, 1915, 1920) life instinct and thus a powerful reminder of the origin and sustenance of the human species. Although each specific embodied manifestation of life is expressed as male or female, life itself cannot be imagined without two sexes. The *Ardhanarishvara* image signifies a sexual composite without dualities. It becomes a firm reminder that while the manifest sex of each person can only express what is biologically and behaviorally possible, at the deepest core of each person there is awareness of his or her psychic bisexuality. *Ardhanarishvara* is therefore not only a religious icon but also the evocative transference anchor of a deeper, latent consciousness in human beings. Indeed, like a wise analytic interpretation, *Ardhanarishvara* simultaneously hints at what already exists in the unconscious and what can become still more overtly "mentalized" (Fonagy and Target 1997). It is a beautiful poem.

Mohini, Harihara, and Ayappa

In ancient times, in order to obtain an immortal elixir, *Devas* (gods) and *Asuras* (demons) collaborated in churning the mythical ocean of milk. Among the gods were Vishnu (who is also called Hari), and Shiva (also called Hara). The elixir materialized through this combined effort, but the gods wanted to keep it all for themselves. Vishnu (a male god) transformed himself into Mohini (a female) in order to distract the demons so that the gods will have complete access to the elixir. In the process, Hara (Shiva) became enamored of Mohini and united with her-him. This composite union of the two male gods, Hari (Vishnu) and Hara (Shiva), as a single figure is the figure of Harihara. Ayappa is the product of the union of Hari and Hara and is therefore also called Hariharaputra. Currently, Ayappa is worshiped by thousands of male devotees in the Southern India state of Kerala.

The Male Devotee and Krishna

Hindus, in general, view the essential human nature to contain both male and female elements. This acceptance of fundamental psychic bisexuality is evident in the prevalence of androgynous myths and icons. Such a view is most pronounced in Tantric practices. Kakar (1982) notes that Tantra claims that a person can become whole when "he annuls sexual differentiation and dissolves gender identity into a certain kind of bisexuality" (p. 156). Fascinatingly, psychoanalysis articulates notions similar to those found in Hinduism. Freud (1930) stated,

> Man is an animal organism with an unmistakable bisexual disposition. The individual corresponds to a fusion of two symmetrical halves, of which, according to some investigators, one is purely male and the other purely female. It is equally possible that each half was originally hermaphrodite. Sex is a biological fact which, although it is of extraordinary importance in mental life, is hard to grasp psychologically. We are accustomed to say that every human being displays both male and female instinctual impulses, needs and attributes; but though anatomy, it is true, can point out the characteristics of maleness and femaleness, psychology cannot. For psychology the contrast between the sexes fades away into one between activity and passivity, in which we far too readily identify activity with maleness and passivity with femaleness. . . . The theory of bisexuality is still surrounded by many obscurities and . . . it has not yet found any link with the theory of instincts. . . . Each individual seeks to satisfy both male and female wishes in sexual life. [pp. 105–106]

A Hindu's prayer is an exercise in self-awareness. In the monist tradition, it aims to help the devotee understand that the phenomenal world of dualities is only *maya* (illusion) and that deeper truths lie beyond it. The meditated god is seen as part of the self, and prayer involves a temporary identification with the god or the god's consort or both. According to O'Flaherty (1980), in Tantric Krishna worship the devotee visualizes himself as both the god and the goddess. A female devotee mostly visualizes Krishna as a male and readily develops a relationship with him. However, when the Krishna devotee is a male, a change in his psychological sex, as it were, seems required and he must assume a somewhat feminine posture toward Krishna. Carstairs (1957), too, feels that "the male [Hindu] worshippers who imagine themselves as *Gopis* have to be open to the charges that their behavior reveals a thinly-veiled longing for him [Krishna] as a homosexual lover" (p. 60).

The mistaken impression of Western scholars that there is a homosexual relationship between such a male devotee and Krishna is because in the West there is a greater degree of congruence between sexual and gender identity and there is no assumption of foundational bisexuality of life. This is an outsider's perspective on a cultural phenomenon different from his or hers. The fact is that in Hindu India there is a general acceptance of psychic bisexuality and delinkage between gender identity and sexual object choice. A god with male and female attributes is intended to convey this essential bisexuality and not intended to imply the worship of some genetically or biologically hermaphroditic or intersexed being. Superimposing Western notions (derived from a view that male and female are fundamental elements of life) onto a Hindu setting, in which the notion of a fundamental bisexuality of life prevails, confuses psychic bisexuality with bisexual behavior.

Sikhandi-Sikhandini

Hindu epics describe many divine and human characters who have undergone sexual transformations or whose souls have transmigrated to bodies of individuals of the opposite sex. *Mahabharata*, the great Hindu epic, tells of the battle between two rivals, the Pandavas and the Kauravas. One of the lead warriors for the Pandavas was Arjuna, and one of the lead warriors for the Kauravas was Bhisma. Bhisma was apparently invincible. Previously Bhisma carried away a young damsel, Amba (who was already betrothed to King Salva), as a bride for his own half-brother Vichitravirya. When Vichitravirya found out that she was previously betrothed, he sent her back to King Salva. But King Salva, on the grounds that she had entered the dwelling of another man, refused to take back Amba. She was consumed with anger for Bhisma and performed penance to Lord Shiva. Lord Shiva informed her that Bhisma would die because of her, in her next birth. Impatient for revenge, she committed suicide.

In her next rebirth, Amba was born to King Dhrupada, as his daughter, and was named Sikhandini. A man named Sthunakarna exchanged his manhood with her and Sikhandini (a woman) became Sikhandi (a man). The battles were fought according to codes of military conduct that did not allow a man to fight a woman. During the war Bhisma revealed that he will not fight Sikhandi because he is a she. Arjuna, taking cover by placing Sikhandi in front of himself, killed Bhisma.

THE SEXES IN ANCIENT INDIA

In ancient India, male homosexuality was ignored, tolerated as an insignificant variation, considered undesirable, or stigmatized. The ancient Indian sexual treaties, *Kama Sutra*, warns against practicing *auparishtaka* (fellatio). The Laws of Manu (4.222; Muller 1886), which constitute the ancient laws of Hindu India, prescribe penance for a man who has swallowed the semen of another man. Sexual activity between men was to be cleansed out of the system by a ritual bath. At other places, too, in Hindu mythology, oral sex is considered to be a perversion. The god of fire, Agni, drinks the semen of Lord Shiva. Shiva says to Agni, "You did a perverse thing to drink my seed" (O'Flaherty 1980, p. 51).

In ancient India, people were classified as male, female, and the third gender. According to Dasa (2003), this division was according to *prakriti*, or nature. These sexes are *purus-prakriti* (male), *stri-prakriti* (female), and *tritiya-prakriti* (the third gender). These three genders are not determined by physical characteristics alone but rather by an assessment of the entire being that includes the physical, psychological body, and social attributes (procreative status). The third sex is described as a combination of the male and female natures to the point that they can no longer be categorized as male or female. There are many examples of this, the most common of which is the Sanskrit word *napumsaka* (literally "not male"), which is used to refer to a man who has no taste for women and thus does not procreate. According to Dasa, while the term *napumsaka* may include children, elderly, neuters, eunuchs, celibates, the diseased, the impotent, and castrated men, the term does not refer to homosexuals.

THE CONTEMPORARY SCENE

Asthana and Oostvogels (2001) clarify that, in the West, the notions of a gay identity and gay community have not developed in India. They suggest that the single, descriptive term "men who have sex with men" (MSM) is more suitable for the Indian context. In contemporary India, the construction of identity is strongly influenced by the notions of gender and power. To be a man is to be a husband and a father; a man may engage in homosexual behavior without compromising his inner sense of masculinity until the time he also (or eventually) marries and fathers children. Consequently, the Indian system can accommodate great fluidity of sexual expression and experience.

There are several overlapping terms used in India to describe or designate people who engage in homosexual behavior. Even in a single state, namely Tamil Nadu, where the Asthana and Oostvogels (2001) study was done, a bewildering set of terms are applied to men engaging in sex with other men: (1) *Panthi* are "real men" with unbridled primarily heterosexual sexual needs. They view sex with another man as a source of additional pleasure. In these sexual acts, they are always the active one. Such sexual activity does not compromise their sexual identity. Passive participation in sexual acts threatens their masculinity and they vehemently reject it. (2) "Double-deckers" are men with a masculine or a neutral identity. They may be involved with women or men. Their sexual activity may be active or passive. (3) *Danga* refers to a man with distinct feminine traits. *Dangas* walk and talk like women. They refer to each other as "she" but retain male clothing. (4) *Hijras* (also called *Ali* in Tamil Nadu and *Kojja* in Andhra Pradesh) are men, many of whom have been ritually castrated. *Hijras* do not fall into the category of male. They dress as women and exhibit exaggerated feminine behavior. *Hijras* claim to be females in male bodies. They may be asexual or practice homosexual prostitution (Nanda 1999, Sharma 1989, Vyas and Shingala 1987).

TWO CLINICAL ILLUSTRATIONS

The Case of Vivek

My initial contact in this case was via Vivek's father. He called me and said that his son, Vivek, aged 20, had recently announced that he was homosexual. He wanted his son to explore the possibility of changing his sexual preference. He prayed and hoped that I could help in this effort, and offered to meet with me along with his wife if necessary. He added that other than the problem with homosexuality, Vivek was a perfect boy. He was always a straight-A student, easygoing, and caused no trouble as a child and adolescent. He asked me, "What is the

next step?" I replied, "If Vivek has any concerns or wants to be in treatment, Vivek should call me. If Vivek calls and decides to seek treatment, I will be his doctor, but our communications will be confidential.
Your concerns are not the same as Vivek's concerns. The outcome of
treatment cannot be predicted." The very next day, Vivek called me
to make an appointment.

Vivek was a handsome young man of slight build who was bright,
articulate, and composed. He explained his problems in a succinct and
clear manner over the next few sessions. Vivek was born in India and
came to the United States as an infant. He came from a very devout
Hindu family that prayed regularly. They often went to temples, and
their social life revolved around religious occasions and festivals. Vivek
noted that he had felt "gay" for as long as he could remember. He had
had a few unsatisfactory homosexual experiences but was looking for a
lifelong and loving gay relationship. Though sex was not a primary
motive in his search, he ached to touch a man and feel the warmth of
a caring person. He clarified that at present he was not involved with
any man. He felt alone and depressed. He was anxious in the presence
of men in authority and preferred to relate to women. Many of his
friends were straight. Mostly he spoke in an unaffected manner. On one
occasion he talked in a high-pitched voice and gestured with a limp
wrist, like the stereotype of a gay man. While he did so, he said that
he often despised gay men. He also said he despised straight guys who
are prejudiced against gays. He alternated between being prejudiced
against gay men and at other times prejudiced against straight men.
Vivek wanted to know why he felt gay and why he felt troubled about
it. He hoped that by talking to me he could gain further insight into
his gayness. I told him that I would be glad to treat him and that his
part of the treatment was to say whatever thoughts occurred to him.
He agreed and we started to meet on a four-times-a-week basis.

Vivek had confided his homosexual leanings a few weeks earlier
to his sister, who was three years older. He was angry that she revealed
it to her parents, though he was not surprised by it. Upon hearing that
Vivek was gay, his father had a discussion with him and asked him if
he had problems of potency with women. Vivek replied that the problem was not potency but lack of a sexual interest in women. His father
was furious and recommended that he try to change his sexual orientation. His father suggested masturbation if he could not change his

orientation. His parents encouraged him to behave like a "normal" Hindu and be heterosexual. They suggested that he should solve the problem by getting married immediately. They offered to look for potential brides. In the face of so many forces, Vivek felt confused about his sexual orientation and decided to seek treatment. His thinking went this way. If he realizes he is truly gay, he will accept his gayness regardless of what his parents or anyone else feels. However, if he comes to realize that he is straight, he will find a woman himself in the Western tradition or ask his parents to arrange a marriage for him. If he does so he will truly change and be true to his wife. He will not live a double life and deceive his wife.

Vivek strongly wished that his parents would adopt a tolerant attitude toward his homosexuality. He reminded his parents that Lord Rama blessed *Kojjas*, who are transvestites in India. Although *Kojjas* were transvestites, Vivek felt that the same applied to homosexuals. Vivek believed that Rama would have accepted gay people. His father, on the other hand, wanted him to be a "normal" Hindu, comply with the normal ideals of Hinduism, and be a heterosexual. In addition, he took umbrage at what he judged to be Vivek's misguided attempts to associate Lord Rama with transvestites or homosexuals. He said that he regretted having come to the United States, and expressed the thought that had they continued to live in India perhaps Vivek would not have become gay. Vivek, on the other hand, is tired of complying with other people's demands. He wanted to be different and unique. His taste in music was New Age, which no one in his family could understand. Vivek felt that he was angry because his parents were trying to force him to change his sexual orientation. They didn't want to know the "real me." Yet he said, "I don't want to hurt my parents."

I indicated to Vivek that I appreciated how he felt himself to be at a crossroads, but that I saw his conflicts regarding gayness within a larger context of negotiating the differences between himself and his parents, of making difficult choices. I agreed that understanding how he came to be the way he is might give us some insights that, in turn, might help him to make decisions that are important to him. Vivek asked, "Have you ever seen anyone whose sexual orientation had changed with treatment?" In a moment two situations flashed through my memory. A man who was the father of two children and subsequently decided he was gay. Another Indian Hindu man, who initially saw himself as gay decided during the course of treatment that he was straight.

While these two cases were buffeting my thoughts, Vivek interrupted me: "I want an answer. Do you know anybody that changed?" I said, "Yes. It looks like you wanted me to answer that question." Vivek said, "Yes." I told him that one was a married man with two children who discovered that he was gay. The other was a man who thought that he was gay but came to realize that he was straight.

Vivek missed his next therapy session. At the subsequent session, he talked about a program on the Phil Donahue television show in which a minister claimed that homosexuality was curable. Vivek was not sure about it. He felt that changing his sexual orientation would mean giving up his own self and conforming to a self that his parents wanted. He felt gayness was a rebellion against parents. If he changed, he would be giving up his independence. I commented on his missing the previous session and wondered if it was a sign of rebellion against me. Vivek noted that he was confused about whether he was seeing me for his parents' sake or his own sake. Vivek wanted me not only to be tolerant of his homosexuality but also to certify to his father that he was normal. I now remembered attending a case presentation of a Hindu man in treatment. The presenter described a young man who was inhibited and came from a progressive Hindu family. After much good work, the man fell in love with a woman of a different caste. Her family was also progressive. With some anxiety, both families came to accept the love marriage and arrangements were being made for the wedding. During this time the patient asked the analyst whether he would meet his bride before the wedding and bless the couple. The analyst readily agreed. I remember feeling that "blessing the couple" comprised ecclesiastical duties that were outside of the line of duty of an analyst.

I told Vivek that I did not think it would be a good idea for me to speak to his father. I acknowledged that Vivek had hoped that I would somehow soothe the tension with his father. Vivek replied that he needs the protection of someone like Lord Rama. He was disappointed that I could not provide it. Upon further reflection, however, Vivek said that even should I agree to do so, it would not change his father.

In the subsequent session, Vivek first talked about his parents' curiosity concerning his therapy. They constantly ask him about his sessions. He wants to talk to them but feels extremely conflicted. "I want them to know the real me, but am afraid that they are so much interested in the image of a perfect family and a perfect son that they can't accept my reality." Finally he related a dream and a few associations: "I was with my family. We were at a train station. We were waiting for the train. I remembered that I forgot to call you about missing my session. My parents told me that there was a pay telephone to call you. Then I realized that I had to pee. I discovered that the place to pee was an open urinal [like in India]. In the dream I began to pee. I woke up and realized that I wet the bed. I was surprised. There was too much wetness. It was not an ejaculation." It was time to end the session, and I commented about his surprise in the dream and his embarrassment about his bed-wetting, which may have caused him to almost forget the dream and report it only toward the end of the session.

During the next session Vivek commented on his reluctance to talk about the dream. He was most embarrassed that he had wet his bed after the dream. It made him feel like a child. I might think less of him because of his bed-wetting and tease him. He recalled that he had been teased as a kid for bed-wetting. He was also always self-conscious about his small height; he would like to have rippling muscles that showed through his tank tops.

At the next session Vivek recalled another dream: "I was in a girl's room and was on the phone. I suddenly saw that someone was jumping off a building to commit suicide. I said to the person that I was talking to that I could not continue the conversation because a suicide was in progress. Suddenly the scene changed. I was at a urinal. It was a peculiar urinal. It had a curtain. Someone was trying to open it and I was trying to keep it closed. I woke up and was glad that I had not wet my bed."

Vivek then noted that he was irritated by his parents' attempts to find out what he discusses with me and fearing that they might somehow get things out of him, he was ambivalent about talking to me about his depression. He both wanted to talk to me and to screen those feelings out. The gods were supposed to cure such fears. He said jokingly, "You failed at being Rama." I smilingly replied, "You do have high expectations of me."

Vivek used the sessions to become more aware of a new aspect of his depression that was related to seeing me. His homosexual interest had decreased. He said, "I can't masturbate easily, it's harder to conjure up pleasant homosexual images during masturbation. I can't even get good erections. You are taking away the one good thing in my life. You are making changes in me too fast. I am not ready for it." I acknowledged the rapidity of the changes he was experiencing and asked him what made him feel that the changes were being caused by me. Vivek noted that he does not have an explanation, but feels that the random thoughts, during the sessions, are somehow responsible. He preferred my talking to his father and removing the problem, the way gods often solve problems.

Vivek subsequently talked about my attitude about his gayness. He thanked me for my attitude, which unlike his father's did not demand a change of his sexual orientation. He added that he had thought about being in treatment with a gay therapist, but could not imagine that a gay therapist would be neutral. He also wanted to understand his desire to be gay. Vivek recalled that a female therapist, whom he met only once, advocated that he had to be himself and accept his gayness. Vivek felt that she was too "pro-choice" and did not understand his family context. He wanted my help, not that of a gay therapist or a therapist who does not understand his family.

Vivek noted that after the previous session he had publicly kissed a well-known gay person at a party at his college. That person advised him to stop treatment with me. I interpreted Vivek's recent open gay involvement as a way of emphasizing his gayness to me. This was probably a reaction to his view that treatment was causing problems with his erections. I said that when he pits his gay friend against me, it's a conflict between us rather than a reflection of his own struggle. He agreed that the screen of his dream also has to do not only with his depression but also with his own attitudes toward homosexuality. He then revealed that he had difficulty having an erection with his gay friend. Now he wondered if he was really gay. He began to express the difficulty in comparing an actual experience with an imagined one. He needed a test to figure out whether he was gay or straight. It was difficult to compare the sexual pleasure actually experienced in anal intercourse with the pleasure that he imagined could be derived from vaginal intercourse. Should he try vaginal intercourse with a woman to find out which is more pleasurable?

Vivek recalled an incident from high school. A football team, on which he played, was celebrating its victory. All the boys piled up in a circle, Vivek ran to join the circle. In the middle of the circle was a *Playboy* centerfold. He noted that the centerfold did not have a penis and exclaimed, "My God!" He exclaimed it in such a way that Vivek thought that his friends understood him to mean "I would like to fuck her," whereas he actually had been shocked by the differences between men and women. Women do not have a penis. This was a fact of life he knew. But he never confronted it. A woman has a vagina. He had expressed his shock in a manner that passed for an erotic comment. I said, "Men and women are different indeed!"

Around this time, Vivek began to study *Bharatanatyam*, a classical Indian dance. His dance teacher was a middle-aged woman who taught at her home. Vivek was excited because she was impressed by his dedication and ability to learn. She also noted that she was particularly interested in him because, unlike most of her pupils, he was male. He felt so excited that he could not sleep. He practiced the dance steps late into the night, and had a feeling of grace as he danced along with her. Once as she taught the dance steps, he was enraptured and looked directly into her eyes. Their eyes met and locked for a series of dance steps. Vivek felt that she looked back and reciprocated his look. He felt surprised and excited. Vivek felt that she looked back like a "lover." He felt aware of "sexual rapport" but broke off the gaze when he remembered that she was married. I said, "It seems that your eye caught a forbidden woman's eye." Vivek nodded in agreement.

Vivek's attention soon changed from his dance teacher to his teacher's pretty daughter. He looked forward to seeing the daughter whenever he went for his dance classes. He imagined marrying the daughter, although he felt no sexual passion for her. He wanted to be a father and wondered about the many ways that he could be a better father than his own father. He wondered about the humiliation he would experience if he were impotent with her. He wondered if women found him attractive.

He felt that some women were making sexual overtures toward him. Then, with great hesitation, he mentioned that a female friend, Mary, had just broken up with her boyfriend. He decided to meet her, as she was sad and lonely. While they were together, Mary said that she would like to have sex with him. "I felt curious, but hesitated. I think she thought that I was shy. Then she said, 'I want to go down on you. When I am finished, there will be lipstick at the root of your penis.' I felt rushed and said, 'No. I am not ready.' We just hugged." Then Vivek asked if I had any thoughts. I said, "You are getting female sexual attention. What were you curious about?" Vivek replied, "I wanted to try the experiment and test the difference between anal and vaginal sex and the difference between a man and a woman as a partner."

Interestingly, the very next session, Vivek expressed the conviction that he was gay. Vivek had read the *Bhagavad Gita*, the great Hindu religious scripture, to seek guidance. He read that ideal life was to be equanimitous and not ruled by passion. He wondered if God meant for an ideal marriage to be between a gay man and a lesbian. They could rear children without the undue influence of passions fueled by hormones, which made heterosexuals out of control. Such a "homosexuality oriented heterosexual couple" can have a reasonable marriage or family with controlled emotions. Vivek also felt puzzled about whether he is truly torn by internal conflicts or simply confused by pressures exerted by others.

I said, "In the past few sessions you have moved from the lock between your dance teacher's gaze and your gaze, to family life with your teacher's daughter, to straight sex with your female friend, and now to gay–straight marriage. Do you feel pressured by me or by changes in the treatment?" Vivek felt that the confusion exists because he thinks I expect him to change. He was deferring to my expectation that he will change his sexual orientation. I said, "So thoughts of marriage and straight sex are caused by me?" Vivek replied, "I am afraid that you will decide my sexuality rather than myself. I am not confused. You may be causing the confusion by your anticipation that I will change." I said, "How do I convey my anticipation to you?" Vivek replied, "By your silence." I replied that we needed to understand what I do that makes him feel that I want him to change or not to change his sexual preference and whether the choice was his or mine.

In the next session Vivek reported a dream. "I dreamt that I was getting married to a girl. It was an arranged marriage that I wanted. The girl was exactly like me. She was the same as me except she was a girl." He then asked, "What do you think of the dream? It would help to know your thoughts." Although I felt that waiting for his associations was important, I decided to comment about the limits that life places on all beings. "It looks like the dream is a test of me. In contrast to all thoughts that you expressed so far, this one is impossible. Gay sex is possible, and straight sex is possible. A relationship with a man is possible, so also a relationship with a female is possible. But a relationship with yourself as a woman is impossible." He responded by saying that perhaps he had been "too imaginative. The fact is I like to be gay, but I also want my own children. This is something that can never happen." He then remembered an incident from when he was about 10 years old. After a tennis match his mother drove home his tennis mate, who had won an important match in a tournament. Vivek, too, had won his match. His mother asked Vivek if he knew the opponent of his friend who had just been beaten in the match. Vivek said no, but that it was his impression that the opponent was "small." His mother then became angry and upset. "I know that boy. He is not small and you are a liar. Why do you diminish your friend's victory?" Vivek felt demolished by his mother's criticism. However, it was still his opinion that his friend's tennis opponent was small, but he decided to agree with his mother and apologized for lying. Here it is important to remember that Vivek's parents were concerned that he is not as tall as his father and maintained the hope that there was a late growth spurt left in him. In fact, they continue to measure his height whenever he came home for vacations.

Once, on the way to his session with me, his mother insisted that he eat a *vada* (Indian fried bagel). She said, "Eat. If there is any more growing left in you, it will help you to grow tall." He ate it but felt coerced by his mother. He felt that coming to see me was also an act of compliance with his parents' wishes. The feeling of being coerced remained with him while driving back and forth to my office. But as soon as he would open the door, he felt that he was coming for himself. As he was telling me all this he suddenly realized he had a choice in life. He told me that after he ate that *vada* and he was driving to my office, he decided to stop treatment. He had been pondering about treatment and his problems for more than a year. Although the resolution was clear and sudden, it was a long time in coming. He said that he had decided to stop and that his problems are as resolved as they can be. He hoped that I would concur with his decision. I said that it was essentially his decision but we might need some time to process his current status and decide when to stop. We set a date about two months away.

In the termination period, Vivek asked me if I thought that gays were normal. I replied, "All beings have a vital spark that is precious." Vivek asked, "Am I normal?" I said, "Normal is a word that means different things to different people. I want to tell you what I think. You came to me depressed; now you are less depressed. You were unsure and conflicted about your gayness; now you seem sure that you are gay. You were very much concerned about being influenced by other people; now you seem less concerned, although you are still somewhat sensitive. You came in wanting to please yourself and also your parents; now I think there is a limit to how much you can accomplish here. You know every choice has its limits. As a straight-A student, you have great potential. I can see many good things in your future."

Vivek agreed. "I decide who I am. I am me. I want to eat *vadas* because I am hungry and I like their taste, not because I will grow taller as my mother imagines. I have been in treatment almost one and a half years. It is time to stop. I will be true to my gayness. My parents will not like it and I will have to live with that. I will not have my own children and I will have to live with that, too. Although I have decided, I will continue to have to deal with challenges. However, you helped me a lot. Even though you did not say it, I feel you let me realize that I am normal." I said, "It was nice to work with you." Vivek, with a smile and a look of gratitude on his face, extended his hand. We shook hands and parted.

The Case of Anesh

Anesh, a Hindu Indian born in the United States, contacted me by phone and said that he needed to see me, as he was experiencing depression and anxiety that he wanted to discuss in detail in person. I was expecting to see someone downcast. I was surprised when I saw Anesh. He was a six-foot-tall, well-built, handsome 19-year-old college student. He was wearing a metal-studded Harley Davidson leather jacket and boots. As he walked in, he intimidatingly glared at me. However, he quickly introduced himself cordially to me. I motioned him into my office and jokingly said, "Are you the same guy I spoke with on the phone? You said you were nervous. Now, you stare at me as if you want me to be nervous." He laughed and seemed to be relieved by my comment. He said, "I have been scared all my life. Now I want to scare others. I have been taking Hapkido lessons for the past six months. It is a Korean art of self-defense and natural healing." He struck a pose. I asked, "How did you get started being scared?"

Anesh reported that his father was hardworking, was often away from home, and had an explosive temper. When he came home, he found fault with everything that his wife did. He blamed her for not serving hot food and threatened violence. He blamed her whenever Anesh got a poor grade. His mother was scared of her husband. She tried to cater to his needs and expected that Anesh, too, would likewise be continuously mindful of his father. Anesh's mother alternated between trying to please her husband and at other times avoiding him. As far back as he could remember, she had been overweight.

"I want to see you because I have become nervous and have a headache that simply has not gone away for about two weeks now. The headache is hard to describe, as it constantly changes. As I describe it, it changes, and I can never fully describe it. Occasionally, I see some strange bright spots in my mind. I also have a metallic taste in my mouth."

I asked him if something had happened two weeks ago. Anesh stared off into space for a few seconds and then said that he could remember nothing unusual. He had returned from a visit to his parents a few weeks ago, and it was a good visit. I noted that his mind drifted away for a few seconds and I completed a medical history, but was not sure if the bright spots and the metallic taste were psychiatric symptoms or some form of an aura related to a neurological condition. I recommended that he also see a neurologist. At his request, I gave him the name of a prominent neurologist covered by his insurance, but whom I had never personally met.

Anesh tried to describe his headache. His head was like the weather map of the world—constantly changing and almost indescribable. After many minutes he would give up in exasperation, convinced that he had taxed my capacity to listen. He felt that I would get angry if he continued to take any more time to explain his headache. The metallic taste in his mouth, equally indescribable, continued unabated. Failing to obtain relief, Anesh turned to describing his life. Throughout his life he had been teased for being overweight. At one time in his high-school years he was as much as eighty pounds overweight. He was interested in Eastern religions and history. These interests occupied him, and he almost totally avoided social and sexual relationships. I acknowledged we were out of touch with the causes of his headaches and metallic taste. I commented that despite the stress of leaving home he joined a Hapkido class. It helped in overcoming his weight problem on his own. I recalled his initial Hapkido pose and said that it gave him a stance toward life. He felt that his problems were medical and held out for some physical explanation for his problems.

When I next saw him, Anesh had made an appointment with the neurologist. With his consent I briefly spoke to the neurologist about his symptoms. His headaches and metallic taste persisted, but his anxiety, in anticipation of the neurologist's visit, had increased. I told Anesh that he had become more anxious as the date for the neurologist's appointment approached. In response, Anesh said that he just remembered a dream he had the previous night. "I went to see Dr. X [the neurologist]. He saw me with another doctor. I told them of my problems. I spoke of my headaches, opened my mouth, and pointed to my tongue inside my mouth. However, instead of examining my head and mouth, he proceeded to perform an anal exam on me. I wanted to hit them, but felt paralyzed. They talked about me and laughed."

Anesh talked about wanting to hit the doctors because they began to laugh at him. He reminded me that his father had threatened to hit his mother. "It may be," I said, "that you are a chip off the old block, your own father. You know that Dr. X and I recently talked. Do you have any thoughts about it?" Anesh suddenly became serious and said, "I am afraid that after the neurological exam he and you may talk and conclude that I am gay. Since I was a child I had that fear. I want to be and am also afraid that I am gay. When I was in high school I was overweight, and did not get involved in any sexual relations. But when I moved to this city in order to attend college, I decided to lose weight and was now in good shape for the first time in my life. I was a virgin when I arrived. After I came back from the visit to my parents, I went to my Hapkido class. Another student invited me over to his apartment. I gave him a blow job. I was reluctant but also excited. He did the same to me. This is my first sexual encounter. Am I now a virgin? Can virginity be lost by a blow job? This incident was so much on my mind soon after it happened. I don't think I told you about the incident. I almost forgot that it happened."

I inquired, "Did the metallic taste in your mouth and headaches begin before or after the blow job?" Anesh then said, "I know what my problem is. I am gay. I am anxious that I am gay. You know the myth of Shiva and Agni. Agni performs a blow job on Shiva. That is the real reason that I started seeing you. The metallic taste was the most un-imaginable taste; it is the opposite of the taste of semen. When I tell my parents that I am gay, my father will explode. However, I feel that is what I am." His face suddenly cleared. The metallic taste immediately decreased and he did not complain about it afterward. His headaches, too, abated. He saw the neurologist, and no neurological basis for his headaches was found.

Anesh recalled an event from his childhood, when he was about 10. His father was a gun collector and hunter. Anesh broke open a bullet and scooped out the gunpowder. He waited until his father was away from home and decided to light the powder. He went into the yard to do so. His mother was often busy and did not like to spend much time with him. She was simultaneously on the phone with one of her friends and was cooking. He could see her through the kitchen window. Anesh set fire to the powder with a match. It suddenly caught fire and neatly burned a circle of skin on his left palm. Looking at his mom, Anesh cried out in pain, "Mom! I burned myself. I have a hole in my hand!" His mom, not taking her eye off her cooking, said, "Anesh, you do not have a hole in your hand. Be quiet and I will be with you as soon as I can." In recalling this event, Anesh said that it was impossible to get his mom's attention even for a moment. I said, "Perhaps the headaches are a test of others. Will I or they listen to your long descriptions of the headache?" Anesh laughed and nodded in agreement.

Anesh no longer complained of anxiety, headaches, or the metallic taste. He mentioned a young lady, his classmate, who seemed to be interested in him. He was anxious but accepted a date she proposed. He wanted to be with her but was afraid that she may reject him. He came to his session one day and announced that he had lost his real virginity! Subsequently, she invited him to meet her parents and they welcomed him. On the basis of his experience, for a while he had been convinced that he was gay. Over a period of time, his concerns about his so-called gayness dissipated. Anesh and his girlfriend began to live together and established a generally satisfactory relationship. However, she complained that Anesh did not help with domestic chores; he did not put away soiled dishes promptly, he did not spontaneously help to take out the garbage. This remained a sore element in their relationship. It was somewhat reminiscent of the relationship between his mother and father. Although he remembered his experience with his male peer, he did not feel gay anymore. Anesh began with the fear that he was gay and ended up being straight.

DISCUSSION

The two cases presented here deal with individuals who sought treatment initially with homosexual-bisexual concerns. They were chosen because of the presence of dysphoric elements vis-à-vis sexuality that were addressed in the treatment with varying degrees of success and different results. Such isolation of sexual concerns produces its own distorting effects. A psychoanalytic working-through usually involves a pattern of assembly of minute details of the case. These include the patient's symptoms, sexual history, relationship patterns, resistances and transferences, and his current cultural milieu and the one in which he grew up. Such a detailed description is not intended, nor are the cases presented as examples of good psychoanalytic technique. The cases presented deal with male homosexuality, but their discussion will make it clear that the notion of fundamental human bisexuality is applicable to both men and women. Based on psychoanalytic and Hindu notions, this discussion is an attempt at cross-cultural integration specifically in regard to what I call the plural Oedipus complex.

Let us first establish, however, that gayness as a social identity definition is now well accepted in the West. In India, on the other hand, the notion of a gay identity has not yet been accepted, even though there are men who have sex with men. Many such men view themselves as desiring women but also engage in sexual activity with men only because they lack heterosexual opportunities. Alternatively, a greater degree of bisexual acceptance seems to be prevalent. However, children reared in the West seem to recognize the notion of a gay identity. Thus, it seems that the notion of a gay identity is culture bound. There are advantages to the notion of homosexuality as defined by erotic imagery (Isay 1993). However, this view has the drawback that a bisexual person with erotic imagery toward both sexes is considered a homosexual person. In addition, it runs the risk of not accounting for the behaviors of chronic homosexual behavior without any gay erotic imagery.

The term "men who have sex with men" (MSM), a classification used in India, is more explicit but disregards the erotic and the unconscious elements of the personality.

A definition of homosexuality or bisexuality should consider several factors, including sexual preference, actual behavior, fantasies, self-definition, and stage of psychological development. Are the person's erotic actions opportunistic, coerced, experimental, chosen, or imposed? Is the person conflicted? Who is labeling him? Is the label assigned by the self or others? Is a person being called a homosexual living in a culture that devalues such a person?

In a categorical model a person is described either as homosexual or not homosexual. In a dimensional model, all people are viewed as having composite identities: there is some degree of heterosexuality, and some degree of homosexuality; there is some degree of gender dysphoria, some degree of congruence between gender identity and biological sex, some degree of acceptance of gender role, and some degree of ambivalence toward the gender of the chosen object.

There seems to be near-universal acceptance that gayness is ultimately a self-identification. However, if the person is in treatment, the analyst has the job of analyzing the reasons that have contributed to a person's sexual identity, the manner of decision making, and the announcement of gayness. The analyst helps the patient become more aware of the range of his choices and their possible implications. If dysphoria is present, it needs to be understood. Vivek, for instance, made the final decision that he was gay and decided to stop the therapy. He recalled that his mother had force-fed him a *vada* and that he also felt forced into the treatment. Although I endorsed his right to decide that he was gay and to stop the treatment, I clarified to him that his decisions were sudden and that he was acting out his mother transference. Anesh displayed symptoms of a metallic taste in his mouth and a headache related to male homosexual activity. His symptoms benefited by being addressed in treatment.

Vivek experienced both homosexual and heterosexual erotic fantasies and was thus beyond a categorical classification. His psychopathology also showed the important role of narcissism. Vivek's mother's preoccupation with his height, his own changing attitudes toward being measured, and his father's acceptance of his short stature all contributed to Vivek's narcissistic vulnerability. Vivek also showed oedipal concerns (when his eyes and his dance teacher's eyes locked). All this goes to show that many perspectives may be useful in understanding the patient to an extent. Overreliance on one or the other of the theories may be unduly reductive.

Vivek revealed that an exploration of his several conflicts led to the establishment of a self-chosen gay identity. In the case of Anesh, the outcome was just the opposite. What this teaches us is that an a priori decision regarding the desired outcome of analysis is neither possible nor advisable. Homosexuality in some cases may be immutable and a fixed trait, but in some other cases it may not be so. However, the choice of homosexuality versus heterosexuality has inevitable outcomes. A patient will need to mourn the loss of the other possibility to achieve an optimal acceptance of the chosen sexual orientation. As a defense against mourning and possible depression, a patient may hold the view that homosexuality is normal. An analyst's attitude, to some degree, may coincide with the patient's—that homosexuality is normal. To that degree, the analyst's stance that homosexuality is only normal may short-circuit useful mourning in relationship to an emerging self-identity and the simultaneous loss of previously held open options for sexual identification.

Freud's notion of bisexuality, as well as subsequent developments in psychoanalysis relating to object relations and narcissism, needs to be integrated into the theory of the Oedipus complex. Without this, it seems that three independent and competing versions of the Oedipus complex continued to exist in our theory.

Freud's understanding of the Oedipus complex was deeply influenced by his belief in bisexuality. Freud (1923) stated:

Closer study usually discloses the more complete Oedipus complex, which is two fold, positive and negative, and is due to the bisexuality originally present in children: that is to say, a boy has not merely an ambivalent attitude towards his father and an affectionate object-choice towards his mother, but at the same time behaves like a girl and displays an affectionate feminine attitude towards his father and a corresponding jealousy and hostility towards his mother. It is this complicating element introduced by bisexuality that makes it so difficult to obtain a clear view of the facts in connection with the earliest object-choices and identifications, and still more difficult to describe them intelligibly. It may even be that the ambivalence displayed in the relations to the parents should be attributed entirely to bisexuality and that is not, as I have represented above, developed out of identification in consequence of rivalry. [p. 33]

Kohut (1977, 1984), in contrast, regarded the Oedipus complex as a pathogenic structure embedded in failures of oedipal selfobjects. Object-relational theorists have their own versions of the Oedipus complex.

In contrast to these psychoanalytic views, Hinduism encourages us to consider a plural Oedipus framework that is insistently perspectival. This is in the spirit of Hinduism's giving freedom to each individual to fashion an individual path toward self-advancement. The concept of *Isthadevata* (a personal god) indicates that each person may seek enlightenment with the help of his own icon. That many people may choose a god with the same-sounding name, does not mean that the guidance sought is identical. However, the devotees of a god do not regard the devotees of another god as misguided. It is understood that the choice of a god may be based on one's stage of development or personal tendency. An action-oriented person seeks an action-oriented god as a model, a contemplative person may seek a contemplative god, or an action-oriented person may seek a contemplative god, and a contemplative person may seek an action-oriented god. Each one of them considers the other person's views and strivings as complementary. A hierarchical, monotheistic, or singular view tends to challenge other competitive views. The notion of perspectival and polytheistic views tends to seek increasing self-definition in light of other views and concedes the plausibility of other views.

In traditional psychoanalytic understanding, input from the father is easily and readily understandable. The father as a source of potential masculine identifications within the oedipal theory means that a boy may or may not identify with such input concerning masculinity from the father. Thus, in the case of Vivek, it is easy to process the father's contributions to his notions of masculinity, namely (1) that a normal man is identified with a male who is capable of having an erection and performing sexually with a woman, (2) that only a man who cannot get an erection with a woman will seek a homosexual partner, (3) that his father (along with Vivek's mother) also willingly offered to arrange a marriage, and (4) that if Vivek cannot find it possible to have sex with a woman, he should seek discharge in masturbation.

In traditional psychoanalytic theory, the father is the source of masculine identifications and the mother is the object of feminine strivings (Meissner 1993). Vivek's mother's input concerning masculinity, that a man naturally loves a woman, is hard to process. How should the mother's input into a child's views of masculinity be processed? For example, the mother held (1) that a man naturally loves a woman, and (2) that she wants Vivek to be taller than his father. In addition, appealing to his male narcissism, she offered to find him a "first-class" bride. All this is difficult to accommodate in the oedipal theory as it developed after Freud and after it abandoned the notion of the bisexual Oedipus complex.

Moreover, the potential identifications emanating from the father include masculine as well as feminine strivings. Feminine messages from the father include the father's acceptance of taking care of the needs of the children and household chores when the mother is menstruating. This acceptance of traditional feminine duties constitutes not only the acceptance of a feminine role, it also includes elements of the recognition of a bisexual identity and is not felt to be sexually dystonic. These potentials for identifications are communicated by the parent through words, actions, attitudes, parental encouragements, or constraints imposed by the parent on the growing child. Such "conversations" do not in themselves cause identifications but they are manifest residues through which a more subtle exploration of the identificatory process can be undertaken.

According to a bisexual theory of the plural Oedipus complex, both father and mother can be sources of a boy's notions concerning masculinity and femininity. The mother, too, through her bisexuality, can contribute to the boy's notions of masculinity. Thus, in Vivek's mother's case, her notions of what is natural for a man and her recognition of a man's narcissistic quest for a "first-class" (high-quality) bride are easily understood as reflecting her notions of masculinity (which Vivek rejected). This does not mean that the son automatically accepts the mother's input, but it indicates that a boy is also guided by his mother's views of masculine strivings.

However, the boy is bisexual, too. Thus, a boy can identity with or reject the feminine aspects derived from the mother and also the father. In Vivek's case, there is an explicit mention of the father's doing "feminine" chores when Vivek's mother was menstruating. This is not to be understood only as the father taking on a mother's role or a feminine role. It also represents the expression of a man's feminine or bisexual tendencies. A bisexual plural oedipal theory offers a clear way to process feminine tendencies derived from a father. In addition, in a bisexual oedipal theory, owing to features in a child's own development, to some degree the Oedipus complex is resolved in a positive manner. To the degree that the Oedipus complex is resolved in a positive manner, the boy derives masculine and male sexual identification with masculine strivings from both the father and the mother. The desired other is a female with feminine qualities derived from both the mother and the father. To the degree the Oedipus complex is resolved negatively, the boy identifies with the feminine identifications derived from the mother and the father, and a masculine object is also chosen.

Owing to the systemic oedipal configuration, each element is potentially influenced by additional sources. For example, Vivek liked his height to be measured as long as he was actively growing, but no longer. His mother intrusively wanted to continue to measure him and wanted him to be taller than his father. His father accepted Vivek's stature. Vivek thought that his father thinks he may want to be taller than his father, but is not demanding regarding his son's height. This is not the most important issue of their relationship. But Vivek felt that his mother thought that he wanted to be taller than his father and that this was very important to him also. Vivek also thought that his treatment with me was like measuring his progress with homosexuality and was angry with me because he thought it was like his mother's measuring of his height. Thus, there are six elements concerning Vivek's height stemming from all the participants in the oedipal drama. According to a plural oedipal framework, the following applies with regard to identifications and the self. A person's plural oedipal self-image is the composite of that person's self-image from several complementary and interactive perspectives of the key people in that person's life. Its constituents may stem from (1) that person's own impressions of who he or she is; (2) the empathic impressions that the mother has of the child's self-image; (3) the child's construction of the mother's views of the child; (4) the father's empathic impression of the child's self-image; (5) the child's construction of the father's views of the child; and (6) if a person is in treatment, the transference revival of such relationships.

To summarize, according to a plural oedipal framework, the following applies with regard to bisexual identifications: (1) A boy will identify to some degree with potential masculine identification derived from two streams: a predominant stream of potential masculine identifications derived from the father and a second stream of potential masculine identifications derived from the mother. (2) Owing to the bisexuality of individuals, a boy will identify with some degree of potential feminine identification derived from two streams: a stream of potential feminine identifications derived from the mother and a second stream of potential feminine identifications derived from the father. (3) To some degree the Oedipus complex is resolved in a positive manner. In a positive resolution of the bisexual Oedipus complex, the child identifies with the masculine strivings derived from both the mother and the father, and takes on a feminine object based on the feminine notions prevalent in the family. (4) To some degree the Oedipus complex is resolved in a negative manner. In a negative resolution of the bisexual Oedipus complex, the child identifies with the feminine strivings derived from both the mother and the father, and takes on a masculine object based on the masculine notions prevalent in the family.

CONCLUSION

Homosexuality and bisexuality are complex and universal phenomena. "Gayness," however, seems to be culture bound. In India, many men who have sex with men do not attach much significance to that activity and easily lead bisexual lives. Only those Indians who have been influenced by Western culture consider themselves as exclusively gay. There is a culture-bound need to separate bisexuality as an abstract concept and to indicate innate latent bisexuality of all humans from behavioral bisexuality. Because of the complex societal consequences of labeling a person as homosexual, it seems desirable for homosexuality to remain a self-definition. A variety of explanations concerning homosexuality and bisexuality are possible. Various psychoanalytic theories seem to offer pertinent insights but exaggerate their claims of understanding and devalue the equally plausible claims of other theories. There are biases in psychoanalytic and cultural discourses concerning homosexuality and bisexuality. One form of bias may tend to consider homosexuality as pathological, whereas another form of bias is that the pathology of a homosexual person is overlooked. A change of sexual orientation and the choice to be or not to be homosexual should always remain within a person's province, but an analyst must seek to understand, clarify, and interpret any conflicts, and enhance adaptation. There are benefits to revisiting the current notions of the Oedipus complex from the point of view of psychic bisexuality. Hindu considerations of the Oedipus complex can enliven the early traditions of psychoanalytic insight that seem to have become dormant. Hindus can gain some understanding about yet another form of human inquiry while marveling at the insights that have been kept alive within their own great tradition for centuries.

REFERENCES

Asthana, S., and Oostvogels, J. (2001). The social construction of male homosexuality in India. *Social Science and Medicine* 52:707–721.

Bergler, E. (1957). *Homosexuality: Disease or Way of Life?* New York: Hill and Wang.

Bieber, I., Dain, H., Dince, P., et al. (1962). *Homosexuality: A Psychodynamic Study of Male Homosexualities.* New York: Basic Books.

Blos, P. (1962). *On Adolescence.* New York: Free Press.

Bollas, C. (1992). *Being a Character.* New York. Hill and Wang.

Carstairs, G. M. (1957). *The Twice Born: A Study of a Community of High-Caste Hindus.* Bloomington, IN: Indiana University Press.

Danielou, A. (1984). *Shiva and Dionysus.* New York: Inner Traditions International.

——— (1987). *While the Gods Play.* Rochester: Inner Traditions International.

Dasa, A. (2003). Tritiya-prakriti: People of the Third Sex. http://www.galva108.org/Tritiya_prakriti.html#footnote18.

Drescher, J. (2002). Causes and becauses: on etiological theories of homosexuality. *Annual of Psychoanalysis* 30:57–68.

Fonagy P., and Target, M. (1997). Attachment and reflective function: their role in self-organization. *Development and Psychopathology* 9:679–700.

Freud, A. (1973). *The Writings of Anna Freud, Vol. 4. Indications for Child Analysis and Other Papers.* New York: International Universities Press.

Freud, S. (1905). Three essays on the theory of sexuality. *Standard Edition* 7:135–243.

——— (1910). Leonardo da Vinci and a memory of his childhood. *Standard Edition* 11:59–151.

——— (1914). On narcissism. *Standard Edition* 14:67–103.

——— (1915). Instincts and their vicissitudes. *Standard Edition* 14:117–140.

——— (1920). Psychogenesis of a case of homosexuality in a woman. *Standard Edition* 18:147–172.

——— (1923). The ego and the id. *Standard Edition* 19:12–68.

——— (1930). Civilization and its discontents. *Standard Edition* 21:59–145.

——— (1933). New introductory lectures on psychoanalysis. *Standard Edition* 22:3–182.

Friedman, R. C. (1988). *Male Homosexuality*. New Haven, CT: Yale University Press.

——— (2002). Homosexuality. *Annual of Psychoanalysis Rethinking Psychoanalysis and the Homosexualities* 30:69–80.

Greenson, R. R. (1967). *Dis-identification from mother: its special importance for the boy*. Presented at the 25th International Psycho-Analytical Congress, Copenhagen, July.

Hajratwala, M. (1995). Twenty years after I grew into your lives. In *Living in America: Poetry and Fiction by South Asian American Writers*, ed. R. Rustomji-Kerns, pp. 51–52. Boulder, CO: Westview.

Isay, R. (1993). Homosexuality in homosexual and heterosexual men. In *The Course of Life, Vol. 5, Early Adulthood*, ed. G. Pollock and S. Greenspan, pp. 179–200. Madison, CT: International Universities Press.

Isay, R., and Friedman, R. (1989). Toward a further understanding of homosexual men. *Journal of the American Psychoanalytic Association* 37:193–206.

Kakar, S. (1982). *Shamans, Mystics, and Doctors*. New York: A. Knopf.

Kohut, H. (1977). *The Restoration of the Self*. New York: International Universities Press.

——— (1984). *How Does Analysis Cure?* Chicago: University of Chicago Press.

Kolodny, R. C., Masters, W. H., Hendryx, J. H., and Toro, G. (1971). Plasma testosterone and semen analysis in the male homosexual. *New England Journal of Medicine* 285:1170–1174.

LeVay, S. (1991). A difference in hypothalmic structure between heterosexual and homosexual men. *Science* 253:1034–1037.

Mahler, M. S., Pine, F., and Bergman, A. (1975). *The Psychological Birth of the Human Infant*. New York: Basic Books.

Meissner, W. W. (1993). Developmental pathology and adult disorders. In *The*

Course of Life, ed. G. H. Pollock and S. H. Greenspan, pp. 233–286. Madison, CT: International Universities Press.

Muller, M. (1886). *The Sacred Books of the East: The Laws of Manu*. New Delhi: Motilal Banarsidass.

Nanda, S. (1999). *Neither Man nor Woman: The Hijras of India*. Belmont, CA: Wadsworth.

O'Flaherty, W. D. (1980). *Women, Androgynes, and Other Mythical Beasts*. Chicago: University of Chicago Press.

Ovessey, L. (1969). *Homosexuality and Pseudohomosexuality*. New York: Science House.

Radhakrishnan, S. (1969). *Eastern Religions and Western Thought*. London: Oxford University Press.

Rado, S. (1940). A critical examination of the concept of bisexuality. *Psychosomatic Medicine* 2:459–467.

Schafer, R. (2002). On male nonnormative homosexuality and perversion in psychoanalytic discourse. *Annual of Psychoanalysis* 30:23–35.

Sharma, S. K. (1989). *Hijras: The Labelled Deviants*. New Delhi: Gian.

Socarides, C. W. (1968). A provisional theory of etiology in male homosexuality. *International Journal of Psycho-Analysis*. 49:27–37.

——— (1978). *Homosexuality*. New York: Jason Aronson.

Stoller, R. (1968). *Sex and Gender*. New York: Science House.

Stutley, M., and Stutley, J. (1917). *Harper's Dictionary of Hinduism*. San Francisco: Harper & Row, 1984.

Subramuniyaswami, S. S. (2002). *Hinduism's Contemporary Catechism*. New Delhi: Himalayan Academy Publications.

Tolpin, M. (2002). Discussion of Ralph Roughton's chapter. *Annual of Psychoanalysis* 30:119–127.

Vyas, D., and Shingala, Y. (1987). *The Lifestyle of the Eunuchs*. New Delhi: Anmol.

Wortis, J. (1954). *Fragments of an Analysis with Freud*. New York: Charter.

SPIRIT

10

Manifestations of God in India: A Transference Pantheon

Dwarakanath G. Rao

> There are assuredly two forms of *Brahman*:
> the formed and the formless,
> the mortal and the immortal,
> the stationary and the moving,
> the actual and the beyond.
> *Brhadaranyaka Upanishad* (II:iii:1–3)

Unity and plurality are the necessary underlying concepts of God in India. Millennia of tradition, many growing in insulated enclaves throughout the country, and forged by foreign and indigenous philosophies and folkways, have led to the vast canvas of ideas and ways of life seen in present-day India. Few have to be reminded of India's staggering diversity of religion, language, race, ethnicity, and socioeconomic status. It is impossible to generalize from such an array of ideas, without necessarily imposing a viewpoint. The burden and task of this chapter is to use a psychoanalytic perspective to understand the concept of God in India.

God in India suggests special meanings not easily applied to God outside India. In keeping with the motif image of this volume—Freudian strollers on the banks of a Hindu river—it will be necessary to examine the admixture of psychoanalytic thought with Indian life, and in the process examine the idea of India as well. Shashi Tharoor (2002), the noted writer and diplomat, describes contemporary plurality in India:

How can one portray the present, let alone the future, of an ageless civilization that is the birthplace of four major religions, a dozen different traditions of classical dance, eighty-five political parties, and 300 ways of cooking the potato? The short answer is that it can't be done—at least not to everyone's satisfaction. Any truism about India can be immediately contradicted by another truism about India. . . . The singular thing about India is that you can only speak of it in the plural. There are many Indias. Everything exists in countless variants. There is no single standard, no fixed stereotype, no one way. You can be a good Muslim, a good Keralite and a good Indian all at once. Where Freudians speak of the narcissism of minor differences, in India we celebrate the commonality of major differences. [Tharoor 2002]

Tharoor stresses the cultivated pluralism of India through the ages, although one is tempted to ask how much of this occurred by happenstance, how much owing to forethought, and how much owing to geopolitical necessity. The celebration of differences, while true, is accompanied by the celebration of differentness as well. This celebratory capacity is adaptational in the psychoanalytic sense, and requires the idea of God being rendered into an adaptational pantheon of many gods.

Tharoor, in the same piece, writes of the political result of Indian pluralism:

So the idea of India is of one land embracing many. It is the idea that a nation may endure differences of caste, creed, colour, culture, cuisine, costume, and custom, and still rally around a democratic consensus. That consensus is around the simple principle that in a democracy you don't really need to agree—except on the ground rules of how you will disagree. The reason India has survived all the stresses and strains that have beset it for fifty years, and that led so many to predict its imminent disintegration, is that it maintained consensus on how to manage without consensus. And so the Indian identity that I believe in celebrates diversity: if America is a melting-pot, then to me India is a "thali," a selection of sumptuous dishes in different bowls. Each tastes different, and does not necessarily mix with the next, but they belong together on the same plate, and they complement each other in making the meal a satisfying repast. Indians are comfortable with multiple identities and multiple loyalties, all coming together in allegiance to a larger idea of India, an India which safeguards the common space available to each identity, an India that remains safe for diversity.

Note Tharoor's stress on what he believes is Indian comfort with "multiple identities and . . . loyalties," and India's political ability to maintain "consensus on how to manage without consensus." A cynical view would hold that this represents political and psychological opportunism and expediency, perhaps turned into a virtue when applied to governing the Indian nation. A psychoanalytic view would concede the idea of political expediency, but only in the context of optimal conflict resolution. What are these conflicts? Why might their resolution require multiple identities, more than one God, and living without consensus? On this brief journey, one might also ask to what degree the quest to delineate one God is in itself a positivistic Western preoccupation.

A BRIEF HISTORY OF RELIGION IN INDIA

India is the name given to the land of *Bharata*, after the Indus River (*Sindhu*), and Hindu is the name given to the people who followed the religions of the land of the Indus. The naming of India by the Greeks and the Arabs is an example of the primal influence of the outsider in the shaping of meaning and history of this land of many faiths and cultures. India is chimerical in this respect, having been defined and redefined according to the preconceptions of the invader *du jour*. Religion, no less than culture, as a consequence, was in the hands of the describer, who is variously regarded as self-serving and unaware, or indigenous and therefore more authentic.

Hinduism

In the millennia that constitutes Indian history, the synthesis of arrays of systems of thought, folklore, as well as mainstream and breakaway groups led to what many believe should rightly be called not Hinduism, but *Sanatana dharma* or eternal *dharma*. *Dharma* can be translated as righteousness or duty, but includes the sense of righteous beingness or way of life. From hoary antiquity to modern times, Indian civilization emphasized the inseparability of the religious and the mundane, *Dharma* itself having both a religious and mundane meaning. God in this context is another word for truth or reality, and God as creator, or supreme being, is a derivative meaning. Both meanings are dialectically balanced in Indian philosophical and religious traditions.

The earliest evidence of religious iconography comes from the Harappan civilization (3000 to 2500 B.C.), also known as the Indus Valley civilization, the earliest to flourish in South Asia, in what is now Pakistan and northwestern India. An orderly, urban civilization with uniform weights and measures, elaborate systems of drainage, and peopled by artisans and artists, it had connections with Mesopotamia. Its people and language are a tantalizing mystery; scholars have suggested proto-Aryan or Dravidian origins. Among the artifacts discovered are figurines of a Mother Goddess indicating a source for what may have later become the Shakti worship of the feminine power in India. A male god in a yoga posture, depicted with three faces and two horns, has been identified with Indra or Shiva, another important figure in later Indian religion. *Lingams*, phallic symbols of Shiva, have also been found.

Around 1500 B.C., the Aryans, a nomadic, warlike people, are said to have come in successive waves, to conquer what are now Iran, Pakistan, and India. Aryan meant the noble ones. They ushered in the *Rigvedic* period (1700–1000 B.C.), named after the *Rigveda*, considered one of the oldest examples of sacred Indian literature. The *Rigveda* was a collection of hymns of praise and rituals of sacrifice, and it shared gods and divinities with Persian culture. The Aryan influence, by now widespread, was further shaped by cultural mixing with indigenous peoples. As this intermixing occurred, there arose the beginnings of the great divisions along the lines of skin color and social standing. The Aryans called the indigenous people *Dasas*, or dark. *Dasa* also means slave or supplicant. These social divisions culminated in the *varna* (color) or caste system. At the top of this hierarchy was the *Brahmin* (priestly class), and in descending order, the *Kshatriyas* (warrior/ruler class), the *Vaisyas* (trader class), and the *Sudras* (servant class).

In the later Vedic period (1000–500 B.C.), also known as the Brahmanic period, priestly ritual controlled every aspect of life. It was also the Epic Age, during which the great epics, the *Mahabharata* and the *Ramayana*, were probably composed, and told of Aryan heroes and cultural values, and their transformation by the Indus cultures. It was also the age of law codes, medicine, mathematics, science, and martial arts. During this period there arose the great commentaries on the *Vedas*, the *Upanishads*.

The *Upanishads* (800 to 400 B.C.), meaning "at the feet of the master," are said to be the most sublime and evocative distillations of Hindu philosophy, and the beginning of the emphasis on experience over learning. The *Bhagavad Gita* (500–200 B.C.), sometimes termed the fifth Veda, because it carries the central message of Hinduism, further consolidated the concept of an impersonal God who could take on many personal forms, and elucidated the meaning of duty, action, morality, and death.

The Persians (500 B.C.) and the Greeks under Alexander the Great (326 B.C.) conquered small parts of northwestern India, but left no great religious impression. The great Mauryan emperor, Chandragupta, taking advantage of a weakening Hellenic sphere of influence, extended his empire westward into large parts of Afghanistan. The most famous Mauryan emperor was Ashoka (circa 304–232 B.C.) (see below under Buddhism), who established the largest empire in India before the advent of the Mughals and the British. Ashoka converted to Buddhism following a particularly bloody battle for Orissa, and subsequently spread Buddhism around the world, specifically to east Asia, Tibet, China, Japan, and Sri Lanka, where it took local forms, including Zen (Sanskrit: *Dhyana*). Eventually Buddhism itself declined in the land of its origin, and gave way to a renewal of *Vedic* religion.

All along, a process of cultural assimilation took place between Aryan and non-Aryan peoples. *Sanatana dharma* seemed infinitely flexible, and able to accommodate any number of new ideas with a degree of tolerance that is touted as the hallmark of Hinduism. One might ask, however, whether calling Buddha the ninth incarnation (Avatar) of Vishnu is a sign of tolerant assimilation or dismissive incorporation of a new idea as if it already existed in Hindu orthodoxy. As a result of centuries of active interaction between the mainstream and the unorthodox, there came to be repeated attempts at reconciliation and new synthesis. One of the outcomes was what is termed the reform movement, beginning, according to some, as early as 2 B.C. as a direct offshoot of the *Vedas*, and more systematized from the fifth century onward. Included in the reform movement are mystics and poets like Kabir, Mira Bai, the Bhakti cults, and indeed the founder of Sikhism.

Vedanta (literally, the end of the *Vedas*) was the name given to the reworking of the *Vedas* by commentators of the *Vedas*, in an intellectual and religious movement that continues to this day. Important among the commentators are Shankara (eighth century), who espoused *Advaita* or nondualism, Ramanuja (tenth century) who rejected Advaita, calling for *Visishtadvaita* or qualified nondualism, and Madhva (twelfth century), who preached *Dwaita* or dualism. Of note is that these commentators, while each claiming the *Vedas* as the source of religious inspiration, differed in their views of the relationship of man to God. The importance of these theological debates lies in the use of logic and experience to acknowledge and evaluate alternative schools of Vedantic thought as well as Buddhism. Of additional interest to the psychoanalyst is that in the explication of the relationship of humans to God, these religious commentators take up what I view as a larger cultural project of examining object relations and object constancy in religious, philosophical, and musical terms (Rao 1994).

The eighteenth century Hindu renaissance movement began with the rediscovery of India by Indologists and Sanskritists like Max Mueller, Monier-Williams, and William Jones, and rekindled interest in India in Indians. In the new struggle to reconcile Western ideas of education and rationality with Indian religion and spirituality, an enlightened cadre of Indians tried to create new institutions and social norms. Raja Rammohun Roy (b. 1773) was a scholar and reformer who started the *Brahmo Samaj*, which eschewed caste and polytheism, forbade idol worship, and formulated a religion based on a universal God-head. A countermovement called the *Arya Samaj* was founded by Swami Dayananda Saraswati. The *Arya Samaj* insisted on *Vedic* insights as fundamental, but allowed non-Hindus to convert to Hinduism, and insisted on removing caste boundaries. The Theosophical Society, founded in 1875, was a collaboration between interested, although sometimes alienated and superstitious, Westerners like H. P. Blavatsky and Annie Besant, and Indians who sought to find legitimacy for *Vedic* ideals. They espoused social reform, independence from the British, and helped to maintain scholarly interest in Hindu thought.

Sri Ramakrishna (1836–1888) was a mystic regarded as realized in God-consciousness. He and his famous disciple, Swami Vivekananda (1863–1902), inspired and educated a generation of Indians by their example of *Vedic* spirituality-in-action. Ramakrishna was pithy, earthy, impatient with philosophical subtleties, and spoke of the experience of God as the only way to quell doubts and questions. Other figures of the twentieth century who appealed to the Western-educated Indian include the mystics Sri Aurobindo and Ramana Maharshi, writers like Rabindranath Tagore, and some would say Mahatma Gandhi, for his very public personal and political struggles to reconcile Indian and Western ideals.

No account of Indian religious traditions is complete without a mention of the innumerable sects, cults, and local variations on every practice and ritual that exist and flourish in present-day India. The *Ajivikas* (500 B.C. to 1400 A.D.) were fatalists who were opposed by Jains and Buddhists, and were followers of an ancient religion that died or was absorbed over time (Basham 1951). Also important in this regard is the history of materialist philosophers of India, an often-neglected group of Indian thinkers. Among them were members of the *Charvaka* school of thought. The *Charvakas*, in a thousand-year lineage, systematically expounded the idea of sense-data as ultimate reality, rejecting mainstream *Vedic* inferences of other worlds and the afterlife. Included in this group of materialists were philosophers and logicians, as well as those who were considered depraved practitioners of the dark arts.

An example of what is considered a dark art is Tantra, an esoteric Hindu and Buddhist tradition of sexual practices accompanied by prescribed use of meat, wine, symbolic speech, symbolic diagrams, and the worship of female deities. Sexual intercourse is used for the awakening of occult powers and divine energies.

Religion in India is intimately associated with Yoga, a term used to denote a variety of practices and philosophies. Seals depicting yogic postures have been traced to the Indus Valley civilization (3000 B.C.). The name associated with yoga is Patanjali (circa 2 A.D.), the author of the *Yoga Sutras*, a compendium of aphorisms concerning the philosophy and practice of yoga whose goal is *Kaivalya*, or liberation. Physical forms of yoga comprise *Hatha* yoga, which is only one aspect of yoga. Yoga (meaning union or joining with) in reality refers to a number of pathways of living, and is used to mean striving and is a kind of practice (*sadhana*). A common classification lists *Raja* yoga (also known as *Ashtanga* or eight-limbed yoga) ascribed to Patanjali, *Jnana* yoga (yoga through knowledge), *Karma* yoga (yoga of living action), *Hatha* yoga (yoga of bodily control), and *Bhakti* yoga (yoga of loving surrender). *Ashtanga yoga's* eight limbs are of interest because of their comprehensive approach to the yogic life. Beginning with *yama* and *niyama* (do's and don'ts regulating ethical thinking and behavior), the other limbs encompass physical body and breathing functions, the practice of reining in the senses, followed by concentration, meditation, and ultimately attainment of the *samadhi* state of consciousness.

Yoga draws the physical and the sensate aspects of human experience into religious aspirations. In this way, yoga exemplifies the Hindu worldview that conceives of four purposes of life: *Artha* (worldly success), *Kama* (pleasure), *Dharma* (righteousness), and *Moksha* (liberation). It becomes understandable why the author of the pleasure treatise known as *Kama Sutra*, Vatsyayana (circa third century), claims to write "in the highest chastity and in the highest meditation" (Smith 2002, section B, p. 9). Pleasure, sexual or otherwise, is coequal with religious experience in the Hindu worldview, thus assigning righteousness, or *dharma*, to every aspect of the lived human life.

Buddhism

The founder of Buddhism, Prince Siddhartha Gautama (born 566 B.C.) was the son of a Nepalese chieftain. A commonly accepted version of his life states that when Siddhartha Gautama was born, a seer predicted that he would become either a great king or a savior. Fearing that his son would not choose to be a king, his father raised Siddhartha in a wealthy and pleasure-filled palace in order to shield his son from any experience of human misery or suffering. This, however, was a futile project, and when Siddhartha saw four sights—a sick man, a poor man, a corpse, and an ascetic—he was filled with infinite sorrow for the suffering of humanity.

Siddhartha then dedicated himself to finding a way to end human suffering. He abandoned his former way of life, including his wife and newborn son, and began a life of extreme asceticism. In this state of wretched concentration, in heroic but futile self-denial, one story goes that he overheard a teacher speaking of music. The teacher said that if the strings on the instrument are set too tight, then the instrument will not play harmoniously. If the strings are set too loose, the instrument will not produce music. Only the middle way, not too tight and not too loose, will produce harmonious music. This chance conversation changed his life overnight. The goal was not to live a completely worldly life, nor was it to live a life in complete denial of the physical body, but to live in a Middle Way. The way out of suffering was through concentration, and since the mind was connected to the body, denying the body would hamper concentration, just as overindulgence would distract one from concentration.

With this insight, Siddhartha began intense meditation beneath the famous pipal tree in Bodh Gaya in current-day Bihar state in north India. In a single night, Siddhartha came to understand all his previous lives and the entirety of the cycle of birth and rebirth, or *samsara*, and most importantly, realized the path that would lead to the end of sorrow. At this point, Siddhartha became the Buddha, or "Enlightened One." Instead, however, of passing out of this cycle himself, he stayed in the world of humanity in order to teach his new insights and free humanity from suffering.

In his first teaching, which took place in what is now known as Deer Park in Benares, he expounded his "Four Noble Truths," which form the foundation of Buddhist belief: (1) All human life is suffering (*dhukka*). (2) All suffering is caused by human desire, particularly the desire that impermanent things be permanent. (3) Human suffering can be ended by ending human desire. (4) Desire can be ended by following the Noble Eightfold Path: right understanding, right thought, right speech, right action, right livelihood, right effort, right mindfulness, and right concentration.

It took nearly four hundred years after the Buddha for his teachings to be written down. Few adherents were to be found, until the great Mauryan emperor Ashoka embraced Buddhism. Ashoka spread Buddhism within India and sent emissaries to all parts of the world. It took root in China, Tibet, Sri Lanka, and Thailand, but sank to a minuscule number of adherents in India. This decline in India is thought to be due to the entrenched Hindu practices within the populace, the changing nature of Hinduism itself, and the advent of the Muslims in the 1100s.

The World Civilizations Web site of Washington State University concludes the section on the Buddha with this passage:

From a metaphysical standpoint, these Noble Truths make up and derive from a single fundamental Truth (in Sanskrit, *Dharma*, and in Pali,

Dhamma). The Buddhist *Dharma* is based on the idea that everything in the universe is causally linked. All things are composite things, that is, they are composed of several elements. Because all things are composite, they are all transitory, for the elements come together and then fall apart. It is this transience that causes human beings to sorrow and to suffer. We live in a body, which is a composite thing, but that body decays, sickens, and eventually dies, though we wish it to do otherwise. Since everything is transient, that means that there can be no eternal soul either in the self or in the universe. This, then, is the eternal truth of the world: everything is transitory, sorrowful, and soulless—the three-fold character of the world.

As pessimistic as this sounds, the philosophy of Siddhartha Gautama contains within it a deeper reality with therapeutic meaning. In fact, classifying it in Western terms is impossible. We think of Buddhism as a religion, which it unquestionably became, but Siddhartha was less concerned with theology or ritual or prayer as he was with providing a tool for individuals to use to escape inner suffering. The goal of this method, the Eightfold Noble Path, is the elimination of one's desires and one's attachment to one's self. Once one has understood correctly the nature of the universe (Right Understanding), and devoted one's life to selfless and altruistic actions (Right Action) and, finally, by losing all sense of one's self and by losing all one's desires, one then passes into a state called Nirvana (in Pali, *Nibbana*). The word means "snuffed out," in the way a fire is snuffed out or extinguished. At this point, the self no longer exists. It is not folded into a higher reality nor is it transported to a land of bliss, it simply ceases to exist. This is the state that the Buddha passed into at his death.

Like Jainism (see below), Buddhism centrally concerns itself with the problem of the eternal birth and rebirth of the human soul. Unlike Jainism, Buddhism in its original form does not posit some transcendent alternative as a goal. In fact, Buddhism in its original form held that the soul actually died when the body died. How, then, could a soul pass from body to body? What passed from body to body was a chain of causes set in motion by each soul; the Buddhist philosopher Nagsena said it was like a flame passing from candle to candle. "The individual, in snuffing out the self, brings those chain of causes to an end" (Hooker 1996).

Jainism

In 500 B.C., Mahavira (the Great Hero) broke away from Brahmanical orthodoxy and canon to found Jainism. A later contemporary, Gautama Buddha (the Enlightened One), established Buddhism. Jainism spread in India, and brought with it the earliest concept of *ahimsa*, nonviolence. Its influence on art and commerce was substantial, but the main contribution came in the new philosophy of no God at all. It was aimed at breaking the stranglehold of Vedic orthodoxy and gathered many adherents. In time, Jainism fused with elements of Vedic Hinduism. Present-day Jains, who number about four million, do not, however, deny the existence of *devas*, deities. These beings are no less than human beings, are considered to be subject to the laws of transmigration and decay, and they do not determine the destiny of humans. Jains believe that souls are individual and infinite. They are not part of a universal soul. Souls and matter are neither created nor destroyed. Salvation is to be attained by the liberation of the soul from the foreign elements (karmic elements) that weigh it down. These elements gain admission to the soul by the individual's acts of passion. Such actions cause rebirth among animals or inanimate substances: meritorious acts cause rebirth among the *devas*. Anger, pride, deceit, and greed are the main obstacles to liberation of the souls, and in resisting or succumbing to these, humans are master of their own destiny. By subduing the self and by doing harm to no being, even to harmful insects, and by leading an ascetic life, a person may achieve rebirth as a *deva*. The moral rules for the devout believer are to show kindness without hope of return, to rejoice in the welfare of others, to seek to relieve the distress of other people, and to show sympathy for the criminal. Self-mortification is believed to annihilate accumulated karma. Jainism is technically a casteless religion; a priestly class is specifically eschewed.

Sikhism

A fourth major religion founded in India is Sikhism. Its founder was Guru Nanak (c. 400 A.D.). Historians and specialists in Eastern religions generally believe that Sikhism is a syncretistic religion, originally related to the Bhakti movement within Hinduism and the Sufi branch of Islam, to which many independent beliefs and practices were added. Some Sikhs believe that their religion is a repurification of Hinduism; they view Sikhism as part of the Hindu religious tradition. Most Sikhs disagree; they believe that their religion is a direct revelation from God—a religion that was not derived from either Hinduism or Islam.

Sikhism believes in one God, prohibits idol worship, is egalitarian, and has no caste system. Its followers, on the one hand, fought many wars (circa 1500) for political and religious freedom from the Muslim rulers of India. On the other hand, theirs is the only Indian religion to embody aspects of Islamic thought, and call for devotion to God without reference to one's religion.

Zoroastrianism

Zoroastrianism is the religion of a persecuted group from Iran who sought refuge in India in the tenth century A.D. Today more than half of the world's Zoroastrians are to be found in India. Many are in the world of business and the arts. Zubin Mehta, the world-renowned classical music conductor, is a member originally of the Indian Zoroastrian community. The religion was founded by Zoroaster (circa 500 B.C.) in what is now Iran. It is thought to be the earliest example of a monotheistic religion. Of note is its connection with Vedic mythology and sacrifice. For example, in the following description of Zoroastrianism, reference to intoxicating drinks called *haoma* is the Persian equivalent of the Sanskrit *soma*, the elixir mentioned in the Vedas.

Zoroaster forbade all sacrifices in honor of Ahriman or of his adherents, the *daevas*, who from pre-Zoroastrian times had degenerated into hostile deities. In the prevailing religious tradition, Zoroaster probably found that the practice of sacrificing cattle, combined with the consumption of intoxicating drinks (*haoma*), led to orgiastic excess. In his reform, Zoroaster did not, as some scholars would have it, abolish all animal sacrifice but simply the orgiastic and intoxicating rites that accompanied it. The *haoma* sacrifice, too, was to be thought of as a symbolic offering; it may have consisted of unfermented drink or an intoxicating beverage or plant. Zoroaster retained the ancient cult of fire. This cult and its various rites were later extended and given a definite order by the priestly class of the Magi. Its center, the eternal flame in the Temple of Fire, was constantly linked with the priestly service and with the *haoma* sacrifice (Encyclopaedia Brittanica, 2004).

Islam

Islam constitutes the religion of 12 percent of the Indian population. The advent of Islam in India began as early as the seventh century A.D. through coastal trader contacts in South India. By 1100 A.D., Muslim conquests of significant portions of India had begun, and with it came the spread of Islam. The Delhi sultanate, and Muslim dynasties that flourished in central and South India, often sought to convert the populace to Islam. The Mughul Empire continued this expansion of Islamic political, cultural, and religious hegemony until the advent of the British. However, in an inevitable dialectic resulting from the meeting of two societies, Islam itself was affected by the prevalent Hindu culture. The impact on Islamic culture is most evident in the realm of architecture and music, and in the birth of a new language, Urdu, which combined Turkish, Persian, and Arabic nouns and adjectives with the vernacular grammars of India. It is of note that Akbar the Great (1542–1605) went so far as to propound a new religion of tolerance called *Din-e-Ilahi*. Although it mixed Hinduism with Islam, the new religion did not win many converts.

Another confluence came from Sufism, the mystical and egalitarian saint-singer movement, which like the Bhakti movement was unwavering in its adherence to transcendent, experiential truth. Sufi saints spoke freely, trying to reach Muslims and Hindus alike. They are said to have influenced the founder of Sikhism, and left a luminous trail of transreligious poetry and philosophy. As Shaikh Abdul Quddus of Gangoh, a renowned Chishti saint of the sixteenth century, admonished his disciples in a letter:

Why this meaningless talk about the believer,
the kafir, the obedient, the sinner,
the rightly guided, the misdirected, the Muslim,
the pious, the infidel, the fire worshipper?
All are like beads in a rosary. [Cited in Nizami 1999]

Judaism

Besides the major religions described above, India is home to Jews who numbered in the thousands until the late 1940s and 1950s, when most left for Israel and other Western countries. There are three main groups, the Bene Israel, the Cochini Jews, and the Baghdadi Jews. A fourth group, consisting of many of the people in the Indian state of Mizoram, claims to have left Palestine in 800 B.C., and traveled via the Silk Route to India. This raises the possibility of their being members of the lost tribe of Israel (Kennedy 2003).

The Bene Israel (children of Israel) claim to be descended from Jews who escaped persecution in Galilee in the second century B.C. The Bene Israel resemble the non-Jewish Maratha people in appearance and customs, which indicates intermarriage between Jews and Indians. The Bene Israel, however, maintained the practices of Jewish dietary laws, circumcision, and observation of the Sabbath as a day of rest. The Bene Israel say their ancestors were oil pressers in Galilee and they are descended from survivors of a shipwreck off the western coast of India. In the eighteenth century they were discovered by traders from Baghdad. At that time the Bene Israel practiced some outward forms of Judaism (which is how they were recognized) but had no scholars of their own. Teachers from Baghdad and Cochin taught them mainstream Judaism in the eighteenth and nineteenth centuries.

The Cochini Jews are thought to be descended from groups of people who came to the southern state of Kerala beginning in the first century A.D. They were businessmen and traders for centuries, and enjoyed the prestige of the ruling class. A local Hindu king created a principality and installed a Jewish prince as ruler, in acknowledgment of the Jewish contributions to local society.

Of note is the peaceful intermingling of Jewish and Hindu peoples. Jews were free to observe religious laws and customs, and many centuries-old synagogues were centers of Jewish culture and religious faith. The several Jewish communities of India are said to have related to one another in a hierarchical fashion, one claiming to be more authentically Jewish than another. Scholars have speculated that the caste system may have influenced divisions among the Jews of India. During the time of the British, some groups of Jews are said to have identified with the British, and became spokesmen for British interests in other countries. The number of Jews in India has dramatically decreased since the creation of Israel in 1948. [See Roland (1998) and Katz (2000) for an account of the Jews of India, and the creation of a miniature caste system within the ranks of the Jews.]

Christianity

Christians in India number close to 30 million and constitute nearly 3 percent of the population. Christianity has a 2000-year history in India, and a complex evolution into modern times. Tradition and legend says it began with the arrival of St. Thomas the Apostle, in 52 A.D. in Kerala. His followers practiced what was known as the Malabar rite, until the late 1500s when the Portuguese attempted to Latinize the rite. Then followed a number of schisms and reconciliations resulting in a number of traditions, including the Syrian Catholic Church. Today, in South India (less so in the north), Christians involved themselves in the fabric of Hindu society, becoming prominent in education, medicine, nursing, and in the social services. Beginning with the Portuguese, and later the Dutch, the English, and the French in more modern times, Christian missionaries were active, providing the impetus for the growth of social services and education in many parts of India. There is no doubt that Christianity found a home in India, and in doing so, acculturated to Hinduism and regional subcultures. The effect of Christian theology on Hinduism is less clear, although Pereira (1976) suggests that Vedantic philosophers of the *Dwaita* (Dualist) school (thirteenth century A.D.) may have been influenced by Christian theology practiced and preached in geographically contiguous areas of South India.

Indigenous Religious Traditions

There are millions of tribal people and other aborigines who are outside the mainstream of modern Indian society and whose culture and religious traditions are poorly characterized and studied. One tribal tradition that has been scrutinized is the *Santal*, whose followers believe in a supreme deity as well as a number of animistic spirits that operate at the village, household, and clan level. Although many members of this and other tribes are converts to Christianity, Hinduism, Islam, and Buddhism, all are influenced by Hindu deities and festivals.

TRANSFERENCE GODS AND GODS OF TRANSFERENCE

In the many religious traditions outlined above, the concept of God in India varies from monotheistic to polytheistic to pantheistic to atheistic. In the Hindu tradition, which will be taken up in this chapter, what is striking is the multiplicity of gods, and the tendency to deify prophets, founders, and gurus of other faiths as well, and invest all things with godliness, in accordance with the juggernaut (from *Jagannath*, Lord of the Worlds) effects of Hinduism within the larger culture. The idea of a roster of 133,000 gods is daunting and incomprehensible except as a case of runaway pantheism. It should be emphasized that while Hindu myths have many gods, Indians frequently pay homage to deities other than their own. These are matters not easily understood in theological and historical contexts alone.

If we were to attempt a psychology of the God concept, and follow Freud in his conclusion that monotheism was the necessary end result of eons of earlier experiments with polytheism, we would be left with the question of how and why India appears to include monotheism as merely one of many possibilities, in sharp contradistinction to the Judeo-Christian world. Freud (1927) observes that "the gods retain their threefold task: they must exorcize the terrors of nature, they must reconcile men to the cruelty of fate, particularly as it is shown in death, and they must compensate them for the sufferings and privations which a civilized life in common has imposed on them" (p. 18). Akhtar and Parens (2001), in their psychoanalytic review of the concept of God, speak of Freud's insistence on God as representing an archaic father, and wonder why not an archaic mother. Freud's antipathy to the irrational ministrations of religion to people with privations and guilt was pointedly made clear when he suggested that a universal (religious) neurosis conveniently replaces a personal neurosis, most tellingly in the obsessional neurotic (Freud 1927). Commenting on Romain Rolland's characterization of the "oceanic feeling" as the origin of religious experience in the Hindu mystic Ramakrishna, Freud (1930) politely but firmly insists that "oceanic" feelings of being one with the world are traceable to early childhood lack of differentiation of self and object and likely representing the "restoration of a limitless narcissism" in the face of the experience of "infantile helplessness" (p. 72).

Freud (1930) goes on to describe the resultant wish to compensate through a wished for god-ideal:

> He [the child-man] formed an ideal conception of omnipotence and omniscience which he embodied in his gods. To these gods he attributed everything that seemed to be unattainable to his wishes, or that was forbidden to him. One may say, therefore, that these gods were cultural ideals. [p. 91]

In this narcissistically flexible vision of God, Freud indirectly suggests what may account for the multiplicity of God images. One reason must lie in the psychological and sociopolitical particulars of India and its history. As even the brief history of Indian religions reveals, there was enormous diversity and disunity among the people of India. An identity with truly collective national or tribal aims or pan-Subcontinental mores was not to be found, nor was it especially sought after. Enclave living on a large scale was the hallmark of Indian life, and celebrated even today. Tolerance, it has been said, led to the peaceful coexistence of many linguistic and ethnic groups at close quarters. Whether or not this was due to tolerance, it is clear that the religious zeitgeist was being continually reinvented locally. From the Aryan influx (1500–2000 B.C.) to British colonization (1608–1947), the most consistently notable effect of foreigners has been a slow but sure assimilation of new ideas. While on certain levels of functioning such as social and philosophical, assimilation was possible and even glorified as unique, I propose that there was a price to be paid. The price was inner counterrevolt. This took the form of an unyielding attachment to every previously held myth and belief, resulting in an unusual passion for preservation of the past. By the rules of compromise formation, when two masters have to be placated, what better way than to appear to please both. The purpose of the compromise, in this case, was to ensure preservation of identity and narcissistic gratification in the face of demands to change to suit the whims of outsiders.

How does this relate to the plethora of gods? First, each god had a distinct sociopolitical beginning. Using the elephant-headed god Ganesha, a popular member of the Hindu pantheon, "a god for all psychic seasons," as Kakar (1978, p. 101) puts it, one may appreciate the layered complexity surrounding the origins and the role of a Hindu God. Ganesha is the son of Shiva the Destroyer (Brahma the creator and Vishnu the protector constitute the other two of the Hindu trinity of supreme gods) and Shiva's consort Parvati. A paradigmatic oedipal situation is unmistakably linked with Ganesha's childhood and his acquisition of an elephant's head. In a commonly told story, Ganesha is asked by his mother not to let anyone in while she is taking a bath. Ganesha, being a devoted and utterly trustworthy son, refuses to let even Shiva, his own father, come in. In a rage, Shiva cuts off Ganesha's head. Only when his mother begs him does Shiva agree to restore Ganesha's life by asking that the head of an available living being be placed on Ganesha's head. As it happens, it is an elephant's head.

Ganesha's birth lends itself to other interpretations. He is variously depicted as Shiva re-creating himself, or as Parvati fashioning Ganesha out of clay or out of her body-dirt. Many myths attest to the extreme difficulty Shiva and Parvati appear to be having with the idea of adding a baby to their family. Upon his birth, the name he receives becomes vital for further understanding of his role. Gana refers to dwarf guardians, and sometimes to people of lower status (Courtright 1985). Ganesha has the further distinction of being the Remover of Obstacles, the possessor of a rather surprising and powerful power for someone who was hardly allowed to be born, and by most accounts, when born was beheaded, leaving him with a grotesque, makeshift head and childlike body. I propose that Ganesha represents, among other things, the symbolic victory of the downtrodden, the childlike, the unfortunate, and the commoner, against rulers and parents who hate him and only reluctantly have permitted his birth. This seems to be an example not only of a child pitted against anxious and envious parents, but also of a child who is disenfranchised and submissive. Note that Ganesha enjoys special popularity among those seeking auspicious beginnings. Ganesha for them has the special power of removing obstacles, and if not propitiated, the power of creating obstacles. Students are said to be particularly helped by Ganesha's blessings; thus among believers, no new venture is undertaken without an auspicious referencing of Ganesha.

Courtright (1985) in his study of Ganesha suggests that the elephant head represents the mascot of indigenous rulers: "Lavishly decorated, the elephant is a magnificent ceremonial vehicle for kings in processions. . . . The king's elephant is an expression of the people's welfare and the king's virtue" (p. 28). He suggests that the Gods of high religion like Shiva and Parvati were being mixed in with the Gods of folk religion. Ganesha, in this respect, was a God virtually created to represent this dialectic. Politically, this would allow the melding of at least two kinds of Gods into one—Shiva of the great tradition, and his son, Ganesha, in the little tradition. The result is perhaps charming, certainly idiosyncratic, but full of portentous meaning, as in the construction of a dream image. But unlike a dream image, the presence of continuing pressures and memories of racial, ethnic, linguistic, or cultural discord, and reverential reliving of a magical solution sanctioned by social approbation, forces the composite, condensed image of Ganesha to live forever, in fervent annual worship, ritual, and prayer. A single religious icon thus came to embody multiple social, psychological, existential, and aesthetic traditions.

Lavy (2003), in a paper on the political use of Hindu gods, argues that the

> popularity of Visnu and other Brahmanical deities was linked to patterns of political authority in pre-ninth century Khmer civilization in present-day Thailand and that the Southeast Asian ruling elite, whether kings or chiefs, utilised images of the gods with these considerations in mind. The deities Visnu and Siva embodied two different conceptions of sovereignty (or leadership in general), and images of these deities were employed to exploit these contrasting notions according to location and styles of rule. These practices are perhaps best understood through analysis of a third case: Harihara, a composite deity generally characterised in ancient Indian and Khmer art by a strict bilateral division between the proper left side with the attributes of Visnu (Hari) and the proper right with the attributes of Siva (Hara). Khmer sculptures of Harihara invariably have four arms and a vertical demarcation of the head into two "half-faces" so that the right side of the head is piled high with Siva's elaborately tangled locks (*jatamukuta*) and the left side is covered by Visnu's tall cylindrical mitre (*kiritamukuta*). By unifying Siva and Vishnu in one anthropomorphic form, Khmer images of Harihara served as a divine analogue for the concentration of the two forms of royal power. Harihara is commonly interpreted, however, as a syncretic deity that brought about the rapprochement of two allegedly "rival" Hindu sects, Saivism and Vaisnavism. [pp. 21–22]

If a god can be represented as a child, or as an adult, or as male, or as composite invocation of political power, a female god is logically necessary to complete the existential and transferential nexus of human life. In the earliest Vedic musings, a male and female principle were present as *Purusha* and *Prakriti*. In India, goddesses and female deities abound. God incarnate as a female personage, embodying virtues and powers, is exemplified by Sarasvati (goddess of learning) and Lakshmi (goddess of wealth). They derive their powers from the *Prakriti* principle as well as from being the consorts of Vishnu and Shiva. Kali, a goddess with a large following is, like Ganesha, an embodiment of an array of virtues, powers, and wishes. Kali often appears as a horrific vision of the divine, with garlands of human skulls around her neck and a severed head in her hand; her bloody tongue hangs from her mouth, and the weapons in her arms drip gore. She dances on the bodies of those she vanquishes. Followers claim that this image attempts to capture the destructive capacity of the divine, the suffering in the world, and the ultimate return of all things to the goddess at death. At the same time, Kali is worshiped for love and maternal succor, no less fervently than Ganesha. The loving and terrifying aspects of this transformational experience are maternal and sexual, usually conspicuously unavailable aspects of god in the Judeo-Christian, Islamic, and Buddhist religions.

A similarly meaningful goddess is Minakshi (the fish-eyed) of South India, described in myths as a dark queen born with three breasts, who set out to conquer the universe. After overrunning the world and vanquishing the gods, Minakshi finally met Shiva and, when her third breast disappeared, accepted him as her lord. This motif of physical power and energy appears in many stories where the goddess is a warrior or conqueror of demons who in the end joins with Shiva. The psychoanalyst with a proclivity for decoding symbols will immediately be struck by the three breasts apparently being required for phallic success, while a symbolic castration suggested by the loss of the extra breast is preparatory to joining with Shiva as female. Androgyny is also represented in Indian god-motifs, most importantly in the image of *Ardhanarishvara* (the god who is half woman). *Ardhanarishvara* may be understood as Shiva in an undifferentiated state of desireless or fulfilled male and female elements. *Ardhanarishvara* can also be understood as representing harmony, resolution, and gender balance. It is important to remember that in the myth of *Ardhanarishvara*, the proto-human being is depicted as fundamentally bisexual in origin, and requiring considerable effort to differentiate into male and female.

Polytheism is much too overdetermined to be explained fully by a few examples. However, syncretistic and novel imagery, condensation, and social mores in the historical context of India are principles that can be applied to the systematic study of God imagery to understand the image content as well as its probative power in the minds of devotees. This leads to a further thought about transference gods. All gods are transferential in nature from a psychoanalytic perspective (Freud 1927, Ostow 2001). In India, however, there appears to be a tendency to create, through the plasticity afforded by polytheism, a God in one's very own image. This is further exemplified by the common practice of *Ishta Devata* or a personal god of one's liking, a god that a family or a family member adopts as personally significant beyond all the other gods. The idea of choosing the form of god to worship or cherish is unique, but not unlike the practice of seeking the blessings of a Christian patron saint. An enigmatic discussion with the sage Yagnavalkya in the *Brhadaranyaka Upanishad* clearly suggests the telescoping of gods into a monotheistic god:

> Then Vidagdha Sakalya began to question him. "Tell me, Yagnavalkya— how many gods are there?" Saying, "As many as are mentioned in the ritual invocation within the laud to the All-gods," he answered in accordance with this very ritual invocation: "Three and three hundred, and three and three thousand." "Yes, of course," he said, "but really, Yagnavalkya, how many gods are there?" "Thirty-three." "Yes, of course," he said, "but really, Yagnavalkya, how many gods are there?" "Six." "Yes, of course," he said, "but really, Yagnavalkya, how many gods are there?" "Three." "Yes, of course," he said, "but really, Yagnavalkya, how many gods are there?" "Two." "Yes, of course," he said, "but really, Yagnavalkya, how many gods are there?" "One and a half." "Yes, of course," he said, "but really, Yagnavalkya, how many gods are there? "One." "Yes, of course," he said, "but then who are those three and three hundred, and those three and three thousand?" "They are only the powers of the gods," Yagnavalkya replied. "There are only thirty-three gods." [*Brhadaranyaka Upanishad* III:ix:1–2, Olivelle (trans.) 1998, p. 93]

Yagnavalkya proceeds to describe the gods identified with natural forces, the vital functions of humans, the animal kingdom, passion, death, sacrifice, water, truth, and on to the subtleties of breath, until he concludes with the famous phrase, *neti, neti* (not this, not this). The conversation is in the nature of an impassioned debate. Being unable to answer Yagnavalkya's final riddle or question, the questioner's head shatters.

If in this Upanishadic teaching, Indian gods are transference gods par excellence, one might go further and say they are also gods of transference, meaning that in a fundamental way Hindu gods extend themselves in turn as transformable beings and transference objects. They do this through the *Avatar* mechanism, usually translated as incarnation or descent (from a more exalted state), a cherished power of Hindu deities that allows for multiple lives, births, appearances, and attributes to suit temporal eras, social customs, and personal wishes. A change of *Avatar* is usually due to a change of eras, and has been likened to a process of evolution. It allows for an unusual attribute of the Indian God, that of changing rapidly rather than being fixed and eternal in form. Thus, arising from an ultimate impersonal godhead is the Hindu trinity— Brahma the creator, Vishnu the protector, and Shiva the destroyer. Vishnu and Shiva manifest themselves in countless avatars befitting the needs of the age, and of the individual. The plasticity of avatars is enhanced further by the tradition of reading historical and overarching meaning into every detail of the deity.

Kamal (1994), in "Esoteric Appellations of Ganapati [Ganesha]," for instance, draws meaning from the words describing the details of the Ganesha icon. One of his appellations is *vakratunda* (broken tusk), which Kamal states is a symbol of Ganesha being beyond duality—the broken tusk represents his broken head against the principle of unbroken *Atman* or cosmic consciousness. This may be an example, incidentally, of the practice of ascribing Vedic meaning into images of regional or folklore importance, thus ensuring continuity in the face of probable discontinuity or dissension. The appellations of Hindu gods are legendary for being even more numerous than the number of gods, and are often sung in hymns and ballads. A much-loved example is the "Vishnu Sahasranama" or the "Thousand Names of Vishnu," a lengthy chant consisting entirely of recitation of the appellations of Vishnu. In the recitation is captured the avatars, exploits, circumstances, and ardent lovers' names. The mood here is one of reverence, familiarity, jocularity, and fondness, bringing to mind Salman Rushdie's remark by an

Indian character who triumphantly announces that the tables have turned, and that he finally has the power to name and describe the British person, just like the British have named and described him. In doing so, the Indian character says, the describer becomes powerful, equal, and takes control of his destiny. Unmistakable here is Rushdie's conviction that the opposite is true as well—one is inferior if one is subject to description. In this respect, it would appear that in India, gods are freqently being cut to size, in a psychologically expectable reversal of creating an exalted, superior being.

In this attempt to be equal to a god, conflicts about aggression and its derivatives inevitably occur and are resolved in characteristic ways. Gods in India are frequently befriended, infantilized, turned into veritable family members, and in the process become objects of transformation (Bollas 1979). In this view, early objects, by virtue of their importance to the child (and adult), can transform and integrate the internal and external world of a patient. Shafranske (1992) extends the idea of transformational object to a universally applicable religious tendency to project momentous experiences of childhood onto adult God representations. The transformational object is related to the transitional object and space, a special psychic playground in which self and other, inner and outer, and real and imaginary have free play. Culture and creativity are claimed by analysts to be located in this space, because transitional phenomena are restitutive adaptations to the profound experience of separation, loss, and fear. The teddy bear and a child's safety blanket are examples of transitional objects. They are objects of love, devotion, apparent indifference, and occasionally of hate. A battered teddy bear is not unusual. A devotee's relationship to a god in India often mimics the relationship to a transitional object. Love and hate are both institutionally feasible to feel toward one's god. God is, through the avatar manifestations, profoundly loving as well as murderously fearsome, as in the dual aspects of Kali, the mother goddess. Superego pressures of both the loving and the punitive kind are enshrined in the same god. Conspicuously absent in the Hindu universe is the idea of the devil or even evil, an organic part of Judeo-Christian and Islamic traditions. Hell and sin are to be found in Hindu discourse, although rarely in a form as intense as the concept of eternal damnation. Guilt, shame, and remorse, however, are ubiquitous in all cultures. It would appear, however, that in India, a transformational god inviting both loving and hateful feelings might render superfluous the idea of the devil. Note, however, that epic battles between gods and demons exist in Vedic and post-Vedic literature. Gods and demons are not considered irreconcilable in these myths. They are opposites but complementary forces. In the eternal cycle of creation and destruction, both are necessary aspects of ultimate reality. In the Vedas *devas* (gods) and *asuras* (demons) were both children of Brahma, the creator, sharing the same origin and nature. Only at the churning of the Great Milk Ocean to obtain the drink of immortality were the *asuras* deceived and denied access to the divine *amrita*; the division between gods and demons is not so much good and evil as an ancient sibling rivalry.

SOCIETY, CASTE, AND THE GODMEN OF INDIA

A feature of the recent history of Hinduism is the attempt to break caste taboos. In this attempt can be seen the inexorable forces of social and political change. Equal access to God became an acceptable ideal, although the conservative forces of society kept matters largely unchanged. The Bhakti movement was a key impetus to bringing to the masses awareness of the excluded and shunned people of Indian society. A charming, if apocryphal, story is told of Kanakadasa, a sixteenth-century south Indian bhakti saint, who as a low-caste youth was not allowed into the temple of his beloved Krishna. He nevertheless devotedly offered his songs and prayers behind the temple, and after one long night, legend has it that Krishna inside the temple turned around to face his most ardent devotee. Records indicate that an earthquake created a crack in the western wall of the temple, which was later made into a window, known as *Kanakana Kindi* (Kanaka's window), which to this day attracts the devout, and enshrines from as early as the sixteenth century the idea of devotion knowing no social barriers.

There are lessons here for the clinical psychoanalyst on the subject of transference and countertransference, their fixity and plasticity, and their optimal use. In some instances, it is likely that patients experience themselves as cherished Gods by the analyst; at other times, they may cherish the analyst as a special God of their own making. This creativity in role playing is evident in the functions of the interlocutors between people and God in India. They can be priests, gurus, and sadhus, some of who attain the status of godmen (and women). Although tradition exhorts one to seek self-knowledge, most traditions give a central role to the guru as guide in what is regarded as uncharted, often dangerous waters. The role of the guru has been described by many, including Ramakrishna, as a veritable incarnation of God (Nikhilanda 1974). Gurus are felt by the student to be a tabula rasa, richly evocative of the analyst who is willing and able to take on the transferential feelings of the patient in a neutral and nonretaliatory manner. While strong feelings of love, rage, dependence, and jealousy are described during the period of intense tutelage, no attempt is made to understand childhood derivatives of such feelings. Strong feelings are understood to be manifestations of the turmoil caused by meditation, the power of past karma, and other extratransferential issues. Long periods of pathological dependency can occur, and opportunities for exploitation by unsophisticated or unscrupulous gurus are a danger inherent in a guru–student relationship. Neki (1979) suggests that Western psychotherapy as well as the guru–student relationship both rely on transference resolution. Idealizing transferences occur in the guru–student relationship because the guru is imputed to have extrasensory powers, and is treated as God in many traditions at least some of the time. I have suggested Krishna plays at being an existential analyst in the *Bhagavad Gita* (Rao 2001), and Reddy (2001) convincingly portrays the *Gita* as a prototypical psychoanalysis.

An extreme example of this type of guru is the phenomenon of the Indian godman. [See Kakar (1982) for a psychoanalytic perspective on gurus and their disciples.] Godmen are typically seen as being a reincarnation of an important guru from the past, are sometimes ambiguous in gender, claim supernatural powers, often have a huge following, and offer spiritual release and help through a variety of techniques and rituals. Organizations of the godmen are cult-like in the Western sense of the word, and allegiance to particular tenets and practices is expected. What is different in India is the meaning of cults. Cults have been cherished and have been revolutionary in their impact on Indian life in general and Hinduism in particular. The singer-saints of the Bhakti movement from the sixth century onward, for example, began as what at the time were heterodox, heretical attempts to radically redefine orthodox Hinduism, what Ramanujan (1981) calls "the Great Shift in Hindu culture and sensibility" (p. 103). Caste was abjured, a personal

relationship with God was seen as the prime goal, Brahmin interlocutors were regarded as obstacles to authentic experience, and a new
democratic way to God-consciousness was celebrated. The Bhakti
movement, along with the message of the *Bhagavad Gita*, swept India,
and is seen as the most recent of the revisions of the teachings of Hinduism. "Loving devotion" introduced a new element into Hinduism
(Zaehner 1966, p. 126).

With this as backdrop, it is easy to see why cults in India are regarded ambivalently—often as stirringly authentic, and just as often as
radically and uncomfortably heterodox. Complicating matters was the
beguiling and emotionally direct message of the Bhakti movement, in
which a love relationship took center stage in the relationship to God.
Logic, argument, definitions, and debate, highly valued qualities of the
orthodox establishment, fell away. A loving relationship to a personal
and personified god was emotionally, and eventually intellectually,
appealing to not just the marginalized, in whom the movement may
have first taken root, but to the orthodox members of the religious establishment as well. The Bhakti movement became an orthodoxy too,
of sorts, and the subversive message of the cult became established discourse in modern times. Modern Hindu cults and charismatic gurus are
only a century away from their Bhakti forbears in the minds of the many
that flock to them. In this sense, the Bhakti movement is still evolving, with a vibrancy and appeal enhanced by modern mass media. Direct experience of God with few intermediaries continues to be its
primary appeal today.

What is the psychological meaning of the Bhakti movement? While
it is certainly an outgrowth of the great tradition of the Vedas and the
Upanishad, its chief distinguishing mark is its identification with the
little traditions. Heesterman (1985), in describing incompatibility
within Indian tradition between ideal and reality, calls it an axial break-
through "that decisively split the unitary order of the world into two
principles; the turbulent order of conflict and the static order of transcendence" (p. 9). Ramanujan (1981) describes a gradual conjoining
of a regional tradition like the Tamilian with that of Sanskrit. He says:

Vedic and Upanishidic notions, Buddhist and Jaina concepts, conventions of Tamil and Sanskrit poetry, early Tamil conceptions of love, service, women, and kings, mythology or folk religion and folksong, the play

of contrasts between Sanskrit and the mother tongue; all these elements
were reworked and transformed in bhakti. [p. 104]

For the historian as for the psychoanalyst, this amalgam of the little
tradition with the great tradition is of crucial interest. It is in this coming together of pan-Indian and regional sentiment that we can appreciate the political, cultural, and psychological tension and their resolution
in blended versions of both.

Politically, Sanskrit conferred the imprimatur of imperial design
on regional kings and chieftains and gave legitimacy through the use
of Brahmin priesthood and patronage.

> Temples are "the most sensitive institution registering changes . . . espe-
> cially of dominance patterns"; they are witnesses to the South Indian
> conception that "human leaders (kings both large and small . . .), and
> the deities installed in temples, *share* sovereignty." South Indian "political
> communities are *communities of worship*. . . . The temple is the cultural
> and ideological context in which men and resources can be controlled,
> authority contested, and kingship revitalized." [Stein 1977, p. 7, italics
> in original]

Heesterman (1985) goes further psychologically, suggesting that
the pressures of inner conflict over the clash with the Muslim state were
responsible rather than the famed Hindu "inclusivity":

> Rather than an integrativeness that accommodates alien elements that
> otherwise might disrupt the coherent fabric of Indian civilization, we see
> here the inner conflict of tradition at work. The open rift between the
> king's order of conflict and the brahmin's, or the renouncer's, absolute
> order of transcendence called for and actually welcomed new ways to deal
> with disruption. It is not so much India's intergrativeness per se as it is
> the inner conflict that allowed the "inclusion" of the Islamic conception
> of transcendent order. [p. 7]

In Heesterman's conceptualization, the psychoanalyst finally hears
a word that changes the discourse—conflict. It is unclear if Heesterman
means inner psychological conflict or social or interpersonal conflict,
but his other writings in the same volume suggest a sophisticated understanding of ritual as dreaded, warded-off action, and of the psychological
accommodation required of different segments of society to allow life

to proceed. A chapter that is particularly trenchant is entitled, "The Case of the Severed Head," and it traces the Vedic meaning of head as the seat of power and knowledge, and related sacrificial ritual, which constitutes significant portions of the Vedas. He begins with human and animal sacrifice in the pre-Vedic or Vedic period, cattle ownership as a measure of prosperity, and ends with a discussion of sacrificial rituals that persist to this day. He is adept at recognizing in these rituals the symbolizing function of these ancient murderous wishes by which to accrue resources and power. He concludes that the rituals involve an ingenious trick: by staging the sacrifice in prescribed ways during a banquet at which the antagonistic parties meet, a true sacrifice of a head never quite takes place. The rituals ensure that through systematic doing and undoing, heads are severed only to be replaced endlessly, thus denying the reality of murderous impulses, covetousness, envy, and death itself. It is, nevertheless, of interest that a directly psychoanalytic approach is never mentioned by Heesterman.

Ganesha's beheading by his father is thus only one, relatively recent, example of the severed head problem, in a lineage that extends back into the earliest sacred writings. The famous adaptation of Thomas Mann in his "Transposed Heads" of the Indian legend involves a double suicide by beheading by two brothers. When the wife of one of the brothers is divinely allowed to reattach the heads, she tragically transposes the wrong heads, leading to a moral dilemma involving incestuous conflict. On a contemporary note, it is interesting to speculate on the implications of the severed head for the problem of Kashmir. Some Indian maps, like the popular pictures of gods, represent Bharata Mata (Mother India), a goddess-like personage, whose arms encompass the western and eastern protuberances of the Indian Subcontinent, her feet reach the very southern tip of the peninsula, and her head is literally pre-1947 Kashmir. To divide Kashmir is presumably then to suffer a severe blow to the head; to have Kashmir leave India is to decapitate India. It is quite likely that in the land of creative and expedient iconography, an unconscious fear of being beheaded is depicted in mass media, drawing upon ancient myth and national pride, and surely informs Indian politics in its dispute with Pakistan.

Culturally, the process of Sanskritization of regional cultures continued, along with de-Sanskritization. High and low cultures mixed. The consolidation of regional languages of India took shape by the tenth century. South Indian (Dravidian) culture was particularly subject to the tensions of this because of Tamil language and culture had ancient origins itself (first century A.D.). As the Muslim saint-poet Kabir (fifteenth to sixteenth century) said, "Sanskrit is standing water, bhasa (vernacular) is flowing water." He was a revolutionary syncretist who forged an unusual alliance between Hindus and Muslims based on Sufi principles of personal, not institutionalized, revelation, a methodology dear to the bhakti tradition.

YOGA

Personal revelation in India is closely linked with the idea of a psychophysiology of God, however fanciful or mystical the underlying assumptions. Yoga is well known for the parallels it draws between the bodily and the transcendent. Breath (*prana*), for example, is regarded not only as a metaphor for life, but also as a concrete way to control the inner forces of life in the practice of meditation. In the same way, focusing attention on an object or word is seen as a way to control forces of the mind to bring about stillness, and a radical resolution of mental strife. Thus, within the conceptual framework of yoga are to be found many ideas, some with surprising relevance for modern times—observing transforms the observer, a concept in keeping with modern physics. Buddhist metaphysics, which carries with it remnants of Hindu ideas (notably dharma, karma, reincarnation, self-realization, guru-preceptor), is often said to be a psychology, perhaps its most radical challenge to orthodox Hinduism. In Buddhism, many feel, Hinduism's true essence was preserved and extended and a meditational psychology consolidated. Yoga's prescriptive emphasis on rote practice was changed to an emphasis on experiential compassion, while both dwelled on the intimate connection between body and mind. Both religions are modally prepared to resort to physiology to understand a god experience; each is concerned with motivation, pleasure, unpleasure, and the seeking of transcendent truth and authenticity by means of general and specific practices to focus and alter consciousness. God in this meditational goal is a feeling state. It is described as a state of hunger satiated, desires fulfilled, anxiety quelled, doubts banished, and the self reconceived as selfless.

There is a growing literature on the relationship of psychoanalysis to Buddhism and related meditation practices (Coltart 1992, Epstein 1995, Rubin 1996). Engler (1986) offers a sophisticated comparison of technical and philosophical differences between meditation and psychotherapy:

> Once attention is stabilized at this level of perception, a further refinement of this insight into the underlying nature of self and object representation becomes apparent. I observe how a self-representation is constructed in each moment as a result of an interaction with an object and only as a result of such an interaction; and conversely, how an object appears not in itself (whatever that might mean) but always relative to my state of observation. I see how preceding causes operate to condition each moment of self-object representation, and how each moment conditions the next moment. In this way I begin to perceive that there are strictly speaking *no constant end-products of representation; there is only a continual process of representing.* I discover that there are actually no enduring entities or schemas at all; only momentary constructions are taking place. [p. 42, italics in original]

Engler's description of perception and the dynamic mindfulness of everyday mentation seem to be identical to much of contemporary psychoanalytic thinking. Clinically, one never enters the same river twice, nor does one look for bedrock as easily as in the early history of psychoanalysis. Engler makes a second comparison of the concept of pleasure/unpleasure between psychoanalysis and Buddhist psychology. He states that in Buddhist psychology, in contrast to psychoanalysis, pleasure/unpleasure is de-linked from the tendency to act. That is, Buddhist psychology believes there is feeling (*vedana*), a "spontaneous sensation of pleasure or unpleasure which accompanies every experience of an object" (p. 45). This has nothing to do with a second step, which is a tendency to respond or act on that sensation (*tanha*). In psychoanalysis, Engler believes the two experiences are usually conceptually and clinically combined as having drive characteristics and are seen as being "innate, automatic, spontaneous, natural; as an autonomic voluntary system response-sequence beyond voluntary control" (p. 45). De-linking *vedana* and *tanha*, the experience of pleasure/unpleasure, and the tendency to respond or act "is a fulcrum point in meditation training. It returns a previously conditioned response to voluntary control and introduces an important principle of delay" (p. 45). This is an example of the conceptual differences in emphasis, detail, and goals between psychoanalysis and meditation. Study and comparison, however, are possible and desirable, because the problems of perception, pleasure/unpleasure, motivation, and reality testing are shared by the two disciplines.

The insistence on a partial or complete unawareness of self is considered the sine qua non of the religious experience in Indian religions. To some degree this is true of strivings in non-Indian religions, although such abnegation is more moral than a function of a state of mind. To the psychoanalyst, it is clear that the idea of self-abnegation must include considerations of narcissism. In this respect, the Sanskrit word *Ahamkara*, or I-maker (colloquially used to refer to haughtiness), is worth examining in the context of the familiar "ego," "self," and narcissistic investment of the self and body. Its opposite, *Shunyata*, in the Buddhist tradition refers to a nothingness, a sought-after state. For the analyst, these polar opposites refer to desires and defenses against them. It is easy to imagine a philosophy in which a painful desirous state might require the ultimate sacrifice of snuffing out of the desire itself. Indian religions are in this sense radical attempts to manage desire and frustration as well as grief through attempts to negate selfhood and desire in the hope of gaining a transcendent self where there are no desires or all desires appear to be fulfilled. The self as God is a majestic refrain in the Vedas and the Upanishads. The self is defined as a cosmic consciousness, unchanging, unborn and undying, eternal. Commentaries on these aphorisms concern themselves with what is meant by self, and how one might realize the self in oneself. The terse Upanishadic aphorism "That Art Thou" is meant to indicate that self-discovery will reveal the oneness of reality and one's self. At the same time, in a cautionary stance, the Upanishads also warn against the elusiveness of this transcendent self with the aphorism "*neti, neti*" ("not this, not this"). Jack Engler, who is a psychiatrist and Buddhist meditator, coined this phrase to describe the paradox of the self concept thus: "You have to be somebody before you can be nobody."

It is of interest that psychoanalysis has not concerned itself with the life of the Buddha as a prototype of ascetic triumph over unbearable affects, a "Buddha complex," which clinicians see from time to time. The fate of aggression in such a transformation would be useful to understand. A colloquial Indian usage of *Hatha* (literally violence) refers to a child's tantrum or obstinacy, as if to suggest that *Hatha* yoga is codified obstinacy or determination, as well as a method of managing associated affects.

CONCLUSION

In this survey of the concept of God in India, it is clear that the central burden of Indian religious thought is existential. With a sustained rigor, Indian exegetists have attempted to discover the boundaries of human functioning, and claim to have found ways to transcend and decondition (Eliade 1969) oneself. The methods are many and range from activities of daily living to esoteric practices. The range of human activity, real and imaginable, encompassed in this endeavor is vast. I conclude with summarizing remarks on topics of interest to the general reader as well as to the psychoanalyst.

1. The concept of God in India as a theological entity in the usual sense is insufficient. Atheistic sentiment is possible to express within the Indian context and still be religious. This is due to a range of God concepts—formless to formed and without attribute to richly endowed with attributes. The concept of merging with an impersonal godhead is juxtaposed against relating to a god of one's choice. God in India can also be personal, transcendent, mundane, eternal, or expedient. The term *henotheism,* meaning belief in, and possible worship of, multiple gods, one of which is supreme, was coined by the Indologist Max Müller to describe Hinduism. Müller believed that a striving toward One was being aimed at by the worship of different cosmic principles, such as *Agni* (fire), *Vayu* (wind), *Indra* (rain, thunder, the sky), and so on, each of which was variously, by clearly different writers, hailed as supreme in different sections of the Vedas.
2. Indian gods are transference gods *par excellence*. Contributing factors are the avatar concept; plasticity of icon and image depending on local culture, language, and tradition; admixture of totemic, pantheistic, and polytheistic traditions; centuries of enclave living with slow assimilation of neighboring cultures, leading to a

surplus of local deities; and absence of pan-Indian religious, political, or linguistic leadership or hegemony, contributing to many small cultures. The gods of the Aryans pitted against the gods of the original inhabitants provided the basis for proxy battles through god mascots interspersed with periods of equilibrium. God mascots being parental and phallic self-representations in this context led to gods competing with one another.

3. The relative absence of a radical monotheism in India leads to questions regarding psychoanalytic explanations for the emergence of monotheism in the Judeo-Christian and Islamic traditions. Sociocultural and complex historical factors are clearly involved. It may be asked, however, if the Indian father is never symbolically killed, in a modal failure of oedipal resolution. By the same token, is the Indian father, hoary and modern, unwilling to exert enough strength to unify and rule? Is this an attitude of conflict avoidance brought on by millennia of invasions causing a relative loss of oedipal will? Is the role of the mother not sufficiently appreciated in Indian life? Kakar (1995) stresses what he calls "maternal enthrallment" (p. 265) in the male patients he sees in India. The plasticity of god imagery speaks to a widened range of representability. The fanciful, imaginative, and syncretistic content of god imagery may be the result of an enlarged sense of transitional space with accompanying diffusion of selfobject boundaries, and heightened action of primary process. Doniger (1984) says, in describing the parallels between dreams and reality, "Latent and manifest content are very close indeed in India" (p. 59). The effects of a "transformational" god on the modal development of the Hindu ego and superego are areas for further research.

4. The prevailing ethos in Indian culture militates against the definition of God in anything approaching Judeo-Christian positivism. Hence, there is an abundance of paradox and not-knowing in the Vedic philosophic tradition. The Upanishadic aphorism "*neti, neti*" ("not this, not this") is a prime example of the ineffability and conceptual difficulty of imagining God. There is a Zen-like insistence on apprehending reality in the correct way. The paradox has been interpreted to mean that the Vedic tradition privileges experience over learning, immediacy

over memory, and being over becoming. The self is used to refer to a transcendently authentic self experience that is regarded as the true search for God.

5. Of interest to psychoanalysis is the privileging of the experience-near "here-and-now" over the past, a technical and theoretical stance taken by analysts in the clinical situation. "Not this, not this" is a phrase most analysts use to pause, rethink, and avoid premature closure in the face of enormous pressure to do so, while looking for the optimally mutative moment of understanding.

6. Ganesha, the elephant-headed God, is an example of the multiple functions, an overdetermined attempt at compromise and resolution of personal, sociocultural, and historical conflicts. Doniger (1998) suggests that the study of myth is accomplished by using a microscope as well as a telescope. She means by this the distinction between the personal and the abstract, which she feels is essential in understanding myth:

> On this continuum between the personal and the abstract, myth vibrates in the middle; of all the things made of words, myths span the widest range of human concerns, human paradoxes. Epics too, so closely related to myths, have as their central theme the constant interaction of the two planes, the human and the divine, as the gods constantly intervene in human conflicts. Myths range from the most highly detailed (closest to the personal end of the continuum) to the most stripped down (closest to the artificial construct at the abstract end of the continuum); and each myth may be rendered by the scholar in its micro- or macro- form. [p. 9]

Doniger provides support for the notion of "myths as political lenses" (p. 18). She believes that theology and politics share the need for dual lenses; each can illuminate the intensely personal as well as the broadly human. Myths, she says, "form a bridge between the terrifying abyss of cosmological ignorance and our comfortable familiarity with our recurrent, if tormenting, human problems" (p. 22).

7. The Ganesha iconology illustrates a wider prevalence of great and little cultures in India. These are related to orthodoxy and heterodoxy, mainstream and breakaway cultures, and inevitably the ruler and the ruled. U. R. Ananthamurthy (2000), a regional Indian writer with a national reputation, feels that

creativity and originality are to be found in the littler, lesser-known cultures. He gives as an example the European literary face-off between the Irish and the English, and Latin and spoken vernacular. He notes that true and authentic literary works required delving into the "little traditions" and resolutely keeping away from the influence of the dominant mode or culture. In India, he describes the great and little traditions as *margi* and *desi* (great path and local path). He feels that in his own writings he relies on yet another psychological dimension of this division—the metaphorical division between the men who dominate the living room in the front of the house, in contrast to the women who stay behind in the inner courtyard of traditional houses. Ananthamurthy says he learned about the intimate life when he was with the women, while he learned to put up an uncreative front when he was with the men.

8. Hinduism, Buddhism, and Jainism and its offshoots offer an atheistic, beliefless technology of self-awareness through the harnessing of ordinary attention. The self is accorded a transcendent meaning and is said to be a form of authentic unity with a godhead. The promise of a technique to achieve awareness invites the study of yogic interiority and related concepts of conditioning by evolutionary, social, and psychological pressures. Psychoanalysis, being itself a tool and purveyor of the interior life, can find a willing and instructive fellow traveler in the Indian *sadhaka* or aspirant.

Tracing the history and origins of the complex web of religious thought in India can never feel complete. It is my hope that the reader has glimpsed some of the richness and nuance of the products of a civilization in its struggle to cope with life. Systematic, cross-disciplinary study of the many psychological issues raised by this subject is necessary. I trust that some readers will be stimulated to do so.

REFERENCES

Akhtar, S., and Parens, H. (2001). *Does God Help? Developmental and Clinical Aspects of Religious Belief*. Northvale, NJ: Jason Aronson.

Ananthamurthy, U. R. (2000). Literary traditions in India. Talk given at the Department of South Asian Studies, University of Michigan, Ann Arbor, MI, April 7.

Basham, A. L. (1951). *History and Doctrines of the Ajivikas, A Vanished Indian Religion.* New Delhi: Motilal Banarsidass, 1981.

Bollas, C. (1979). The transformational object. *International Journal of Psycho-Analysis* 60:97–107.

Coltart, N. (1992). *Slouching Towards Bethlehem.* London: Guilford.

Courtright, P. B. (1985). *Ganesa: Lord of Obstacles, Lord of Beginnings.* New York: Oxford University Press.

Doniger, W. (1984). *Dreams, Illusion and Other Realities.* Chicago: University of Chicago Press.

——— (1998). *The Implied Spider: Politics and Theology in Myth.* New York: Columbia University Press.

Eliade, M. (1969). *Yoga. Immortality and Freedom.* Bollingen Series, vol. 56. Princeton, NJ: Princeton University Press.

Encyclopaedia Britannica. (2004). Encyclopaedia Britannica Premium Service. http://www.britannica.com/eb/article?eu=80561.

Engler, J. (1986). Therapeutic aims in psychotherapy and meditation. In *Transformations of Consciousness: Conventional and Contemplative Perspectives on Development,* ed. K. Wilber, J. Engler, and D. Brown, pp. 17–51. Boston: Shambhala.

Epstein, M. (1995). Thoughts without a thinker: Buddhism and psychoanalysis. *Psychoanalytic Review* 82:391–406.

Freud, S. (1927). The future of an illusion. *Standard Edition* 21:3–66.

——— (1930). Civilization and its discontents. *Standard Edition* 21:57–145.

Heesterman, J. C. (1985). *The Inner Conflict of Tradition: Essays in Indian Ritual, Kingship, and Society.* Chicago and London: University of Chicago Press.

Hooker, R. (1996). http://www.wsu.edu:8000/~dee/Buddhism/sidd.htm.

Kakar, S. (1978). *The Inner World: A Psycho-analytic Study of Childhood and Society in India.* Delhi: Oxford University Press.

——— (1979). *Identity and Adulthood.* Delhi: Oxford University Press.

——— (1982). *Shamans, Mystics and Doctors: A Psychoanalytic Enquiry into India and Its Healing Traditions.* New York: Alfred A. Knopf.

——— (1995). Clinical work and cultural imagination. *Psychoanalytic Quarterly* 64:265–281.

Kamal, J. K. (1994). Esoteric appellations of Ganapati. *The Kalyana Kalpataru* 60:34–40.

Katz, N. (2000). *Who Are the Jews of India?* Berkeley: University of California Press.

Kennedy, M. (2003). The Jews of India: A Lost Tribe? National Public Radio, December 24.

Lavy, P. (2003). As in heaven, so on earth: the politics of Visnu, Siva and Harihara images in Preangkorian Khmer civilization. *Journal of Southeast Asian Studies* 34:21–39.

Neki, J. S. (1979). Panel discussion. In *Psychotherapeutic Processes. Proceedings of the seminar held at the National Institute of Mental Health and Neuro Sciences*, ed. M. Kapur, V. N. Murthy, et al., pp. 142–143. Bangalore, India: NIMHANS.

Nikhilanda, S. (1974). *The Gospel of Ramakrishna*. Madras, India: Sri Ramakrishna Math.

Nizami, K. A. (1999). The contribution of Indian Sufis to peace and amity. In *Culture of Peace*, ed. B. Saraswati. New Delhi: IGNCA and D. K. Printworld Pvt. Ltd. http://ignca.nic.in/cd_09019.htm.

O'Flaherty, W. D. (1984). *Dreams, Illusion and Other Realities*. Chicago: University of Chicago Press.

Olivelle, P. (1998). *The Early Upanishads: Annotated Text and Translation*. New York: Oxford University Press.

Ostow, M. (2001). Three archaic contributions to the religious instinct: awe, mysticism, and apocalypse. In *Does God Help? Developmental and Clinical Aspects of Religious Belief*, ed. S. Akhtar and H. Parens, pp. 197–233. Northvale, NJ: Jason Aronson.

Pereira, J. (1976). *Hindu Theology: A Reader*. Garden City, NY: Doubleday.

Ramanujan, A. K. (1981). *Hymns for the Drowning. Poems for Visnu by Nammalvar*. Princeton, NJ: Princeton University Press (Trans.).

Rao, D. G. (1994). The acoustic merger experience and the Indian musical drone: drive, defense, and adaptation. Unpublished.

——— (2001). God playing psychoanalyst: some lessons from the *Bhagavad Gita*. In *Does God Help? Developmental and Clinical Aspects of Religious Belief*, ed. S. Akhtar and H. Parens, pp. 177–196. Northvale, NJ: Jason Aronson.

Reddy, S. (2001). Psychoanalytic reflections on the sacred Hindu text, the *Bhagavad Gita*. In *Does God Help? Developmental and Clinical Aspects of Religious Belief*, ed. S. Akhtar and H. Parens, pp. 153–176. Northvale, NJ: Jason Aronson.

Roland, J. R. (1998). *The Jewish Communities of India: Identity in a Colonial Era*. New York: Transaction Publishers.

Rubin, J. B. (1996). *Psychotherapy and Buddhism: Toward an Integration*. New York: Plenum.

Shafranske, E. P. (1992). God-representation as the transformational object. In *Object Relations Theory and Religion: Clinical Applications*, ed. M. Finn and J. Gartner, pp. 57–72. Westport, CT: Praeger.

Smith, D. (2002). A new Kama Sutra without Victorian veils: book review of *Kama Sutra*, by W. Doniger and S. Kakar. *New York Times*, May 4.

Stein, B., ed. (1977). Special number on South Indian Temples. *Indian Economic and Social History Review* 14:1–7.

Tharoor, S. (2002). A culture of diversity. *Resurgence Magazine*, February 16. http://resurgence.gn.apc.org/articles/tharoor.htm.

Zaehner, R. C. (1966). *Hinduism*. New York: Oxford University Press.

Psychoanalytic Process in a Sacred Hindu Text: *The Bhagavad Gita*

Satish Reddy

Yea! Son of Kunti!
For this flesh ye see is *Kshetra*, is the field where life disports;
And that which views and knows it is the Soul, *Kshetrajna.*
In all fields, thou Indian Prince,
I am *Kshetrajna.* I am what surveys!
Only that knowledge knows which knows the known.
Be the knower!

Bhagavad Gita

The *Bhagavad Gita*, literally meaning "The Song of the Lord," is one of the most sacred, influential, and profound texts of Hinduism. Widely considered the apogee of Hindu theological and philosophical thought, the *Gita* is a small part of the great Hindu epic the *Mahabharata*, which recounts the story of a fratricidal war between the five Pandava brothers and the one hundred Kaurava brothers. The *Gita* is a dialogue between the Pandava prince and warrior Arjuna and his charioteer and god incarnate Krishna. The *Gita* is a religious text, a mystical poem, a philosophical treatise, and a practical manual for living. It was the first Sanskrit text translated into English—in 1785 by Charles Wilkins. It has no author and, though a source of much debate, it is thought to have been composed circa 500 B.C. (Radhakrishan 1929).

Before the war, Arjuna despairs and refuses to fight. He is paralyzed by fear and guilt. He tells Krishna that he cannot fight. Overwhelmed by his condition, he asks Krishna to help him. Arjuna is not aware of Krishna's divinity. He thinks of him as his friend and counselor. Krishna's teachings to Arjuna constitute the core content of the *Gita*. In eighteen terse and dense chapters, a dialogue ensues between Krishna and Arjuna that leads to the resolution of Arjuna's crisis and his existential transformation.

The *Gita* is a precise text. Each word and stanza is carefully and deliberately placed. The structure of the chapters as well as the details of the dialogue has an important sequence, logic, and consistency. Hindu commentaries on the *Gita* explain each word in relation to its stanza and each stanza in relation to the chapter (Radhakrishnan 1948, Sampatkumaran 1969, Sastry 1979). The chapters are explained and dissected in relation to each other and to the text as a whole. Both Hindu and Western interpretations of the *Gita* allow for a multiplicity of religio-philosophical positions, ranging from theism to atheism and agnosticsm. The *Gita* accommodates and supports monotheism, polytheism, and henotheism as well as the more uniquely Indian philosophical traditions of *Vedanta* and *Yoga*. The beauty, elegance, and endurance of the *Gita* through centuries lies in its capacity to support a multiplicity of interpretations while maintaining the central core teaching that embodies the essence and everyday practice of Hinduism.

The logic of the structure and teachings of the *Gita* can be seen as constituting a transformative dialogue that, while culturally and idiomatically distinct, is akin to a psychoanalytic process. Loewald (1960) states:

> By psychoanalytic process I mean the significant interaction between patient and analyst that ultimately leads to structural changes in the patient's personality. . . . If structural changes in the patient's "personality" means anything, it must mean that we assume that ego development is resumed in the therapeutic process in analysis. And this resumption of ego development is contingent on the relationship with a new object, the analyst. [p. 16]

In the *Gita*, Krishna functions as Arjuna's teacher (*Guru*) and psychoanalyst. Krishna's analytic (therapeutic) function is not interpretive per se but more as an object that facilitates Arjuna's ego (psychic) development and maturation. Specifically, it is Krishna's allowing Arjuna to use him as a transformational object (Bollas 1979). The transformational object, by its capacity to transform, becomes a potential sacred object. The object, by actually eventuating a transformation, becomes sacred, an object of *Bhakti* or devotion. From a psychoanalytic viewpoint, the cardinal techniques of abstinence, anonymity, and neutrality are both observed and violated by Krishna. The pivotal and transformative violation of anonymity in Chapter 11, by Krishna's self-disclosure, promotes the therapeutic regression and psychic reorganization that leads to Arjuna's existential transformation.

THE CONTEXT OF THE *GITA*

The *Gita* consists of 600 stanzas and occurs within the 200,000 stanzas that comprise the vast Hindu epic the *Mahabharata*, the longest epic in the world. It consists of eighteen books (*Parvans*), each subdivided into chapters. The *Gita* occurs in the sixth book, the *Bhishmaparvan* (*Book of Bhishma*), in a chapter entitled the *Bhagavadgitaparvan* (the *Book of the Bhagavadgita*). The plot of the epic revolves around Bhishma's voluntary renunciation of his kingship by a vow of celibacy so that his father might marry a lower caste woman. Bhishma's renunciation leads to progressive problems in succession to the throne that climax in the war between the Pandavas and the Kauvaras.

Bhishma's actions can be viewed as both positive oedipal submission and negative oedipal affection for his father. From a Hindu perspective, it is veneration and respect for the father's wishes but at an extremely high cost. Bhishma does what he does to spare his father the penultimate suffering-separation from the loved object. His motives for doing so are complex and beyond the scope of this work. Suffice it to say that Bhishma relinquishes his duty (*Dharma*) to be the rightful heir to the throne. He is celebrated and revered for his action to remain celibate and is given the blessing of the gods. The name *Bhishma* means the one who keeps his vows. Bhishma's acts are complex psychologically; politically, they are simple folly. Bhishma's voluntary renunciation to his throne eventuates the war between the Pandavas and the Kauvaras. It is notable that in the *Mahabharata*, Bhishma knows all along Krishna's true identity and agenda. His knowledge of this point underscores the extraordinary and complex persona that Bhishma represents.

Bhishma, revered by both warring parties, becomes the first general of the Kaurava army. *The Book of Bhishma* chronicles the killing of Bhishma by Arjuna. It is the thought of killing Bhishma that precipitates Arjuna's crisis. The *Book of the Bhagavadgita* begins with the announcement by Sanjaya to his patron, the blind king Dhritarashtra (father of the Kauvaras), that Bhishma has fallen in battle. Dhritarashtra, stunned by the news, questions Sanjaya how this happened. The *Gita* occurs midway in the *Book of the Bhagavadgita*. Its positioning here in the epic is psychologically important. "It is not just a successful narrative device that the death of Bhishma is first reported as an accomplished fact, then juxtaposed with the prior teaching of the *Gita* which in the end seeks to justify the killing of him: each one is the condition of the other" (Van Buitenen 1980, p. 1). Chronologically, before the *Gita* begins, Arjuna has already slain Bhishma. The dialogue of the *Gita* begins *ex post facto*:

> The preamble tells us that Bhishma is dead, that Arjuna's reluctance to fight in this war was therefore fully justified, and that consequently a need existed to override Arjuna's reluctance with a higher truth, so that in fact *that* will come about which we know is *already* the case. [Van Buitenen 1980, p. 3]

This highlights a crucial point: time in the *Gita* is not linear. This is a salient motif that recurs in the *Gita* to which I will later return. Timelessness has a significant corollary to Freud's notion of the unconscious:

> The processes of the system *Ucs.* are timeless; i.e., they are not ordered temporally, are not altered by the passage of time; they have no reference to time at all. Reference to time is bound up, once again, with the work of the system *Cs.* The *Ucs.* processes pay just as little regard to *reality*. They are subject to the pleasure principle; their fate depends only on how strong they are and on whether they fulfill the demands of the pleasure–unpleasure regulation. To sum up: *exemption from mutual contradiction, primary process, timelessness* and *replacement of external by psychical reality*—these are the characteristics which we may expect to find in the processes belonging to the system *Ucs.* [Freud 1915, p. 187]

ARJUNA'S DESPONDENCY

Arjuna's inhibition to fight and his crisis occur on three different and overlapping levels: (1) the moral and ethical dilemma of killing in general; (2) the oedipal guilt of (displaced) parricide in particular; and (3) the existential questioning of "who am I," with the "I" connoting the psychophysically conditioned self, the grammatical "I," the empirical ego that is based on self-identifications. In Kohut's (1977) terms, Arjuna is both "guilty man" and "tragic man."

On the level of morality, Arjuna's reluctance to fight is understandable. He is distressed by the carnage that war will bring. However, Arjuna was a warrior who had fought and killed many times before. Why was engaging in a war and killing so paralyzing to him now, at this point in his life? Before the war, Arjuna did not have to kill those who were close to him—the people he loved and respected. The emotional valence of aggression against loved objects underscores Arjuna's oedipal inhibitions, particularly the killing of Bhishma and Drona. Arjuna is guilt ridden and reluctant to fight against Bhishma, his adopted father, and Drona, his teacher (guru).[1]

Arjuna's moral inhibition is based on the psychological guilt of killing loved objects, and the prospect of killing his loved objects reveals the deepest layer of his existential crisis: Who am I that is going to kill? What is my responsibility in this situation, and what choice do I have in the matter?

> Drive my chariot, Krishna immortal, and place it between the two armies. That I may see those warriors who stand there eager for battle, with whom I must now fight at the beginning of this war. That I may see those who have come here eager and ready to fight, in their desire to do the will of the evil son of Dhritarashtra. [*Gita* 1, 21–23]

---

1. In Hinduism, the teacher or "guru" occupies a role equivalent to the father. In the *Dharmasastra*, the Hindu scripture on laws, sleeping with the guru's wife is considered to be one of the most heinous sins, equating the role of the father to the guru. The guru is considered a conduit between the father and God, elevating his position above the father and below God—a broker between the paternal and the divine. See Kane (1974).

Krishna positions the chariot between the two armies, facing Bhishma and Drona. They personify Arjuna's identifications. His predicament is that he must kill the ones he loves or be killed by those who love him. In the calculus of psychic dynamics, Arjuna is in a no win situation. No wonder that he does not want to fight. "In a war, Arjuna could have again easily defeated both of them, but they were inviolate, one because he was his grandfather, the other because he was his teacher" (Karve 1991, p. 126).

> I owe veneration to Bhishma and Drona. Shall I kill with my arrows my grandfather's brother, great Bhishma? Shall my arrows in battle slay Drona, my teacher? Shall I kill my own masters who, though greedy of my kingdom, are yet my sacred teachers? I would rather eat in this life the food of a beggar than eat royal food tasting of their blood. [*Gita* 2, 4–5]

Bhishma, though fighting on the opposing side, is revered and loved by Arjuna. Prior to the enmity that develops between the cousins, the Pandavas and the Kauravas grow up in the same house with Bhishma as the head of the household. A special affection develops between Arjuna, the child, and Bhishma. Krishna is well aware of this attachment and Arjuna's profound ambivalence in killing Bhishma. He consistently and repeatedly prompts Arjuna to kill Bhishma, yet Arjuna resists.

> How, Krishna, shall I fight in battle, with the venerable and aged preceptor of the Kurus, the grandsire of accomplished understanding and intelligence? Krishna, while playing in the days of childhood, I used to soil the garments of the high-souled and illustrious one by climbing on his lap with my body smeared with dust. Krishna, in my childhood, climbing on the lap of the high souled father of Pandu (our father), I used to say "father." "I am not your father, but your father's father, Arjuna," were the words he used to say in reply to me. Oh how he used to treat me thus; how could he be now slain by me. [*Mahabharata*, Book 6, Chapter 108, verses 90–93]

After Bhishma's fall, Drona becomes the commander of the Kaurava army. Similar to Bhishma, Arjuna's inhibitions against killing Drona run deep. Drona too has inhibitions against killing Arjuna, his favorite and most accomplished pupil. Drona tells Duryodhana, "You keep Arjuna away, and I will wipe out the rest of the Pandavas" (Karve 1991, p. 127). Drona was saying this not out of fear in fighting Arjuna but rather out of his affection for him. Arjuna is Drona's protégé. Drona has a profound narcissistic investment in Arjuna. Arjuna does not kill Drona. The general of the Pandava army, Dhristadyumna, kills him. When Dhristadyumna is about to kill Drona, "Arjuna saw what was happening and cried, 'Stop Dhristadyumna, don't kill our teacher.' While Arjuna was still speaking, Dhristadyumna took his sword and cut off Drona's head" (Karve 1991, p. 129).

Bhishma and Drona are Arjuna's two principal oedipal figures. It is Arjuna's identification with Bhishma and Drona that underlies both his moral dilemma of killing in general, and the more specific oedipal interdictions.

> Indeed, the first to fall is Bhishma, the most venerable guru of the family, the only survivor of the grandfather generation, hence "grandfather par excellence," who, by his lifelong honoring of his oath of celibacy, is the paragon of rectitude and truthfulness, the benefactor and sage advisor of all. He is the first to be sacrificed in this war, and is it a wonder that Arjuna shrinks from sacrificing him as well as Drona, Krpa, etc.? Arjuna's dilemma is both a real one, and despite Krishna's sarcasm, an honorable one. In effect, on the level of Dharma Arjuna will be proved to have been right; but in the *Gita*, Krishna offers him the choice of another level of values, which will absolve him from guilt. [Van Buitenen 1980, p. 3]

KURUKSHETRA: THE BATTLEFIELD AS THE PSYCHOANALYTIC SETTING

In the original Sanskrit, the first stanza of the *Gita* reads: "*Dharmaksetre kuruksetre samaveta yuyutsavah mamakah pandavas caiva kim akurvata Samjaya.*"[2] The translation reads: "On the field of truth, on the battle-field of life, what came to pass, Sanjaya, when my sons and their warriors faced those of my brother Pandu?" (*Gita* 1, 1). Antonio de Nicolas (1970), in *Avatara*, writes:

---

2. *Dharma* means "duty, law, righteousness, virtue, and honor." *Ksetre* means "in the field, on the field."

The first line of the *Gita* identifies for us the problem, the human problem of Arjuna. The "field of the Kurus" and the "field of Dharma" are the same: "Dharmaksetre kuruksetre." In the field of the Kurus, in the field of Dharma, the crisis of Arjuna unfolds. What is at stake is not the battle alone, but his whole social and conceptual scheme, his whole life. He has literally no ground to stand on. [p. 179]

The setting of the *Gita* is the battlefield. The *Gita's* occurrence in the "middle" of the battlefield is noteworthy, as middle connotes neutrality. The middle or center is a neutral place to observe and contemplate action. Middle connotes not only neutrality but also equidistance of intrapsychic domains vying for dominance. Mahler's developmental notion of the necessity of "optimal distance" between a growing child and his parents speaks to this point (Mahler et al. 1975; see also Akhtar 1992). In a different vein, Anna Freud (1966) comments on this notion by her recommendation that technically and ideally, the analyst should be positioned equidistant from the analysand's id, the ego, and the superego.

The middle or center characterizes Krishna's perspective. He is centered and grounded within himself, neutral and impartial, both to himself as the agent of the action and to the fruit of the action. This is the doctrine of selfless action, known as *Karma Yoga*. In contrast, Arjuna is not centered. He identifies himself as the agent of the action. His identifications, the root cause of his problems, lead to his dejection, pity, and inability to act. Krishna says, "Do thy work in the peace of Yoga and, free from selfish desires, be not moved in success or in failure" (*Gita* 2, 48). In Van Buitenen's (1980) translation, this reads:

> Your entitlement is only to the rite, not ever to its fruits. Be not motivated by the fruits of the acts, but also do not purposely seek to avoid acting. Abandon self-interest, Dhanmjaya, and perform the acts while applying this single mindedness. Remain equable in success and failure—this equableness is called the application, for the act as such is far inferior to the application of singleness of purpose to it. [*Gita* 2, 48–49]

It is significant that the *Gita* occurs in the battlefield, as *Kuruksetre* refers not only to the literal battlefield but also metaphorically to Arjuna's intrapsychic and interpersonal battlefield. In contrast to the calm setting of the analytic office with the patient lying on the couch, the dialogue between Krishna and Arjuna occurs in a chariot positioned in the middle of two armies, amidst all the noise and clamor. Freud (1940), in his *Outline of Psychoanalysis*, likened the analytic situation to a civil war:

> The ego is weakened by the internal conflict and we must go to its help. *The position is like that of a civil war which has to be decided by the assistance of an ally from the outside.* The analytic physician and the patient's weakened ego, basing themselves on the real external world, have to band themselves together into a party against the enemies, the instinctual demands of the id and the conscientious demands of the superego. We form a pact with each other. The sick ego promises us the most complete candor—promises, that is, to put at our disposal all the material which its self-perception yields it; we assure the patient of the strictest discretion and place at his service our experience in interpreting material that has been influenced by the unconscious. Our knowledge is to make up for his ignorance and give the ego back its mastery over lost provinces of his mental life. *This pact constitutes the analytic situation.* [p. 173, italics mine]

It is not the quietness and distraction from external stimuli that defines the analytic setting but rather the capacity of the analyst to create a safe "holding environment" (Winnicott 1960). In the hostile and dangerous space between two armies, Krishna creates the safe "holding environment" where Arjuna's transformation occurs. Franklin Edgerton (1972), a notable translator of the *Gita*, dismisses the setting of the *Gita* in the middle of the battlefield as a "dramatic absurdity" (p. 105). Despite his otherwise meticulous approach, Edgerton misses the psychological "battlefield" where the *Gita* occurs.

KRISHNA BECOMES ARJUNA'S ANALYST

In the first chapter of the *Gita*, Arjuna's crisis unfolds. The second chapter begins with Sanjaya's description of Arjuna's despondency and Krishna's initial response to his condition:

Whence this lifeless dejection, Arjuna, in this hour, the hour of trial? Strong men know not despair, Arjuna, for this wins neither heaven nor earth. Fall not into degrading weakness, for this becomes not a man who is a man. Throw off this ignoble discouragement, and arise like a fire that burns all before it! [*Gita* 2, 2–3]

The relation between Krishna and Arjuna here is not analytic. Arjuna has not yet asked for Krishna's help. Krishna is acting as any warrior's exhortative charioteer would do at a time of battle and crisis. Arjuna is not convinced by the traditional charioteer's role in raising his spirits. Appeals to his *Kshatriya* (warrior) duties and heavenly rewards fail to motivate him. His crisis runs much deeper and necessitates a different approach and instruction. He is not a warrior with cold feet shying away from battle. Arjuna is existentially questioning himself. The battle is but a moment exemplifying his self-doubt. Arjuna's refusal to be convinced by the usual supportive appeals from his charioteer is an indication for a higher level of instruction and analysis. Krishna is using traditional techniques to prompt Arjuna to fight. He is also testing Arjuna's level of crisis and qualifications for a deeper instruction. It is as if Krishna is evaluating Arjuna as a potential analysand. Arjuna formally asks for Krishna's help: "In the dark of night of my soul I feel desolation. In my self-pity, I see not the way of righteousness. *I am thy disciple, come to thee in supplication: be a light unto me on the path of duty*" (*Gita* 2, 6–7, italics mine). This marks the beginning of a new object relation—a psychoanalytic relationship. It begins with a resistance and an implicit transference that Krishna cannot help. In the verses immediately following his plea for help, Arjuna states:

> For neither the kingdom of the earth, nor the kingdom of the gods in heaven, could give me peace from the fire of sorrow which thus burns my life. When Arjuna the great warrior had unburdened his heart, "*I will not fight, Krishna*," he said and then fell silent. [*Gita* 2, 8–9, italics mine]

Arjuna is not seeking insight or understanding. He wants Krishna's approval to not fight. He is asking Krishna to justify his existential stance. This is analogous to an analysand coming to an analyst for help and then saying, "I can't do what you ask of me" and "I am not sure you can help me anyway." Arjuna is a naive and skeptical analysand. Krishna is aware of this and proceeds accordingly, as indicated by his response in the next verse:

Krishna smiled and spoke to Arjuna—there between the two armies the voice of God spoke these words: Thy tears are for those beyond tears; and are thy words words of wisdom? The wise grieve not for those who live; and they grieve not for those who die—for life and death shall pass away. [*Gita* 2, 10–11]

Krishna's smile signifies Krishna's understanding of Arjuna's resistance and his intellectualizations. Krishna's smile is striking. It is not an appropriate analytic response and suggests a patronizing attitude. However, the smile is an expression of empathy and love for the subject, analogous to a parent's response to a child whose locutions are incongruent with his emotional state. Krishna's smile highlights the initial object relation—that between a child and a parent. It is not a coincidence or a dramatic interlude that Krishna's counsel to Arjuna begins with a smile. It is an expression of Krishna's understanding of the initial transference. By smiling, Krishna is accepting both the felt and the repudiated state of Arjuna's psychic experience. Krishna's smile conveys that he knows what Arjuna is feeling and what Arjuna is capable of feeling.

TEACHING UP AND TEACHING DOWN

Trevor Legget (1955), an eminent Hindu and Buddhist scholar, in his commentary on the *Gita* notes:

The usual way of teaching a subject is to build up information to higher and higher levels, each resting on the lower ones, which cannot be dispensed with. It would be called Teaching Up. But there is another method, *Teaching Down*, for cases where the final knowledge is already there but not recognized. This method is used extensively in the *Gita* and by Sankara following the *Gita*. In the *Gita* as a whole, first the highest truth of the self is presented . . . the basis of the Teaching Down Method is that there is already a submerged intuition of the truth, which has to be stimulated by increasingly detailed instructions. The aim of the instructions is not to give information but to awaken half sleeping knowledge. [p. 18]

Freud's cites an exquisite expression of Leonardo da Vinci's, "*per via di levare*," as in sculpting, as opposed to "*per via di porre*" as in painting. In sculpting, the "true self" is inherently present in the material. In painting, it is created by adding to the canvas. In one, we chisel; in the other, we paint. Truth is revealed as opposed to created. Teaching up is painting and teaching down is sculpting.

The notion of sculpting, of chiseling, to reveal the true self has a profound history in Hindu thought. It is the leitmotif of Hinduism that the "true self" is not created but discovered. The principle is that individual contains the truth within himself that must be revealed by chiseling away the layers of ignorance (*Avidya*). Nothing is created—what is inherent in the individual is revealed and exposed. Quoting Legget:

> The order of the chapters, and the presentation of instruction, is not casual. A special technique is being used, which can be called *Teaching Down*. This kind of teaching is the opposite of building up a body of information and methods of applying it. Teaching down is concerned with removing illusions. The method is, that the final truth is declared first. If the pupil can "see" it, and actually embody it, further instruction is needless. If he does not "see" it, an additional pointer is given, and if necessary further and further indications. [p. 23]

In the *Gita*, the nature of the self is articulated to Arjuna in Chapters 2 and 3. The rest of the *Gita* is reworking the material that has been posited in Chapters 2 and 3. If Arjuna understood, the *Gita* would have ended by Chapter 3. However, Arjuna does not understand. The next fifteen chapters explicate and amplify Chapters 2 and 3 from the perspectives of *Karma Yoga* (selfless action), *Jnana Yoga* (knowledge), and *Bhakti Yoga* (devotion).

It is notable that the techniques of psychoanalysis, despite Freud's analogy between sculpting and painting, follow the teaching-up method. The analyst does not say to the analysand in the initial sessions that this is what the issues are (i.e., you are suffering from oedipal conflicts that are resulting in your inhibitions in work and love). From an analytic perspective, this will result in premature intellectualizations inhibiting emotional and affective processing, promoting resistances, and impeding analytic work. In distinction, the technique followed in the *Gita* is teaching down. The full teaching is articulated explicitly in the beginning and subsequently reiterated. It is not that resistances and intellectualizations do not occur in the teaching-down method. They occur and are dealt with accordingly. In the *Gita*, the technique of teaching down highlights the point that there is one "truth," Krishna's truth, which is revealed to Arjuna. Psychoanalysis admits to multiple "truths." In the *Gita*, knowledge is absolute; in psychoanalysis, it is relative. These are two radically different existential paradigms.

THE LOGIC AND STRUCTURE OF THE *GITA*

The *Gita* consists of eighteen chapters in the form of a dialogue between Krishna and Arjuna. The first ten chapters consist of Arjuna's crisis and Krishna's attempts at resolving Arjuna's crisis. Chapters 2 and 3 are the core teaching of the *Gita*. However, Arjuna's resistances are powerful and lead to Krishna's continuation of his teaching. This may be seen as the initiation to mid-phase of analysis. Chapter 11 is the pivotal chapter where Arjuna undergoes a profound psychic regression and metamorphosis through a vision of Krishna's divinity. The transference is one of fear and awe. Chapter 11 is the fulcrum on which the *Gita* oscillates. When Arjuna asks Krishna who he is in his divine form, Krishna responds, "I am all powerful time." Chapter 11 negates, transcends, and collapses chronological time; it takes us into Krishna's timelessness.

Chapters 12 to 18 are a continuation of Krishna's teaching, but with a difference. Arjuna has gained insight. He is at a higher grade of ego development and maturation. Arjuna's development of *Bhakti* (devotion) becomes a prominent theme. Krishna, the charioteer and friend, becomes for Arjuna an object of devotion. Krishna, the transformational object, becomes the sacred object. Arjuna's questions and doubts remain but at a higher level of awareness and consciousness. This may be seen as the working through phase. Each stage is replete with its corresponding resistances and transferences. Chapters 1 to 10 have an intellectual tone, Chapter 11 a uniquely mystical transfiguring aspect, and Chapters 12 to 18 develop *Bhakti*, the devotional dimension.

RESISTANCE AND TRANSFERENCE

Arjuna employs three principal resistances in the *Gita*: asking questions, remaining silent, and not reacting. "In typical traditional pictures of the *Gita* scene, Arjuna is shown with palms joined in reverence, looking at Krishna in an attitude of devotion and faith. But this is not what is described in the *Gita* itself, in which Arjuna shows from the very beginning that he does not really recognize Krishna as a teacher or as a god. For a long time, he has little confidence in what he is told" (Legget 1955, p. 38). Arjuna is not aware of and does not believe in Krishna's divinity, even though Krishna reveals this to Arjuna. It is not until Chapter 11 that Arjuna emotionally comprehends the true identity and nature of his teacher. This is like the analysand who comes to his analyst regularly and diligently with the hope for change but believes on an unconscious level that the analyst cannot really help. The analysand comes to analysis to prove to himself his unconscious conviction that the analyst is unable to help.

Arjuna's resistances are evident from Chapter 2. Immediately after asking for Krishna's help, Arjuna states, "I will not fight." This is not only a resistance but also Arjuna's initial transference to Krishna: Arjuna is saying: "You cannot help me!" In Chapter 4, Krishna reveals the first signs of his divinity:

I revealed this everlasting yoga to Visasvan, the sun, that father of light. He in turn revealed it to Manu, his son, the father of man. And Manu taught his son, King Ikshvaku, the saint. Then it was taught from father to son in the line of kings who were saints; but in the revolutions of times immemorial this doctrine was forgotten by men. Today, I am revealing to thee this Yoga eternal, this secret supreme; *because of thy love for me, and because I am thy friend.* [*Gita* 4, 1–3, italics mine]

Grounded in linear time, Arjuna cannot fathom the realm of eternity and timelessness in which Krishna moves. The countertransference, as the text suggests, is overtly paternal. However, Arjuna has no reaction to the affection that Krishna displays. He says: "Thy birth was after the birth of the sun: the birth of the sun was before thine. What is the meaning of thy words: 'I revealed this Yoga to Vivasvan'?" (*Gita* 4, 4). Arjuna is incredulous and dismissive. The transference is negative. I say this because Arjuna's silence suggests that he implicitly rejects Krishna's affection or at least does not recognize it. His response to Krishna is a blunt rational question. As the unmoved mover, Krishna responds:

I have been born many times, Arjuna, and many times hast thou been born. But I remember my past lives, and thou hast forgotten thine. Although I am unborn, everlasting, and I am the lord of all, I come to my realm of nature and through my wondrous power I am born. When righteousness is weak and faints and unrighteousness exults in pride, then my sprit arises on earth. For the salvation of those who are good, for the destruction of evil in men, for the fulfillment of the kingdom of righteousness, I come to this world in the ages that pass. *He who knows my birth as god and who knows my sacrifice, when he leaves his mortal body, goes no more from death to death, for he in truth comes to me.* [Gita 4, 5–9, italics mine]

Krishna explicitly reveals his divinity. Arjuna is inquisitive and more emotionally interested in what Krishna has to say. He is engaged in the analytic process. But doubts remain. Arjuna asks:

Thou has told me of a Yoga of constant oneness, O Krishna, of a communion which is ever one. But, Krishna, the mind is inconstant: in its restlessness, I cannot find rest. The mind is restless, Krishna, impetuous, self-willed, hard to train: to master the mind seems as difficult as to master the mighty winds. [Gita 6, 33–34]

From Arjuna's statement, one may well wonder who is teaching whom. An intersubjective dialectic sets in where the distinction between the teacher and disciple is temporally and temporarily blurred. Showing resilience in the face of such flux, Krishna acknowledges that the mind is indeed restless and expounds on how to control it. Arjuna continues:

And if a man strives and fails and reaches not the end of Yoga, for his mind is not in Yoga; and yet this man has faith, what is his end, O Krishna? Far from earth and far from heaven, wandering in the pathless winds, does he vanish like a cloud into air, not having found the path of God? Be a light in my darkness, Krishna: be thou unto me a Light. Who can solve this doubt but thee? [Gita 6, 37–39]

Arjuna is asking for Krishna's help but in a different context. What if I cannot do this? What will happen to me? He wants reassurance and permission to fail! Arjuna develops an idealizing transference (Kohut 1971). This transference is a defense against his inner void and an attempt to contain his doubts about his teacher. It is an attempt to maintain his narcissistic equilibrium. Arjuna is trying to fill his sense of powerlessness and lack of understanding by projecting onto Krishna omnipotence and omniscience (Ferenczi 1913). Krishna, as the object that possesses these qualities, will protect and care for him. Arjuna asks: "Speak to me again in full of thy power and of thy glory, for I am never tired, never, of hearing thy words of life" (*Gita* 10, 18). The idealizing transference reaches its apex in the beginning of Chapter 11.

> In thy mercy thou hast told me the secret of thy Spirit, and thy words have dispelled my delusion. I have heard in full from thee of the coming and going of beings, and also of thy infinite greatness. I have heard thy words of truth, but my soul is yearning to see: to see thy form as god of this all. If thou thinkest, O my Lord, that it can be seen by me, show me, O God of Yoga, the glory of thine own Supreme Being. [*Gita* 11, 1–4]

What Arjuna will see will shock and transform him. The sensory modalities of vision and speech in the realm of secondary process are transformed and transfigured to the synesthestic primary process of the unconscious in the "Manifestation of the World Form."

THE MANIFESTATION OF THE WORLD FORM

Chapter 11 is called "*Visvarupadarsanam*." *Darsana* means view, vision, and comprehension, and is derived from the Sanskrit root *drs*, which means to see, to contemplate, to comprehend. *Visva* means world and *rupa* means form. Hence, *Visvarupadarsanam*—Manifestation of the World Form.

> See now the whole universe with all things that move and move not, and whatever thy soul may yearn to see. See it all as One in me. But thou never canst see me with thy mortal eyes: I will give thee divine sight. Behold my wonder and glory. [*Gita* 11, 7–8]

Arjuna sees Krishna's divine form:

> If the light of a thousand suns suddenly arose in the sky, that splendor might be compared to the radiance of the Supreme Sprit. And Arjuna

saw in that radiance the whole universe in its variety, standing in a vast unity in the body of God of gods. Trembling with awe and wonder, Arjuna bowed his head, and joining his hands in adoration he thus spoke to his God. [*Gita* 11, 12–14]

Arjuna says: "Reveal thyself to me! Who art thou in this form of terror? I adore thee, O god supreme: be gracious unto me. I yearn to know thee, who art from the beginning: for I understand not thy mysterious works" (*Gita* 11, 31).

Krishna responds:

I am time grown old to destroy the world,
Embarked on the course of world annihilation:
Except for yourself none of these will survive,
Of these warriors arrayed in the opposing armies.
Therefore raise yourself now and reap rich fame,
Rule the plentiful realm by defeating your foes!
I myself have doomed them ages ago:
Be merely my hand in this, Left-Handed Archer!
[*Gita* 11, 32–33; Van Buitenen 1981, italics mine]

Krishna's response is agency redefined. He is saying: "Do not arrogate your actions to yourself: I am orchestrating the play." Arjuna's reaction to Krishna's theophany is fear and awe as well as reverence, humility, and respect. There is diffusion and obliteration of ego boundaries. All egos are consumed by Krishna, "as moths swiftly rushing enter a burning flame and die" (*Gita* 11, 29). Arjuna regresses and prostrates before Krishna. Unable to withstand Krishna's true nature, he begs Krishna to take his benign human form.

In a vision I have seen what no man has seen before: I rejoice in exultation, and yet my heart trembles with fear. Have mercy upon me, Lord of Gods, Refuge of the whole universe: show me again thine own human form. [*Gita* 11, 45]

Dwarkanath Rao (2001), an Indian psychoanalyst, in his essay on the *Gita* writes:

In verse after verse, Krishna is at once sublimely metaphysical, lovingly compassionate or terrifyingly dangerous. The nearest mundane parallel is the child looking up at a parent. One wonders if the cosmic vision of Krishna can be understood as the terrifying, omnipotent, omniscient parent of vulnerable childhood. [p. 183]

Rao suggests that Arjuna's reaction to Krishna's theophany depicts the awe of the child before the parent. His observation is salient and warrants a brief digression into the human experience of awe.

The *Oxford English Dictionary* (OED) (1971) defines *awe* as a noun and a verb. As a noun, awe is (1) "Immediate and active fear; terror, dread." (2) "From its use in reference to the Divine Being this passes gradually into: Dread mingled with veneration, reverential or respectful fear; the attitude of a mind subdues to profound reverence in the presence of a supreme authority, moral greatness or sublimity, or mysterious sacredness." Phyllis Greenacre (1956) wrote about the "awe reaction," suggesting that it was derivative of the phallic phase, specifically awe of the father's phallus. At the end of her paper "Experiences of Awe in Childhood," she stated, "One of the most interesting parts of the awe reaction is its association with inspiration, with creativity, and *with religious feelings*" (p. 30, italics mine). More recently, Irving Harrison (1975) in his paper "On the Origins of Maternal Awe," observed that in contrast to the paternal phallic awe that leads to feelings of dread, maternal awe leads to the feelings of wonder and lacks the feelings of dread and terror. A still more contemporary contribution is that of Mortimer Ostow (2002). In his paper "Three Archaic Contributions to the Religious Instinct: Awe, Mysticism and Apocalypse," Ostow comments on the role of awe in the formation of religious sentiment:

> The sense of awe derives from the newborn's nondeclarative memory of his impressions of his adult, giant parents. The tendency to mysticism derives from the infant's wish to undo the process of separation-individuation, that is, to merge back into the mother. Apocalyptic thinking is created by externalization of early mood swings, before, and to the extent that it fails to achieve, perfect homeostasis. Together, awe and mysticism create an affect that is generally described as religious. [p. 231]

Returning to Arjuna's transferential reaction to Krishna, we note its similarity with that of a child to a powerful paternal *and* maternal figure. The transference is modulated by affects of fear and dread mingled with excitement. Arjuna says to Krishna:

Father of all. Master supreme. Power supreme in all the worlds. Who is like thee? Who is beyond thee? I bow before thee, I prostate in adoration; and I beg thy grace, O glorious Lord! As a father to a son, as a friend to his friend, as a lover to his beloved, be gracious unto me, O God. [*Gita* 11, 43–44]

Note the multiplicity of transferences exhibited by Arjuna: maternal, paternal, idealizing, romantic, dependent, and fearful. A profound alteration takes place in Arjuna's ego. His sense of "I" is radically changed. Arjuna experiences Krishna in his totality—and this experiencing diminishes, if not obliterates, Arjuna's sense of himself. The "I" as the doer of the action, Arjuna's empirical ego, is transformed and integrated with Krishna. Arjuna's "awe reaction" to Krishna's theophany derives from paradigms of maternal love and paternal dread as well as maternal dread and paternal love. The Hindu goddess *Kali* best approximates this complex of paternal and maternal object relations, particularly Melanie Klein's concept of the creative and destructive mother. Arjuna, in his "awe," fully experiences the maternal and paternal vicissitudes of creation and destruction. The creative and destructive emotional states occur through projective identifications with the father *and* the mother. Maternal and paternal identifications precipitate the fear and love that constitute the object relations of the "awe" reaction.

THE TRANSFORMATIONAL OBJECT AND *BHAKTI*

Arjuna's metamorphosis and his new relation to Krishna occur through Krishna's allowing Arjuna to use him as an object that facilitates transformation. Krishna's neutrality and empathy are an integral part of this transformative process. In self psychology terms, Arjuna has undergone a "transmuting internalization" (Kohut 1971). Subject and object have been integrated and internalized. Arjuna understands that he is a part of Krishna and that Krishna is a part of him. Arjuna appreciates what he failed to understand in Chapter 10 when Krishna tells him: "Of the children of Vrishni I am Krishna; and of the sons of Pandu I am Arjuna" (*Gita* 10, 38).

The *Gita* teaches that the divine exists within the true self and the true self is part of the divine. The "ego" or the empirical self, the grammatical "I," obstructs the realization of the true self.[3] In the *Gita*, the ego is called *Ahankara*, the ego function. Heinrich Zimmer (1969), in his *Philosophies of India*, eloquently elucidates the concept:

> *Ahankara*, the ego function, causes us to believe that we feel like acting, that we are suffering, etc.; whereas actually our real being, the Purusha, is devoid of such modifications. *Ahankara*, is the center and prime motivating force of "delusion." *Ahankara*, is the misconception, conceit, supposition, or belief that refers all objects and acts of consciousness to an "I" (*aham*). *Ahankara*—the making (*kara*) of the utterance "I" (*aham*)— accomplishes all psychic processes, producing the misleading notion "I am hearing; I am seeing; I am rich and mighty; I am enjoying; I am about to suffer." etc., etc. It is thus the primal cause of the critical "wrong conception" that dogs all phenomenal experience; the idea, namely, that the life-monad (purusha) is implicated in, nay is identical with, the processes of living matter (*prakti*). One is continually appropriating to oneself, as a result of the Ahankara, everything that comes to pass in the realms of the physique and psyche, superimposing perpetually the false notion (and apparent experience) of a subject (an "I") of all the deeds and sorrows. [p. 319]

Krishna's theophany alters Arjuna's ego—his *ahankara*. This transfiguration occurs after his terrifying vision (*darshan*) of Krishna. The benevolent analyst reveals his destructive side. The creative and the destructive are two sides of the same coin. Arjuna internalizes the complete object—Krishna in his multiplicity of forms and functions. The defensive splitting of the libidinal and aggressive components is integrated, comprehended, and internalized by Arjuna.

Krishna's primary analytic function in the *Gita* is not interpretive but as an object that facilitates self-alteration. Bollas (1979), in his paper "The Transformational Object," elaborates the point:

> Thus, in adult life, the quest is not to possess the object: it is sought in order to surrender to it as a process that alters the self, where the subject-as-supplicant now feels himself to be the recipient of enviro-somatic caring, identified with metamorphoses of the self. . . . This anticipation of being

---

3. Note the striking overlap to Winnicott's (1960) views on the true and false self.

transformed by an object—itself an ego memory of the ontogenetic process—inspires the subject with a reverential attitude toward the object, so that, even as the transformation of the self will not take place on the scale it did during early life, the adult subject tends to nominate the object as sacred. . . . Of course this may lead to the object's achieving a secondary idealization—as in the legend of Christ—but making the object sacred occurs after the object's transformational potential has been declared. [p. 97]

As Bollas suggests, Arjuna's metamorphosis leads to Arjuna's considering Krishna as a sacred object. The relation between Krishna and Arjuna continues as analyst and analysand, but another parallel object relation develops in and after Chapter 11—that between devotee (*Bhakta*) and God. Krishna says to Arjuna:

Thou hast seen now face to face my form divine so hard to see: for even the gods in heaven ever long to see what thou hast seen. Not by the Vedas, or an austere life, or gifts to the poor, or ritual offerings can I be seen as thou hast seen me. *Only by love can men see me, and know me, and come unto me. He who works for me, who loves me, whose End Supreme I am, free from attachments to all things, and with love for all creation, he in truth comes unto me.* [Gita 11, 52–55, italics mine]

This is *Bhakti* defined by Krishna himself. *Bhakti* means devotion or "love of God." It is not an intellectual love but an intense emotional and affective experience. *Bhakti* is a personal relation between the individual and God, without the middleman, the priest. A necessary condition for true *Bhakti* is surrender to the object of *Bhakti*. The ego suspends and transcends itself to a state where it becomes selfless and egoless. In other words, self-love (narcissism) is directed toward the love of God. In drive theory, narcissistic libido becomes totally invested in object libido, the object being God. Freud (1914) noted that such a condition occurs in only one instance—the state of being in love. Analogous to Plato's concept of forms, Radhakrishan (1929) noted:

The *Gita*, however, recognizes nirguna bhakti, or devotion to the quality less, as superior to all else. Then the absolute becomes the most ultimate category. When devotion is perfected, then the individual and his God become suffused into one spiritual ecstasy, and reveal themselves as aspects of one life. Absolute monism is therefore the completion of the dualism with which the devotional consciousness starts. [p. 656]

From a psychoanalytic stance, *Bhakti* and the religious sentiments accompanying it are often seen as defenses against infantile dependence and narcissistic regression to a primordial blissfull dyadic infant–mother state. This is a reductionistic viewpoint that does not allow for the possibility of a developmentally advanced and healthy source of faith and religious belief and negates the possibility of a primary religious instinct. Compare Freud's notion of thanatos, or the death instinct, to Krishna's description of who he is: "I am all-powerful time which destroys all things." Ferenczi (1938), in his work *Thalassa*, considers Freud's concept of the death instinct and regression to symbiotic union with the mother in a manner that more closely approximates the Hindu essence of *Samsara*— the cycle of birth and death to which we are destined until we attain release. Ferenczi wrote:

> There does not exist an absolute life without any admixture of symptoms of death, biology has long asserted; and it is but a short while since that that Freud demonstrated the operation of the death instinct among all living things. "The goal of all life is death," for "lifelessness was here before life was." What if, however, death and dying were not anything absolute, if germs of life and regressive tendencies lay hidden even within inorganic matter. If Nietzsche were right when he said, "All inorganic matter has originated out of the organic, it is dead organic matter. Corpse and man," then we should have to drop once and for all the question of the beginning and end of life, and conceive the whole inorganic and organic world as a perpetual oscillating between the will to live and the will to die in which an absolute hegemony on part either of life or of death is never attained. [pp. 94–95]

This is where psychoanalysis reaches its self-imposed theoretical limits. The oscillation and eternal recurrence between life and death (*Samsara*) can be transcended. Indeed, the summon bonnum, in Hinduism, is to overcome the eternal recurrence of birth, death, and rebirth. This goal is seen in psychoanalysis as the wish to reunite with the primordial mother. From a developmental point of view, this is a regressive tendency directed toward a blissful infant–mother dyad. Religious emotions and mystical experiences are reduced to hypothetical and regressive defensive states of infant–parent dyadic bliss.[4] Karl Marx noted that

---

4. It is worth noting that monotheistic religions as compared to polytheistic religions have a different developmental emphasis and ontogenesis. The monotheis-

religion was the "opiate of the masses" and Freud believed that religion is a defense against infantile dependence. It is important to ask why religion, in psychoanalytic theorizing, is viewed necessarily as a defensive posture as opposed to a developmentally advanced position that is not only adaptive but perhaps has an intrinsic instinctual origin.

CONCLUSION

In this chapter, I have approached the *Gita* as a psychological discourse. I have shown that the interaction between Arjuna and Krishna can be viewed through a psychoanalytic lens as constituting a psychoanalytic process, replete with resistances and transferences. I have assiduously not dealt with the content of the *Gita*, because the *Gita* as a religious text contains assumptions that psychoanalysis does not admit. The *Gita* to the Hindus is parallel to the Gospels of the Christians, the Torah of the Jews, and the Koran of the Muslims. Most observant Hindus would dismiss a psychoanalytic approach to the *Gita* as a superfluous intellectual exercise that detracts from the religious essence and beauty of the work. While there might be merit in this point of view, I believe that psychoanalysis has much to offer for understanding the *Gita* without repudiating its sacredness and profundity.

NOTE

All references to the *Bhagavad Gita* are from Juan Mascaro's translation, unless otherwise noted. References to the *Gita* are in the form

---

tic religions (Judaism, Christianity, and Islam) are based on the father imago—the paternal figures prominently, if not exclusively, in the monotheistic faiths. In Christianity, the Holy Trinity consists of the Father, Son, and Holy Spirit. The maternal, Mary, is conspiciously absent. In contrast, polytheistic religions are based on the maternal element. In Hinduism, the maternal encompasses both the maternal and the paternal, blurring the distinction between father and mother. This is perhaps best exemplified by one of the forms of the God Shiva, known as *Ardhanarishawara*, who is half man and half woman. A parallel concept is found in Plato's *Symposium*, where the original human is a composite of the male and female, until Zeus, threatened by such an entity, separates it into male and female.

of chapter, followed by the verse. For example, *Gita* 2, 1–3 means Chapter 2, verses 1 to 3. This allows the reader to readily cross-reference the citation to any of the multiple translations of the *Gita* that are available.

REFERENCES

Akhtar, S. (1992). Tethers, orbits, and invisible fences: clinical, developmental, sociocultural, and technical aspects of optimal distance. In *When the Body Speaks: Psychological Meanings in Kinetic Clues*, ed. S. Kramer and S. Akhtar, pp. 21–57. Northvale, NJ: Jason Aronson.

Bollas, C. (1979). The Transformational Object. *International Journal of Psycho-Analysis* 60:97–107.

De Nicolas, A. T. (1970). *Avatara*. New York: Nicolas-Hays.

Edgerton, F. (1972). *The Bhagavad Gita*. Cambridge, MA: Harvard University Press.

Ferenczi, S. (1913). Stages in the development of the sense of reality. In *First Contributions to Psychoanalysis*, pp. 213–239. New York: Brunner/Mazel.

―――― (1938). *Thalassa: A Theory of Genitality*. New York: Norton.

Freud, A. (1966). *The Ego and the Mechanisms of Defense*. New York: International Universities Press.

Freud, S. (1914). On narcissism. *Standard Edition* 14:73–102.

―――― (1915). The unconscious. *Standard Edition* 14:166–204.

―――― (1940). An outline of psychoanalysis. *Standard Edition* 23:143–207.

Greenacre, P. (1956). Experiences of awe in childhood. *Psychoanalytic Study of the Child* 11:9–30. New York: International Universities Press.

Harrison, I. B. (1975). On the origins of maternal awe. *Psychoanalytic Study of the Child* 30:181–195. New Haven, CT: Yale University Press.

Kane, P. V. (1974). *History of Dharmasastra: Ancient and Medieval Religious and Civil Law*. Poona, India: Bhandarkar Oriental Research Institute.

Karve, I. (1991). *Yuganta: The End of an Epoch*. Hyderbad, India: Disha.

Kohut, H. (1971). *The Analysis of the Self*. New York: International Universities Press.

―――― (1977). *The Restoration of the Self*. New York: International Universities Press.

Leggett, T. (1995). *The Bhagavad Gita Yogas*. London: Kegan Paul.

Loewald, H. (1960). On the therapeutic action of psychoanalysis. *International Journal of Psycho-Analysis* 41:16–33.

The Mahabharata. (1994). Trans. M. N. Dutt, Delhi, India: Parimal.

Mahler, M. S., Pine, F., and Bergman, A. (1975). *The Psychological Birth of the Human Infant*. New York: Basic Books.

Mascaro, J. (1962). *The Bhagavad Gita*. New York: Penguin.

Ostow, M. (2001). Three archaic contributions to the religious instinct: awe, mysticism, and apocalypse. In *Does God Help? Developmental, Psychological, and Technical Aspects of Religious Belief*, ed. S. Akhtar and H. Parens, pp. 197–233. Northvale, NJ: Jason Aronson.

Oxford English Dictionary. (1971). Oxford, England: Oxford University Press.

Radhakrishan, S. (1929). *Indian Philosophy*. London: Allen and Unwin.

———— (1948). *The Bhagavad Gita*. London: Allen and Unwin.

Rao, D. G. (2001). God playing psychoanalyst. In *Does God Help? Developmental, Psychological, and Technical Aspects of Religious Belief*, ed. S. Akhtar and H. Parens, pp. 177–195. Northvale, NJ: Jason Aronson.

Sampatkumaran, M. R., trans. (1969). *The Gitabhasya of Ramanuja*. Madras, India: Prof. M. Rangacarya Memorial Trust.

Sastry, A. M., trans. (1979). *The Bhagavad Gita with the Commentary of Sri Sankaracharya*. Madras, India: Samata.

Van Buitenen, J. A. B. (1980). *The Bhagavad Gita in the Mahabharata*. Chicago: University of Chicago Press.

Winnicott, D. W. (1960). Ego distortion in terms of true and false self. In *The Maturational Processes and the Facilitating Environment*, pp. 140–152. New York: International Universities Press.

Zimmer, H. (1969). *The Philosophies of India*. Princeton, NJ: Princeton University Press.

12

Psychoanalytic and Buddhist History and Theory

Jeffrey B. Rubin

"Early in the day it was whispered that we should sail in a boat, only thou and I, and never a soul in the world would know of this pilgrimage to no country and no end."

Rabinadranath Tagore (1911)

Buddhism arose in the sixth century B.C. in India. This epoch was a watershed in the intellectual and spiritual development of the world. The Greek rationalist philosophers, the Jewish prophets, Confucius in China, and Buddha in India all illuminated human history during this time.

The history of India is shrouded in obscurity. The archeological record is incomplete. Buddhism's fundamental "ahistoricity," in which time and place become irrelevant to those who seek to dwell in the presence of the infinite, make historical reconstruction difficult (McNeill 1963). Early Buddhist works suggest traces of aristocratic and republican polities comparable to the Greek city-states. But in the Ganges valley, centralized monarchical states began to dominate the scene from about the eighth century B.C. By about the sixth century B.C., these monarchies were either absorbed or had established their control over most of the small republican states of northern India.

From all accounts, the India of Buddha's time was in transition and ferment. There was "rapid social change. . . . So hitherto significant ordered collectivities, and the individuals within them, were no longer able to construe or guide their own fate" (Carrithers 1985, p. 254). The local tribal republican government and aristocratic society were disrupted by new social and political forces. As territorial subordination replaced tribal bonds and agriculture came to replace cattle tending, the old tribal solidarity was compromised. The aristocratic style of life, expressed politically in the tribal republics, crumbled under the pressure of urbanism and centralized monarchy. In a world in which traditional social structures had vanished, there were those who probably joined the victors and became servants of the ascending monarchies, while others may have sought a spiritual resolution to their worldly frustration, joining religious orders. It has been suggested that the breakup of the local tribal units and their replacement by kingdoms eroded ethnic ties and the sense of security they fostered, which led to fundamental psychological turmoil.

It was a time of enormous suffering and narcissism (cf. Roccasalvo 1982). Dissatisfaction was prevalent. There was a "great wave of pessimism" (DeBary 1972, p. 5). The sources were varied. Daily life was enormously difficult and unappealing. "Life in the home," noted Buddha, "is cramped and dirty" (quoted in Carrithers 1983, p. 21). Drought, disease, and hunger were ubiquitous menaces. Every year, floods destroyed hard-earned crops wrung from the earth; monsoons spawned droughts, famine, dysentery, cholera, and countless other ills, weakening people for the predatory beasts (cf. Stryk 1968, p. xxxiii).

That narcissism may have been prevalent in Buddha's India and was a concern of Buddhism is suggested by the frequent references in the Pali Buddhist texts to two narcissistic conceptions of human beings held by the "uneducated manyfolk" and Buddha's contemporaries. A central facet of Hinduism, which was the predominant philosophical and religious perspective in India prior to Buddhism, was the belief in *Atman*, an unchanging self. Buddhism was, in certain fundamental ways, a protestation against certain aspects of Hinduism, including its emphasis on the primacy of the self. Buddha unequivocally opposed Eternalism or self-immortality, the view that the soul is "permanent, steadfast, eternal, and not subject to change" (Roccasalvo 1982, p. 209), and the equally self-preoccupied Annihilationism, the view that the body is the "final locus for utter and complete dissolution" (Roccasalvo

1982, p. 208). These positions are illustrated by Buddha's descriptions of two types of teachers:

> Here a certain teacher sets out soul as something real and permanent in the present life as well as in the future life. Again, another teacher sets out soul as something real and permanent as far as this world is concerned but does not say so with regard to any future existence. . . . The teacher of the first order is to be understood as a teacher who upholds the doctrine of Eternalism . . . the teacher of the second order . . . the doctrine of Annihilationism. [Roccasalvo 1982, p. 210]

The Buddhist doctrine of *anatta*, the essential selflessness of humans, which served as the cornerstone of Buddhist teachings, opposed these two narcissistic theories.

Because of the pervasiveness of suffering, Indians had a "passionate desire for escape, for unison with something that lay beyond the dreary cycle of birth and death and rebirth, for timeless being, in place of transitory and therefore unsatisfactory existence" (Basham 1988, pp. 44–45). Escape from one's condition in life was virtually nonexistent because India was ruled by the estates system. The estates prescribed an orderly, preordained hierarchical relationship between people, with each person having certain responsibilities toward others. The estates defined a person's position in life. The world of India was hierarchically ordered in a prescribed manner: those who labor, those who fight, and those who pray. The servants, who occupied the lowest position, were ineligible for the benefits of the sacrificial religion and were compelled to a life of servitude by the three other estates. The commoners were the producers. The Warriors, whose duty it was to rule, fight, and pray for sacrifice, wielded power. The Brahmans were the priests of the sacrificial religion and the intellectuals.

Buddhism presented a fundamental and plausible refutation of the estates theory. Success and fate are the result of good deeds. The good deeds of the poor will garner their just desserts in the next life, while those who abuse power will be punished. Whether one was destitute or favorably endowed by birth, successful in business or defeated in battle, this theory could explain it. This offered Indians a release from the squalid exigencies of daily existence.

BUDDHISM

Siddhartha Gautama, the Buddha, was born around 536 B.C. in a small province in northern India on the border of present-day Nepal. His title—the Buddha—became his message. The Sanskrit root *Budh* connotes both to wake up and to know. Buddha means the "Awakened One" or the "Enlightened One." While the vast majority of humans lived as if they were emotionally "asleep," unable to escape from stifling patterns and unending suffering, Buddha roused himself from psychological slumber. Buddhism is the ethical psychology based on his discoveries.

Legend has it that before he was born, his father, Suddhodana, the head of the Shakya clan and ruler of the principality of Kapilavastu, received a disturbing prophecy about his future son. A choice between two diametrically opposed destinies lay before the rajah's heir: he might become a great sovereign or a famous ascetic. Fearing the latter, Gautama's father attempted to prevent him, at all costs, from witnessing misery or unhappiness. Gautama lived amid great luxury and was shielded from exposure to sickness, old age, and death.

In his 20s he disobeyed his father's injunctions and left the sheltered palace compound. In the streets of Kapilavastu he encountered four sights: an old man, a corpse, a sick man, and a holy mendicant—known in Buddhism as the "four signs"—which fundamentally transformed the direction of his life. He was bewildered and horrified by the realization that old age, sickness, and death were the common fate of humankind. Before returning to the palace, he saw a peaceful wandering ascetic. In the serenity of this recluse, Gautama sensed the only response to his growing disillusionment.

After witnessing these three disturbing signs of human suffering and mortality, he returned to the splendor of his home. He fell asleep. When he awoke, his attendants, who usually entertained him with dance and song, were asleep. As he observed their "bodies wet with trickling phlegm and spittle; some grinding their teeth, and muttering and talking in their sleep" (Warren 1977, p. 61), he was filled with aversion. His home "began to seem like a cemetery filled with dead bodies impaled and left to rot" (p. 61). He felt that "life in the home is cramped and dirty, while the life gone forth into homelessness is wide open" (Carrithers 1983, p. 21). He said out loud to himself: "how oppressive and stifling is it all. . . . It behooves me to go forth on the Great Retirement this very day" (Warren 1977, p. 61).

Once he had perceived the inevitability of illness, bodily pain, and mortality, he could not return to the normal pleasures of worldly pursuits. He said,

> Why, since I am myself subject to birth, ageing, disease, death, sorrow and defilement, do I seek after what is also subject to these things. Suppose being myself subject to these things, seeing danger in them, I were to seek the unborn, undiseased, deathless, sorrowless, undefiled, supreme surcease of bondage, the extinction of all these troubles. [Carrithers 1983, p. 21]

Since he felt life was inevitably painful and enslaving, renouncing worldly life seemed, in his view, the only way to escape human bondage. His encounter with old age, sickness, and death was so troubling that he decided to forsake his life of ease, leave his home, his wife, and his children that very evening, and become a spiritual seeker.

His quest lasted six years and exposed him to a variety of spiritual teachings and practices. It is said that his journey occurred in three phases. First, he studied yoga and philosophy with two Hindu masters who propounded ascetic and sensualistic practices. But he did not find what he sought; pursuing neither self-mortification nor self-indulgence released him from suffering. Recognizing that neither method extinguished the flame of desire or led to the liberation he sought, he devoted the final phase of his search to religious contemplation and meditation.

He decided to explore a more moderate path involving intensive self-scrutiny in the hopes of "destroying passion's net" (Warren 1977, p. 76). One evening he sat in a lotus position under a tree in northern India, south of the town now known as Patna, vowing that he would not move until he solved the vexing problems that besieged him,

After six days, it is said that his eyes opened on the rising morning star and he experienced a profound clarification of his searching: an understanding of the riddle of human existence, a freedom from crippling psychological illusions, and a vision of the path to eradicating human suffering and attaining freedom.

His self-investigations led to what he termed an "exalted calm" and a blissful self-emancipation. He said:

Through birth and rebirth's endless round,
Seeking in vain, I hastened on,
To find who framed this edifice
What misery!—birth incessantly!
O builder! I've discovered thee!
This fabric thou shalt ne'er rebuild!
The rafters all are broken now,
And pointed roof demolished lies!
This mind has demolition reached,
And seen the last of all desire. [Warren 1977, p. 82]

After this experience he eventually returned to the quotidian world and became a religious teacher. He taught that suffering pervades human existence and is caused by one's attachment and clinging to an illusory belief in the notion that there is an independent, abiding self. He claimed that there is no self and there is no inner director in control. Psychic reality, in his view, is created by what we think, not by a self or an external world: "The mental natures are the result of what we have thought, are chieftained by our thoughts, are made up of our thoughts" (Buddha 1950, p. 58).

Through purity of thought and deed he maintained that it is possible to escape the tormenting cycle of rebirth with its unending suffering and inevitable death. Unwholesome thinking usually leads to unwholesome actions that create negative consequences such as creating another life and body and causing one to be reborn: "'To be born here and die here, and die here and be born elsewhere, to be born there and die there, to die there and be born elsewhere . . . this is the round of existence. . . . He that still has the corruptions is born into another existence; he that no longer has the corruptions is not born into another existence.'" Awareness, Buddha maintained, is the path to the *deathless*: "Vigilance is the abode of eternal life, thoughtlessness is the death. Those who are vigilant (who are given to reflection) do not die" (Buddha 1950, p. 66).

Buddha's teachings can best be understood against the background of Hinduism of which they arose. Buddhism was, as I briefly alluded to earlier, an Indian Protestantism in the original sense of witnessing (*testis*) for (*pro*), and in the more recent connotation of protesting against something else. Buddhism began as a revolt against six aspects of Hinduism: authority and tradition, ritual, speculation, grace, mystery, and a personal God. Buddha felt each had gotten out of hand (cf. Smith 1986).

Slavish adherence to authority and tradition had justified and perpetuated the privilege and dominance of the ruling Brahman class. Spiritless performance of rituals and preoccupation with metaphysical questions had become a sterile substitute for authentic religious experience. Concepts of divine sovereignty and grace had promoted passivity rather than spirituality. Religious mystery had degenerated into religious mystification.

Onto this sterile religious stage Buddha emerged and forged a religion devoid of each of these six elements. His attack on authority and tradition was unequivocal: "Do not accept what you hear by report, do not accept tradition, do not accept a statement because it is found in our books, nor because it is in accord with your beliefs, nor because it is the saying of your teacher. . . . Be a lamp unto yourselves" (Burtt 1955, pp. 49–50).

Ritual and speculation fared no better. Buddha advocated a religion without ritual. In fact, "belief in the efficacy of rites and ceremonies" is one of the ten fetters, or obstacles, to spiritual practice in classical Buddhism. Buddha was not uninterested in metaphysical questions—he had given them close attention—but he felt that "greed for views" on such questions tended "not toward edification" (Burtt 1955, p. 15) and detracted from the crucial concerns of reducing human misery. There is some evidence that when abstract inquiries were put to him, he remained silent or directed the interrogator toward the more important subject of how best to lead one's life.

Buddha's concerns were pragmatic and therapeutic. His primary focus was psychological and ethical. He was more interested in alleviating human suffering than in satisfying human curiosity about the origin of the universe or the nature of divinity.

For Buddha, neither God's grace nor divine intervention could aid in this endeavor. He condemned all forms of supernatural divination and soothsaying. The fatalism and passivity that God's sovereignty and grace often fostered was replaced by an encouragement to intense personal effort. He took pains to emphasize to his followers that none of them was to look upon him as a divine savior; that he only pointed out the path to freedom; that they had to "work out their salvation with diligence" (Burtt 1955, p. 49).

His central teaching was the Four Noble Truths. This doctrine delineates the symptom, diagnosis, prognosis, and treatment plan for addressing human suffering.

The first Noble Truth presents the salient characteristic of human life, *Dukkha*, a Sanskrit word for awryness, unsatisfactoriness, and suffering. It refers to an "axle which is off-center with respect to its wheel" and to a "bone which has slipped out of its socket" (Smith 1986, p. 150). Life, according to Buddha, is dislocated, out of joint, and full of suffering.

According to Buddha there are three types of suffering. There is the ordinary suffering of old age, sickness, and death. This is similar to what Freud (1895) referred to as the great inevitabilities of fate. Then there is the suffering caused by change. Change—personal, relational, environmental, occupational—can be unsettling. The third type of suffering parts company with Western psychological understandings. Buddha maintains that all conditioned states of mind inevitably lead to suffering. By becoming attached to what changes, humans, according to Buddhism, sow the seeds of their own suffering.

The second Noble Truth presents the cause of suffering: desire, attachment, and craving. There are three types of desire: desire for sense gratification, existence or nonexistence, and the clinging to self. The first type of desire corresponds to Freudian perspectives on pleasure-principle functioning. The second relates to issues familiar to psychoanalysts treating patients suffering from issues related to the continuity of the self and selfhood in relation to others. The third type of desire in the Buddhist scheme is similar to narcissistic issues in psychoanalysis.

A brief synopsis of the Buddhist model of the mind helps place the second Noble Truth in perspective. Mind, according to Buddhism, is composed of three elements: (1) consciousness of (2) one or more of the five senses—seeing, hearing, tasting, touching, smelling—plus thinking (which in Buddhism is considered a sixth sense), and (3) a reaction of attachment, aversion, or impartiality to whichever of the six facets of experience one is aware of. Reading this paragraph, for example, there is either aversion, affection, or neutrality toward the thoughts that are arising. In this impersonal theory of mind, every instant of seeing, hearing, tasting, touching, smelling, or thinking is responded to with pleasure, unpleasure, or neutrality, but without anyone *having* those experiences.

Suffering, according to the Buddhist account, derives from our difficulty acknowledging a fundamental aspect of life: that everything is impermanent and transitory. Suffering arises when we resist the flow of life and cling to things, events, people, and ideas as permanent. The doctrine of impermanence also includes the notion that there is no single self that is the subject of our changing experience.

The third Noble Truth is that suffering can be eradicated. It is possible, according to Buddhism, to extricate oneself from psychological imprisonment and to reach a state of complete awakening or liberation called Nirvana, which means "to blow out" or "to extinguish." What is extinguished is personal desire. In this state, grasping and suffering have disappeared and the oneness of all life is evident. There is no equivalent in the history of Western psychology. "Health" in Western psychology, whether Maslow's self-actualization or the fully analyzed patient of psychoanalysis, is an arrested state of development according to Buddhism.

The fourth Noble Truth provides the map of how to experience enlightenment: the Noble Eightfold Path, which comprises right understanding or accurate awareness into the reality of life; right thought or aspiration; right speech, speaking truthfully and compassionately; right action, abstaining from killing, lying, stealing, adultery, and misuse of intoxicants; right livelihood, engaging in occupations that promote rather than harm life; right effort, or the balanced effort to be aware; right mindfulness, seeing things as they are; and right concentration, or meditative attentiveness.

The Theravadin ideal of spiritual development was Nirvana or complete awakening and liberation. The *Arahant*, or one "worthy of praise" for conquering the enemies of awareness and wisdom, that is, greed, hatred, and delusion, attained this state and was believed to have escaped from reincarnation.

None of Buddha's teachings were recorded during his lifetime. In the first few centuries after his death, several Great Councils were held by the leading members of the Buddhist order at which time the entire Buddhist teachings were recited aloud and interpretative disputes were addressed.

During the rainy season after Buddha's death, it is said that 500 of his leading disciples convened the First Great Council. Ananda, Buddha's attendant, repeated all of the sutras or sermons and discourses; Upali recited the *Vinaya*, the 250 rules of morality and discipline; and Mahakashyapa presented the Abhidharma, the higher philosophical and psychological teachings.

Buddhism, like psychoanalysis, developed partisan schools and schisms. At the Second Great Council a schism developed regarding how strictly to follow the Vinaya rules. Ten thousand monks were expelled from the Council. They formed a school called the Mahasanghika, which flourished in Northern India. The remaining Buddhists, the Theravadins, or the school of the elders, Buddha's contemporaries (often erroneously known as the Hinayana, or the "small vehicle"), banded together in the south of India. The Theravadins continue to this day in Southeast Asia and parts of India and the United States. The Mahayana or "great vehicle" spread to the north and east and was eventually transplanted to Korea, Japan, Nepal, China, Tibet, and the United States.

Each school was termed a *yana*, or raft, that carried Buddhist practitioners across the sea of life to the shore of enlightenment. The words *small* and *great vehicle* refer to the respective restrictions and latitude of interpretation and practice of Buddhist doctrine. The Mahayanists, who do not object to being designated as the large vehicle, adhered less closely to early Buddhist teachings. The Hinayanists, who prefer to characterize their brand of Buddhism as Theravada, or the Way of the Elders, observed more of the letter of Buddha's teachings. In doing this, they claim to represent the original unadultered Buddhist teachings as taught by Buddha. They maintain that spiritual practitioners are "on their own" with progress being based on one's own efforts. Emancipation is not contingent on the salvation of others. No God or intercessory powers are available (Ross 1966).

Mahayana Buddhism encompasses doctrines ranging from religious faith in the teachings of Buddha to elaborate philosophies and complex cosmologies. Unlike the Theravadins, Mahayanists believed in a personal God and a divine savior. For the Mahayanists, unlike the Theravadins, emancipation is contingent on the salvation of others. Grace and love are the sine qua non of the path.

For the Mahayanists, the Theravadin ideal was selfish. The proper focus of spiritual life should be on refraining from entering Nirvana in order to help others ascend the ladder of reincarnation and escape from the suffering of existence. The Theravadin ideal of spiritual development—the *Arahant*—was replaced with the Bodhisattva, "one whose essence (*sattva*) is perfected wisdom" (*bodhi*), a being who forsakes the quest for enlightenment for him or herself alone, but has vowed to help all other beings attain enlightenment. Bodhisattvas were believed to inhabit a heaven of their own making. Pointing to its doctrine of grace and its wider accessibility for laypeople, Mahayana Buddhism claimed to be the larger vehicle of the two. Theravadin Buddhism remains a unified tradition, while Mahayana has splintered into five schools that stress such elements as faith, intellectual study, reciting ritual formulas, and intuitive understanding.

In the past a great deal of attention in the West has been devoted to Mahayana Buddhism. Theravada Buddhism has usually been mentioned in terms of early Buddhist history and scriptures. Yet, Theravada monks and nuns and millions of lay disciples in Southeast Asia form the largest living Buddhist tradition in the world (Kornfield 1977). The practices taught by the Theravadin Buddhist meditation masters in Thailand, Burma, and Sri Lanka are based on the original Pali scripture and subsequent transmission. It is this tradition that my study is primarily based on. References to Zen and Tibetan Buddhism, however, will appear throughout the text.

My choice of focusing on one tradition should not be construed as a judgment on the other schools of Buddhism. Different schools are different vehicles. Buddha's reflections bear repeating:

> Would he be a clever man if out of gratitude for the raft that has carried him across the stream to the other shore, he should cling to it, take it on his back, and walk about with the weight of it? Would not the clever man be the one who left the raft (of no use to him any longer) to the current stream, and walked ahead without turning back to look at it? Is it simply a tool to be cast away and forsaken once it has served the purpose for which it was made? In the same way the vehicle of the doctrine is to be cast away and forsaken once the shore of Enlightenment has been attained. [Quoted in Smith 1986, pp. 209–210]

As he was dying, Buddha is reported to have said to his attendant, Ananda: "Be a lamp unto thyself; pursue your deliverance with diligence" (cf. Burtt 1955, p. 49). No one was selected to teach or govern the Buddhist community that outlived him. The *Dharma*, the teachings of the truth of how things are, not a person or institution, would be the teacher (Kornfield 1977). In the next section I present an overview of psychoanalysis.

PSYCHOANALYSIS

Four character ideals have vied for center stage in the history of Western life, according to sociologist Phillip Rieff (1963): the "political" subject of classical antiquity who participates in public life; the "economic" subject who retreats into a search for private fulfillment while enjoying the fruits of citizenship; the Hebraic and Christian "religious" person who substitutes faith for reason; and the late nineteenth- and twentieth-century "psychological" subject, who eschews any redemptive external doctrine or creed, whether political or religious, and attends to the workings of his or her own private universe of thoughts, feelings, dreams, and symptoms.

Psychoanalysis arose from the soil of the modern period in which there was a "despiritualization" of subjective reality (cf. Kovel 1991), by which I mean a devaluation, marginalization, and pathologization of the spiritual. Spirituality does not flourish in a world in which science rather than religion is viewed as the ultimate arbiter of the nature of reality.

The "psychological" subject monopolized the stage of intellectual life in the West during the formation and development of psychoanalysis. "In the age of psychological man, the self," notes Rieff (1963), "is the only god-term" (p. 23). Selfhood, according to Baumeister (1987), became a problem in the modern period:

> During the Victorian era (roughly 1830–1900), there were crises with crises with regard to . . . four problems of selfhood . . . how identity is actively or creatively defined by the person, what is the nature of the relationship between the individual and society, how does the person understand his or her potential and then fulfill it, and how and how well do persons know themselves. . . . Early in the 20th century, themes of alienation and devaluation of selfhood indicated concern over the individual's helpless dependency on society. [p. 163]

For psychological man, self-maximization, not participation in the polis, is the chief vocation. Interest in the workings of one's psyche replaces commitment to the life of the commons. Psychotherapeutic concern for the meaning of symptoms replaces questions about meaning or "ultimate concern." Better living, not the Good Life, becomes the main psychoanalytic preoccupation (Rieff 1963).

Psychoanalytic assumptions about the self, whether classical or contemporary, are underwritten by Western values, particularly the "Northern European/North American cultural values and philosophical assumptions involving individualism" (Roland 1995, p. 4). The individual in individualism is sacred: "The supreme value in and of itself, with each having his or her own rights and obligations. . . . Society is considered to be essentially subordinate to the needs of individuals, who are all governed by their own self-interest" (p. 6). Psychoanalysis is an exemplary psychological version of Western individualistic thought.

The history of psychoanalysis is the story of competing and often opposing visions of why humans suffer and how they might be helped. Each school of psychoanalysis offers a different account of the former and a different answer to the latter. Since Freud made his groundbreaking discoveries over 100 years ago, psychoanalytic theory and practice have evolved into a continuously expanding framework for the understanding of the mind and the treatment of psychopathology. Five main psychoanalytic viewpoints have been espoused: drive–conflict theory, developmental ego psychology, Sullivanian interpersonal psychoanalysis, British object relations theory, and self psychology. Each of these schools of thought focuses on and illuminates certain crucial aspects of theory and technique.

Greenberg and Mitchell (1983) have suggested that two distinct and incommensurable paradigms underlie these schools: the drive–structure model and the relational model. Classical psychoanalysis and ego psychology are examples of the former, while object relations theory, interpersonal psychoanalysis, and self psychology are exemplars of the latter.

In the drive–structure model, humans are viewed as driven, autonomous, conflicted creatures who are shaped by their historical past and struggle to mediate between endogenously arising, asocial, somatically based, hedonic impulses and the demands of conscience and external reality. Creating a neutral, nonimpinging environment for the disavowed past to emerge, the drive–structure model offers the patient an opportunity to gain a measure of clarity and control over his troubling past. Drive theory was intellectually compatible with the intellectual Weltanschauung of the world in which psychoanalysis arose with its Darwinian flavor, philosophy of science and brain physiology, and neuroanatomy (Mitchell 1988).

Since the late 1940s, there has been an increasing emphasis in psychoanalysis on relations with others, past and present, actual and imaginary, as an alternative framework for understanding human development as well as the therapeutic process. Within the heterogeneous relational fold, some have emphasized self-experience and organization (Kohut 1977), some attachment (Bowlby 1969), and some interpersonal interactions (Sullivan 1953). From Melanie Klein's (1975) depiction of the human struggle between malevolence and envy, love and gratitude, to Ronald Fairbairn's (1952) account of the human propensity for seeking attachment and relatedness, to Winnicott's (1960) illumination of the human struggles to fashion a life of authenticity and aliveness rather than conformity and deadness, to Kohut's (1977, 1984) emphasis on the development and vicissitudes of self organization in the matrix of parental responsiveness, the reality and ubiquity of relationships have placed a conceptual strain on the drive model. Many studies comparing psychoanalysis and Buddhism unfortunately equate the former with the drive–structure model and neglect newer views of development, self, and the therapeutic process dictated by relational theories.

Freud (1917) claimed that psychoanalysis was the third great blow to humankind's narcissism. Copernicus demonstrated that the earth was not the center of the universe, Darwin revealed that humans are descendants of animals, and psychoanalysis illuminated the myriad ways that humans are unconscious of vast facets of their thoughts, feelings, fantasies, and conduct and thereby not even masters of their own minds (cf. Freud 1917, p. 143). The notion of unconsciousness, as Phillips (1994) notes, makes a mockery of the idea of self-mastery. We are shaped by hidden motivations and often behave in ways that are counter to our avowed wishes and conscious intentions. Buddhist teachers and students, no less than analysts and patients, may, for example, engage in self-compromising behaviors or treat others in ways that clash with their conscious ideals. Or, to cite another possible example, our characteristic ways of pursuing freedom may inadvertently lead to self-enslavement, as we place a Buddhist or psychoanalytic doctrine or a Buddhist teacher-psychoanalyst on a pedestal and trust them more than ourselves.

It was Freud's singular genius to detect and articulate the variety of ways that we are self-delusive and opaque to ourselves. Since Freud, we are more aware, for example, of the variety of strategies or defensive processes (Kohut 1984) that we employ to ward off pain and buttress self-esteem, such as denial, repression, projection, displacement, intellectualization, rationalization, and identification with the aggressor. We may, for example, deny and remain silent about intolerance or corruption in the psychological or spiritual communities we inhabit so as not to "rock the boat" with colleagues or friends and risk censure or disapproval. Or, we may rationalize or intellectualize away limitations in the psychotherapeutic or spiritual disciplines we are committed to out of a fear of being independent and free.

Since Freud, we are much more aware of the way that our present is deeply shaped by our past. Because of a ubiquitous psychological phenomenon Freud termed *transference*, we may perceive figures we encounter in the present, including analysts or Buddhist teachers, in a manner that does not befit them, as if they are formative figures from our past. The Buddhist teacher's detachment can be interpreted by his or her students as if, among other things, it is a sign of a negligent parent. The analyst's silence can be experienced as if it is the condemnation of a critical parent.

Not only do we transfer onto others in the present thoughts, feelings, and fantasies we originally experienced with significant others in our past, we may unconsciously reenact such forms of relatedness or nonrelatedness (cf. Sandler 1976). The spiritual seeker who was sexually traumatized as a child may, for example, not only fear a traumatogenic repetition with people in the present, which might include his or her spiritual teacher, he or she might move toward unconsciously recreating such situations.

Psychoanalysis has taught us that analysts, as well as Buddhist teachers, have countertransferences or counterreactions to their patients' and students' transferences. Analysts who were treated as children as if they were invisible might experience a patient's self-centeredness as an intolerable perpetuation of a disturbing form of interpersonal connection. Spiritual teachers who were sexually exploited or starved for emotional closeness or sustenance as children might respond to a student's interest as a longed-for validation of their being, which might result in initiating an intimate relationship and thus enacting and perpetuating their earlier history and trauma rather than exploring its meaning and impact on their current life.

Another important aspect of psychoanalysis is its recognition of psychic complexity or multidimensionality (Stolorow et al. 1987): the fact that any aspect of emotional life may have multiple causes and meanings as well as serve multiple functions (cf. Waelder 1936). Generosity may hide ambitiousness and self-aggrandizement, and self-denial and self-abasement may also partake of nonattachment in the spiritual sense of the term.

The special conditions of the psychoanalytic situation are designed to promote the optimal unfolding of the patient's unconscious subjective life. Freud's investigative method consisted of a transformative context and a special methodology for investigating and illuminating conscious and unconscious aspects of human subjectivity. The context I am referring to is the self-reflexive dialogue of analyst and analysand, and the methodology is the special way of speaking and listening that the analysand and the analyst engage in. The analysand "free associates" or says whatever comes to mind without concern for social propriety or logical coherence. The analyst listens to the analysand with a special quality of heightened attentiveness that Freud (1912) termed "evenly hovering attention."

The analytic situation and the methodological principle of speaking and listening with a minimum of constraints and preconceptions creates an altered state of consciousness for both analyst and analysand that is akin to an imaginative, dreamlike state. This encourages the optimal emergence of the patient's characteristic patterns of seeing and relating to him- or herself and others as well as the analyst's capacity for creative listening. Although this process is literally unpredictable, it often has a similar result.

As the analysand is less concerned with logical consistency, social decorum, self-judgments, pride, and shame, his or her thinking and speech take on a more spontaneous and unfettered form. This opens up the possibility of experiencing previously hidden aspects of self. The patient's discourse is not transparent and lacks a self-evident meaning. The analyst's conception of the analysand is shaped, at least in part, by the analyst's own theoretical models and desires. The Freudian method thus leads not to the truth about who the patient really is but to a variety of ways, including formerly unconscious ones, of conceiving of his or her life. The recurrent unconscious principles and patterns of relating to self and other from the patient's past that shape and delimit him or her, or transference, then appear with greater clarity.

In recommending that the analyst listen afresh to the patient and her associations—and, as it were, dream along with the analysand—the Freudian method can destabilize "fixed" theories including Freudian ones. When the analyst's understandings of the patient's material emerge out of the mutual dialogue between analyst and analysand, a nonauthoritarian psychoanalytic climate is promoted and the analyst is encouraged to have a less narcissistic relationship to his or her theories and practices (Rubin 1995).

Contradictions, gaps, inconsistencies, and displacements in the taken-for-granted narrative that the analysand brings to analysis are more readily recognized when the analyst listens in this way to the analysand's free associations. As alternative conceptions of one's life become possible, and one's sense of one's self becomes more complex and less rigid and one-sided (Schafer 1992). This alters the analysand's sense of her past as well as enriches the possibilities for her present and future. When excessive and inappropriate guilt or shame, for example, is analytically questioned and ultimately mitigated, one may exchange a life lived under an oppressive cloud for an undreamt of sense of freedom. Or, as the unconscious apathy or passivity resulting from disclaimed responsibility for one's life becomes more conscious, a greater sense of personal responsibility and agency may flourish.

Psychoanalysis can foster an enriched sense of "I-ness," an enhanced mode of self-care, and improved kinds of relatedness. In the concluding section of this chapter I shall reflect on what we might learn from our review of psychoanalytic and Buddhist theory and practice.

PSYCHOANALYSIS AND BUDDHISM

"It is just as absurd," claims Hegel (1952), "to imagine that a philosophy can transcend its contemporary world as it is to fancy that an individual can overleap his own age, jump over Rhodes" (p. 11). Psychoanalysis and Buddhism are usually decontextualized from their historical and personal roots and treated as universally valid insights about human life. When they are disconnected from both the specific cultures in which they developed—fifth-century B.C. India and nineteenth-century Europe—and the particular conditions and difficulties that they were designed to address (e.g., suffering and narcissism and dehumanization and alienation, respectively), it is easier to believe that they offer eternally satisfactory solutions to dilemmas that peoples in different cultures and ages such as our own confront. Unfortunately, this may not always be so.

Let us briefly reflect on certain important historical and personal influences on both traditions so as to more properly contextualize them. This will help us more readily evaluate what they might offer people in twenty-first-century North American and European culture.

Earlier I argued that Buddhism was a kind of Indian Protestantism in the sense of witnessing against and protesting various facets of Hinduism such as authority and tradition, speculation, grace, a personal God, and narcissism. In this section I will say a little more about Buddhism's reaction against narcissism and then add one more important factor that Buddhism appears also to have been reacting against: history, particularly the traumatic fact of human finitude and mortality.

Buddhism's critique of egocentricity and advocacy of a life of detachment was certainly salutary. It provided a path out of the jungle of suffering and narcissism that pervaded Buddha's India. Detachment became a strategy for dealing with the dearth of available possibilities for living.

Tolerance and ethics cannot flourish in a world in which egocentricity reigns. A less solipsistic and more compassionate way of being is important in an age like our own that is pervaded by a sense of scarcity, rampant selfishness, and hardheartedness. Buddhism's concern for the other as well as the self can offer an alternative perspective to the politics of blame and scapegoating that permeate contemporary reflections on society.

"The central construct in a theorist's account of human nature and the human condition," as Atwood (1983) notes, "mirrors his [or her] personal solutions to the nuclear crises of his [or her] own life history" (p. 143). The central construct in Buddha's account of human nature and the human condition is the nonexistence of the self in a world of tremendous suffering. The central conflict that seems to have thematized his young adult life was the horror and fear occasioned when he first encountered as a sheltered young man the human misery and mortality that are a part of human history. He found old age, disease, and death terrifying and profoundly disturbing. It filled him with disgust and dread. He felt life was "oppressive and stifling," enslaving and debilitating. Life was, in a word, deadly. He responded to this terrifying specter by immediately fleeing from the world and pursuing a renunciate life. He then formulated a death-defying philosophy-psychology of self-denial and self-immortalization: He both denied the reality of personhood—"Misery only doth exist, none miserable" (Buddhaghosa 1976)—and affirmed the possibility of a "deathless" realm beyond history, human suffering, and mortality: "Vigilance is the abode of eternal life," Buddha (1950) says in the *Dhammapada*, "thoughtlessness is the abode of death. Those who are vigilant (who are given to reflection) do not die" (p. 66).

But of course this is quixotic because there is no deathlessness in a human life. No one eludes death. Buddhism's strategy for coping with this intractable fact is to depersonalize mind and human history by viewing them as a process without a subject or self, thereby denying the reality of human existence. By eliminating human existence, which obviously disengages subjects from affective life and the world, Buddhism attempts to avoid and ward off human finitude and misery.

Whether or not the revolutionary strategy Buddha fashioned for addressing the historicity of human existence did or did not partake of a defensive escape from excruciatingly painful realities of human existence that might be worthy of further investigation with his meditative method of radical self-inquiry, what does seem clear is that it had within it some potential liabilities. With its emphasis on selfhood's insubstantiality, Buddhism promotes self-nullification, which can preclude questions of human agency and inhibit political engagement. For if there is no subject, then there is no one who is exploited or alienated and no oppression to challenge or contest.

The emphasis in psychoanalysis on the development of the psyche of the "psychological" subject offered psychological grounding and comfort for the psychologically dehumanized and alienated early twentieth-century citizen. But its individualistically oriented psychological theory of persons can promote an excessively self-centered view of self (Rubin 1995) and an incomplete view of relationships and morality. This view may eclipse aspects of self-transcendence and spirituality, that which goes beyond the autonomous, separate self, as well as foster a sense of alienation, disconnection, and isolation. A world that excludes spirituality seems impoverished. The increasing nihilism, alienation, and disconnection in our world may be related, at least in part, to our neglect of the spiritual.

The conceptions of subjectivity that arose to deal with the narcissism and suffering of Buddha's India and the threats to identity in Victorian Europe are particular and partial. In overemphasizing, respectively, detachment from affective life and a reified, solidified, egoistic-possessive individualism, Buddhism and psychoanalysis each necessarily eclipse certain of subjectivity's features and possibilities, and complicate coping with certain facets of twenty-first-century life in the West.

(UN/POST?) MODERN TIMES

We live in different and difficult times. Certain of the familiar coordinates by which previous ages mapped themselves have been challenged in recent years. In our world there are no absolute foundations for knowledge; there is no totalizing logic of the social world, by which I mean that it is impossible to describe the social structure from the vantage point of a "single, or universal point of view" (Laclau 1988, Mouffe 1988); there is a despiritualization (Berman 1981) and functional stratification (Luhmann 1986) of the social landscape, with individuals experiencing multiple "subject positions" (Mouffe 1988) or a plethora of kinds of roles and self states; and there is a sense of profound rootlessness, disconnection, and ontological "homelessness" (Berger et al. 1973). Let me elaborate.

An important consequence of modernism is a sense of what Max Weber termed a "disenchantment" of the world. In the premodern world it was widely assumed that the universe was an intrinsically meaningful and hierarchically ordered whole, with every entity and form of being, including animate and inanimate objects, animals, humans, and God, having a preordained status, significance, and function. One's responsibility was to ascertain and live in accordance with this inherited social and moral framework, which was constitutive of the person's identity and lent a coherence and direction to human lives.

The ascendancy of modernism involved a discrediting of this conception of the world. But the increased individual freedom resulting from decreasing allegiance to this inherited sacred order was purchased at the cost of eliminating the comforting, meaning-giving moral and cosmic horizons that had guided human choices and actions. Without the social and cosmic framework of reference that had guided people in the premodern world, the conduct of modern citizens became anormative, devoid of a shared standard of values and conduct. Instead, human conduct often became guided by individualistic and essentially self-centered needs and attitudes. This led to both "flattened" and "narrowed" lives of "self-absorption" (cf. Taylor 1991, p. 4) and a sense of personal alienation.

We inhabit a world that is, according to Luhmann (1986), "functionally differentiated" rather than "stratified" (p. 318). In stratified societies, the individual is ordinarily placed "in only one subsystem" based on "social status (condition, qualité, état) [which] was the stable characteristic of an individual's personality." In a society like ours, which is "differentiated with regard to politics, economy, intimate relationships, religion, sciences, and education," this is no longer possible. Nobody lives "in only one of these systems" (p. 318). In fact, we often live in many.

A single person thus inhabits a "multiplicity of subject-positions" (Mouffe 1988, p. 34). We are always "multiple and contradictory subjects," who inhabit "a diversity of communities," depending on such things as "the social relations in which we participate and the subject-positions they define." We are thus "constructed by a variety of discourses and precariously and temporarily sutured at the intersection of those subject-positions" (p. 44). A person is thus, in Pynchon's (1973) evocative phrase, a "crossroads, a living intersection" (p. 625) of multiple psychological, sociocultural, and historical influences, intersecting in complex and sometimes conflicting ways.

There is some evidence that a configuration that Cushman (1990) terms the "empty self" is a subject position that predominates in the post–World War II era in the United States. By "empty self," Cushman means a self that experiences a significant "absence of community, tradition and shared meaning. . . . It is empty in part because of the loss of family, community and tradition. . . . It experiences these social absences and their consequences 'interiorly' as a lack of personal conviction and worth, and it embodies the absences as a chronic undifferentiated emotional hunger. . . . It is a self that seeks the experience of being continually filled up by consuming goods, to acquire and consume as an unconscious way of compensating for what has been lost: It is empty" (p. 600).

These unprecedented features in our postmodern world necessitate more expanded conceptions of subjectivity that neither psychoanalysis' focus on the self-centered individual nor Buddhism's emphasis on the agentless subject can sanction, let alone imagine.

REFERENCES

Atwood, G. (1983). The pursuit of being in the life and thought of Jean-Paul Sartre. *Psychoanalytic Review* 70(2):143–162.

Basham, A. L. (1988). Jainism and Buddhism. In *Sources of Indian Tradition, Vol. I: From the Beginning to 1800*, ed. A. Embree, pp. 41–199. New York: Columbia University Press.

Baumeister, R. (1987). How the self became a problem: a psychological review of historical research. *Journal of Personality and Social Psychology* 52:163–176.

Berger, P., Berger, B., and Kellner, H. (1973). *The Homeless Mind*. New York: Random House.

Berman, M. (1981). *The Reenchantment of the World*. New York: Bantam.

Bowlby, J. (1969). *Attachment*. New York: Basic Books.

Buddha, G. (1950). *Dhammapada*. London: Oxford University Press.

Buddhaghosa, B. (1976). *The Path of Purification*. Berkeley, CA: Shambhala.

Burtt, E. (1955). *The Teachings of the Compassionate Buddha*. New York: New American Library.

Carrithers, M. (1983). *The Buddha*. New York: Oxford University Press.

——— (1985). An alternative social history of the self. In *The Category of the Person*, ed. M. Carrithers, S. Collins, and S. Lukes, pp. 234–256. Cambridge, England: Cambridge University Press.

Cushman, P. (1990). Why the self is empty: toward a historically situated psychology. *American Psychologist* 45:599–611.

DeBary, W. (1972). *The Buddhist Tradition in India, China, and Japan*. New York: Random House.

Fairbairn, R. (1952). *An Object-Relations Theory of the Personality*. New York: Basic Books.

Freud, S. (1895). Studies on hysteria. *Standard Edition* 2:255–305.

——— (1912). Recommendations to physicians practicing psycho-analysis. *Standard Edition* 12:111–120.

——— (1917). A difficulty in the path of psycho-analysis. *Standard Edition* 17:135–144.

Greenberg, J., and Mitchell, S. (1983). *Other Relations in Psychoanalytic Theory.* Cambridge, MA: Harvard University Press.

Hegel, G. (1952). *Philosophy of Right,* trans. T. M. Knox. Oxford, England: Clarendon Press.

Klein, M. (1975). *Love, Guilt and Reparation and Other Works 1921–1945.* London: Hogarth.

Kohut, H. (1977). The *Restoration of the Self.* New York: International Universities Press.

——— (1984). *How Does Analysis Cure?* Chicago: University of Chicago Press.

Kornfield, J. (1977). *Living Buddhist Masters.* Santa Cruz, CA: Unity.

Kovel, J. (1991). *History and Spirit: An Inquiry into the Philosophy of Liberation.* Boston: Beacon.

Laclau, E. (1988). Politics and the limits of modernity. In *Universal Abandon?: The Politics of Postmodernism,* ed. A. Ross, pp. 63–82. Minneapolis: University of Minnesota Press.

Luhmann, N. (1986). The individuality of the individual: historical meanings and contemporary problems. In *Reconstructing Individualism: Autonomy, Individuality, and the Self in Western Thought,* ed. T. Heller, M. Sosna, and D. Wellbery, pp. 313–324. Stanford, CA: Stanford University Press.

McNeill, W. (1963). *The Rise of the West: A History of the Human Community.* Chicago: University of Chicago Press.

Mitchell, S. (1988). *Relational Concepts in Psychoanalysis: An Integration.* Cambridge, MA: Harvard University Press.

Mouffe, C. (1988). Radical democracy: Modern or postmodern? In *Universal Abandon?: The Politics of Postmodernism,* ed. A. Ross, pp. 31–45. Minneapolis: University of Minnesota Press.

Phillips, A. (1994). *On Flirtation: Psychoanalytic Essays on the Uncommitted Life.* Cambridge, MA: Harvard University Press.

Pynchon, T. (1973). *Gravity's Rainbow.* New York: Viking.

Rieff, P. (1963). Introduction. In *Freud: Therapy and Technique.* New York: Macmillan.

Roccasalvo, J. (1982). The terminology of the soul (atta): a psychiatric recasting. *Journal of Religion and Health* 21(3):206–218.

Roland, A. (1995). How Universal Is the Psychoanalytic Self? Unpublished manuscript.

Ross, N. (1966). *Three Ways of Asian Wisdom: Hinduisim, Buddhism and Zen and Their Significance for the West.* New York: Simon & Schuster.

Rubin, J. B. (1995). *The Blindness of the Seeing I: Perils and Possibilities in Psychoanalysis*. New York: New York University Press.

Sandler, J. (1976). Countertransference and role-responsiveness. *International Journal of Psycho-Analysis* 3:43–47.

Schafer, R. (1992). *Retelling a Life: Narration and Dialogue in Psychoanalysis*. New York: Basic Books.

Smith, H. (1986). *The Religions of Man*. New York: Harper & Row.

Stolorow, R., Brandchaft, B., and Atwood, G. (1987). *Psychoanalytic Treatment: An Intersubjective Approach*. Hillsdale, NJ: Analytic Press.

Stryk, L., ed. (1968). *World of the Buddha*. New York: Grove Weidenfeld.

Sullivan, H. S. (1953). *The Interpersonal Theory of Psychiatry*. New York: Norton.

Taylor, C. (1991). *The Ethics of Authenticity*. Cambridge, MA: Harvard University Press.

Waelder, R. (1936). The principle of multiple function. *Psychoanalytic Quarterly* 35:45–62.

Warren, H. C. (1977). *Buddhism in Translations*. New York: Atheneum.

Winnicott, D. W. (1960). Ego distortion in terms of true and false self. In *The Maturational Processes and the Facilitating Environment*, ed. D. W. Winnicott, pp. 140–152. New York: International Universities Press.

13

Advaita Vedānta, Psychoanalysis, and the Self

Madhusudana Rao Vallabhaneni

The Self is the dearest of all things, and only through Self is anything
else dear.
The self is the origin of all finite happiness, but it is
itself pure bliss, transcending definition. It remains unaffected
by deeds, good or bad. It is beyond feeling and
beyond knowledge, but it is not beyond the meditation of the Sage.
Brihadāranyaka Upanishad (*The Upanishads, p. 79*)

The concept of self is not new, having existed in various guises in
psychiatric, psychoanalytic, religious, and philosophical systems. Psychoanalysis is one of the most prominent discourses of our times, which
has explored various aspects of self experience in depth and with great
precision. While much of traditional metaphysical philosophy emphasizes the pursuit of truth, psychoanalysis emphasizes the pursuit of the
life-shaping truths about ourselves in search of autonomy, instinct-
mastery, self-integration, self-fulfillment, and the acceptance of the
inevitability of loss, pain, and death. Psychoanalytic concepts of self are
psychological. Ancient Indian concepts of self are spiritual. *Advaita
vedāntic* philosophers believe that the embodied self (*jeevātma*) continues through a cycle of birth and rebirth in different bodies until it attains a state of self-knowledge (*Ātmadarshanam*) and then the cycle
ends. This view is radically different from that of modern scientific

thought but somewhat similar to the view held by the ancient Greek philosopher Plato (Phaedrus, Timaeus).

Freud (1930) expressed the view that the "oceanic feeling" that Romain Rolland assumed to be a common and fundamental religious experience is a defensive regression that revives memories of elational, fusional states prior to subject/object differentiation and is a continuation in the child's helplessness. Many psychoanalysts who have followed Freud have upheld his view (for example, Sperling 1958, Hanly and Masson 1976). This view expresses the disregard of spirituality in psychoanalysis. Rubin (1998) is of the opinion that "the plethora of analysands and analysts who are pursuing various forms of spiritual practice, the increasing number of conferences and articles on spirituality and psychotherapy, and perhaps the burgeoning attention to subjectivity and relationship issues in treatment suggests we may be witnessing a hunger for and a return of the (spiritual) repressed in contemporary psychoanalysis" (p. 133). Although several pioneer analysts showed interest in exploring Eastern philosophies like Buddhism, the worlds of *vedāntic* thought and psychoanalysis have remained remarkably insulated from each other over the years with very few exceptions (Hanly and Masson 1976). This is possibly due to the language barriers between authors and teachers of these ideas, but it may be that the most important factor is the radical differences in the fundamental premises about the nature of reality that this contribution seeks to clarify.

This chapter is an attempt to compare and contrast the psychoanalytic and *vedāntic* concepts of self and open up a dialogue that is long overdue. At the outset, I would like to make it clear that this is not, by any means, an exhaustive description or criticism of either of these systems of thought but a brief outline in order to open up discussion for further investigation by the readers should they choose to do so. In this chapter, the words *self* and *I* are used interchangeably to take advantage of the universal associations they generate. However, when *vedāntic* concepts are presented the word *Ātman* (self) is used because it denotes a set of unique ideas that are inseparable. The word *spiritual* is used not as in theology but as opposed to materialism. The readers may find the language used in translation of *upanishadic* and *vedāntic* thought atypical due to an active attempt to avoid reifying the concepts of *Ātman* and the *upanishads*.

THE SELF IN PSYCHOANALYSIS

Freud

Of the manifold contributions Freud made to psychology, the most important are his fundamental hypotheses of psychic determinism and unconscious mental processes (Brenner 1973), the metaphorical structural model of the mind, the psychoanalytic method, and the psychoanalytic situation including free association. His anatomy of the soul consisted of three mental agencies: id, ego, and superego. The id refers to unwanted wishes formed by libidinal and aggressive drives along with repressed memories and fantasies in which they find expression and through which they seek satisfaction. The id is ruled by the pleasure principle and is only interested in discharging tensions. It "contains everything that is inherited, that is present at birth, that is laid down in the constitution—above all, therefore, the instincts, which originate from the somatic of organization and which find a first physical expression here [in the id] in forms unknown to us" (Freud 1940, p. 145). The id is more or less controlled by both conscious aspects of the ego and by the superego.

Freud (1923) described the ego "as the coherent organization of the mental processes" (p. 17) within each individual representing "reason and common sense" (p. 25). It is "essentially the representative of the external world of reality" (p. 35) and "tries to mediate between the world and the id to make the id pliable to the world" (p. 56). It is governed by the reality principle. The conscious aspect of the ego is the "executive organ" of the psyche, responsible for the integration of perceptual data and decision making. The unconscious aspect of the ego contains defense mechanisms, such as repression, which are necessary to counteract the powerful drives of the id. The ego is like "a man on horseback, who has to hold in check the superior strength of the horse (the id)" (p. 25). For Freud, the ego is "first and foremost a body-ego" (p. 26) arising from bodily excitations and sensations. Identifications with parents and their surrogates also contribute to the formation of the ego. With its qualities of reason, adaptation, sense of reality, and anxiety and the defense mechanisms, the ego is able to gain a limited mastery of the unconscious instinctual forces that affect it.

Superego refers to conscience and ego ideal. The former dictates what one should not do and the latter commands what one ought to do and strive to be. It provides guidelines for morally acceptable behavior. The superego is more sensitive to the strivings of the id and hence more immediately connected with the unconscious than the ego. Freud (1923) considered the origins of superego as both "historical" and "biological" arising from "the lengthy duration in man of his childhood helplessness and dependence and the fact of his oedipus complex" (p. 35). The superego is heir to the Oedipus complex. As the child negotiates successfully through the oedipal phase, he or she renounces the possessive sexual longings for the parent of the opposite sex and the hostility toward the same-sex parent, by strengthening the identification with the latter. Sexual and hostile feelings give way to affectionate functioning toward the parents.

The self in Freud's formulation is irreducibly historical, social, and familial (Rubin 1998). An individual's ideals, fears, hopes, and affections arise and are perpetuated in relations with parents, siblings, and their surrogates. Freud's multidimensional view of self acknowledges that human motivation is shaped by multiple external and internal forces, including the body, history, the family, culture, relationships, ideals, desires, fantasies, guilt, self-unconsciousness, internal conflicts, and reason (Flax 1990).

How then does a notion of self fit into Freud's tripartite metapsychology? It must be noted that Strachey's translation of *das Ich* by the latinate English word *ego* has been criticized (Bettelheim 1982, Orneston 1982) because it fails to do justice to Freud's concrete, earthy, and metaphorical use of the former. Strachey (1961) acknowledged that in some of Freud's works the ego seems to correspond rather to the self. This use of the term to denote self experience may have become lost in translation.

That certain forms of psychic pathology and health have psychological, developmental, and relational causes does not alter the yet more fundamental reality of the psyche's dependence for its existence on the living body. In terms of the philosophical concepts of substance, according to Freud, the body is the substance of the mind. Thus Freud thought about the self in two fundamental mutually compatible ways. Freud's self is a psychological concept. As such, we can characterize it as the totality of id, ego, and superego. This totality is equivalent to psychological self-hood and thus captures the meanings of Freud's *das Ich* that may have been lost in Strachey's translation. However, Freud's thought is grounded in philosophical materialism. Hence there is also at work in his thinking a more comprehensive notion of self as the unity of psyche and soma in the individual. Ultimately psychic life owes it exis-tence to the living human body. Freud's notion of self eschews any form of spiritual transcendentalism. For him, psychic reality is only made of the mental activities of living human beings.

Winnicott

Winnicott's 1960 notion of true and false selves can be seen as a psychological elaboration of Polonius's exhortation to his son Laertes, "To thine own self be true" (*Hamlet* I:iii). Although Winnicott ac-knowledged that the concepts already existed in the literature, he gave sharper and richer connotation, as well as focus and emphasis, to them. He (1960a) linked the idea of false self with earlier formulations of Freud: "In particular I link what I divide into true and false self with Freud's division of self into a part that is central and powered by the instincts (or by what Freud called sexuality, pregenital and genital) and a part that is turned outwards and is related to the world' (p. 140). Winnicott's work provides an account of the developmental basis for integrity, authenticity, and a deeply assimilated and personal bodily foundation for one's self experiences (Akhtar 1992).

According to Winnicott (1960b), the true self is the "inherited potential which is experiencing a continuity of being and acquiring in its own way and at its own speed a personal psychic reality and a per-sonal body scheme" (p. 46). He (1960a) held that the true self "comes from the aliveness of the body tissues and the working of the body func-tion and is, at the beginning, essentially not reactive to external stimuli, but primary" (p. 148). Winnicott emphasized that the infant is a "psycho-somatic being" (p. 144). He (1960b) suggested that the true self is the source of the infant's spontaneous gestures and ideas. It (the true self) becomes a "living reality" (only) when the "mother is good-enough" pro-viding a "live adaptation to the infant's needs" (p. 54), meeting the in-fant's omnipotence by empathically and responsively making sense of it. Here Winnicott appears to be relying on Ferenczi's (1913) account of parental rapport with the phase-appropriate narcissism of the child. The true self mode of being is characterized by "spontaneity, aliveness, and creative originality" (Winnicott 1960a) including the use of symbols and play.

If the mother fails to "decode his gestures and substitute her own gestures which are to be given sense by the infant," the true self withdraws and the infant is forced into a compliance that dissociates him from his authentic assertiveness. "This compliance on the part of the infant is the earliest stage of the false self, and belongs to the mother's inability to sense her infant's needs" (Winnicott 1960a, p. 145). This imposed compliance results in the infant living falsely. "Compliance is then the main feature, with imitation as a specialty" (p. 147). This will result in inauthenticity and in being dominated by the expectations of others rather than by one's psychosocial needs (Winnicott 1960a). Winnicott referred to this mode of inhibition as the "false" self.

The adult false-self organizations fall into five hierarchical categories: (1) The false self sets itself up as the real personality. (2) It defends the true self serving as a caretaker, which hides the true self by compliance with the object's demands (Winnicott 1960a). (3) The false self searches for conditions in which the true self can be allowed a safe emergence. If such conditions cannot be found, then there emerges a new defense against exploitation of the true self. The result is suicide: "suicide in this context is the destruction of the total self in avoidance of annihilation of the true self by others" (Winnicott 1960a, p. 143). (4) The false self is built up on the identifications, which are not in sync with one's inherent potentials and aptitudes. (5) Finally, the false self is represented by good manners, compliance, obsequiousness, and excessively polite and ingratiating social attitudes.

For Winnicott, as for Freud, the self cannot be adequately conceptualized in terms of self representation alone. Such a conceptualization is useful, so far as it goes, since it accounts for self-deceptive self images, beliefs, and feelings but the self also involves impulses, desires, needs, aversions, anxieties, and identifications, and it is involved in relationships. It is this self of which the self representation(s) is a true or false representation. For Winnicott, as for Freud, the self is not an institution or agency in its own right, made independent of id, ego, and superego by a drive such as narcissism, which gives it efficacy. Winnicott's thinking about the self agrees with Freud's and differs from Grunberger

(1971), who treated the self as a fourth agency—the vehicle of narcissistic development. However, in the end, Grunberger's conception of the self is not inconsistent with Freud's because his theory assigns to it a relative status with the ego and superego and is energized by narcissistic libido at the expense of object love. Freud (1923) can be understood as having implied such a concept of relative independence when he affirmed that the superego inherits infantile narcissism and when he speaks of the conversion of sexual libido into narcissistic libido as a stage in the resolution of the Oedipus complex and the formation of sublimations. The more telling contrast is with Kohut's psychology of the self.

Kohut

Kohut (1977) considered self as the "center of initiative and recipient of impressions" (p. 99) in human beings and as "a locus of relationships" (Goldberg 1981, pp. 6–30). According to Kohut (1977), the beginnings of the self emerge at the point where "the baby's innate potentialities and the [parent's] expectations with regard to the baby converge" (p. 99). However, this nascent self of the infant has no structure or continuity and requires participation of others to provide cohesion, constancy, and resilience. Kohut terms these needed others as "selfobjects," since they are objectively separate people who serve functions that will later be performed by the individual's own psyche. Kohut (1977) noted: "The child's rudimentary psyche participates in the self object's highly developed psychic organization; the child experiences the feeling states of the self object—they are transmitted to the child via touch and tone of voice and perhaps by still other means—as if they were his own" (p. 86). Empathic responsiveness of the selfobject is necessary for the healthy development of self. In the usual course of development, the child displays his evolving capabilities with a sense of omnipotence and grandiosity, seeking approving responses from the mother. Kohut termed this stage of normal development as the "grandiose-exhibitionistic" self. He used the term *mirroring* to describe the caregiver's appreciative and affirming responses to the child's actions and new developmental initiatives. Such responses are essential to provide a sense of self-worth, wholeness, and self-regard.

Greenberg and Mitchell (1998) noted

> in the course of optimal development, two relational configurations emerge sequentially: grandiose, exhibitionistic self images become connected to "mirroring" self objects ("I am perfect and you admire me"), toned-down imagery of the self become fused with idealized self-objects ("You are perfect and I am part of you"). [p. 354]

By idealized selfobject, Kohut meant the caregiver's availability, strength, calmness, and wisdom for the child to identify with and draw sustenance from. Parents are bound to fail at times to mirror the child or to be ideal. If this failure is minor, sporadic, and gradual over time, the child can effectively internalize the selfobject relations resulting in the development of a stable, autonomous psychic structure, the self. Kohut termed this process "transmuting internalization." Chronic failure by the parents to be adequately empathic leads to maldevelopments. Under optimal circumstances, the grandiose self is transformed into healthy ambitiousness and pleasure seeking while the parent-imagos become internalized as ideals and values (Kohut 1971).

Kohut (1977) describes the nuclear self that emerges from this process as a "bipolar self" comprising "patterns of the basic ambitions and ideals that were laid down in two polar areas" (p. 49). A tension arc of talents and skills lies between these two poles: "The abiding flow of actual psychological activity that establishes itself between the two poles of the self, i.e., a person's basic pursuits towards which, he is 'driven' by his ambitions and 'led' by his ideals" (p. 180). The self, Kohut now suggested, is a supraordinate bipolar configuration that is conceptually independent of the "mental apparatus" and its "agencies" and their principles, functions, and content. This expanded view of the bipolar self, along with its correlated concepts and theories, constitutes the "psychology of self in the broader sense" (Orenstein 1978, p. 97).

Kohut disagreed with Freud's (1914) view on the connection between narcissistic and object-related libido by proposing separate lines of their development. In contrast to Freud's description of "Guilty Man in conflict over his pleasure seeking drives," Kohut (1975) conceptualized man as "blocked in his attempt to achieve self realization—[as] Tragic Man" (p. 101). In his last book, *How Does Analysis Cure?*, Kohut (1984) extended his conceptualization of self as "tripolar," by adding another pole of selfobject needs that he described as "twinship" or "alter ego." This third pole of the self is traced to its origin in a child's wish for the merger with the idealized selfobject, which is gradually transformed into imitative behavior.

Kohut considered the oedipal conflict, including its murderous rage or parricidal competitiveness, to be a "breakdown product" of selfobject failure. The fundamental anxiety, according to self psychology, is disintegration anxiety. This anxiety is a fear that one's self will be fragmented by inadequate selfobject responses. With these formulations, Kohut replaced the drives as the basic constituent of mental life with factors derived from the earliest relationships between the child and his/her objects (Greenberg and Mitchell 1998).

Thus Kohut's idea of self is in fundamental disagreement with Freud's idea with respect to both the structure and the dynamics of the psyche. Kohut's self is not simply the unity of the three psychic agencies sustained by the body as in Freud. Kohut's self is supraordinate in the sense that it sustains the three agencies and determines the quality of their functioning. This difference has far-reaching theoretical implications. To take but one example, the aggression of the id becomes parricidal, not because of a vicissitude of the sexual instinct (Freud 1923, 1926), but as a consequence of a failure of parental empathy.

Because Kohut passes over in silence the question of the biological origins of the self, he appears to leave the door open to the possibility of a philosophy of spirit. This is also true of Kohut's concept of cosmic narcissism, which might be thought to imply a cosmic narcissistic totality that unites the narcissistic human selves. Here we come upon a possible contradiction concerning the nature of the self in psychoanalysis. Is this contradiction fundamentally the result of a philosophical disagreement? Let us keep this question in mind as we explore the *advaita vedāntic* concept of self.

THE SELF IN *ADVAITA VEDĀNTA*

Many systems of philosophy developed in India consider the *vedas* as their sources. *Veda* in Sanskrit means knowledge. The *vedas* are believed to be books of knowledge compiled by the *rishis* (seers) containing truths regarding the soul, the universe, and ultimate reality. They contain *mantras* (hymns) that were captured by the *rishis* in the deep states of meditation but not authored by them. There is no agreement among scholars regarding the date of the *vedas*. The great sage Krishnad-vaipayana, also known as Vyasa, codified the *vedas* into four books: *Rig*, *Yajur*, *Sama*, and *Adharva*. Vyasa lived at the time of the *Mahabharata*, a renowned Indian epic. The *vedas* had been in existence for many centuries prior to Vyasa, who was only the codifier but not the author. So, Hindus believe that the date of codification of the *vedas* was about 5000 years ago, which corresponds to the beginning of the Kaliyuga,[1] as per the Hindu *yuga* calendar (the *vedas*).

Each *veda* comprises a *samhita*, a compilation of *mantras* (hymns), and a *brahmana*, an exposition of the *vedic* mantras by the *rishis* (Daya-nanda Saraswati 1998, p. 229). The *Brahmanas* include *aranyakas* and *upanishads*. Those who continue their studies without marriage are called *aranas* (ascetics). The forests where the *aranas* live are *aranyas*. The books that contain the philosophical speculations of the *aranas* are called *aranyakas*.

The word *upanishad* is derived from *upa* (near), *ni* (down), and *shad* (sit). These books are learned by students sitting down in front of their teacher. Also, Indian scholars give different deeper meaning to the word *upa-ni-shad*. By reading the word *shad* to mean approach, the word *upanishad* means a literature that helps the student to attain supreme wisdom, which leads him closer to self realization (*Ātmadar-shanam*). Because they are the concluding chapters (*anta*) of the *vedas*, *upanishads* are called *vedānta*. The system of philosophy based on the *upanishads* is also called *vedānta*. Altogether, there are about 280 *upanishads* (Swami Chinmayananda 1978) so far unearthed, and the scholars are still continuing their research in determining their authenticity. Of the 108 *upanishads* that are already accepted as authentic, eleven

---

1. *Kaliyuga: Yuga* is a period of time measured in eons. The Hindu calendar of *yugas* describes each cycle of creation of the universe in terms of four *yugas*, which are measured in terms of eons: *Krita, Treta, Dwapara*, and *Kali*. The current *yuga* is *Kaliyuga*, which is deemed to have started at the time of death of Sri Krishna, the Acharya (teacher) of the great Hindu philosophical treatise, the *Bhagavad Gita*. Sri Krishna lived during the period of the *Mahabharata*, the great Indian epic, authored by the *rishi* Vyasa, as the history was unfolding. After *Kaliyuga*, the cycle of creation repeats again start-ing from *Krita yuga*.

are considered major: *Aitareya, Taittiriya, Chandogya, Brihadāranyaka, Mundaka, Māndukya, Iśa, Kena, Katha, Praśna,* and *S'vetāśvatara.*

The main theme of the *upanishads* is a philosophical inquiry into the nature of the soul, universe, and *Brahman (Ātman).* The wisdom contained in the *upanishads* is referred to as *Atmavidya,* the knowledge of *Ātman* or the self. *Ātman,* which is the true spirit in man, is of the nature of pure consciousness and is identical with *Brahman* (Supreme Self). It is assumed that if one lives according to the dictates of the *vedas,* one could acquire purity of thought and mind, and then could turn to the study of the *upanishads* to explore and experience the ultimate reality. In the ordinary course of life, taking up the study of the *upanishads* corresponds to the third quarter of life and the effort could continue into the fourth quarter. Thinkers such as Vyasa, Gaudapada, Sankara, Ramanuja, and Madhva developed the *vedāntic* system of philosophy from the *vedas, upanishads,* and *darshanas.*

The philosophical thought of ancient India is ordered and summarized in six main systems called *darshanas—poorva meemamsa, uttara meemamsa, sankhya, patanjala, nyaya,* and *vaiseshika*—ascribed to the *rishis*—Jaimini, Vyasa, Kapila, Patanjali, Gautama, and Kanada, respectively. The *poorva meemamsa* describes the role and relevance of the *vedic* rituals. The *uttara meemamsa* is based on the *upanishads* and deals with the understanding and realization of *Brahman* (supreme self) as the only reality. The *sankhya* deals with the universe and life through the three principles: *jeeva* (individual soul), *Purusha* (God), and *prakriti* (nature). The *patanjala* deals with *yoga,* a systematic approach to physical, psychological fulfillment and self realization. The *Nyaya* deals with science, logic, and metaphysics and the *vaiseshika* provides a scientific view of the universe (Prasad 2002). The *darshanas* are called orthodox systems of philosophy not because they believe in God as the creator or the ultimate reality, but because they all derive their authority from the *vedas* and maintain the existence of *Atman* or the self as distinct from and independent of the body and mind (Swami Nikhilananda 2002).

In addition to the *upanishads, vedāntic* literature includes other books such as the *Brahmasutra,* the *Bhagavad Gita,* and the commentaries elucidating these texts. The *Brahmasutra* is a basic text, which contains *sutras* (aphorisms) composed by the sage *Badarayana.* The central theme of the upanishads is epitomized in the Brahmasutra in a very cryptic manner in the form of brief aphorisms. The Bhagavad Gita is a philosophical treatise, which occurs in the book of Bheeshma in the great Indian epic the Mahabharata authored by Vyasa. The Bhagavad Gita outlines in a condensed form the philosophy of the vedas and the upanishads and hence is also given the status of an upanishad. The upanishads, the Brahmasutra, and Bhagavad Gita are referred to as the Prasthanatraya (three principal sources) of vedānta. Interpretations of these basic books resulted in two different subsystems of vedānta: the nondualism or monism (advaita) of Sankara, and the theism of Ramanuja, Madhva, and other philosophers.

The principal premise of advaita (nondualism or monism) is that Brahman (Ātman), pure consciousness, alone is real. The universe is unreal in itself, and the individual soul (jeevātma) is no other than the universal soul (Brahman). Sankara rejected the notion of a personal God. He believed that the universe of names and forms cannot be denied as a fact of everyday experience for people under the spell of ignorance. But he held that from the standpoint of Brahman the ultimate reality, the phenomenal world, including a personal God, is not real in itself. Therefore, as long as a man sees multiplicity, he must work, play, worship, reap the results of actions, and experience happiness and unhappiness but should also strive for self realization (Ātmadarshanam).

The theists accept a personal God as ultimate reality; God is related to the universe and embodied souls (jeevātmas) in varying degrees and ways. Ramanuja, the proponent of qualified nondualism (visishtadvaita), held the view that the reality is Brahman, but the individual souls are also real, being parts of Brahman or modes of His manifestations; Brahman, with the universe and the individual souls, constitutes the whole of reality. According to Madhva, the dualist, the universe and the living souls are separate from God. While the universe is a material entity, the souls are spiritual in nature. The souls, though separate from God, cannot exist without Him. Their existence is entirely dependent on God (Swami Nikhilananda 2002). In this chapter, only the concepts of self in the nondualistic system are discussed because they are the most popular and accepted by the vast majority of Indian thinkers. Sankara lived in the eighth century A.D. He propagated advaita (nondualism), which, having permeated the Indian culture, is still current and very much alive today.

Sankara

Sankarāchārya, popularly known as Sankara, was born in the township of Kaladi in the Province of Kerela on the West Coast of India. After completing the study of the *vedas*, he renounced the world at an early age in the quest of truth and was initiated into a monastic life (*sanyasa*) by the great ascetic Govinda Pada. A seer and a spiritual genius, Sankara, whose life span extended over only thirty-two years, wrote commentaries on the *Bhagavad Gita*, the *Brahmasutra*, and the principal *upanishads*. He traveled throughout India teaching *advaita vedānta* (nondualistic philosophy) and established monasteries in Sringeri in the south, in Puri in the east, in Dwaraka in the west, and Josi Math in the north. Sankara organized the ancient *vedic* order of *sanyasis* (monks) and assigned to it the spiritual leadership of the Hindu society (Swami Nikhilananda 2002). During his lifetime, Sankara met opponents from other schools in open debates, refuted their views, and established the supremacy of *advaita vedānta*. At that time the Buddhist faith in the Indian Subcontinent, having passed through many stages of rise and fall over a period of 1000 years, was ruinous. The orthodox systems of philosophy, which derived their authority from the *vedas*, had become enfeebled. The vitality, the advent, the career, and the life work of Sankara rejuvenated faith in the *vedic* philosophy and tradition.

Sankara's monumental commentaries on the *Brahmasutra*, the *upanishads*, and the *Bhagavad Gita* provided a solid foundation for the revival of *advaita vedānta*, a very ancient philosophical system. Sankara did not newly propound *advaita* for the first time, but instead had imbibed it from the *vedas*, *upanishads*, *Brahmasutra*, and a distinguished lineage of seers. He taught *advaita* with extraordinary clarity, reasoning, and eloquence. The analytical power, argumentative ability, and refuting capacity of this 32-year-old monk put the *vedic* philosophy at center stage where it still continues at the present time. Sankara completed commentaries on sixteen well-known books of *advaita vedānta*: the *Brahmasutra*, twelve *upanishads*, the *Bhagavad Gita*, the *Vishnu Sahsramama* (thousand names of *Vishnu*), and the *Sanatsujatiya*, all philosophical masterpieces. Sankara also wrote small philosophical treatises such as the *Atma Bodha*, the *Viveka-Cudamani*, and the *Tatva Bodha* and composed many *stotras* (hymns) in praise of Hindu deities, in order to inspire longing for the spiritual life. Sankara's *stotras* are known for their melody and devotion, whereas his philosophical writings are known for their clarity and reasoning. A seer, a man of self-realization, a philosopher, a poet, and a reformer, Sankara occupies a unique place in the hearts of Indians. Having permeated the spiritual culture of India for the last several centuries, Sankara's *advaita vedānta* has become the philosophy of many religions in India.

According to Sankara's nondualistic theory, there is nothing that exists outside the Universal Knowing Subject, *Ātman*. *Brihadāranyaka upanishad* states, "*Ātman* [the Supreme Self], who alone exists, is the knowing subject in us, and as such sustains the whole universe of conceptions, in which is everything and beyond which nothing, and with the knowledge of the *Ātman*, therefore all is known" (Duessen 1966, p. 257). However, Sankara makes a distinction between two states of *Ātman*: *Paramatma*, the supreme self, and *jeevātma*, the notional individual embodied self. The *Ātman*, in the *Paramatma* state, is Omniscient, Omnipotent, and Omnipresent, and in the *jeevātma* state is limited in knowledge, power, and capacity of movement. The former (*Paramatma*) is neither active nor passive, and is free from the very beginning. The latter (*jeevātma*) is active and receptive and is therefore entangled in the external cycle of change (*samsara*) and stands in need of self realization, that is, de-individualization.

In *advaita* thought, self realization (*Ātmadarshanam*) refers to the *jeevātma* realizing that in reality, it (*jeevātma*) in its full and complete measure is the Supreme *Ātman* itself. The real nature of the Supreme Self, which manifests itself, is concealed by the superimposition of the conditionings (*upādhis*) of physical organs and mental structures. The process of superimposition is referred to as *adhyāsa* or *adhyāropa* and the product of that process is called *upādhi*. The *upādhis* (conditionings of physical organs and mental structures) are not a real transformation of the Supreme *Ātman* but temporary appearances that obscure it.

Adhyāsa denotes the illusory superimposition, through *avidya* (nescience) on account of which one thing is perceived as another and the properties of one thing are attributed to the other. Thus, for example, if an individual sees a rope in semidarkness, through *adhyāsa*, it appears to be a snake and also to possess the characteristics of a snake. "In the same manner, the attributes of the non-self (*anatma*) are falsely attributed to the self (*Ātman*) and as a result, the self which is eternal, immortal, ever pure, beyond time and space, untouched by the law of causation and of the nature of pure consciousness appears as *jeeva* (embodied self), a phenomenal being, a physical entity subject to hunger and thirst, disease and death and other limitations of the relative world" (Swami Nikhilananda 2002, p. 44). In the same manner, the attributes of the self are falsely attributed to the non-self (*anatma*). Thus, due to *adhyāsa* (illusory superimposition), the consciousness and bliss that really belong to *Ātman* are falsely attributed to the nonself comprising the body, the senses, and the mind, which by nature are insentient (*jada*). Thus, *Ātman* the pure consciousness appears to be of limited consciousness (ignorant), and appears as the universe of multiple forms and as the individual soul (*jeeva*)—this is an error. This illusion, due to *adhyāsa*, is universal in all *jeevas* and, as such, their thoughts and actions in the phenomenal world are determined by it.

The process of superimposition (*adhyāsa*) is happening only on the *jeeva's* mind and body. True self's reality of awareness is incorrectly attributed to mind—it is an error. The consciousness in the mind is considered as true self and this is an error. Consciousness belongs to *Ātman*. Individuality belongs only to man. *Adhyāsa* is a double superimposition in the sense it is false attribution of the characteristics of non-*Ātman* to *Ātman* and the characteristics of *Ātman* to non-*Ātman*.

Aapavada (negation) is the elimination, through discrimination, of falsely superimposed attributes (*adhyāsa*) in order to discover the true nature of a thing. Thus, only by negating the attributes of the illusionary snake, seen in the semidarkness, the true nature of the rope is discovered. Likewise, only by negating through discrimination (*apavāda*) the attributes of the nonself, one discovers the true nature of the self (*Ātman*) and by negating the nature of the relative phenomenal world, the true nature of *Brahman*. The words *Ātman* and *Brahman* are synonymous. The attributes due to the superimposition upon a thing do not belong to it and cannot truly affect its nature. Likewise, the *upādhis*, due to *adhyāsa*, cannot change the true nature of *Ātman* (self), which is *Sat* (existence), *Chit* (knowledge), and *Ānanda* (bliss).

It is only after attaining a state of supreme awareness (*jnana*) that the individual self (*jeevātma*) overcomes the delusional state of empirical reality (*ajnāna*), recognizes its own real state (*swaswaroopa*), and attains pure consciousness (*Ātmadarshanam*). This is the state of realization of the individual self (*jeevātma*) to be the supreme self (*Paramatma*) in its true state. The *upanishads* describe this state as "the one without a second," meaning that Ātman is the subject of all individual subjectivity. The individual embodied self (jeeva) is a combination of four constituents: the supreme self (Ātman), the mind (manas), the intellect (budhi), and the reflection (ābhāsa) of Ātman in the mind and intellect. Because of the reflection of Ātman, the mind (manas) and the intellect (budhi) become conditionings (upādhis). The reflection of Ātman in mind and intellect is further reflected onto the body and senses. Thus, some writers would include body in the definition of jeeva.

Sankara acknowledged that the universe of names and forms cannot be denied everyday experience for people under the spell of ignorance (ajñāna), but he held that, from the standpoint of the Supreme Self (Brahman), the phenomenal world is nonexistent (Swami Nikhilananda 2002). When a man mistakenly perceives a rope to be a snake in semidarkness, that mistaken perception is very real to him at the time. To Sankara, the world is real and it is Brahman (the Supreme Self), but it is the multiplicity that is not the reality. Vidyaranya Saraswati described two aspects of reality in every individual: an outer reality and an inner reality. The outer reality refers to the forms of the phenomenal object world and apparent individuality, which is ultimately an illusion. The inner reality refers to "being," which is present in every individual. To Vidyaranya, the outer reality is an illusion and the inner reality, "being," is real and refers to the Supreme Self (Ātman).

According to Swami Nikhilananda (2002), Sankara did not believe that the individual soul or ego creates the nonego or the universe. In that regard, Sankara is not a subjective idealist. Sankara's advaitic thought gives rise to the natural question—how can the Absolute (Ātman) have produced the relative? Swami Nikhilananda (2002) notes, "Sankara maintains an attitude of enlightened agnosticism that is to say he (Sankara) sees the logical impossibility of determining the precise relationship between Brahman (Supreme Self) and the relative universe, for there cannot be any relationship between reality and appearance, but the ignorant sees the manifold universe" (p. 50).

Sankara explains that the illusion of the world as collection of manifold individual objects is due to avidya (nescience). Avidya has no beginning. Sankara also emphasized that nescience (avidya) can only be inferred from the effects it produces, which include the misperceptions of the world as a collection of individual objects and the misperceptions of mind that the body and self are the same. Under the influence of avidya, the pure consciousness (*Ātman*) appears as individualized self (*jeeva*). Nescience (*avidya*) is due to non-knowing (*ajnāna*) of the Absolute (*Ātman*). Though *avidya* has no beginning, it ends with self realization. From this *advaitic* premise, a natural question arises—how can *avidya*, which has no beginning, have an end? Sankara explains that nescience (*avidya*) has an end because upon attaining Ātman, one realizes that *avidya* is only an illusion arising from non-knowing (*ajnāna*). Sankara held that nescience (*avidya*) can be seen through like the mistaken idea of the snake (*sarpabhranti*) in semidarkness is removed by discriminating and establishing the reality of the rope. In *advaitic* literature, the word *māya* is also used to indicate *avidya*. To Sankara, *māya* and *avidya* are synonymous (*Viveka-Cudamani* 2000, p. 34). Both words, *māya* and *avidya*, are used in some *upanishads* and in the language from the later period of *advaita* to denote cosmic illusion on account of which the pure consciousness (*Brahman*) appears as the creator of the universe. The writers of the later period of *advaita* tend to use the term *avidya* in the context of individual self and *māya* for the cosmic process.

Sankara describes the *Ātman* by first describing what it is truly not (*anatma*). He states that *Ātman* truly is not the subtle body (*sukshma sareera*), not the gross physical body (*sthula sareera*), and not the causal body (*karāna sareera*), as they are the objects of the knowledge of the knowing subject "I." The gross body (*sthula sareera*) is the medium through which *jeevātma* physically interacts with the world. The subtle body includes the instruments of experience of the individual self (*jeevātma*): the three organs of action (hands, legs, and vocal organs) owing to their tendency to work; the five sense organs (ears, skin, eyes, nose, and tongue), which help the individual to perceive objects; the mind (*manas*), the intellect (*budhi*), the ego (*ahankāra*), the inflated sense of I, the memory (*chitta*) that recollects the past experiences; and the vital forces (*prana*). The words *skin, ears, eyes, nose*, and *tongue* refer to only sensory experiences of touching, hearing, seeing, smelling, and tasting, but not to physical organs.

The faculties of mind, intellect, memory, and ego are described as the individual's inner instruments (*antahkarana*). *Manas* (mind) refers to the faculty of considering the pros and cons of a thing. *Budhi* (intellect) refers to the faculty of determining the truth of objects. *Ahankāra* (ego) refers to its identification with the body falsely considering it (body) as the true self. *Chitta* (memory) refers to the faculty of remembering things it is interested in (Swami Madhavananda 2000). Metaphorically, the mind has its seat in the organs such as the eyes, as well as the body, identifying with them and endued with a reflection (*ābhāsa*) of *Ātman*. Ego (*ahankāra*) identifying itself with the body becomes the doer or experiencer. When sense objects are favorable, *ahankāra* becomes happy and it becomes miserable when the case is the opposite, but happiness and misery are characteristics of *ahankāra*, not of *Ātman*, which is ever blissful. Causal body (*karāna sareera*) is the abode of all *vāsanās*, which are the latent impressions of past actions (*poorva karmas*) in the past lives. These bodies are only metaphorical concepts. *Vāsanās* are also concepts, and as such they cannot have a real abode outside the mind. *Karāna sareera* is supposed to be outside the mind and subtler than the mind (*Viveka-Cudamani* 2000, pp. 33–35).

Jeevātma has five sheaths: the sheath of gross material particles (*annamaya kosa*), the sheath of vital forces (*pranamaya kosa*), the sheath of mind (*manomaya kosa*), the sheath of knowledge (*vijnānamaya kosa*), and the sheath of bliss (*ānandamaya kosa*). The *kosas* are not real structures but metaphorical envelopes that conceal the true nature of the *Ātman*. The concept of *kosas* should not be interpreted to mean physical envelopes, because such an interpretation results in reifying *Ātman*, which in reality can never be reified. *Kosas* are figuratively described as one inside the other, the physical sheath (*annamaya kosa*) being the outermost and bliss sheath (*ānandamaya kosa*) the innermost. The first and the outermost sheath, *annamaya kosa*, is the gross body (*sthula sareera*); the next three sheaths, *pranamaya*, *manomaya*, and *vijnānamaya kosas*, constitute the subtle body (*sukshma sareera*), and the last sheath, *ānandamaya kosa*, forms the causal body (*karāna sareera*). The subtle body is permeated by the ignorance (*avidya*) of the causal body. The *kosas* are the limiting adjuncts of *Ātman*. They have no existence outside *Ātman* but, because of ignorance (*avidya*), they obscure *Ātman*. They are metaphorically called sheaths because *Ātman* manifests itself through them. The sheaths of the body, from the outermost *annamaya kosa* to the innermost *ānandamaya kosa*, become subtler and subtler reflecting more and more of the true nature of the *Ātman*, and this is only a metaphorical description. It is only by eliminating these sheaths by practice of negation (*apavāda*), by discrimination, that *jeevātma* realizes its true nature, not to be one with any of all of these sheaths but one with the *Ātman*.

The *annamaya kosa* constitutes the gross physical body. The *pranamaya kosa*, the sheath of vital force, enters the body after conception, leaves the body after death, and produces the feelings of hunger and thirst. The *manomaya kosa* experiences different forms of objects in the outer world. The seedbed of desires, the mind (*manas*), impels senses to activity for their fulfillment. The *vignanamaya kosa*, the sheath of intelligence (*budhi*), is the discriminative faculty. Though insentient (*jada*) by nature, because of the reflections (*Ābhāsa*) of Ātman whose nature is chit (pure intelligence), *jeevātma* appears intelligent and conscious. Subject to *vāsanās*, the latent impressions of actions (*karmas*), *jeevātma* assumes different bodies, determined by the desires of previous births, a process referred to as incarnation. *Ananadamaya kosa* is the condition of blissful ignorance. The bliss of *Ātman* naturally arises in the absence of ego (*ahankāra*). The fullest manifestation of *ānandamaya kosa* is experienced in deep sleep and partial manifestations in wakefulness because of coming into contact with pleasurable objects and in a dream state due to pleasant memory impressions. The dreamless sleep is blissful because one is given a break from the burdens of ego. *Kosas* are not real in themselves, but they appear real because of the substratum of *Ātman*. *Ātman* has no real coverings. Individualization of *Ātman* is not real but only due to *ābhāsa* (reflection of itself in *kosas*) or *adhyāsa* (superimpositions of *upādhis*).

The *Jeevātma* has three states: the waking state (*jagrut*), the dream state (*swapna*), and the deep sleep state (*sushupti*). In the waking state, *jeeva* functions in the world of objects and in all *kosas*. In the dream state, *jeeva*, through the subtle body, experiences its own thoughts, and is not conscious of the physical body. The inner three *kosas* (*prananamaya, monomaya, vijnānamaya*) are present in the dream state and are permeated by the ignorance of *ānandamaya kosa*. In the deep sleep state (*Sushupti*), *jeevātma* does not exist in ego (*ahankāra*) form. The two realms of wakeful and dream states get absorbed into the causal condition in the deep sleep state (Swami Chinmayananda 1978). *Jeevātma* identifying itself with the sheath of intelligence (*vijnānamaya kosa*) experiences misery and unhappiness in the waking state and their absence in the dreamless sleep (*sushupti*). In the state of deep sleep, *jeeva* presents itself as the *ānandamaya kosa*.

The *Māndukya upanishad* describes the infinite consciousness as *Turiya*, the fourth:

> *Turiya* is not that which is conscious of the inner (subjective) world, not that which is conscious of the outer (objective) world, not that which is a mass of consciousness, not that which is unconsciousness, it is unperceived by any sense organ, incomprehensible (to the mind) unrelated (to any object), non-inferable, unthinkable, and indescribable. It is essentially of the nature of pure consciousness, constituting the self (*Ātman*) alone, and is the negation of all phenomena. It is peace, bliss and one without a second (the subject of all individual subjectivity). This is *Ātman* and it has to be realized. [Swami Nikhilananda 2002, pp. 65–66]

Turiya is called the fourth in relation to the three states of consciousness of embodied self (*jeevātma*), but by itself has no numerical significance. The waker, dreamer, and deep sleeper are ignorance (*avidya*) and are not *Ātman*. *Turiya* is the unrelated witness (*sakshi*), the pure consciousness present through all the three states of *jeevātma*.

According to Sankara, *Turiya* is equivalent to *nirvikalpa samādhi*, a state of formless meditative concentration in which there is no phenomenal world. This is only a temporary state in the process of self realization during which all the mental activities are under suspension and the aspirant has no subject–object discrimination. *Turiya* cannot be described in words. Self realization is attaining *Ātman* (*Ātmadarshanam*) in all *kosas* and in all states of *jeeva*, and as such, a self realized person operates in the universe with continuous awareness at all times. Such a state is referred to as *jeevanumkta* (the one with self realization in this life and still is operating in the phenomenal world in the human body). This is the ultimate goal for life in *advaita vedāntic* thought.

Although it is of the nature of Eternal Truth (*Satswaroopa*), due to *adhyāsa* (the mistaken attributions of *upādhis* of all non-*Ātma*, subtle body, gross body, and causal body), the Supreme Self (*Ātman*) feels perishable and although of the nature of pure consciousness (*Chitswaroopa*), it (Supreme Self) feels ignorant. The *Ātman*, the true nature of which is absolute bliss (*Ānanda Swaroopa*), owing to *adhyāsa*, which is due to *avidya*, feels sorrowful and bound. Only by seeing through the illusionary imposition of mistaken attributes and by recognizing them to be unreal, the individual self (*jeevātma*) overcomes the identification with nonself (*anatmani atma budhi*) and realizes its own true nature, the eternal truth, the pure consciousness, and the absolute bliss. However, the individual self (*jeevātma*) cannot see through the mistaken attributions (*adhyāsa*) intellectually. Self realization (*Ātmadarshanam*) can only be attained by meditative discipline. Meditation on the *Ātman* is possible only when the senses and mind are calm.

Sankara describes a fourfold means (*sādhana chathushtaya*) for preparing oneself to take up meditation (*Tatva Bodha* 1998): discrimination (*viveka*) between self (*Ātman*), which is eternal, timeless, and unlimited, and nonself (*anatma*), which is noneternal, time bound, and limited; dispassion in objects (*virāgh*); yearning for liberation from *adhyāsa*, the superimpositions (*mumukshatvam*); and finally sixfold disciplines (*Shat sampatti*) to overcome the agitations of mind. These disciplines include staying composed in mind (*sama*); control of external sense organs (*dama*); remembering to return to *sama*, *dama*, and observance of one's own duties to oneself and others (*uparama*); having endurance toward the pairs of opposites like sorrow and happiness (*titiksha*); dedication and trust in the sources of knowledge, teacher, and books (*sradha*); and pointedness of mind to keep the flow of thoughts in the direction of only one object at a time (*samādhanam*). An individual whose mind becomes calm and pointed with the above-described means can now begin to meditate on *Ātman* in order to realize that he in fact is *Ātman*. Sankara emphasizes that meditation should be taken under the guidance of a teacher (guru) who has attained *Ātman* (self realization) and is well versed in the scriptures, calm, self-controlled, and compassionate (*Viveka-Cudamani* 2000).

During meditation, one will have to gradually discriminate between the "seer" (*drik*) and the "seen" (*drisya*), the subject (*visayi*) and the object (*visaya*). The seer is the perceiver, identical with the subject whose nature is pure consciousness. The seen is that which is perceived, identical with the object which is insentient (*jada*) by nature. All entities from the tangible objects in the outside world must be of the nature of the seen (the object) and by nature are insentient and changing, but the *Ātman*, or the pure consciousness, is the true seer (or subject), and the unchanging knowledge. *Ātman* is never insentient (*Atmabodha* 2002). The mind and the world are unreal in themselves and their genuine reality is the *akhanda* (undivided) *Brahman* (*Ātman*). All is *Brahman*!

Sankara advises the spiritual aspirant to meditate on *Mahāvākyas* (the great sentences) and be guided by them constantly in meditation in order to attain *Ātman*. There are four *vedic* statements described as *Mahāvākyas* (the great sentences), through contemplation of which the mind is led from the phenomenal world to *Brahman*. They are *Prajnāman*, *Brahma* (*Brahman is Consciousness*) from *Rigveda*; *Aham Brahmasmi* (I am *Brahman*) from *Yajurveda*; *Tatva masi* (that thou art) from *Sama veda*; and *Ayamātmā Brahma* (this self is *Brahman*) from *Adharva veda*, contained, respectively, in *Aitareya*, *Brihadaranyaka*, *Chandogya*, and *Mandukya upanishads*. All these *Mahāvākyas* indicate that the *jeevātma* in its true state is in fact the Supreme Self.

In the *Kaivalyopanishad*, the *Ātman* that is to be meditated upon is described as unthinkable (*achintyam*); unmanifest (*avyaktam*), possessing of endless forms (*anantharoopam*), ever auspicious (*sivam*), peaceful (*prasatam*), immortal (*amrutam*), without beginning and end (*adimadhyanta viheenan*), one (*ekam*), all pervading (*vibhum*), knowledge and bliss (*chidanadam*), formless (*aroopam*), and wonderful (*vichitram*). *Ātman* is described as unthinkable, because it is not an object of perception or emotions but the subject. There is no other subject to which *Ātman* becomes an object. It is described as unmanifest because it is not perceivable. *Ātman* is described as one with endless forms, because it manifests in the pluralistic world as objects of perceptions; ever auspicious because it is free of sorrow gained through the *upādhis* of body, mind, and intellect; as peaceful because it is beyond the disturbances and agitations of the mind and intellect. It is described as immortal because it is a changeless constant experience, and one without beginning, middle, and end because it is not conditioned by time. Time is a concept of intellect. Pure self is experienced only when intellect is transcended. *Ātman* is also described as one without a second because it is the subject of all individual subjectivity and hence all pervading and formless. That which is all pervading cannot have a form, because form denotes limitations by space. Space is in *Ātman*, but *Ātman* is not in space. *Ātman* is described as wonderful because it is inconceivable by intellect (*Kaivalyopanishad* 1978). This meditation moves from the third person where *Ātman* is referred to as He or It to the second person where *Ātman* is addressed as Thou to the first person where *Ātman* is acknowledged as I.

Sankara describes the experience of his self realization:

I have no form or fancy:
The all pervading am I;
everywhere I exist,

and yet am beyond the senses;
neither salvation am I,
Nor anything to be known;
I am Eternal Bliss and Awareness;
I am Siva! I am Siva!
[*Nirvana-Shatkam* 2002, verse 6]

Thus we can see that in Sankara's view, self is neither an idea nor a mental structure. His thought is grounded neither in philosophical materialism as in Freud, nor in philosophical idealism as in Plato (*The Republic*). *Ātman* is neither matter nor an idea but pure consciousness. While the psychoanalytic self is psychological, a part of nature, Sankara's self is spiritual and ontologically, although not spatially or temporally, beyond nature, in the sense that nature, including man's psychic nature, is only an appearance. To Sankara *Ātman* is the ultimate reality, the substratum of all that is in the universe and *jeeva*. If *advaita* is the vantage point, the spiritual is fundamental in the universe as it is the ultimate reality and matter is unreal despite its apparent reality. The psychoanalytic psychological self is confined to the body and mind, whereas Sankara's *Ātman* is the substratum of body, mind, and intellect. Freud is a psychologist and Sankara is a philosopher. Freud's material philosophy is implicit in his psychology while Sankara's psychology is implicit in his spiritual philosophy. Despite philosophical differences, is there, in Sankara, an implicit psychology of significance for psychoanalysis?

DISCUSSION

In comparing various concepts of psychoanalytic self and *advaita vedāntic* self, one faces a twofold dilemma concerning (1) the methods of observation and (2) the terminology used to articulate the concepts. First, psychoanalytic data are obtained from clinical observations and from the study of normal development. *Advaita* philosophical concepts, in contrast, are derived from experiential data obtained in deep meditative states. The validity of the former can be tested in the clinical setting and that of the latter through meditation. *Advaitins* (believers of *advaita*) also advance logical refutations of the rival views of self, including the materialistic view based on premises drawn on meditation.

Upanishads describe *Ātman* as unthinkable, unmanifest, formless, non-inferable, and indescribable. These considerations pose the question as to how *vedāntic* meditative experiences can provide premises from which philosophical materialism can be logically refuted. Conversely, from the psychoanalytic side of the controversy about mind and matter, Freud (1927) held that a psychoanalytic explanation of the genesis of a contemplative state or a religious belief does not by itself falsify the idea inherent in the state or belief.

Second, the terminology to articulate concepts poses a major problem for both disciplines. It is not uncommon to get lost in the discussions of various schools of psychoanalysis due to unfamiliarity with the terminology. Avoiding getting lost becomes no less difficult when it comes to articulating the complexities of *advaita vedānta*. The various orthodox systems of Indian philosophical thought, which maintain that *Ātman* exists independently of body, mind, and intellect, derive their authority from the *vedas*, which have their own complex terminology. Adding further to the complexity, there are two systems of Sanskrit grammar: the *vedic*, which is primarily etymological, and *laukika*, which is primarily conventional. If the *veda* is interpreted by non-*vedic* grammar, the words in mantras fail to give correct meanings, resulting in misinterpretations. The great *vedic* scholar Swami Dayananda Saraswati (1998) pointed out that the confusion present in various orthodox systems of Indian philosophy, including *vedānta*, is mainly due to the misinterpretations of the *vedas* as a result of the use of non-*vedic* literary grammar by both Eastern and Western scholars. If such is the difficulty in reconciling differences in interpretations among the systems of Indian philosophy due to language and terminology, one could imagine how daunting a task it is to compare psychoanalytic concepts with *advaita* philosophical concepts. Describing *Ātman* and *Ātmadarshanam* (the experience of self realization), which are indescribable, and translating the language of *upanishads* and *advaita* into English or any other language, poses a great challenge, because one runs the risk of reifying *Ātman* and the concepts of *vedānta*; but still, an attempt is in order to see if one system can inform the other.

Freud's focus is the investigation of the intrapsychic processes and interpersonal relations, and Sankara's focus is self realization through recognition of the ultimate reality of *Ātman*. Freud emphasized instincts, conflict, self-development, and object relations, while Sankara emphasized the universality of the spiritual. For Freud, spirit is an appearance and the body is real. For Sankara, it is the opposite; Ātman is real and the body is not real. Here we come upon the fundamental ontological difference between Sankara and Freud. Sankara viewed Ātman as the substratum of body, mind, and intellect, while Freud viewed the body as the substratum of mind. For Freud, mind exists only so far as the body is alive. In Sankara's thought, while the body dies, Ātman is eternal. *Advaitins* believe in reincarnation. What really gets reincarnated, of course, is not a particular body or even a mind but a continuing set of nonmanifest *vāsanās* (desires emanating from memories) that express themselves through a succession of minds and bodies. To Sankara, gross body and subtle body are *upādhis* and not real in themselves.

Freud's thought is based on two fundamental hypotheses (Brenner 1973): dynamic unconscious and psychic determinism. Freud's unconscious has no sense of time. But unconscious psychic processes themselves are enclosed in time, and have a beginning and ending in time. By contrast, Sankara's Ātman is eternal, beginningless, endless, and all pervading. Ātman is not in space or time, but time and space are in Ātman. Opposites such as love and hate can exist side by side in the unconscious of Freud. Ātman has no opposites in it, as the opposites are only the products of *upādhis*. Sankara's concept of *vāsanās* is similar in some respects to Freud's unconscious. *Vāsanās* are the latent impressions of patterns of thought and behavior from the past, but the individual does not recognize or understand them, somewhat as in Freud's unconscious. For this reason, they can have the quality of compulsions. The deepest *vāsanā* is to take oneself to be an individual, whereas psychoanalysis is the psychology of the individual. Reincarnation in *advaitic* thought is subject to a type of determinism, in the sense that the bodies and mind that follow in succession are determined by the *vāsanās* from the past life. However, Ātman itself has no unconscious as it is pure consciousness, and is not subject to determinism because it is neither reified nor embodied, a fundamental difference from Freud. Thus, the entire apparatus of mind in Freud with its agencies and drives is only an *upādhi* (conditioning) for Sankara and unreal in itself. Ātman is the pure universal eternal subject, a conception similar to the One as conceived of by the neoplatonic, third-century philosopher Plotinus (Enneads).

While instinctual mastery and psychic harmony are goals in psychoanalysis, they are prerequisites for starting self-realizing meditation for Sankara. For Freud, the best method of instinct mastery is the satisfaction of mature instincts, and for Sankara, practicing due control of restraint of external sense organs (*sama, dama*) is a necessary prerequisite for preparing for meditation. To Sankara, there is nothing wrong with satisfying the basic instincts of hunger, thirst, sex, and aggression, but he adds that such satisfactions are necessary for the sustenance and the pleasure of body and mind, but they are not the ultimate goal of life. A temporary suspension of drives is necessary to practice meditation. Practicing *sama* and *dama* is not "withdrawal of interest from the natural world"; it is avoiding becoming lost in the sensual pleasures of life.

Hanly and Masson (1976) noted that Indian culture is strikingly similar to the Western philosophical traditions stemming from Parmenides, Plato, and Aristotle, in that

> in every case there occurs, in association with the withdrawal of interest from the world and the lack of willingness to rest content with the gradual construction of a deeper knowledge of the world by means of its empirical investigation, a derogation of the epistemic, ontological, moral and aesthetic worth of natural objects. [p. 59]

Advaitins would argue the opposite: the phenomenal world both inside and outside is not real in itself and its apparent existence is the result of *avidya*; restraining the external sense organs from the natural world and contemplating Ātman through meditation is not negating the construction of a deeper knowledge of the world, but affirms that the deepest knowledge of the world is the realization that Ātman is the ultimate reality. In this there need be no derogation of nature and its empirical investigation. On the other side of the question, the psychoanalyst might ask, if Sankara understood the deepest nature of selfhood, how did he fail along the way to uncover some of the truths about psychic life discovered by Freud? Freud, for his part, eschewed any form of psychic or spiritual transcendentalism.

For Winnicott and Freud (but not for Kohut), self is not an institution or an agency in its own right made independent of id, ego, and superego by narcissism. While Winnicott's basic idea of self, as articulated in his thesis about true and false selves, is consistent with Freud's, it differs from that of Sankara. Winnicott's self, as in Freud, comes from the aliveness of body tissues, thus the body becomes the overall substratum for the self. When there is failure of empathic responses from parents, the true self withdraws and is separated within from the mother or her surrogates and in this way, a developing child can lose touch with one's own body and with both one's physical and psychic needs. The child's developing ego becomes the locus of a false self that dominates the child's object relations. One might suppose that Winnicott's distinction between the true self and false self at least parallels Sankara's distinction between *Ātman* and *ahankāra*. However, to Sankara, Winnicott's true and false selves are both false in that they are not real in themselves. Winnicott's true self is also an "appearance" in Sankara's thought. They both correspond to *ahankāra* (the ego, I) in *advaita*. To Sankara the "normal" *ahankāra* is an experience of *avidya*. Winnicott's true self is a deeper *ahankāra*, which needs to realize its true nature, *Ātman*. For Winnicott, good-enough parenting is necessary to facilitate the development of an authentic self; for Sankara good-enough teaching is a necessary requisite to facilitate meditation for self realization. Sankara's *Ātman* cannot be precarious in the way Winnicott's true self is because it is the immutable foundation of all being, including the fully realized true self of Winnicott.

In contrast with Freud and Winnicott, Kohut's self is a supraordinate structure in the sense that it sustains Freud's three psychic agencies as well as Winnicott's true and false selves and determines the quality of their functioning. To Kohut, the infant needs the empathic responses and mirroring from the idealized parental objects to provide cohesion in the nuclei of the infant's nascent self and to facilitate its development into an enduring structure. Sankara's *Ātman* is also supraordinate in the sense that it is the substratum of all that there is including the universe and *jeeva* (individualized soul), which are only appearances. Sankara's *Ātman*, being pure consciousness, is not a structure and can never be reified. Being the only and universal subject, there is no other self other than the *Ātman* for *Ātman* to be internalized. Nothing can be in *Ātman* and *Ātman* is in everything. Because Sankara's *Ātman* is self-illuminating (*swayam prakāsam*), it does not need a mirror to reflect itself nor is there one to reflect it. And because *Ātman* is *akhanda* (indivisible) and eternal, it is neither fragmented nor needs to be made cohesive. While *ahankāra* (the inflated ego) could be narcissistic and grandiose, *Ātman* is not grandiose as in Kohut's theory. Grandiosity is a feeling, mental state, and characteriological feature; thus it is only mental.

Kohut (1966) proposed an independent developmental line for narcissism and assumed that there are higher forms and transformations of narcissism that are free of psychopathology but are essential to ego maturation; among them is "a new expanded transformed narcissism: a cosmic narcissism which has transcended the bounds of individual" (p. 265). He drew a distinction between the oceanic feeling and cosmic narcissism: "in contrast to the oceanic feeling, however, which is experienced passively (and usually fleetingly), the genuine shift of the cathexes towards a cosmic narcissism is the enduring, creative result of the steadfast activities of an autonomous ego, and only very few are able to attain it" (p. 266). Hanly and Masson (1976) argued that the narcissistic libidinal organizations and object libidinal organizations are dynamically interdependent, and the so-called higher transformations of narcissism (cosmic narcissism) mask libido, regressed to or fixated at preoedipal stages of development.

These authors also point out that Kohut did not make a distinction between oceanic feeling and cosmic narcissism. Agreeing with Freud's (1930) remarks on religious beliefs in the context of oceanic feeling as regressive, Hanly and Masson (1976) concluded that oceanic feeling and Kohut's cosmic narcissism are regressive and defensive. Reviewing Freud's writings on narcissism, Parens and Saul (1971) concluded that Freud's ideas regarding the origin of religious belief are compatible within the framework of normal symbiosis formulated by Mahler (1965). They suggested that infant's symbiotic experience would be a reasonable antecedent explanation for the oceanic feeling, as described by Romain Rolland—feeling one with the universe, a feeling of something limitless, an indissolvable bond, and being one with the external world. Mahler (1965), Lichtenstein (1961), and Jacobson (1964) held that this symbiotic yearning for such an experience continues throughout life. Grunberger (1971) traced all forms of transcendental utopian experience and thinking to longing to return to the effortless bliss of the womb and of neonate orality.

Upanishads describe experiences of meditation that are similar to and that are different from the oceanic feeling as described by Romain Rolland. Particularly of note are two experiences: the Hiranyagarbha state and the Jeevanmukta state. During meditation, ahankāra (ego) can expand to cosmic proportions. This state is described in two different ways. Some describe it as ahankāra becoming Hiranyagarbha (effulgent); others describe this as a merger with the "world soul" or the soul of the deity. Saint Rama-krishna Paramahamsa described this state as merger with the "cosmic mother" Kali (Ramakrishna). In the *Hiranyagarbha* state, *Chitta* (which is a substance of mind) is expanded cosmically because normal ego (*ahan-kāra*) is suspended. Sankara warns that the *Hiranyagarbha* is another version of illusion and so should not be pursued, but if it occurs in the meditative states, it should be ignored, as it is only a temporary state. To Sankara, *hiranyagarbha* is only one half of a duality, that is, this state has an opposite; the opposition is with the small conventional ego or with absolute nothingness; duality is still present in the form of expanded ego and nothingness. From the psychoanalytic point of view, the *Hiranya-garbha* can be compared to the ego in an expanded narcissistic state. This expanded *anhankara* (ego) is similar to but not the same as cosmic nar-cissism in Kohut. Sankara cautions that *Hiranyagarbha* could be a trap and advises to ignore it if it happens. From the descriptions of Saint Rama-krishna (Ramakrishna), it appears that *Hiranyagarbha* is also similar to but not the same as the symbiotic experience described by Mahler (1965), Lichtenstein (1961), Jacobson (1964), and Parens and Saul (1971), which persists in and is yearned for by adults. The *Hiranyagarbha* is an ecstatic but subtler blissful state. The contentment states of the baby are not the same as the blissful state of the *Hiranyagarbha*. To Kohut such a state might well be considered to be a higher transformation of narcissism. To Freud it is a regressive state and to Sankara, the *Hiranyagarbha* is a distraction in the path to *Ātmadarshanam* (self realization).

Jeevanmukta is the term used to describe an individual liberated in the current life and still functioning in the human body. This is the ultimate goal of meditation. It is a state in which *jeeva's ahankāra* is present and functioning but is not taken to be I (ego). This state is also referred to as *Atma bodhi* (the one with self realization) the ultimate reality, the true knowledge. Sankara describes the *Jeevanmukta* as a state beyond all duality because it is beyond the distinction between being and nothingness. This state cannot be described in words. The closest any psychoanalytic concept comes to this state is Kohut's cosmic nar-cissism but it could be argued that cosmic narcissism is much akin to the *Hiranyagarbha*. From the psychoanalytic point of view, the *Jeevan-mukta* is beyond object relatedness of psychoanalytic thought. The *Jeevanmukta* functions in all *kosas*. It is different from *nirvikalpa samādhi*, which is a fleeting state. In the *Jeevanmukta* state, there is a continuous awareness of *Ātman* while the individual is functioning in the phenomenal world in the human body; *ahankāra* is normal and present but without a break in the awareness of *Ātman*, the pure consciousness. Sankara describes this to be beyond the comprehension of mind and intellect, indescribable and wonderful (*vichitram*). The *Jeevanmukta* still functions in the world of objects. In psychoanalytic theory the *Jeevanmukta* state has no pride of place and perhaps even no place. Psychoanalysis analyzes only *ahankāra* (ego). The *Jeevanmukta* state is unique to *advaita* system of philosophy. It is not a regressive state in the pejorative sense of the word. It is neither a merger state nor an expanded ego state such as the oceanic feeling. The *Jeevanmukta* state is the goal of all the teachings and practice of *advaita* philosophy. Although the *Jeevanmukta* state described by Sankara is without any anxiety, whether it be neurotic or ontological, from a psychoanalytic point of view perhaps the absence of anxiety is only apparent because of the defensive nature of the state itself. Psychoanalysis emphasizes the pursuit of individuality, autonomy, self regulation, and the acceptance of loss and death. Accordingly, psychoanalysis would make at least two basic criticisms of Sankara's *advaitic* thought: first, *advaita* denies the reality of death, and second, *advaita* also denies separation and individuation.

Advaitins would argue that validity is established by reason, while truth is found through experience. But psychoanalysis could argue that such a proof is circular or mystical. To psychoanalysts the position of *advaitins* regarding validity and proof is a circular argument. Psychoanalytic thought seeks to be scientific, whereas *advaitic* thought is philosophical. From a scientific point of view, *advaitic* thought may be considered to be irrational and impossible to validate. In response, *advaita* could criticize psychoanalysis for being so limited to *ahankāra* that it fails to realize the real self, which is *Ātman*.

CONCLUSION

In psychoanalysis, a clinical pursuit, the analyst and the analysand have to deal with the analysand's pursuit of the understanding of the analysand's unconscious mind and his ego ideals, which are explored on an individual, unique basis. The truth, which is pursued, is relative to the individual analysand. The domain of knowledge demanded of the psychoanalyst is that of understanding the human nature of the analysand and the human nature of the analyst so as to minimize the confounding effect of countertransference in this pursuit. On the other hand, the corresponding goal of the student in the student–teacher relationship of the *advaita* system is *Ātmadarshanam* (self realization), which is not defined according to the individual, but according to the established doctrine. The truth, which is pursued, is absolute. The domain of the teacher is that of the knowledge of the doctrine of the system and the truth, which it describes and prescribes. The method in psychoanalysis is free association, leading to the resolution of the conflicts through the discovery of the unconscious. In *advaita*, the method is one of preparing oneself by *Sādhana Chatushtaya* (*vivekh*, *virāgh*, *shatsampatti*, and *mumukshutvam*) and meditation on *Ātman*. Meditation, unlike free association, is discrimination of the subject and object and concentrating on *Mahāvākyas*, a combination of didactic and experiential techniques. Transferences and countertransferences are harnessed in psychoanalysis while they would be considered as distractions in *advaita* thought and either bypassed or ignored as nonreality but not explored as part of the process of meditation.

Despite fundamental differences, the pursuit of instinct mastery and psychic harmony are at least, to some extent, shared goals of psychoanalysis and *advaita*. Here, one can note a possible common interest, which may be a common point from which both systems of thought can inform each other.

Let us turn from these relatively abstract considerations to the human situation and the analytic situation. Analysis inevitably requires two people, each with his or her own history, conflicts, strengths, aspirations, and good or bad fortune. The analytic dyad also inevitably involves a certain complexity. The analyst is required to empathically observe the analysand, but he must always be aware of both himself and how the analysand is experiencing him. The analysand is expected to progressively tolerate more and more of him- or herself and to become increasingly aware of the nature of his or her relation to the analyst. Complexities of this sort are inescapable. This realization poses a question of what contribution, if any, *advaitic* concept of the self can make to the analytic process. The most profound problem suggested by our exploration is precisely that of the polar differences between the concepts of self, elaborated in *vedāntic* and in psychoanalytic thought. However, according to the personal testimony of certain analysts (Coltart 1992, 1996, Rubin 1996), their therapeutic acumen has been sustained if not improved by their practice of Buddhistic meditation. Perhaps the same could apply to *vedāntic* meditation. Finally, there may be analysands even after successful analysis who find *vedāntic* meditation helpful in their struggle with the inevitable ontological as distinct from the neu-rotic anxieties of life. We should not forget that Freud's statement of the goal of psychoanalysis is to replace neurotic suffering with ordinary human unhappiness. And Freud (1927) noted that the psychological explanation of the idea inherent in a meditative state or religious be-lief does not by itself falsify the idea.

Our exploration of the self in psychoanalysis and *vedānta* gave rise to two questions: Are the concepts of self in current psychoanalytic theory satisfactory? Or can an understanding of *advaitic* thought improve them? Alternatively, does the psychoanalysis provide a completely ade-quate naturalistic explanation(s) of *vedāntic* meditative experience?

Yogarato vaa, bhogarato vaa
Sangarato vaa, sangaviheenah
Yasya Brahmani ramate chittam
Nandati, nandati, nandatyeva!
[Sankara, *Bhajagovindam*, verse 19]

Let one revel in yoga (meditation on the self), let him revel in *bhoga* (enjoyment of worldly objects), let one seek enjoyment (of company of others) or let him revel in solitude away from the crowd, he, whose mind revels in *Brahman* (in the self), he enjoys, verily he alone enjoys. [trans. Swami Chinmayananda 1978]

No, our science is no illusion. But an illusion it would be to suppose that what science cannot give us we can get elsewhere. [Freud 1927, p. 56]

ACKNOWLEDGMENTS

I am indebted to Professor Charles Hanly, with whom I discussed psychoanalytic and philosophical aspects of the topic, and to Alan Jones, with whom I discussed aspects of *vedāntic* thought. Professor

Hanly is a training and supervising analyst at the Toronto Institute of Psychoanalysis and professor emeritus, Department of Philosophy, University of Toronto. Jones is a retired diplomat living in Ottawa, Canada. He was posted to India for two years during his active service. He has been engaged in the study of *vedānta* for over twelve years.

REFERENCES

Akhtar, S. (1992). *Broken Structures: Severe Personality Disorders and Their Treatment.* Northvale, NJ: Jason Aronson.

Atmabodha: Self Knowledge of Sri Sankaracarya. (2002). Translation and explanation by Swami Nikhilananda. Sri Ramakrishna Math, 16, Sri Ramakrishna Math Road, Madras-600 004 India, pp. 14–66 and 256.

Bettelheim, B. (1982). *Freud and Man's Soul.* New York: Vintage.

Bhajagovindam of Sri Sankaracarya. (1979). Translation and commentary by Swami Chinmayananda. Madras: Chinmaya Publications Trust.

Brenner, C. (1973). *An Elementary Textbook of Psychoanalysis.* Garden City, NY: Anchor/Doubleday.

Coltart, N. (1992). *Slouching Towards Bethlehem.* London: Free Association Book.

——— (1996). A conversation with Anthony Molino in "Slouching Towards Buddhism." In *The Couch and the Tree: Dialogues in Psychoanalysis and Buddhism,* ed. A. Molino, pp. 170–179. New York: North Point Press, a division of Farrar, Straus and Giroux.

Dayanand, Saraswati. (1998). *An Introduction to the Vedas.* New Delhi: Sarvadeshik Arya Pratinidhi Sabha.

Duessen, P. (1966). *The Philosophy of the Upanishads.* New York: Dover.

Ferenczi, S. (1913). Stages in the development of the sense of reality. In *First Contributions to Psychoanalysis,* pp. 213–252. New York: Brunner/Mazel, 1980.

Flax, J. (1990). *Thinking Fragments.* Berkeley, CA: University of California Press.

Freud, S. (1914). On narcissism: an introduction. *Standard Edition* 14:67–102.

——— (1923). The ego and the id. *Standard Edition* 19:3–66.

——— (1926). Inhibitions, symptoms and anxiety. *Standard Edition* 20:75–124.

——— (1927). The future of an illusion. *Standard Edition* 21:5–56.

——— (1930). Civilization and its discontents. *Standard Edition* 21:64–145.

——— (1940). An outline of psychoanalysis. *Standard Edition* 23:145.

Goldberg, A. (1981). One theory or more. *Contemporary Psychoanalysis* 17: 626–638.

Greenberg, J. R., and Mitchell, S. A. (1998). *Object Relations in Psychoanalytic Theory.* Cambridge, MA, London, England: Harvard University Press.

Grunberger, B. (1971). *Narcissism.* New York: International Universities Press.

Hanly, C., and Masson, J. (1976). A critical examination of the new narcissism. *International Journal of Psycho-Analysis* 57: 49–66.

Jacobson, E. (1964). *The Self and Object World.* New York: International Universities Press.

Kaivalyopanishad. (1978). Discourses by Swami Chinmayananda. Madras: Chinmaya Publications Trust.

Kohut, H. (1966). Forms and transformations of narcissism. *Journal of the American Psychoanalytic Association* 14:243–272.

——— (1971). *The Analysis of the Self.* New York: International Universities Press.

——— (1975). Remarks about the formation of the self. In *The Search for the Self,* vol. 1, p. 101. New York: International Universities Press, 1978.

——— (1977). *The Restoration of the Self.* New York: International Universities Press.

——— (1984). *How Does Analysis Cure?,* ed. A. Goldberg. Chicago: University of Chicago Press.

Lichtenstein, H. (1961). Identity and sexuality. *Journal of the American Psychoanalytic Association* 9:179–260.

Mahler, M. S. (1965). On the significance of the normal separation-individuation phase. In *Drives, Affects, and Behavior,* vol. 2, ed. M. Schur, pp. 161–169. New York: International Universities Press.

Nirvana Shatkam by Sankara in *Atma Bodha: Self Knowledge of Sri Sankaracarya.* (2002). English translation with notes, comments, and introduction by Swami Nikhilananda. Madras, India: Sri Ramakrishna Math

Orneston, D. (1982). Strachey's influence: preliminary report. *International Journal of Psycho-Analysis* 63:409–426.

Ornstein, P. H. (1978). *The Search for the Self: Selected Writings of Heinz Kohut,* vol. 1, pp. 97, 150–178. New York: International Universities Press.

Parens, H., and Saul, L. J. (1971). *Dependence in Man: A Psychoanalytic Study.* New York: International Universities Press.

Plato. *Republic.* (circa 360 B.C.). Translated by A. D. Lindsay. New York: E. P. Dutton, 1935.

———. *Timaeus.* (circa 360 B.C.). Translated by Benjamin Jowett. New York: Bobbs-Merrill, 1949.

———. *Phaedrus.* (circa 360 B.C.). Translated by W. C. Helmbold and W. B. Rabinowitz. New York: Bobbs-Merrill, 1956.

Plotinus. (250 A.D.). Enneads. In *Philosophical Classics Volume I. Thales to Saint Thomas*, ed. Walter Kaufman, pp. 576–579. Englewood Cliffs, NJ: Prentice-Hall.

Prasad, M. G. (2002). Multifaceted vedic Hinduism. www.salagram.net/sstp-mgpuja3.html

Ramakrishna. (1942). *The Gospel of Sri Ramakrishna*. Translation and introduction by Swami Nikhilananda. New York: Ramakrishna-Vivekananda Center. (Original: Mehendranath Gupta, ed., Sri Sri Ramakrishna Kathamrita, 5 vols. Calcutta: 1932–1987.)

Rubin, J. B. (1996). *Psychotherapy and Buddhism Toward an Integration*. New York: Plenum.

——— (1998). *A Psychoanalysis for Our Time: Exploring the Blindness of the Seeing I*. New York: New York University Press.

Sperling, S. J. (1958). On denial and the essential nature of defense. *International Journal of Psycho-Analysis* 39:25–38.

Strachey, J. (1961). Editorial introduction. *Standard Edition* 19:7,8.

Swami Chinmayananda. (1978). *Discourses on Kaivalyopanishad*. Madras: Chinmaya Publications Trust.

Swami Madhavananda. (2000). *Viveka-Cudamani of Sri Sankaracarya*, text with English translation, notes, and index. Calcutta: Advaita Ashrama Publications Department.

Swami Nikhilananda. (2002). *Atmabodha: Self Knowledge of Sri Sankaracarya*, an English translation with notes, comments, and introduction. Madras: Sri Ramakrishna Math.

Tatva Bodha of Sankaracarya. (1998). Translation and explanation by Swami Dayananda Saraswati and R. G. Coombs. Saylorsburg, PA: Arshavidya Gurukulam.

The Upanishads. (1948). Translation by Swami Prabhavananda and F. Manchester: *Breath of the Eternal*. New York: New American Library.

Viveka-Cudamani of Sri Sankaracarya. (2000). Pp. 33–35. Calcutta: Advaita Ashrama Publications Department.

Winnicott, D. W. (1960a). Ego distortion in terms of true and false self. In *The Maturational Processes and the Facilitating Environment*, pp. 140–152. New York: International Universities Press, 1965.

——— (1960b). The theory of the parent–infant relationship. In *The Maturational Processes and the Facilitating Environment*, pp. 37–55. New York: International Universities Press, 1965.

——— (1962). Ego integration in child development. In *The Maturational Processes and the Facilitating Environment*, pp. 56–63. New York: International Universities Press, 1965.

EPILOGUE

14

The Ganges River:
Metaphor and Mythopoeisis

Prajna Paramita Prasher

> With every wave, another story pours into time's flood.
> She's history, my Ganga.[1]
>
> *Jan Nisar Akhtar (1975)*

Work within a visual medium, film, makes one constantly aware of the persistence of self-reference, the image of an image building its way into the psyche and supplanting the experience with the vicarious, the virtual, and the mediated rather than the immediate. Visual language, the coding that brings forward into a form we can negotiate the inchoate impulse toward order, is as social an activity as is verbal language, and shares with words the capacity to compress into the symbolic realm divergent, even discordant, meanings in ways that conceal construction and naturalize the created. In the age of mechanical reproduction, a creation, film in the present case, develops new meaning, dependent on its origins but separate from them, which then goes on, like a new word in language, to alter the way those origins themselves are experienced. In this, the growing public library of popular

---

1. My translation of the famous twentieth-century Urdu poet of India, Jan Nisar Akhtar (1914–1976).

record might be seen as something like an analyst's notes, a series of transferences whose recording is both steps in a process and the evidence of one moment there. To wit, they are pieces of art that are inescapably also the tangible evidence of transference both of the artist who made them and, because they are functions of a market economy, also of that artist's accurate intuition of the countertransference of his audience.[2] A pilgrimage to the river Ganges (rendered in Hindi as *Ganga*, from here on) then becomes a complex idea composed in small part of actual experience and in large part of re-creations themselves richly inflected by the depictions she inspired in artists whose metaphors (conscious and otherwise) we have previously internalized. This multiple way of experiencing—our awareness of what is there conditioned by what we've been told should be there—already endemic to urban life follows the urbanite out of town. James Sanders's (2001) *Celluloid Skyline* suggests that New York is experienced doubly, both as the city that real people live in and as the legendary one known through images, sets, and films; Sanders considers these not options but more like parallel universes. The "screen memory" is applicable here: just as we may in childhood cover some events with other preferable versions, rendering the originals unavailable, so too do we reassemble the memory

---

2. "There is neither such a thing as reality nor a real relationship, without transference" (Loewald 1960, p. 32.) Transference as a psychoanalytic dynamic is the insertion of the analysand's developmental tasks and unrecognized desires into the therapeutic situation. Countertransference is the insertion of the analyst's recognized and unrecognized responses to the client's transference and can, like transference, become a productive part of the analysis only if acknowledged, a positive twist to the inevitabilities of inserting past into present. Film's past into present expands transference/countertransference in that it provides an utterly dependable, utterly neutral analyst, a "blank screen" that is never blank. Laura Mulvey's (Sabbadini 2003) insight that Freud found film uninteresting assumes that film is not itself a reference point (analyst) into which we insert private meaning. The "artificial blindness" Freud suggested in a letter to Lou Andreas Salome is more accurate as a descriptor of our relationship to popular film. More on the complex dynamics of transference and countertransference as photographic negative and copy can be found in Freud (1912). I am drawn to Jean Laplanche's formulation of transference being akin to "metaphor"—the fact that this understanding draws our attention not only to the carrying over of something from the past into the present, that is onto another site, but also to "the continuity of its rhythm" that we "never stop holding with ourselves and which is held with us," so allowing the meaning of transference to move away from reductions such as "fantasmogorias" (Laplanche 1976, p. 138). See also Poland (1996) and McLaughlin (1981).

of place. Our inherent capacity to redesign, when nudged by the vividness of the secondary experience of filmic rendering, readily substitutes the created for the experienced. Much connection to the Ganga is through these prefab screens (movies), their imagery superimposed not only over but also into our relation to the river. Freud (1899) writes, "A screen memory may be described as 'retrogressive' or as having 'pushed forward' according as the one chronological relation or the other holds between the screen and the screened-off." (p. 320)

REPRESENTATION INTERNALIZED

The protection the screen memory provides to the developing personality is similar to the shelter popular images offer in grappling with overwhelming affect. Shaken by the power of the water rushing under *Lakshman Jhoola*, I "see" it in terms of film versions whether of *Lakshman* or of other heroes. My experience is a twisting mix of the present, the remembered, and the suggested. What further complicates this screen memory, the one whose screen is of images created and distributed like any other merchandise, is that such memory not only is powerful enough to supplant private alternatives, desirable or not, but also becomes itself a language form. The silver screen image increasingly becomes the way we see a thing. Try to imagine 1960s sexuality without Marilyn Monroe, or Mother India without *Nargis*. It is very difficult.

Wrestling the overwhelming into the comprehensible in a search for recognition is an experience Freud metaphored elsewhere by comparing it to the mechanical action of a telescope, but within popular culture, as the mirrors shift, the eye and the object can exchange ends. It is in this sense that the experience of watching a film could as well be compared to a Kleinian enactment,[3] with the film itself, static in

---

3. In "The Origins of Transference," Klein (1940) writes, "It is my experience that in unraveling the details of transference it is essential to think of total situations transferred from the past into the present, as well as emotions, defenses, and object relations" (p. 52). The resonance with "hpho" (Tibetan word meaning "transference" of the sum total, or aggregate, of karmic propensities, or bound up with personality and consciousness) suggests that film's function here translates through Tibetan and Indian cultural form an experience already recognized (Evans-Wentz 1960). Strachey (1934) draws on Klein's notions of projection and introjection to suggest that both

each separate moment of its linear change, standing in the analyst's position. As we insert ourselves into the narrative, each member of the audience becomes a separate analysand. Over time, however, these positions can be reversed; a retrospective critical review can turn analysand to analyst as signs of the construction of the film become more available, drowning the overt messages. It is with this understanding that I hope to investigate some popular depictions of Ganga, focusing in these representations not on Ganga herself but on the convex end of the glass, on the eyes of those looking. And before I try to assess anybody else's adventure into mythic space, I'll first take a look at my own.

A journey to the Ganga is a willing insertion into mysticism made as real as moving light on water. I remember going many times with my parents. They went as a couple and we went as a family. We went carrying ashes and carrying picnics. My father and I stopped there after going to Benares for my TOEFL.[4] On the boat of my memory—not the one I see as a picture in a book—what I focus on most is the sound of the oars on the water, the light, and the look of my father up at the prow, facing the sunrise with his eyes closed but seeing everything. So many images of the gods and goddesses are with their eyes closed, or half closed. Is this an acknowledgment of the limits of the visual? Was it in that mode that he dreamed the dream, the god who dreamed us both, the father who dreamed me? With my eyes open, I saw him, his joyous face. What did he see, radiant, with his eyes closed? We had come on a trip into my distant future. Into this memory I now pour possibilities. What was he holding for me with that interior look?

My mother and I went one year in a rain so cold that we couldn't get warm afterward, and huddled in our dripping saris, pitiful as mendicants. Vacation and a pilgrimage at once, each visit was both something we had planned and something we were available to.[5] If the effect of a visit to grandmother's house in the home village could be conjoined with a Catholic's visit to Notre Dame, and if both could be made at

---

internal and external objects are transferred. For enactment, containment, projection, and identification as they relate to transference and countertransference within a Kleinian framework, see Joseph (1988), Hinshelwood (1999), and Schafer (1994).

4. The acronym stands for Test of English as a Foreign Language—the English competency test required of all international students hoping to study in the United States.

5. For an examination of the contemporary uses of pilgrimages see Poland (1996).

once on a hectic, jostling Indian train, that is the journey to Ganga. The frenzy of arrival makes its own contribution. Once there, whatever the season, Ganga is the one in motion and human life is stalled in place, individuality gradually washing away in the rush from glacier to sea. In rainy season the water is so forceful that roads may be closed to *Rishikesh*, and even in *Hardwar* (two holy cities on the bank of the Ganges where the river leaves mountains and enters plains) immersion is done carefully, and clinging to a support. Cold in August, the water is frigid in January. My tall father would immerse himself repeatedly, with each dunking announcing the names of those who hadn't come with us. I would follow his example, eager to imitate him in anything, but following as well some interior insistence that was both my own and nobody's at all. It's a doorway to nothing and everything, that brief collapse into the silence within the lively, silty water. If ever I felt in touch with vastness, it would be on the return to air, Ganga clinging to me like another skin. This hugeness I am a part of welcomes me on each return, and each one is different. I have been back since my father's death, a woman with a family of her own. Joy and grief collect in my throat like the pool on the downstream side of a *ghatt* (the riverbank). Mourning: its corner of stillness is another illusion. A dropped flower dawdles briefly and then inches toward the current until it is caught and disappears out of sight, gone on or gone under, vivid life in a transformation of its own. These unmediated experiences contain within them transferences I have absorbed from art and from media, but they are distanced by the rush of water and the nearness of family. Most of the exchanges are immediate, instantaneous, even preverbal. I could say I return to this mother like any baby, but that explanation is its own transference.[6] The river reflects back the self like a mirror, a primal

---

6. In gendering the river, in calling her "mother," I am externalizing Mahler, Klein, and Winnicott's suggestion that our most significant connections replicate the drama of mother/infant as a unified whole. They highlight the physicality of this connection and its responses, known as instincts. Dyadic rather than triadic dynamics are particularly relevant to the atomized experience of a filmic audience. For Mahler, mother-infant interactions move from primary narcissism or autism to symbiosis, i.e., from "an inborn unresponsiveness to outside stimuli"—an elaboration of Freud's fiction of the bird's egg and primary fusion to "a dim awareness that need-satisfaction cannot be provided by oneself, but comes from somewhere outside the self." Psychological birth, for Mahler, mimics the hatching process of infant–mother "holding

environment whose return gaze with its promises of creative response turns everyone into a child.

TRANSFER POINT: IMAGES IN THE DARK

It is with a sense of thievery, then, that I go forward with a film-maker's discussion of the river, The River, the Ganga. I want to remain aware of the violence of this act, that in representing her at all I am channeling off a little rivulet of her abundance and then, because I can put a name to this trickle, calling it my own. The re-creating I do, writing down these memories, shoves that trickle through a narrow passage indeed, for I have only words to represent how rich they are, and how full of meaning. Launched out into the world they are only secondary revision notations on a dreamscape brought forward into public discourse (Freud 1900).

As Freud (1925) made explicit with his reference to the mystic pad, when one is talking about internal matters, the way to bring them up to the surface through language is by a comparison. The wax bed is his image of what brain activity might be like. Chaotic, unreadable, but nonetheless present traces of old information lie under a clean surface. I'd like to borrow this idea to talk about how cultural ideas become imprinted and then unrecognizable. Freud also used Greek myth as he used the telescope and the mystic pad, all ways to put into the visual a universal interior passage. *Oedipus Rex* is a drama about maturation, but any theatrical production of it now is also a lot of other things, many of them more closely connected to Freudian ideas than to the less scientific, more mystical world that produced this play (Freud 1925). Representation (words, pictures, stories), as it puts form onto the formless, also substitutes the representation for the ungraspable real and becomes an action of destruction and diminishment as well as of expansion and

---

behavior" (Mahler et al. 1975, pp. 49–56). "Wouldn't it be awful if the child looked into the mirror and saw nothing?" Mirroring and holding for Winnicott is "the only way in which a mother can show the infant her love." It is a dynamic process of "mother-infant mutuality," "playing," and change (Winnicott 1965, p. 49). Klein's part-object theorization is from the infant's point of view and takes into account the infant's internal and/or phantasied relationship to the breast, i.e., seeing the whole mother as the loving breast and the "hated withheld breast" (Klein et al. 1952, pp. 239–240).

knowledge. We do not have a choice about whether we participate in this process, but can try to be alert to it. Film as a popular form has a significant difference from the film on the surface of the mystic pad. New movies do not supplant or erase their predecessors, but overwrite them, reinscribing or recoding their meanings. By review, we watch ways of seeing develop. In his lifelong search for a metaphor various enough to fit his theories, Freud might well have come eventually to popular film.[7]

COMPANY STYLE[8]: EARLY COMODIFICATION OF THE GANGA

This review itself can begin very far back indeed, since depictions of Ganga appear as early as Vedic times.[9] But before considering early mythic/historical accounts, I'd like to stop at the more recent way stations of her representation by early travelers. If my own medium, film, could be said to have an immediate antecedent, it would be photography, and before that, landscape art. Many British landscape artists, including the prolific William Hodges and Thomas and William Daniell, not

---

7. For a larger exploration of this idea, see Parasher (2002).

8. The Company Style refers to watercolors, drawings, and etchings produced in India as a colonialist project and intended for reproduction and sale in Europe. J. Zoffany, Tilly Kettle, T. Boys, the Daniell brothers, Prinsep, and others applied Romanticism to Indian landscapes, bringing notions of individuality rooted in the dominance of subjective reason into conflict with Eastern artistic anonymity and its focus on intuitive response. Klein (1936) notes on the aggressive process of colonization: "We know that in discovering a new country aggression is made use of in the struggle with elements, and in overcoming difficulties of all kinds. But sometimes aggression is shown more openly; especially was this so in former times when ruthless cruelty against native populations was displayed by people who not only explored, but conquered and colonized. Some of the early phantasied attacks against the imaginary babies in the mother's body, and the actual hatred against newborn brothers and sisters, were expressed in reality by attitude towards the natives. The wished-for restoration, however, found full expression in repopulating the country with people of their own nationality" (pp. 104–105).

9. The River Hymn in the Rig Veda: "*imam me gange yamune sarasvati sutudri stonam sacata purusnya asiktaya marudvrdhe vitastaya arjikiye srnuhya susomaya*" (invocation to Ganga, Yamuna, and other rivers). (Griffith 1889, pp. 251–252.).

only spent years painting and drawing the river and other scenes of India, but also published them at home, where a desire for the picturesque insured a ready market. *Oriental Scenery* (Mahajan 1984) appeared two hundred years ago, but looking at these aquatints today I can see in the framing, the perspective, the implication of action in human figures, and full sails—an artistic tradition I have internalized as natural: Ganga touching the geometry of *ghatts* and supporting rich shipping, already subdued to the agency of men. This applied visual Ganga, the information of maps and schoolbooks, resides comfortably inside my head alongside other kinds of knowledge, its parallel course not interfering with the twelfth century A.D. Ganga I see in a *Hoysala* panel at Nuggihalli, Mysore (Sivaramamurti 1976), or with the Ganga I've experienced in person. What touches me now, reviewing the souvenirs of eighteenth- and nineteenth-century travelers, is how much more recognizable the century is than the river. A Daniell budgerow, for instance, shows fifteen scantily dressed Indian sailors working at tasks, and, amidships, Daniell and his nephew in jackets and boater hats at ease under an awning. Three of the five sails have fully caught the wind, though the water is glassy and the flag (nation uncertain) hangs limply over the stern (Mahajan 1984). A retrospective eye doesn't immediately recognize the obvious coding in the details, and when it does, isn't startled. What is startling is the ready acceptance of image as real, or as the only "real" there is. This imaginary craft floats forward into my century, immortality of a sort for the Daniells. Do the anonymous sailors, in their life after death, force us to recognize what their picturation thoughtlessly but not mindlessly repressed? A trace of what that world was, the picture reads like any other archaeological find or dream shard, rich with the implications within the calligraphy of its own facticity. An Oriental wonder the painter recorded for Europe is stalled here in my life like a pot of sacred water, pretty container for the unknowable, a transference I cannot return.

I could extend this picture's arbitrary tranquility with the panoramic hubbub of Prinsep's lithograph, *Eve of an Eclipse of the Moon*, a view of Varanasi in 1825 (Mahajan 1984). An anonymous crowd mills before the viewer, the faces far less distinct than the details of the surrounding buildings, which seem to herd them together. There is a bit of small street business in the foreground, and then a curiously empty, unoccupied distance at the forward edge, as if the artist didn't want to get too close. One would assume, from the way the temple and other buildings are situated, that the Ganga was at the far left, but the flow of figures seems to be moving right as much as left, a real swarm. Following the rules for perspective drawing, one's eye goes to the low center of the field, and finds there in a little clearing a man with a dagger, a woman with a baby, and a pair of rough looking dogs. Centered directly above them, the temple dome features a few scraggly saplings sprouting from the masonry. Long shadows in the foreground and deep shade under the awnings suggest gloom despite the bright white of much of the clothing. The overall effect is of curiosity and activity, but even more, of a distanced gaze of them. There is no way in the melee we can pick out individual stories, as one can with a Breugel. This is chaos. Another Prinsep work, *The Ram Lila Festival*, is similar (Mahajan 1984). Darkness abounds, shading much of the crowd and lodging deeply into the bodies of the elephants on the right. The dancers in the middle, bearing tails and fire and dwarfed by the surrounding effigies, are a Dantean circle under a billowing sky. The crowd faces away from their recording. Nothing of the framing invites the viewer in. In recording what he thought he saw, Prinsep made permanent an interior self and a viewing heritage at odds with its new location.

If one looks into these period depictions with an eye toward seeing Mother Ganga, one risks sharing this mistake, of seeing the expected rather than the presented. Most of the views are not of the Ganga at all, but from the Ganga, views of the shoreline, often of buildings and *ghatts*. Rigid geometrical lines, even when softened by trees and human figures, upstage the river, which is frequently only a soft wash in the foreground. Such focus on human activity, so different from a sculpture of Ganga in human form,[10] denies the transitional space of representation and leaves little room for mystery or reverence, substituting instead an illusion of accuracy.[11] But they were not meant for local use.

---

10. Early sculpture of Ganga cited in Shrimali (1983).

11. Freud's "watching agency," or narcissism transformed via repression into conscience, becomes for Winnicott transitional space or the "third area of experience." It is neither fantasy nor real, but the space available for play and creativity, a place where "a separation . . . is not a separation but a form of union." Because it is not part of a binary, it is neither here nor there, therefore free to be occupied in whatever way is useful to the moment. For the importance of transitional space remaining provisional, paradoxical, unchallenged, and inconclusive see Winnicott (1967, 1971b).

They were the postcards of their time, souvenirs in a European form for a European market. What they offer now, in investigation of the use of Ganga in film, is an inflection of landscape art in the High Romantic mode, an illusory celebration of the natural, which is inevitably unmasked as centered around the human when the acknowledgment and recording of wonders supplant the wonders themselves as the more evident subject at hand. The sentimental implicits of romanticism—nature as background—are but a short step to those of romance in, as it were, the vulgate: movie love stories. The lone adventurer with his pencil and brush centers these nineteenth-century scenes; they seem surprisingly gentle in retrospect. On the screens of the mechanized twentieth century, man's centrality is even more demanding; in addition to capturing landscape, he must also capture a woman. The glamorization of this fairly ordinary conquest theme runs unevenly into historic usages so that Ganga as mother and Ganga as potential wife vie within films for primacy. The most obvious distinction in the filmic and the static depictions is that landscape and woman are played separately; that is, the river plays mother (supporting environment) and the playful young Ganga is portrayed by the ingenue. And so, in functions fragmented and isolated, the central figure, the romance, becomes the potential vacancy into which projections (intended or unintended ideas and attitudes of the artist) must flow.

The advantage for filmic tension and excitement is that a love story, a story that centers on the beginnings of attraction and bonding, positions itself in a permanently suspended moment. All possibilities are contained within it. Within the movie convention, this suspended moment draws the psyche of the viewer and supplants with its obviousness the sense of partialness, of being ridiculous before a mystery, which reminds one that gods not only do not look, but frequently have enigmatic names or are kept within the even plainer enigma of having no utterable name at all. Using Ganga as a personal name[12] or using the Ganga as a place through which a human story flows reverses the process, claiming a parallel between finite and infinite that is recognizable within the feeling of being in love, but separated from the mys-

---

12. For a detailed list of names and meanings for Ganga, see Shukla and Shiva (1995). See also Dowson (1973).

tic. Visuality, with all its dazzle, cannot accommodate the void, and cannot make the leap of the Sufi poets into rapture as absence. Libido, out there adventuring on its own, assumes the viewer into its own maverick worldview and thus must maintain, with ever-increasing glamour, the illusion that this particular love connection is a magnificence, a peak experience. It is conventional for the visual splendor of Ganga—scenery—mother-of-all—to embrace (kindly, one assumes) the romance. We absorb this relationship as readily as we do the crowds and the dark shadows in the nineteenth-century paintings. Places of transference, they contain what they are given, something into which meaning is poured. The river is the mystic pad onto which has been written "Goddess. Mother." With this aspect of womanhood assigned, in each film the other woman, she who is wooed and won, is available for other transference. She is a vessel of meanings and contains the hero's potential family as well as the audience's vicarious desire to be or to own that potential. The practical unavailability of this vessel makes it an ideal transference because it is an exchange that can never be finished and thus never out of the idealized state—being in love forever, seeing the same movie over and over again.

SOLID IDEA: RIVER GODDESS ABSTRACTIONS

The transference inherent in insertion into the symbolic provides a vast field for negotiation. Before movies, before visiting landscape painters, Ganga's life in representation was already a complicated series of transformations whose origin and mooring points in a body of moving water had to vie for precedence with one another in the personifying eyes of those narrating her tale.[13] In a chapter investigating the nature of representation, I need grounding in these enduring representations; that is, I need to consider the way Ganga has previously been treated by her neighbors. The language I'm using will be of that origin, and deal with figures who are sometimes translated into English

13. The episteme of psychoanalysis is rooted in a universal scientific spirit of Enlightenment ideals, "universe" as a different understanding from the metaphysics of Indian premodern systems of thought. The aid and comfort these two can offer one another on their joint pilgrimage into the postmodern and beyond is yet to be discovered.

as "gods." It might be more appropriate, and more accurate too, in an international context, to call them "powers," to consider them as earth-bound, the creations of artists who knew, as we do, that intent and achievement are never the same, and that the history embedded in each statement, whether of stone or syllable, would be in process of transforming even before it became familiar. The Ganga representation most directly available to the academic is the one from the *Puranas*. If one speaks of the persistent urge to personify one's landscape as another sort of secondary revision, then this record of Ganga's adventures is less the screen memory represented by a hoarding of film stars on an urban corner than the agreed-upon language one uses for indicating a multiplicity. The daughter of Snow Clad Himalayas, talkative, aggressive, and self-willed, annoys *Brahma* until he curses her with the water form. Still she speaks, her waves chatter as extraordinary action. These ideas, too complex for single visuality, generate iconography with distinct form as indistinct, tenor and vehicle of the idea comfortably shifting places as they may within the lines of words. There are, therefore, abundant variations in the way the story proceeds. In one version, coaxed to come down to earth to purify the ashes of the Sagara family,[14] she is poured from a *kamandalu* onto Vishnu's foot by *Brahma*, a Puranic explanation for how her water comes to be so pure. Descending from the foot, she falls onto Shiva's locks, combining her playful self-flitting around his face with her forceful one, both dispersed and contained by his hair. These containments—Brahma's pot, Vishnu's foot, Shiva's locks—all suggest a desire to own one's creation. Ganga is after all a daughter, a gender-bound encryption of the roiling relationship between ego and id.

Because they already know Ganga, another sphere, another space, the skies, the sages have been asked to manage her descent. She has to be caught by something or someone who can bear her fall and prevent complete earthly devastation. Within this story are both awe and terror, the child's upward glance at the mother's incomprehensible size and strength. Visible within its self-evidence is the subplot of girlish Ganga, willful, playful, oblivious, and aware of her own strength. As a torrent

---

14. Discussed in many Puranas, e.g., *Visnu Purana*, Book IV, Chap. 3; *Brahmanda* Book III, Chap. 48. Also found in the *Mahabharata, Ramayana, Harivamsa, Bhagvata Purana*, and *Vayu Purana*.

contained in Shiva's hair[15] she is only just a manageable idea of a power. Can we say it is a transference by agrarian peoples who took this landscape as their own, and so were aware that they could not know it but only try to incorporate its behavior by applying the family story? This goddess is one way of envisioning what has so long drawn Hindu pilgrims to her banks, to bathe, to worship, to rejoin Mother at death. A river goddess is not so distant as a celestial one. The everyday manifestation of the mythic shows itself in Abul Fazal's written records of Akbar's and subsequent emperors Jahangir's and Aurangzeb's preference for Ganga's water. By having it carried to their court for drinking and cooking (Mahajan 1984), they participated in the effect of legend without direct connection to the legend itself, that is, they incorporated received representation into their understanding of the self-evident.

It was the arrival of the Mughals, and the Persian garden aesthetic, that began adding new theoretical designs to Ganga's wildness. They wanted courtyard gardens with natural fountains, paths for elegant canters, irrigation for a tapestry underfoot as well as before the dazzled eye. Its simultaneous now, this historical moment; arches and slender minarets have become seamless with mango, banyan, and pipal trees, whether in miniature painting from the thirteenth century or beside a paved highway. This mixed geometry of inheritance touches the water, where fluid sounds seem cheerfully indifferent, Mother Ganga still. Representation: everything mentioned leaves so much else aside. Perhaps Ganga's indecipherable voice, with its seductive gritty edge, is composed of the invisible, the lost. Were these scraps of driftwood a fruitful courtyard tree, and then a bier? Fragments of the past invade the present, things and thoughts constantly in motion. At dusk at *Hardwar* when the *diyas* (oil lamps) begin to float, the transience of their small light is multiplied by the ripples and eddies until starlight appears to come from below as well as above.[16] Stone and water blur their boundaries. We are in the middle of it all, our presence altering the flow. In the middle of what?

---

15. Gangavataran or the descent of the Ganga—one of the earliest sculptural representations, fantastic in its vastness and detail, narrates the *Puranic* lore at Mamallapuram, Tamilnadu. For details see Ramaswami (1975).

16. Mirza Asadullah Khan Ghalib's (1797–1869) famous poem "Chirag-i-Dair" ("Temple Lamps") echoes in Persian the metaphorical/spiritual affect of Ganga and who she meets.

Is a waking experience, remembered, different from a dream or is this act of recall incapable of fixing meaning, and only an act of secondary revision?[17]

FILM'S GANGA: MOTHER/BRIDE SEPARATIONS

The loss within representation is unavoidable, real meanings soaking into the dry lines of text. The Ganga feels alive. I box up my hubris like so many holiday sweets and do a conscious experimental transference. I examine what she might think of the way we portray her: "Ganga is my Mother's name. My Father's name is the Himalayas. [*Ganga meri ma ka naam, Baap ka naam Himalaya*]." As long as I am going into philosophical impossibilities anyway, let me get down to points via a popular song. It's quite touching, really, the way we want to see landscape as a reflection of ourselves rather than the other way around. This book is titled *Freud Along the Ganges*. By putting the German doctor beside the great lady here, I'm more than risking making comedians of them both, and myself too. It's so interesting, the way we all say "Mother Ganges" when the mythological tracery describes her as the Himalaya's daughter. Psychological language offers cumbersome ways of describing this cultural transition, and has the additional load of being largely the language of psychic disorder. Such implications! Such fears! But there it is; that's what's happened. The Puranas present her as a girl, and it's her young womanhood we see in sculpture, but "mother" is how she appears in language. Is it the visual/instinctive that is so discordant or is something else afoot here? Suppose that the use of Ganges follows not Freudian patterns of the discovery of self but Kleinian? Imagine how a baby sees mother at 3 to 6 months of age. Is it a mature woman, or a lively beauty full of vitality that the baby is loving? Any mother who

---

17. It is Girindrasekhar Bose's letter to Freud in 1921 that reminds us that flows of thought, like the flow of rivers, can meet and join but cannot meet and remain separate. Bose's correspondence with Freud is the first attempt in Indian psychoanalytic discourse to reframe the Oedipus complex, castration anxiety, bisexuality of the subject, and the theory of opposite wish as an explanation of repression and of anxiety, within the specificity of an Indian cultural context. The Indian Psychoanalytical Society was founded in 1922 in Calcutta. See Sinha (1966).

remembers the infant staring into her eyes with a passion unmatched by their shared man will recognize the intensity, and the glamour, of this moment. Could Mother Ganga be a psychic window into elemental attachment at a level previous to any structured understanding of relationships? (Mahler 1979, 1982). Using language to put the mountain and the river into a family is both a courage builder and a metaphorical claim on place and power. Though not on the scale of Kiplings's view of the English dam as "Mother Gunga—in irons" (Prakash 1999, p. 168), it does share with the novelist the need to create fictions that channel and control the flood of the uncontainable that drove him to words. We each find our rapprochement where we can. Mahler's description of accepting separateness becomes transformed in the specular to a celebration of that distinction so noisy that it reverberates with dishonesty—Yes, we are not the same, and your individuation has driven you from me.

Already rich with cultural meaning, the Ganga was an obvious location around which to organize popular films as soon as the technology was adroit enough to incorporate location shots. New iconography arises with a new medium and out of the plethora of Ganga/woman films produced, I'd like to choose a pair of central ones through which to trace her passage into celluloid.[18] Actor/director/writer Raj Kapoor is all but synonymous with the creation of the Bollywood form; in two films, one early and one late in his career, the evolving parataxis of multiple planes can be seen to collide and separate as well as to blend and evolve. Representation, with its apparent intent to move outward, quickly returns to source, having more to say about speaker than subject. In film (another river, but of frames and sprockets) the metonymy of Mother Ganga blurs into a glimpse of the unconscious of the making. Even when present primarily as a gesture toward place as in *Jis desh Mein Ganga Behti Hai* [*The Country on Which the Ganga Flows*] (Raj

---

18. A visual conflation that reaches disturbing new areas in Prakash Jha's *Gangajal* (2003), where the holy water has turned to acid, moreover, an acid used as a proletariat weapon of revenge. For other examples see *Gangavataran*, 1937; *Ganga Maiya*, 1955; *Ganga Ki Lehren*, 1957; *Ganga Jamna*, 1961; *Ganga Tera Pani Amrit*, 1971; *Ganga*, 1974; *Ganga Ki Kasam*, 1975; *Ganga Ki Saugandh*, 1978; *Ganga Aur Suraj*, 1980; *Ganga Dham*, 1980; *Ganga Meri Maa*, 1982; *Ganga Teri Shakti Apaar*, 1985; *Ganga Jumuna Saraswati*, 1988; *Ganga Ka Vachan*, 1992.

Kapoor 1960), she is a figure rich in the kind of meaning that must hang just out of reach. Real location shots, a calm barge at the beginning of the film and a precipitous rocky gorge toward the end, bracket an interior studio-set pool. These interior water scenes, predictably sexualized and gendered, when gangetic by inference, imply an extension of swimming and love lyrics into the national, and a national expressed in the traditional. Such meanings are made complex, now in one way and now in another, by context. The love story set within a *dacoit* (bandit) community has its own current of assumptions—love will prosper, outlaws will reform—with sheltering Ganges-as-nation making its plot arrival as a crowd of uniformed police. The love interest shares with her marginalized community the burden of the transfer of the sociopolitical onto the human body. And indeed, the heroine, Padmini, contains as much motherliness as seduction since she's wise against Kapoor's fool, resourceful when he is helpless. Looking back on film with the same long-lens approach used with the watercolors, one focuses on a clearer understanding of what is being transferred. The extraordinary passivity of the hero in his own trip up-river for a bride flags an incomplete process, a transference stopped at the maximum point of desire for the analysand and the largest responsibility for the analyst. The romance text and the mythic join in allowing the all-will-be-possible moment to stay suspended; mother will care for us and nobody has to grow up. A truncated process reveals itself over time. Reliquary of young nationalism, *Jis Desh Mein Ganga Behti Hai* seems now to have so simplified and subverted Indian questions of class and gender as to be almost as transparent as the watercolors of a century earlier.

Kapoor may have been uneasily aware of this himself. A later work within his canon, *Ram Teri Ganga Maili* [*Ganga, Your Water Is Dirty*] (1990), displays an increasingly overt/complex ability to manage the visual so as to combine historical and psychosocial languages; the Freudian and the mythological unite in Ganga, the pure mountain maiden from Gangotri. The opening suggests a mostly conscious management of image as we are introduced to Calcutta and the mouth of the river sludgy and full of flotsam. But the camera lingers on floating bodies and the effect becomes both archaic and foreign. Corpses have been an important reference point not among Hindus but with visitors, whose revulsion, like Mark Twain's in *Following the Equator*, often overrode other impressions. Could Kapoor's vision be doubled, functioning as soothsayer in the Shakespearean fool/clown tradition? The possibility is enticing; we are warned against the blandishments of politicians as the scene shifts to the glamorous digs of an industrialist ready-coded as villain of the piece. The interpolation of social disorder into the family romance is almost complete as we meet wheelchair-bound but beautiful *Dadima* (grandmother) and a restless son who does not share his father's values. Kapoor's recollection of his inspiration for this film is firmly set not within the family but in a conversation between two *sadhus*—"Totapuri Maharaj said: '*Ram yeh teri Ganga kitni maili hai!* [Ram, this Ganga of yours is dirty.]' Sri Ramakrishna replied: 'Maharaj, this is but natural. As she flows down from *Rishikesh* to here, she does nothing but wash away the sins of human beings.' This incident remained in my mind and eventually led me to make *Ram Teri Ganga Maili*" (Nanda 1991, p. 86). Eruptions from the pressure necessary to force philosophy into the shape of romance will startle both artist and viewer throughout the film.

Instinctive conscientiousness (the mother figure at the mouth of the river is disabled but carries value) does nothing to aid him in his own helplessness as an incarnation of the exploiting father, not the resistant son, in the matter of irreverent use. The issue of the violence of representation itself surfaced (Is it a log? Is it an alligator?) in the predictable fuss made over nubile near-nudity at the origin of the river. A public peek at Mandakini's nipples, in retrospect, makes them into inverted commas. The sentimental love story, the only story there is, if we were to take popular film as a measure, a limited, and limiting, vessel to contain either the awkward move from pre- to postindustrial or from mythic past to aggressive present. Essentialist Freudian readings fall easily into this format, as do essentialist historical ones. Naren, the hero, after an invocation to *Dadima*, is singing, "I have come to find Ganga and I will take her back with me." Music in Hindi film often carries complexities not visible in the prose narrative, but in this case, multiplicity is visualized. He is carrying the *gangajalli* pot[19] that his

---

19. The pot can be seen as Winnicott's transitional object in a multiple sense: it is Naren's connection to his grandmother, the film's symbolic motif realized, and in traditional iconography, a pot, an urn shape, at the bottom of a temple column or centering a frieze is an invocation of the female. Winnicott's transitional object has resonances with Klein's mental concept of the internal object. Winnicott suggests that

grandmother has given him, and in his excitement, drops it. As he chases his irreplaceable pot downhill through the flowering bushes, Freudian, historical, and cinematic language roll together and are caught—of course—by womanhood at the edge of a dangerous cliff. The dialogue is full of authority and self-confidence and double-edged awareness: "If you play with death, how will you take Ganga back with you?" "Who are you?" he asks—one need not note this is rhetorical.

The break happens between Gangama and Ganga. The moment she reveals herself in a name, metonymy overrules symbol and mystery is unveiled as ordinary. Catastrophe to the religious and the sexual, such unveilings are the current that propels cinematic romance. Larger transferences must be sacrificed to maintain the banal one of erotic desire. The burden that places on the shoulders (or elsewhere on the specularized body) of the ingenue limits her enunciations to diminished platitude— "Your Ganga has become dirty"—inherent in a hymeneal reading of the unspoiled.

Kapoor abandons a more comprehensive fertility story to one only of joining, and the kind of jointure that eliminates one part, the female. This was his last film, and starred his youngest son. Despite the beauty of its vista and sets, despite the charm of the subject and the players, there is a darkness about it, a despair in the wooden characterizations of the secondary players and in verisimilitude of some of Ganga's more sordid passages. In many places his use of the usual language of film suggests this bleaker awareness. The required fight scene, for instance, happens at night, in low light, and just outside the temple where love is being consecrated. Such specular pleasures rupture the seriousness of the premise and place the audience, miserably, in the position of the Calcutta family. Kapoor's apparent recognition of this misplacement, the unfittedness of feminine youth, innocence, and beauty as trope for the ecological and the spiritual, puts his incarnation of Ganga solidly in the Freudian, but with a recognition, undeveloped, of the possibility of Mahler pushing her heavy barge along the shallows. Ganga's sexu-

---

the transitional object "is a possession. Yet it is not an external object either" (Winnicott 1971, pp. 9–10). Kapoor's erasure of the most obvious mother (Naren's) in favor of the potential mother (Ganga) and the remembered mother (*Dadima*) suggests Bion's (1962) ambivalent "binocular vision" and isolation of the *gangajalli* pot as a transitional object.

ality at *Gangotri* (the origin of the Ganges River) is conventional, but also forceful and whole-hearted. She appears to recognize the lover's oneness immediately, calling him to her as if separation and rapprochement were only a bad dream. In her dogged determination to find her husband again, she rewrites this psychic drama over and over, but only one player's view of it. The baby who accompanies her downstream is only a prop, since it is his father's completion the story documents. Whether it is by marrying, that is, leaving virginity, or by traveling, that is, by leaving the source, that Ganga puts herself in danger is not clear, but also not important, because the field of discourse is despoilment and she its vehicle rather than its subject.

Motherhood as declared and as imaged bifurcate again. (Is this a filmic backward glance or are there implied in this view of a healthy, beautiful actress the newsreel images of famine-ravaged mothers and their empty-eyed babies?) The milk has dried up, and her song (!) cannot solace the wailing infant on the train. [Are we seeing a good breast here? (Klein 1957). What kind of a good is indexed by a breast voyeuristically sound and biologically censured?] "Get some water," recommends the traveling grandmother, but Ganga conspires against Ganga when this woman will not share the water she is carrying home for the rites around her own potential demise. "If it were ordinary water, I would have given it to you." The manipulation of symbol can arrive as a bitter joke over time and acquire unanticipated resonance. If there is a Kleinian reparation in this assignment of the film's central motif to the uses of death, our recognition is extra-textual (Klein and Riviere 1937). Life must win out over death, so the heroine leaves to find ordinary water at a tap, but to rescue her child she has stepped off the train literally as well as emblematically and into another trial. Transport metaphor, like the pot that began this travel, maintains Ganga, remarkably, as vessel, transference location, and never as the "body" of water the primary metaphor claims. It is a cinematic slippage that might reveal a too-direct dependence on Freudian assumptions.

In Ganga's dirtying, Kleinian recognitions, a background note thus far, come to full visuality. At Benares she accepts a life on the terrace: "The child does not have the protection of a father. Let your sacrifice give him sustenance." Good mother = bad woman. It works in the sentimental but not in the psychological or commercial. As the value of a sign, as a fetish figure, any agency she earns is outside the frame of the story, and belongs to whoever owns her in this extra-text level of cinematic experience that the public search for an actress has already acknowledged. In the blank return gaze of her inexperience Kapoor could place only convention. Enter the oblivious in-laws. When the object of their crude acquisitiveness is directly a woman they are supposed to protect, the didactic point takes some of the zing out of her danger, at least in the linear. Melodrama's misrecognition should be a space-maker, leaving voids in the narrative into which alternative possibilities bleed. Mandakini, prone upon a mat, is framed by the columns of a pleasure pavilion, with the river and its lamps twinkling in the background. A couple of insipidly dressed dancers draw attention to the remains of her red costume. Beyond the colonnade, the river twinkles, and the scene is intercut with images of people worshiping, launching lamps on leaf boats. Lewdness in the foreground, spirituality in the background, music over their hiatus. The image isn't static though, and must be forced into the larger narrative of the plot.

"We do not carry evidence of our sins in the market." "But you sit in the same market all right." "Scream or people will say that Ganga did not protest when stripped." It's an abrupt exchange, Ganga maintaining her legendary tart tongue, and the men of the plains their flatlander vision. To separate the dynamics of plot from the extra-frame dynamics of seeing and being seen, it may be necessary to go back here. As the two Gangas leave the Himalayas separately, a joined pair of anthropomorphic attitudes toward landscape also begin to diverge. There is scant evidence in the mythological trace of Ganga that she herself had any particular interest in becoming useful to mankind, but the filmic version has lost all personhood in pursuit of her destiny—a husband. (In being the more forward one in the early part of the romance, she was still mythic.) Applying such intention to her character's behavior separates this Ganga—she is now a mother, remember—from the maiden at the beginning, but only partially. The conventions of film are abrasively colliding with the conventions of Mother Ganga. The actress, regardless of the baby in her arm, is unchanged. Her visual appeal as sexually desirable both anticipates the kind of exploitation she will meet and keeps the viewer implicated by making her vulnerability itself a come-on as we continue to get peeps at her maternal body. Sudhir Kakar's (1990) acknowledgment of this part of the film as a rape fantasy is important. Not only does that depiction code national distress about the changing nature of use of landscape, but it also recognizes in the overt documentation of a near-child in the sex trade an ugly aspect of patriarchal control of women. What Kakar does not also investigate is the joining of the two in the commodification of woman as vessel of desire, with the audience's unavoidable position as aggressor and the actress's as willing victim. Once off the mountainside, Kapoor can neither maintain his premise nor get out of it. For the mother–son relationship that originates in the Calcutta part of the story to become thematic, the focus at this point would have to move to the baby, and away from the seducers of Ganga. Alas, the baby gets his bit, but still as an appendage of his mother: as present to excuse more peeping, and to lend drama to the largest violation scene, in which Mother Ganga's child is sidelined by, even violenced by, the men whose point of view the film cannot escape. And it is not a fully adult one.

TRANSFERENCE/COUNTERTRANSFERENCE AND THE CASH IN BETWEEN

Does this mean that the marketplace is also not an adult realm? The superficial answer is yes, since the story line accuses the potential exploiters of both girl and river. But that's the part of the floating log that's showing. There's a lot of rotten wood just under the water. As Ganga absolves the father-of-origin from further responsibility, we are left with an oedipal drama whose moral location (chorus voice in Greek) becomes ambivalent to the point of frustration. Her new father figures are not worthy. They glory in the potential for incest, and they don't get punished. An avuncular figure intervenes, suggests she save herself, that she use her dirtiness as entertainment to test the godlike forbearance of the man who has abandoned her. In turning Ganga to *Meera* (ancient Indian poet who wrote devotional poetry about Krishna) at this test, invoking water over fire, "One mad with love, the other wounded by it; one loved his face and form, the other worshipped his image," Kapoor manages to loop in *Parvati* (divine consort of Shiva) and Ganga over Shiva (it happens with all major figures in wedding clothes) and appears to solve the symbolic journey as Radha (divine consort of

Krishna) blesses the union. All mirror work. *Meera* and *Radha* readily exchange places, the transference of Oedipus, a boy living at home. In fact, he has been immobilized there while his woman has her adventures in the flesh trade. Only at this point does he become an active figure, not reclaiming the transference, but at least moving into its implications. The magnificence of Oedipus's story is in his desire to avoid an unconscionable fate; it's heroic, sexuality being only a part of what he negotiates. In this film, the woman, not the man, is making that journey; she makes it, however, as he would like to imagine (a transference so flawed one would giggle were the stakes not so large).

Kapoor's own untenable position as aligned via the camera with the exploitative fathers keeps becoming more obvious. A film has at least some of dream's potential to allow subjectivity to meander about. From the point of view of the projection, it would be interesting to take cognizance of what has been introjected. Like a dream's upside-downness, the oedipal exchanges here are displaced. The viewer's enticement is the fear that the fathers will violate the son's wife. By providing such thrills, the film itself participates in the rapine that its text pretends to abhor. Leering in-laws approach Ganga, nursing on the porch. "Did you think in this manner when drinking at your mother's breast?" she accuses, still with the sharp tongue of the Brahma's retribution. Verbal and specular intentions diverge; she uses the sari to shield herself from the actors as she draws in toward her exposed breast the eye of the camera, the unmentioned and unavoidable other tool of reproduction, the monstrous baby of pure capitalism. It is as consumers, not as devotees, we know Ganga, adults placed in the baby's position and given only the language of the schoolyard with which to acknowledge distress.

As long as romance, not married life and procreation, is the primary text of film, the positionality of adolescence is inescapable, and so, for viewers, the subtle frustration of an incomplete adulthood. In the metaphorical collision of Mother Ganga and father Oedipus, two tributaries disappearing into the mainstream of anthropomorphic understandings of landscape, gendered difference is at risk to distract away from shared meanings lodged elsewhere in the psyche than with sexuality. The suspended moment of romantic love as an opportunity for transference imposes its text onto whatever it is forced to contain. The rapprochement that would finish this psychological exchange is not possible. Because the point of view remains sexuality and not mothering, the conflation of the Gangas disallows separation or individuation.[20]

Excessive sight could be a displacement of oedipal blinding, but oedipal penance was also indirect, his eyes the sacrifice for the errors of the rest of his body. It was not what he had seen but what he had done that he wished to escape. For the purpose of this chapter, it is important to remember that Oedipus arrives in contemporary culture through a theatrical presentation, and the Grand Guignol effect is a principal part of the performance. Excess. Stage hyperbole can carry meaning only when it arrives to balance and thus reacknowledge litotes to this point unrecognized. It is the pairing of the exaggerated and the minimalized that provides the tense interior space of the protagonist's psyche into which we wish to insert our understanding. Remember the surging crowds and the dark shadows of the aquatints? Film, as an inheritor of this tradition, has access to different visualities, close-ups for instance, but must still depend on visualizing interior conflict, on primary and secondary significations. When Ganga and babe find succor on death's steps, or in the hands of a charlatan blind man, the hyperbole of the melodramatic plot is in the same figure a minimalization of the danger she meets and in non-extraordinary circumstances, would have to succumb to. Beyond the displacement of ecological catastrophe onto the incapable body of one youthful actress are the multiple additional displacements of her fetching near-miss rescues, all made at least superficially intelligible through paralleling the ideas of sexuality and dirt. Grotesqueries in the film text "we will plunge into the Ganga" that require her to be the vessel for the sins of others are matched with ordinary movie star visuals that strip the idea of force and make it ordinary, tawdry, not a comment upon victimization and exploitation but a participant therein.

---

20. Balint's (1965) formulation of "instinctual interdependence" of mother and child and "what is good for one is right for the other" allows us to move focus from sexuality to motherhood, and from the oral, anal, and genital to "something on its own," primary love as "a quiet tranquil sense of well being" different from primary narcissism and the prescribed erotogenic zones that it entails (pp. 84–85). See Mahler (1979, 1982).

CONCLUSION

How else? The blinding within melodrama is conventionalized, the audience agreeing to believe that characters do not see the perfectly obvious. Such structure can do much with minor chords—fearsome death turning gentle and respectful, for instance, or the father figure being murdered as the woman consummates her marriage—but collapses as the deeper meanings of its prime metaphor implode into unintentional comedy. The difference between Mother Goddess and Sex Goddess is, one could say, a matter of how she's used. The emotional cleansing intended by a production of Oedipus is obviated in *Ram Teri Ganga Maili* by foreshortening the distance the audience has to travel, by substituting the facile youth = truth = beauty for the despairs and conundrums of an adult who has met his disagreeable fate. The possibilities for transference, limited by the size of the vessel, cannot contain the political/ecological claim of the title, let alone the interior psychic ones a theatrical experience anticipates.

I am drawn to old films the way one is drawn to family letters and photographs, and recognize here a foolish desire to reenter the lost past. But in the recognition of that past's distance is the transparence of its making. I leave the computer and open the jug of Ganga water. It pours like ordinary tap water over my fingers and I feel it entering me, origin returning. There is no space but half the world between representation and real. The river writes upon its landscape—geophysical fact both practical and metaphorical. The flow of water, within and without, is not only life itself but also the expression of that life, effects and their expression inextricably bound one to another. A stylized row of scallops, whether under a painted fish or within Shiva's hair, points to this knot of meanings but doesn't disentangle them. Because it is my own medium, my yearning toward film is always a little nervous, uneasy, suspect. Do I know what part of the transference I am enacting? Touching these wordless ions of water, facing *Gangavataran*, I feel safe, inserted into transitional space, not doing representation but within it. Freud's interest in the telescope was as a device that could contain an image and make it available, enable but never own or hold what it contains. The flow of image that is a film, a flow of representations, is both transitory and permanent, but in a different way from the river. The specificity that is each film's life—each new story, each actor—is a containment, shoreline, not the river itself. Like the aquatints, they cannot be recovered, only reexperienced, each time with increased recognition of their fragile constructed inability to capture mystery by giving it a face.

ACKNOWLEDGMENTS

With gratitude, I put on record the inspiration and intellectual support from Salman Akhtar, James McLaughlin, and Sandy Sterner.

REFERENCES

Akhtar, J. N. (1975). *Pichhlay Pehar*. New Delhi: Mahtaba Jamia.

Balint, M. (1965). *Primary Love and Psycho-Analytic Technique*. New York: Liverpool Publishing.

Bion, W. R. (1962). *Learning from Experience*. London: Heinemann.

Dowson, J. (1973). *Classical Dictionary of Hindu Mythology and Religion, Geography, History and Literature*. New Delhi: Navchetan.

Evans-Wentz, W. Y., ed. (1960). *The Tibetan Book of the Dead*. London: Oxford University Press.

Freud, S. (1899). Screen memories. *Standard Edition* 3:320.

———— (1900). The interpretation of dreams. *Standard Edition* 4/5:1–626.

———— (1912). The dynamics of transference. *Standard Edition* 12:99–108.

———— (1924). The dissolution of the Oedipus complex. *Standard Edition* 19:173–182.

———— (1925). Note on the mystic writing-pad. *Standard Edition* 19:228–229.

Griffith, R. T. H., ed. (1889). *The Hymns of Big Veda*, vol. 4. Benares: Ranish Mayo.

Hinshelwood, R. D. (1999). Countertransference. *International Journal of Psycho-Analysis* 80:797–813.

Joseph, B. (1988). Object relations in clinical practice. *Psychoanalytic Quarterly* 57: 626–642,

Kakar, S. (1990). *Intimate Relations: Exploring Indian Sexuality*. New Delhi: Penguin.

Klein, M. (1931). *Psychoanalysis of Children*. London: Hogarth.

———— (1936). Love, guilt, and reparation. In *Love, Hate, and Reparation*, ed. M. Klein and J. Riviere, pp. 57–113. New York: W. W. Norton.

———— (1940). The origins of transference. In *The Writings of Melanie Klein*, vol. 3, pp. 48–56. London: Hogarth, 1975.

———— (1957). *Envy and Gratitude*. London: Tavistock.

Klein, M., Heimann, P., Isaacs, S., and Riviere, J. (1952). *Developments in Psychoanalysis*. London: Hogarth.

Klein, M., and Riviere, J. (1937). *Love, Hate, and Reparation*. London: Hogarth.

Laplanche, J. (1976). *Life and Death in Psychoanalysis*. Baltimore, MD: Johns Hopkins University Press.

Loewald, H. W. (1960). On the therapeutic action of psychoanalysis. *International Journal of Psycho-Analysis* 41:16–33.

———— (1980). The transference neurosis: comments on the concept and the phenomenon. In *Papers on Psychoanalysis*, pp. 302–314. New Haven, CT: Yale University Press.

Mahajan, J. (1984). *The Ganga Trail: Foreign Accounts and Sketches of the River Scene*. Delhi: Clarion.

Mahler, M. (1979, 1982). *The Selected Papers of Margaret S. Mahler*, vol. 1: *Infantile Psychosis and Early Contributions*, and vol. 2: *Separation-Individuation*. New York: Jason Aronson.

Mahler, M., Pine, F., and Bergman, A. (1975). *The Psychological Birth of the Human Infant*. New York: Basic Books.

McLaughlin, J. T. (1981). Transference, psychic reality, and countertransference. *Psychoanalytical Quarterly* 50:639–664.

Nanda, R. (1991). *Raj Kapoor: His Life and Films*. Moscow: Iskusstvo.

Parasher, P. P. (2002). *Retrospective Hallucination: Echo in Bollywood Modernities*. New Delhi: USBPD.

Poland, W. (1996). *Melting the Darkness*. Northvale, NJ: Jason Aronson.

Prakash, G. (1999). *Another Reason*. Princeton, NJ: Princeton University Press.

Ramaswami, N. S. (1975). *Mamallapuram*. Department of Archaeology, Government of Tamilnadu, Madras.

Sabbadini, A. (2003). *The Couch and the Silver Screen*. London: Brunner–Rutledge.

Sanders, J. (2001). *Celluloid Skyline: New York and the Movies*. New York: Knopf.

Schafer, R. (1994). The contemporary Kleinians of London. *Psychoanalytic Quarterly* 63:409–432.

Shrimali, K. M. (1983). *History of Pancala: A Study*, vol. 1. New Delhi: Munshiram Manoharlal.

Shukla, A. C., and Shiva, V. (1995). *Ganga: A Water Marvel*. New Delhi: Ashish.

Sinha, T. C. (1966). Development of psycho-analysis in India. *International Journal of Psycho-Analysis* 47:427–439.

Sivaramamurti, N. (1976). *Ganga*. Delhi: Orient Longman.

Strachey, J. (1934). The nature of therapeutic action of psychoanalysis. *International Journal of Psycho-Analysis* 15:275–293.

Winnicott, D. W. (1958). Primitive emotional development. In *Collected Papers: Through Paediatrics to Psychoanalysis*, pp. 145–156. London, Tavistock.

——— (1965). *The Maturational Processes and the Facilitating Environment*. London: Hogarth.

——— (1967). The location of cultural experience. *International Journal of Psycho-Analysis* 48:368–372.

——— (1971a). Mirror-role of mother and family in child development. In *Playing and Reality*, pp. 111–118. London: Routledge.

——— (1971b). *Playing and Reality*. London: Tavistock.

Index

Printed in the United States
by Baker & Taylor Publisher Services